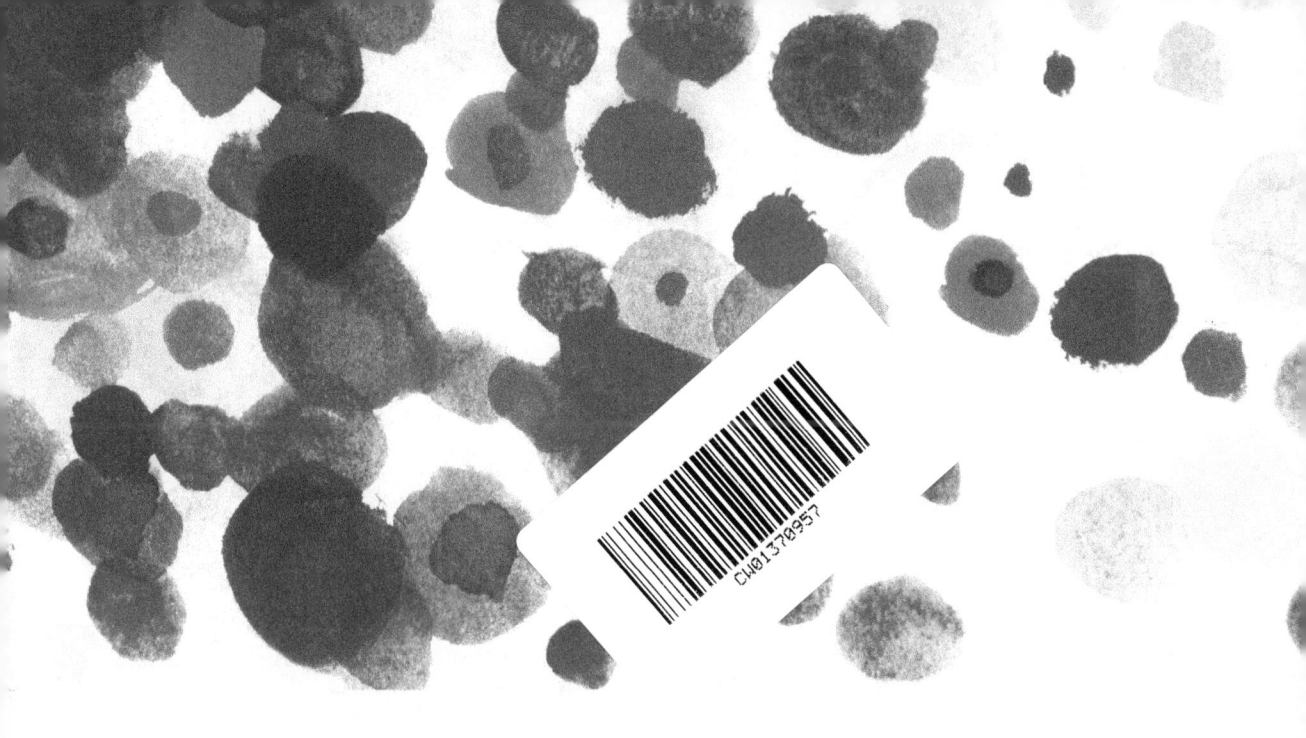

# ADDICTION
## A BIOPSYCHOSOCIAL PERSPECTIVE

## CHRIS CHANDLER
## & ANITA ANDREWS

**$SAGE**

**SAGE**

Los Angeles | London | New Delhi
Singapore | Washington DC | Melbourne

SAGE Publications Ltd
1 Oliver's Yard
55 City Road
London EC1Y 1SP

SAGE Publications Inc.
2455 Teller Road
Thousand Oaks, California 91320

SAGE Publications India Pvt Ltd
B 1/I 1 Mohan Cooperative Industrial Area
Mathura Road
New Delhi 110 044

SAGE Publications Asia-Pacific Pte Ltd
3 Church Street
#10-04 Samsung Hub
Singapore 049483

Editor: Robert Patterson
Editorial assistant: Katie Rabot
Production editor: Imogen Roome
Copyeditor: Aud Scriven
Proofreader: Brian McDowell
Indexer: Adam Pozner
Marketing manager: Lucia Sweet
Cover design: Wendy Scott
Typeset by: C&M Digitals (P) Ltd, Chennai, India
Printed in the UK

© Chris Chandler and Anita Andrews 2019

First published 2019

Apart from any fair dealing for the purposes of research or private study, or criticism or review, as permitted under the Copyright, Designs and Patents Act, 1988, this publication may be reproduced, stored or transmitted in any form, or by any means, only with the prior permission in writing of the publishers, or in the case of reprographic reproduction, in accordance with the terms of licences issued by the Copyright Licensing Agency. Enquiries concerning reproduction outside those terms should be sent to the publishers.

**Library of Congress Control Number: 2018957101**

**British Library Cataloguing in Publication data**

A catalogue record for this book is available from the British Library.

ISBN 978-1-84920-800-0
ISBN 978-1-84920-801-7 (pbk)

At SAGE we take sustainability seriously. Most of our products are printed in the UK using responsibly sourced papers and boards. When we print overseas we ensure sustainable papers are used as measured by the PREPS grading system. We undertake an annual audit to monitor our sustainability.

For John, Jai and Sharmila (Anita)

For Max, Guy and Diane (Chris)

# CONTENTS

*About the Authors* — vii
*Acknowledgements* — ix
*How to use this book* — xi
*Preface* — xiii

1  Addiction Defined — 1

2  Psychopharmacology of Addictive Substances — 23

3  Biological Theories of Addiction — 51

4  Genetics of Addiction — 79

5  Psychological Theories of Addiction — 103

6  Pharmacotherapy for Addiction — 127

7  Psychological Treatments — 155

8  Non-Substance Addictions — 177

9  Society, Policy, Law and Ethics — 199
   *Jai Andrews*

*References* — 223
*Index* — 259

# ABOUT THE AUTHORS

### Anita Andrews

Anita is an independent academic research scientist holding a PhD in Biochemistry from Imperial College, London, and holds a second PhD in the field of Addiction Psychology from London Metropolitan University, where she is a visiting lecturer. Anita is an advocate of inter-disciplinary research, considering it crucial to fully understanding psychology and health. She is particularly interested in the link between stress and addiction. She is currently training to be a counsellor and works part-time at an addiction charity in London.

### Chris Chandler

Chris is Head of Psychology at London Metropolitan University. Prior to that he worked at the Institute of Psychiatry and worked on nicotine addiction. His research interests are in the neuropsychology of addiction and he has published on this topic. He is also author of the BPS textbook *Psychobiology* (Blackwell Wiley, 2015) and *The Science of ADHD* (Blackwell Wiley, 2010).

### Jai Andrews

Jai is a law graduate from Birkbeck College, University of London, and also holds an LLM in Criminal Justice and Criminal Law from the University of Leeds. As a Family Engagement Worker based in London prisons he worked directly with offenders and their families, many of whom struggled with addictions.

# ACKNOWLEDGEMENTS

Thanks to all those at Sage for their time and patience. Thanks also to Dr Jo Lusher who helped shape initial proposals of this book and to the reviewers for their kind words and encouragement.

# HOW TO USE THIS BOOK

This book, *Addiction: A biopsychosocial perspective*, provides students with an evidence-based approach to addiction, covering a broad range of information and perspectives about addiction. It is full of helpful, easy-to-use features to guide you through your studies. In every chapter you will find chapter summaries, learning aims, and end of chapter questions to help you to go further in your studies, and save time when prepping for exams and assignments.

## EVIDENCE-BASED DISCUSSION OF ADDICTION

Focusing on theory and evidence helping the reader acquire knowledge that can act as a platform for further enquiry. These are designed to provide you with practical insights that arise from contemporary evidence-based discussions of addiction.

## CHAPTER OVERVIEW AND LEARNING AIMS

This provides you with a quick overview of what will be covered in this chapter. This will introduce you to the key ideas and breakdown the chapter so you know what to expect. This will help to put the content in context. The learning aims provide you with 3–4 bullet points, by the end of the chapter you should refer back to this list.

## CHAPTER SUMMARY AND QUESTIONS

This section encourages you to review what you have learned and engage with the core content of each chapter. There are discussion questions – designed to stimulate reflection on the key issues addressed in each chapter.

# PREFACE

Another book on addiction! Is this really necessary? Having taught the topic of addiction for many years and researched aspects of addiction, surprisingly, there was a real lack of books laying out the subject *clearly*. There were no books that provided coverage of the areas *we* wanted to cover; most books typically had a North American focus, and many books centred around therapy (many therapies having failed in their goals) or supporting someone's particular theory (we do not have a theory we are selling, but we do have a *view*).

In the UK, addiction remains a great concern for many; from health professionals, to crime agencies, to the angry people populating the column inches of the letter pages of tabloid newspapers. In the UK we joined the US War on Drugs, and arguably, we have lost (or certainly haven't won). Governments fearful for voters' future behaviour routinely ignore the ramifications of the science of addiction. Not long ago, the one-time Prime Minister of the UK, David Cameron, rejected a call for a discussion on drug policy – not a change in policy, merely a dialogue with an evidence base. This book aims to provide an *evidence-based discussion of addiction* which will provide readers with knowledge that can act as a platform for further enquiry and ultimately change lives and society, if there is the will to do so.

This book aims to provide a broad range of information about addiction, including content on its psychological, biological and societal aspects. The amount of research and information on this subject is vast and, as a result of trying to provide a broad range of information, it is necessary to acknowledge that the subject coverage is not comprehensive, but we have picked out what we consider to be the most salient features at present. However, we hope that the information we have included will enable readers to grasp the complexity of addiction, and appreciate how research from different disciplines and theoretical perspectives has contributed to our improved understanding of this subject.

Due to the pervasive presence of alcohol in our society there is a greater emphasis on alcohol in some of the chapters that follow. Addiction, in all its forms, affects a huge number of people and their families. It blights lives. We hope that our book will encourage readers to find out more, explore areas of specific interest further, and develop an informed view of addiction.

*Chris Chandler & Anita Andrews, 2018*

# ADDICTION DEFINED 1

## CHAPTER OVERVIEW

This chapter will initially provide a brief overview of what addiction is currently understood to mean, and how this meaning has evolved over time. It will then describe the various constituent components of addictive behaviour, and how this behaviour is influenced by interacting biopsychosocial factors. Finally, the psychiatric classification systems that are clinically utilised to diagnose addiction will be described and considered.

This chapter will:

- Outline the use of terminology in addiction
- Outline the components of addiction
- Discuss factors contributing to addiction
- Describe diagnostic nomenclature

ADDICTION

> **LEARNING AIMS OF THE CHAPTER**

- To understand factors in addiction
- To appreciate the elements of diagnosis and the use of different diagnostic systems
- To understand the main components that the addiction concept is comprised of

# WHAT IS ADDICTION?

First consider these three illustrative people:

## CASE 1

Cynthia is a 55 year old woman. She grew up in a household where both parents were regular heavy drinkers. Cynthia was bullied at school and lacks confidence in herself. She is divorced and lives alone, and supports herself by working in a low paid administration job. She has three grown up children who rarely visit, and a strained distant relationship with her elderly mother who lives in the area. Cynthia is a daily drinker, and wine is her drink of choice. She feels nervous if she thinks her supplies are running low. She drinks roughly three quarters to one bottle of wine a day. She has a few friends that she goes drinking with a couple of times a month, but the rest of the time she drinks alone. Cynthia is able to turn up for work on time and carry out the duties required in her job, although she sometimes makes minor errors. She is often moody, and snaps at her work colleagues if she is challenged about her work. On occasional nights out with friends or colleagues she can easily consume three bottles of wine over the course of the evening. She feels tired and overwhelmed by life sometimes. Her children worry about her drinking and have tried to persuade her to cut down. Cynthia considers her alcohol use her own business and completely acceptable. She would not dream of ever touching cannabis, cocaine, ecstasy, heroin or any other 'drug'. She considers these other drugs as dangerous and unacceptable and has little sympathy for their users. She would never consider seeking help for reducing her alcohol intake, and does not consider that drinking may have contributed to other problems in her life.

## CASE 2

Michael is a young man aged 23. He started to use alcohol and other drugs around age 14. Michael is shy and socially awkward. He has always felt different from other people, and finds it hard to communicate his feelings. Alcohol and other drugs alter his mood and help him to feel accepted by his peers. However, Michael is unable to control his drink and drug use. He has ended up in hospital Accident and Emergency departments several times as a consequence of excessive use. He is well aware that his substance use causes significant problems in his life, and his own pattern of use differs from the way his friends use substances. Although he has sought professional help for his problems, and has a loving and supportive family, he has so far been unable to prevent the repeating cycle of abstinence and relapse that has dominated recent years. Michael fights what he describes as a constant battle with the side of himself that wants to use and the side that wants to stop. This struggle drains his energy and makes him feel tired and depressed. Sometimes he contemplates suicide as a way to end this struggle. He finds it difficult to tell new people that he meets about his problems with alcohol and other drugs for fear of being distrusted and judged. As a young person living in a society in which the majority of socialising involves alcohol use, or takes place in venues where alcohol is readily available, he finds it very difficult to put this problem out of his mind. Even if he switches on the television or opens a magazine he is exposed to frequent images and references to alcohol.

## CASE 3

Peter is a 35 year old marketing executive living in London. He grew up with a father who was a cocaine and heroin addict, and a mother who was twenty years younger and had severe mental health problems. Although his parents were not deliberately abusive, he was neglected regularly, and was exposed to a world of crime and drugs from a young age. As a child he developed an extrovert and entertaining persona as a way to gain attention and avoid the feelings of disconnection he experienced. Peter has used cocaine, amphetamines and alcohol to varying degrees, since around age 13. Despite his outwardly happy and outgoing persona, he feels deeply out of place in the world, and suffers from strong feelings of self-loathing. He uses substances to manage and numb these uncomfortable feelings. He also frequently gambles, seeks out casual sex and uses prostitutes, for the same reasons.

Peter has many acquaintances but no close friends. He has never had a stable relationship, though he has had many one-night stands. He tells those around him this is a lifestyle choice, but deep down he feels lonely and ashamed at his inability to connect with the world around him. Although his substance use has led him to be erratic and unpredictable at times, natural ability and charm have allowed Peter to do reasonably well at work. He has drunk alcohol and used drugs at work for many years, however in his line of work people doing this is not entirely uncommon. Recently his substance use has escalated, and he is regularly not turning up to work at all, and risks losing his job. Peter knows he has a problem. He wants to stop his addictive behaviours, but he does not know how to live in any other way.

We have included these three cases (loosely based on actual people with personal details altered) at the start of this chapter because they illustrate some of the complexity around defining addiction. Subjective judgements are involved both on the part of the addicted individual and others, and these judgements cannot fail to be influenced by peer group and societal norms.

Come back to consider the following questions in relation to some or all of these three cases when you have finished reading this chapter and the other chapters in this book.

- Do you think Cynthia is addicted to alcohol?
- Are other people affected by these individuals' substance use?
- Do you consider Cynthia's attitude to alcohol use compared to the use of other substances to be reasonable? If so why?
- Where have Cynthia's opinions and assumptions about substance use originated? Where have your own opinions come from?
- Do you think that genetic vulnerability and/or an underlying psychiatric disorder may be influencing substance use in these particular cases? Why do you think so?
- What are the similarities and differences between Cynthia's, Michael's and Peter's substance use?
- Who do you think stands a better chance of recovery?
- How much responsibility should society take for the 'choices' made by Cynthia, Michael and Peter? Who is to blame? Where does responsibility lie?

The term 'addiction' is defined according to the historical, social and cultural context in which it is used, and it can be defined in slightly different ways for different purposes. The meaning and assumed implication behind the use of this word have also changed throughout history (Alexander, 2008). At various points in time, addiction has been thought of as a moral weakness, a medical condition, a socially determined behaviour, and the product of a dysfunctional brain (Rehm, 2014). There is still no clear consensus on the definition of the word because it involves both objective and subjective elements. Addiction is generally understood to mean a loss of self-control and compulsion with regard to an activity or substance.

In the current context, addiction can be defined as:

> A repeated powerful motivation to engage in a purposeful behaviour that has been acquired as a result of previously engaging in that behaviour, with significant potential for unintended harm. (adapted from West and the EMCDDA, 2013)

This definition manages to define addiction, but does not try to explain or describe the underlying mechanisms and associated symptoms, which can vary in their presence and severity between individuals and between different addictive agents (e.g. behavioural addictions and substance addictions).

Addiction can refer to the pathological consumption of alcohol, tobacco and other drugs, but can also encompass other behaviours, for example, compulsive eating, gambling, shopping and internet use. There is evidence for some underlying commonalities in the neurotransmitters and brain circuits involved in some substance and non-substance related behavioural addictions such as gambling (which will be explored in Chapter 8), however, throughout this book we will be primarily referring to drug addiction (*inclusive of alcohol addiction*) unless otherwise stated.

Consider the American Society of Addiction Medicine's (2018) definition of addiction, which is described in their Public Policy Statement (released April, 2011) as follows:

> Addiction is a primary, chronic disease of brain reward, motivation, memory and related circuitry. Dysfunction in these circuits leads to characteristic biological, psychological, social and spiritual manifestations. This is reflected in an individual pathologically pursuing reward and/or relief by substance use and other behaviours.
>
> Addiction is characterized by inability to consistently abstain, impairment in behavioural control, craving, diminished recognition of significant problems with one's behaviours and interpersonal relationships, and a dysfunctional emotional response. Like other chronic diseases, addiction often involves cycles of relapse and remission. Without treatment in recovery activities, addiction is progressive and can result in disability or premature death.

This definition of addiction acknowledges what has been learned about the underlying neuroanatomical, neurocognitive and neurochemical basis of addiction through scientific research in recent decades. This definition could be interpreted as reductionist if it is applied without thinking about the influence of the wider socio-cultural context within which it was originally formulated and is currently placed. This definition is widely influential in the addiction field.

It is worth thinking critically about how this definition is worded. Dysfunctional brain circuitry is described as leading to the various manifestations of addiction. However, although dysfunctional brain circuitry is clearly involved in addiction, the interrelationships between contributory factors to addiction are not clear-cut. There is also an inherent danger in defining addiction as a disease in that it overemphasises the biological explanation, at the expense of psychosocial explanations, and consequently may adversely influence the formulation of effective treatment strategies. It has been argued (Booth Davis, 1997; Peele, 1985; Pickard et al., 2015; Satel & Lilienfeld, 2013) that the 'brain disease' model of addiction obscures the dimension of personal choice, the capacity to respond to incentives, and the fact that people use drugs for often valid reasons, such as self-medication of emotional states, or to tolerate the otherwise intolerable aspects of themselves and/or their lives. It also does not explain or encompass factors that influence treatment-free recovery. There is no doubt that defining addiction will remain a controversial area because it has at its core the concept of personal responsibility (and its perceived erosion).

Different explanations of addiction can be simultaneously accurate and compatible with each other. Seemingly divergent aspects of addiction are worthy of exploration and potentially useful in aiding overall understanding of this condition and its variation both between individuals and within individuals. Addiction is best understood from an interdisciplinary perspective and examined at multiple levels of explanation, from the biological through to the societal.

## COMPONENTS OF ADDICTION

There are certain features which are traditionally associated with addiction and it is thought that an individual will repeatedly cycle through these stages which are outlined below:

- Initial use, which is usually associated with pleasure and reward
- Escalating use/binge/intoxication
- Increasing dependence, tolerance, and loss of control
- Adverse effects if substance use or activity ceases or is prevented (including physical withdrawal effects)
- Craving for the substance or activity
- Relapse to substance use and repetition of behaviour

The addictive cycle is initially driven by impulsive use, and over a period of time the behaviour becomes increasingly compulsive. Initial use is often associated with short-term pleasure and reward, whereas as addiction takes hold over time; behaviour becomes increasingly motivated by alleviation of the discomfort associated with abstinence.

Much of what was originally understood about addiction came from early research on heroin and alcohol addiction, and much has been learned subsequently, with regard to addiction to these, and other drugs. This early research led to a definition of addiction which focused on the ability of a substance to produce physical withdrawal symptoms. When a person takes a substance for a period of time their body adapts to the substance and they become physically dependent on the substance to feel 'normal'. Alcohol and heroin both result in distinctive and identifiable physical symptoms when their regular heavy use is discontinued. For example, the effects of heroin include euphoria, constipation and relaxation. Habitual users of heroin become physically dependent on the drug and develop what is known as *tolerance* to some of the drug's effects. Drug tolerance is when larger and larger amounts of the drug are needed in order to experience the same effects.

This is caused by compensatory mechanisms that occur in the body as a result of drug intake and are the body's attempt to achieve homeostasis (maintain a biologically optimum steady state). These compensatory mechanisms are opposite to the effects of the drug itself, so when drug use is abruptly discontinued these effects are experienced acutely and are felt as *withdrawal* symptoms.

In the case of heroin use, withdrawal is experienced as agitation, diarrhoea, vomiting and anxiety, amongst other symptoms, which are opposite to some of the drug's effects. The severity and length of the withdrawal syndrome will vary according to drug type, individual difference factors, drug dose and duration of use.

It was originally believed that the drug addict was driven to take the drug to alleviate these unpleasant withdrawal symptoms, resulting in a feeling of physical *craving* (a powerful feeling of longing for, or 'wanting') which would drive further drug-seeking and drug-taking behaviour. Although alleviating unpleasant withdrawal symptoms undoubtedly contributes to drug addiction, it does not explain why relapse to drug use often occurs a long time after the physical withdrawal symptoms cease. It is now thought that physical withdrawal, although unpleasant, is not what drives addictive behaviour. Many addictive drugs such as cocaine, marijuana and amphetamines are highly addictive in the absence of prolonged or severe withdrawal symptoms, and these drugs have therefore been described as psychologically addictive. Physical and psychological withdrawal can be important components of addictive behaviour but other factors are also involved.

The exact mechanisms underlying the addictive process are not well understood, and the study of addiction is complicated by the fact that it encompasses the study of the harmful effects of many different drugs, with both overlapping and distinct modes of action. Although the contribution of differing factors varies between individuals and with different drugs, research evidence has identified that different drugs of abuse also share many common features at the neurobiological and behavioural levels (Kelley & Berridge, 2002).

## THE ROLE OF COGNITION IN ADDICTION

Cognitive processes such as attention, perception and memory, both explicit and implicit, are considered to be central to drug addiction (Baker et al., 2004; Tiffany, 1990), and cognitive control can be recruited to either support or inhibit drug use (Curtin et al., 2006). One of the commonalities of addictive drugs is their ability to invoke reactivity to environmental drug cues. Cue reactivity is the array of responses that are observed when drug users or former drug users are exposed to stimuli previously associated with drug effects. These cues could include particular people, places, or drug-associated behavioural rituals, for example, always lighting a cigarette whilst talking on the phone, or always having a drink with a smoke. Over time using the phone would automatically cause a craving for a cigarette through repeated association, and having a drink would cause a craving to smoke. Cues could also include particular emotions associated with drug taking such as low mood, depression and anxiety. Associative learning (involving perception, attention and memory processes) is thought to play a crucial role in drug craving and relapse to drug use in the absence of acute physical withdrawal. This is proposed to occur through the mechanisms of classical and instrumental conditioning to drug cues. These drug associated cues can themselves elicit powerful neurophysiological effects in the absence of the drug itself.

Several theories of addiction propose that reactivity to drug-related cues is an important feature of drug dependence. The incentive-sensitisation theory (Robinson & Berridge, 1993) incorporates associative learning but places particular emphasis on the *sensitisation* of brain motivational systems to drugs and drug associated cues. Sensitisation is a process whereby, over repeated exposure, a greater effect is observed. Addictive drugs produce both positive and negative reinforcement effects on behaviour depending upon at which stage of the addictive cycle they are taken. Reinforcement refers to the effect that a particular stimulus has on a behaviour that preceded it, and it means that the behaviour is more likely to be repeated. That behaviour is effectively strengthened. This is particularly true for behaviour resulting in immediately rewarding effects, and drugs that produce an immediate 'high' (or other pleasurable effect) are more positively reinforcing and addicting (Volkow et al., 2000). Negative reinforcement occurs when an unpleasant stimulus is removed as a result of the preceding behaviour. In the case of drug consumption, this can be escape from an unpleasant emotional state, such as low mood, or from unpleasant psychological and/or physical withdrawal symptoms. Negative reinforcement is considered to be an important factor in driving drug use, craving and relapse (Baker et al., 2004).

# WHICH PARTS OF THE BRAIN ARE INVOLVED IN ADDICTION?

Research on addiction has shown that addictive drugs can interact with, subvert and alter neural circuits in the brain which are associated with naturally rewarding motivated behaviours such as eating, drinking and sexual activity (Kelley & Berridge, 2002). These behaviours have evolved to be motivationally potent to ensure survival. In particular, the mesotelencephalic dopamine system is implicated in mediating the pleasurable effects of drugs.

The release of the neurotransmitter dopamine is thought to occur in response to nearly all addictive drugs, and also in response to drug-associated cues. Large and rapid increases in dopamine in the limbic system are involved in the initial reinforcing effects of most drugs of abuse. Research has focused on dopamine, but other neurotransmitter systems including serotonin, glutamate and GABA are also known to be important in the transition to addiction. Neuro-adaptive changes resulting from chronic drug use may result in changes in dopamine receptor levels which drive further drug consumption. Recent research using a neuroimaging technique has shown that individuals at high familial risk of addiction show a blunted dopamine response following a dose of amphetamine, suggesting a possibility that this diminished response either develops early in drug use history or is a pre-existing familial vulnerability trait (Casey et al., 2014).

Evidence from neuroimaging studies has greatly enriched understanding of brain regions and processes involved in addictive behaviour (Goldstein & Volkow, 2002; Volkow et al., 2003). The findings from both human and pre-clinical research have shown that much of the neural circuitry involved in addiction is involved in motivation, the processing of rewards, and in reward-related decision making and impulse control (Bechara, 2005; Kalivas & Volkow, 2005). Circuits necessary for insight and social behaviours are also affected, resulting in addicted individuals making poor behavioural choices despite awareness of their negative consequences (Forbes & Grafman, 2010; Volkow et al., 2011). Disruption of this circuitry is thought to result in the development and maintenance of addiction, with different addictive substances influencing different parts of this circuitry (reviewed by Reid & Lingford-Hughes, 2006).

# WHAT FACTORS INFLUENCE THE TRANSITION TO ADDICTION?

Of the large numbers of people who are exposed to, experiment with and regularly use addictive drugs, it is only a small minority in whom drug use escalates to addiction. There are many factors that interact to increase or decrease the likelihood that an individual will become an addict, but there is no clear causal pathway.

Risk factors for addiction vulnerability include some of the factors considered below that *interact with each other* to a greater or lesser degree and with the pharmacological properties of the drug itself. Ultimately addiction will result if the factors that confer addiction vulnerability outweigh the factors that may protect against it. This list is not exhaustive and these and other factors influencing addiction vulnerability will be considered in more detail in subsequent chapters in which theoretical models of addiction will be examined.

## GENETIC PREDISPOSITION

There is no single gene that predisposes a person to addiction. As addiction can involve numerous different substances and behaviours, any genetic influence is a result of differences in multiple genes. For example, genes may influence pharmacological factors such as individual differences in the regulation of enzymes involved in drug metabolism. This may indirectly affect how sensitive an individual is to a particular drug effect and how it is subjectively experienced, and hence its addictive potential for that individual. Genes affecting individual differences in the expression of dopamine receptors and other neurotransmitters and their receptors may also influence addiction vulnerability in this manner.

The genetics of addiction have been studied using family, adoption and twin studies, and the role of heritable influences has been estimated for different substances and also across substances. For example, the variation in liability to nicotine dependence has been estimated at between 33–71% (Edwards et al., 2011; Kendler et al., 1999; Lessov et al., 2004; Lyons et al., 2008) and alcohol dependence at between 48–66% (Heath & Martin, 1994; Heath et al., 2001; Kendler et al., 1992). Another study (Merikangas et al., 1998) has shown that the percentage of relatives with a substance use disorder is approximately eight times higher in those related to an addicted person compared to those related to a non-addicted person.

## DEVELOPMENTAL FACTORS

Developmental factors are important components of addiction vulnerability and there is increasing evidence that the adolescent brain is a critical period of heightened vulnerability to any environmental insult, including exposure to potentially neurotoxic drugs. This is because adolescence is a developmental period during which significant physiological, psychological and behavioural changes occur, including puberty, and its associated hormonal and emotional challenges.

The adolescent brain is still extensively developing and maturing which may make it particularly sensitive to drug effects and also to social and environmental pressures. In adolescence synaptic connections undergo a 'pruning' process, increased myelination of nerve cells occurs, and the communication between key regions of the brain is enhanced and becomes more efficient. Importantly, the frontal lobes (and their connections) – which are critical to complex thought, decision making and inhibition of more impulsive behaviour – are still undergoing development. This developmental period coincides with an increased desire to engage in and ability to access what are perceived as more adult social behaviours, including drug use. Increased peer-directed social interaction and influence typify the teenage years, and increased rates of impulsivity and risk taking occur in adolescence (Spear, 2000). Increased sensitivity to drug reward and a decreased sensitivity to drug withdrawal also occur at this time (O'Dell, 2009). Disruption of the brain circuits involved in behaviour control by addictive drugs during this critical developmental period may cause lasting damage, which increases the risk for the onset and maintenance of mental health problems, including addiction.

Most research on the developmental effects of drug use has been carried out on alcohol and nicotine, because these addictive drugs are legal in most societies and so are more easily accessible to teenagers and are usually the first drugs they try.

Recent longitudinal studies on adolescent alcohol use suggest that there are both preexisting differences in the brains of those who later engage in heavy alcohol use and also damaging effects of this use. This has been demonstrated for working memory (Squeglia et al., 2012), response inhibition (Wetherill et al., 2013) and brain regions impacting on behaviour control, language and spatial tasks (Squeglia, Rinker, et al., 2014). A recent study (Squeglia, Jacobus, et al., 2014) showed that compromised inhibitory functioning in 12 to 14 year olds was related to more frequent and intense alcohol and marijuana use by late adolescence (17 to 18 years). These authors suggest that tests of inhibitory performance could help to identify those at risk for initiating heavy substance use during adolescence. Prospective and longitudinal studies on adolescent exposure to nicotine also suggest that adolescent exposure to nicotine increases the risk of mental health disorders, including anxiety and depression, and increases the risk for developing addiction (reviewed by Counotte et al., 2011).

## SOCIAL CONTEXT

Social learning and social and cultural context play an extremely important role in vulnerability to drug use and addiction. How a drug is experienced is related to an interaction between the pharmacological properties of the drug itself, the set (personal factors) and the setting, including the views and beliefs of family and the wider social and cultural community towards a particular substance, as well as the views and beliefs of minority drug-using subcultures (Zinberg, 1986).

An example of the importance of social context and context specific drug use is provided by a unique study of heroin use by American servicemen in the Vietnam War (Robins et al., 1975). Heroin was considered at the time to be one of the most addictive and dangerous drugs. American servicemen in Vietnam were widely exposed to heroin and many became addicted after regular use. This led to a belief that on returning to America there would be problems relating to heroin use in this population. In reality these fears did not materialise, and only a small percentage of war veterans had heroin use problems on their return. These studies showed the widespread use of heroin by soldiers in Vietnam was related to specific contextual factors, such as easy access to high quality heroin, drug-using peers, the lack of alternative recreational substances, the absence of social censure, and the fact that serving in Vietnam (and its related stresses) were seen as unrelated to their lives in America (Robins, 1993).

It has been claimed that modern industrial capitalism, with its associated social upheavals such as rapid urbanisation, mass migration and modern warfare, has led to a dismantling of the cultural structures and social ties that would have more easily helped to control drug use in the past (Samson, 2004). It has also been argued (Alexander, 2008), that from a historical perspective, addiction is better understood as a societal rather than an individual problem. Alexander's 'dislocation theory of addiction' attributes the current increase in both substance and behavioural addictions to a lack of psychosocial integration (referred to as social dislocation) in the modern world. Psychosocial integration, in this context, means an interdependence between an individual and their society, and is proposed to fulfil the human need for both individual autonomy and social belonging. The competition and individualism inherent in the current globalising free market economy is proposed to have resulted in increasing feelings of alienation in both rich and poor, and an attendant poverty of the spirit. This is more readily visible when the powerful presence and influence of a majority culture adversely affects a minority indigenous culture, for example, as has happened to ethnic Canadian Indians in Vancouver, where it is argued that social dislocation has led to increases in drug and alcohol problems.

A number of studies have examined drug self-administration in laboratory rats housed in spacious and sociable conditions compared to isolated rats housed in standard laboratory cages (e.g. Alexander et al., 1978; Bozarth et al., 1989; Hadaway et al., 1979; Raz & Berger, 2010). These experiments aim to model the effect of social and environmental deprivation, and its associated stress, on drug use in humans. The results of these studies show a marked decrease in drug self-administration in animals housed in socially-enriched environments compared to isolated animals in standard cages, and provide indirect evidence to support the effect of social and environmental stress in the pathogenesis of addiction (see below).

## STRESS AND THE CO-OCCURRENCE OF OTHER PSYCHIATRIC DISORDERS WITH ADDICTION

The role of both acute and chronic stress in triggering drug use and relapse is confirmed by the personal accounts of many people. Stress can manifest itself through traumatic life events and through unhappy or disrupted social relationships, for example with family, work colleagues or peer group. Evidence from animal and human research studies has repeatedly demonstrated that the hormonal system involved in regulating the stress response – the hypo-thalamic-pituitary adrenal axis (HPA axis) – is critically important in drug use, relapse and addiction (Koob, 2010; Koob & Le Moal, 2001; Lovallo, 2006; Stephens & Wand, 2012). The HPA-axis controls secretion of the hormone cortisol, which is a 'master hormone' that not only responds to stress, but also regulates multiple body organs for optimal functioning, as well as being involved in regulating mood and emotions.

Large-scale epidemiological studies (Grant, Hasin et al., 2004; Grant, Stinson et al., 2004) have revealed comorbidities of 21–29% for mood disorders, 22–25% for anxiety disorders, and 32–70% for personality disorders. All these disorders are associated with aberrations of HPA axis function. Thus, pre-existing factors which impact on biological stress systems may precipitate drug use. For addicts with co-morbid psychiatric disorders it is likely that substance use provides a habitual and temporarily effective means for coping with psychological stress in the short term, and is consistent with a self-medication view of addiction (Khantzian & Albanese, 2008).

# HOW IS ADDICTION DIAGNOSED?

There are two main systems that are currently used to diagnose mental disorders, including addiction, which comes under the definition of 'substance use disorder' in these systems. These systems are the ICD and the DSM. The ICD is an abbreviation of *International Statistical Classification of Diseases and Related Health Problems* (World Health Organisation, 1992), and is the official classification system used throughout the world. The current version is the ICD-10, and a revised version (ICD-11) is in process at the time of writing and expected to be completed in 2018. The ICD is the system that is used to classify most disorders in medicine, including substance dependence and other mental disorders which come under the section called 'Mental and Behavioural Disorders'. The DSM is an abbreviation of the *Diagnostic and Statistical Manual of Mental Disorders*, and is the standard classification of mental disorders used by the American Psychiatric Association for clinical diagnosis in America, and is also used worldwide. The current version of the DSM is DSM-5, which was released in 2013. Some of the differences between the DSM and the ICD are given below (adapted from Tyrer, 2014):

1. The ICD is the official world classification, whereas the DSM is the US classification (although it is also used in many other countries).
2. The ICD is intended for use by all health practitioners, whereas the DSM is used primarily by psychiatrists and researchers.
3. Special attention is given in the ICD to primary care and low- and middle-income countries, whereas the DSM is focused mainly on secondary psychiatric care in high-income countries.
4. The ICD-11 is planned to focus on clinical utility and intends to reduce the number of diagnoses, whereas the number of diagnoses has increased with each successive revision of the DSM (although there was a reduction of three diagnoses between DSM-4 and DSM-5).
5. The ICD provides diagnostic descriptions and guidance but does not employ operational criteria, the DSM depends on more clearly defined operational criteria: as a result of this the DSM is considered by some to be a more reliable (but not necessarily more valid) system, while the ICD allows for more clinical discretion in making diagnoses.

## THE ICD-10

In the ICD, harmful use is distinguished from the dependence syndrome which can be considered analogous to addiction. The block (labelled F10 – F19) covers mental and behavioural disorders due to psychoactive substance use covering: alcohol, opioids, cannabinoids, sedative hypnotics, cocaine, other stimulants including caffeine, hallucinogens, tobacco, volatile solvents, multiple drug use, and use of other psychoactive substances.

The following extract shows the ICD-10 definitions for harmful use and dependence syndrome, and letters in brackets refer to ICD codes:

> Harmful use
>
> A pattern of psychoactive substance use that is causing damage to health. The damage may be physical (as in cases of hepatitis from the self-administration of injected drugs) or mental (e.g. episodes of depressive disorder secondary to heavy consumption of alcohol).

The diagnosis requires that actual damage should have been caused to the mental or physical health of the user. Harmful patterns of use are often criticized by others and frequently associated with adverse social consequences of various kinds. The fact that a pattern of use or a particular substance is disapproved of by another person or by the culture, or may have led to socially negative consequences such as arrest or marital arguments is not in itself evidence of harmful use. Acute intoxication (see F1x.0), or "hangover" is not itself sufficient evidence of the damage to health required for coding harmful use. Harmful use should not be diagnosed if dependence syndrome (F1x.2), a psychotic disorder (F1x.5), or another specific form of drug- or alcohol-related disorder is present.

This next extract comes from the ICD-10 diagnostic guide for *dependence syndrome:*

A cluster of physiological behavioural, and cognitive phenomena in which the use of a substance or a class of substances takes on a much higher priority for a given individual than other behaviours that once had greater value. A central descriptive characteristic of the dependence syndrome is the desire (often strong, sometimes overpowering) to take psychoactive drugs (which may or may not have been medically prescribed), alcohol, or tobacco. There may be evidence that return to substance use after a period of abstinence leads to a more rapid reappearance of other features of the syndrome than occurs with nondependent individuals.

Diagnostic guidelines: A definite diagnosis of dependence should usually be made only if **three or more** of the following have been present together at some time during the previous year:

a. a strong desire or sense of compulsion to take the substance;

b. difficulties in controlling substance-taking behaviour in terms of its onset, termination, or levels of use;

c. a physiological withdrawal state when substance use has ceased or been reduced, as evidenced by: the characteristic withdrawal syndrome for the substance; or use of the same (or a closely related) substance with the intention of relieving or avoiding withdrawal symptoms;

d. evidence of tolerance, such that increased doses of the psychoactive substances are required in order to achieve effects originally produced by lower doses (clear examples of this are found in alcohol- and opiate-dependent individuals who may take daily doses sufficient to incapacitate or kill nontolerant users);

e. progressive neglect of alternative pleasures or interests because of psychoactive substance use, increased amount of time necessary to obtain or take the substance or to recover from its effects;

f. persisting with substance use despite clear evidence of overtly harmful consequences, such as harm to the liver through excessive drinking, depressive mood states consequent to periods of heavy substance use, or drug-related impairment of cognitive functioning; efforts should be made to determine that the user was actually, or could be expected to be, aware of the nature and extent of the harm.

(Extract from *The ICD-10 Classification of Mental and Behavioural Disorders: Diagnostic Criteria for Research*, 2018, © WHO.)

## THE DSM

The DSM was first published in 1952 and has been revised several times. Since its inception it has had widespread influence in the USA and elsewhere on how disorders are diagnosed, treated and investigated. The current version, DSM-5, was published in 2013 after a fourteen-year revision process which aimed to overcome some of the problematic issues identified in DSM-4-TR (Hasin et al., 2013). This involved literature reviews and extensive new data analyses by a work group consisting of 12 scientists and clinicians with additional input from consultants and advisers, and through comments obtained through the DSM-5 website.

The revised chapter in the DSM-5 is now called 'Substance Related and Addictive Disorders'. This change in terminology has been implemented to avoid the potential confusion that had arisen from earlier versions of the DSM, which had favoured use of the term 'dependence' over 'addiction'. Some scientists had considered 'addiction' to be derogatory and 'dependence' was chosen by a narrow margin of only one vote for the DSM-3-R in 1987, and subsequently incorporated unchanged into the the DSM-4-TR in 1994 (O'Brien, 2011). However, dependence does not necessarily mean addiction, and can be used to refer purely to the physiological adaptation that occurs when a substance is taken over time, rather than the compulsive drug-seeking behaviour that characterises addiction.

The major change implemented in the DSM-5 is the combining of DSM-4 abuse and dependence criteria into a single disorder, measured on a continuum from mild to severe. Other changes included: dropping legal problems as a diagnostic criterion because of its poor diagnostic utility; adding craving as a diagnostic criterion to increase consistency with ICD-10 (where it is included); adding cannabis and caffeine withdrawal syndromes; aligning tobacco use disorder criteria with other substance use disorders; and including gambling disorders in the same chapter as substance-related disorders. Gambling disorder is the sole condition in a new category on behavioural addictions, and is included in the same chapter as substance use disorders in recognition of research findings that have provided evidence for similarities between these disorders in their clinical expression, brain origin, co-morbidity, physiology, and treatment (APA, 2013).

Section III of the manual includes disorders for which further research is required before they can be considered as diagnosable disorders, and internet gaming disorder and caffeine use disorder are included in this section in DSM-5. Each specific substance is addressed as a separate use disorder (apart from caffeine, which is not considered as a diagnosable substance use disorder at present), but the same overarching criteria are used for diagnostic purposes. There are ten separate classes of substances included: 1) alcohol; 2) caffeine; 3) cannabis; 4) hallucinogens – phencyclidine or similar acting aryl cyclohexylamines; 5) inhalants; 6) opioids; 7) sedatives, hypnotics and anxiolytics; 8) stimulants; 9) tobacco; 10) other.

The overarching criteria used for diagnosis of substance use disorder in the DSM-5 are listed below using alcohol as an example of a substance use disorder:

> A problematic pattern of alcohol use leading to clinically significant impairment or distress, as manifested by at least two of the following, occurring within a 12-month period:
>
> 1. Alcohol is often taken in larger amounts or over a longer period than was intended.
>
> 2. There is a persistent desire or unsuccessful efforts to cut down or control alcohol use.
>
> 3. A great deal of time is spent in activities necessary to obtain alcohol, use alcohol, or recover from its effects.
>
> 4. Craving, or a strong desire or urge to use alcohol.
>
> 5. Recurrent alcohol use resulting in a failure to fulfil major role obligations at work, school, or home.

6. Continued alcohol use despite having persistent or recurrent social or interpersonal problems caused or exacerbated by the effects of alcohol.
7. Important social, occupational, or recreational activities are given up or reduced because of alcohol use.
8. Recurrent alcohol use in situations in which it is physically hazardous.
9. Alcohol use is continued despite knowledge of having a persistent or recurrent physical or psychological problem that is likely to have been caused or exacerbated by alcohol.
10. Tolerance, as defined by either of the following:
    a. A need for markedly increased amounts of alcohol to achieve intoxication or desired effect.
    b. A markedly diminished effect with continued use of the same amount of alcohol.
11. Withdrawal, as manifested by either of the following:
    a. The characteristic withdrawal syndrome for alcohol
    b. Alcohol (or a closely related substance, such as a benzodiazepine) is taken to relieve or avoid withdrawal symptoms.

## CONSIDERATION OF CURRENT CLASSIFICATION SYSTEMS

Substance use disorders in both systems are defined by a set of criteria, where no single criterion is necessary or sufficient to diagnose addiction. Considerable overlap is observed between the DSM-5 and ICD-10 dependence criteria as would be expected, and this is desirable for diagnosis of the same condition. However, this also means that similar criticisms are applicable to both systems.

A major change in the DSM-5 has been the move away from splitting abuse criteria and dependence criteria as separately diagnosable syndromes. This has resulted in a more continuous classification system, with severity being measured by the number of diagnostic criteria. This move towards a more continuous system, and removal of the abuse diagnosis as a separate syndrome (which was previously considered to precede the diagnosis of dependence), is supported by statistical analysis, indicating that they represent the same underlying condition (Hasin et al., 2013). However, diagnostic criteria are not weighted in either the

DSM or the ICD systems, and a diagnosis is based on an individual having a minimum number of criteria. For DSM-5 the threshold is set at two or more for mild, four or five for moderate, and six or more criteria for a diagnosis of severe substance use disorder. It is therefore possible for people with very different defining criteria to be given an identical diagnosis. Both systems involve a degree of subjective interpretation, both by the individual being diagnosed and by the clinical or research practitioner. They are essentially a set of descriptive symptoms that provide a common language for diagnosis, and their major drawback is their lack of specificity (see Lilienfeld et al. 2013 for a detailed review of further problems associated with the DSM system).

Some of this diagnostic subjectivity could be addressed if objective measures, applicable to substance use disorders, were available. However, although there are biological correlates of addiction, these are currently of no diagnostic value in either system. Unlike mental disorders, many medical disorders have an identifiable biological basis that can confirm disease. Although the threshold of diagnosis can be arbitrarily defined even in medical diseases, defining a threshold for diagnosis is more subjective for mental disorders. The evidence for the use of biomarkers for substance use disorder diagnoses was reviewed for possible inclusion in DSM-5, but was rejected. This decision was based on the inability of current biomarkers to be diagnostically useful. For example, although useful for detection and confirmation of drug use, the limited time window applicable for current measures of drugs and associated metabolites in blood, urine, sweat, saliva and hair, prevents their use for diagnosing substance use disorder. Despite the repeated association of certain genetic variants with substance use disorders, these associations cannot be used for diagnosis due to their small effects and inconsistency across different populations. Also, evidence from neuroimaging studies such as positron emission tomography (PET) and functional magnetic resonance imaging (fMRI), showing group differences between substance users and controls, is not considered specific enough to diagnose substance use disorders in individual cases, and there is also considerable overlap with other psychiatric disorders. This absence of any reliable or valid biomarker for the diagnosis of addiction is ironic, considering the widespread influence of the prevailing biomedical paradigm.

## OTHER DIAGNOSTIC SYSTEMS

### RESEARCH DOMAIN CRITERIA

The Research Domain Criteria project (RDoC) was initiated by the US's National Institute of Mental Health (NIMH, 2008). It is an expansive framework for organising research from different scientific disciplines and across different levels of analysis. It differs considerably in its approach compared to the ICD and DSM systems, and is compatible with a biologically-based conceptualisation of addiction as a disorder of dysfunctional brain circuitry.

This extensive research framework is in its infancy at present, but it is hoped that eventually it will lead to a more precise classification system for psychiatric diagnosis (Insel, 2014). The RDoC framework comprises a matrix of broad psychobiological domains that correspond to brain-based circuits that are relevant to psychopathology. These domains include negative valence systems (e.g. fear, anxiety, loss) and positive valence systems (e.g. approach motivation, reward responsiveness, reward learning, habit), with different sub-categories in each domain (see Cuthbert, 2014). These domains can be experimentally studied using different types of research tools and strategies. The research paradigm under which the investigation is being conducted is also taken into consideration.

An example of this approach is a recent review of abnormal reward functioning across substance use disorders and major depressive disorder (Baskin-Sommers & Foti, 2015). This review synthesised available data from preclinical, electrophysiological and neuroimaging literature on reward processing, and organised information under the key reward constructs within the Positive Valence Systems domain of the RDoC matrix. These authors suggest that examining reward functioning across clinically diverse samples, rather than within limited diagnostic categories, may ultimately be more clinically useful.

Although this approach will undoubtedly increase understanding of the biological correlates of addiction, it also faces several methodological and conceptual challenges, and has been criticised for underplaying the importance of the social, cultural and psychological dimensions of mental health (Bracken et al., 2012; Lilienfeld, 2014).

## HEAVY USE OVER TIME

In Europe there has been a drive by some scientists to implement the concept of *heavy use over time* as the key criterion for defining substance use disorders (Rehm et al., 2013). Proponents of this view argue that this concept underlies all current definitions of substance use disorder criteria. It is argued that the physiological, psychological, social, behavioural, and other health consequences of substance dependence, as defined by the current DSM and ICD criteria, are nearly all associated with 'heavy use over time'. For example, tolerance and withdrawal are argued to be physiological consequences of heavy use over time, whereas craving is argued to be a psychological consequence. Other consequences of heavy use over time include relinquishing social, occupational, and recreational activities in favour of drug use. It is also argued that physical and health consequences arise from heavy use over time, in a dose-dependent manner, for example, diseases such as cirrhosis of the liver result from increasing heavy alcohol use over time. Data obtained from epidemiological surveys demonstrate a high correlation between level of consumption and criteria used for diagnosis of substance use disorders. It is also argued that high levels of consumption are more associated with adverse mortality and morbidity outcomes than current diagnostic criteria, and are therefore far more relevant to public health. Proponents of 'heavy use over time' suggest that a definition based on a continuum such as consumption level (with defined thresholds for diagnosis, as currently occurs for example with blood pressure) will reduce the stigma attached to the current diagnoses of substance use disorders.

Although there is undoubtedly some merit in this approach, it is not without criticism. Heather (2013) argues that the addiction concept is necessary to direct theory and research towards understanding the essential paradox of addictive behaviour – continued use despite knowledge of harmful consequences – and this is not addressed by invoking 'heavy use over time'. Saunders (2013) also questions the ability of 'heavy use over time' to replace the concept of substance use disorders, because it fails to capture the clinical experience as described through cognitions, behaviours, actions and physiological responses, and argues that a quantification of heavy use is problematic in itself. For example, although commercial alcohol and tobacco products can be accurately quantified, underreporting of use is a common problem in clinical practice, whereas other features of the dependence syndrome can be more readily communicated by substance users and observed by others (e.g. impaired control, continued use despite harmful consequences). Quantification with regard to illicit substances presents an even greater challenge, where the absence of quality control means that it is difficult to ascertain the amount of drug taken. Bradley and Rubinsky (2013) advocate that consumption measures should be included in the diagnostic criteria for substance use disorders rather than replace them, and suggest that this approach would lead to the identification of a greater number of people who could be helped to reduce their high-risk drinking.

# SUMMARY

- Addiction is thought to result from a combination of biological factors that interact with environmental contexts. The definition and popular understanding of what addiction means have varied throughout history.

- Addiction generally consists of several stages through which an affected individual repeatedly cycles. These stages broadly consist of initial use, escalating use, tolerance, abstinence, craving and relapse. Initial substance use tends to be motivated by reward seeking (positive reinforcement), but in its later stages substance use can often end up being motivated by relief from discomfort (negative reinforcement).

- The exact mechanisms underlying the addictive process are not well understood. It is likely that the contribution of differing factors varies between individuals, and also within an individual, depending on which stage of the addictive cycle they are engaged in. Factors which influence addiction include: genetic predisposition; developmental factors; social context; exposure to stress; and co-occurring psychiatric problems. These factors are not mutually exclusive and interact to varying degrees.
- The current classification systems used to diagnose addiction are the DSM-5 and the ICD-10. These classification systems are not ideal, due to the fact that they are descriptive and entail subjective judgement. There is general agreement that some kind of classification system is necessary, but the nature and content of these systems will continue to evolve, and there is potential for future revision as more information becomes available.

# QUESTIONS

- What is addiction?
- How is addictive behaviour diagnosed?
- Who becomes addicted?

# PSYCHOPHARMACOLOGY OF ADDICTIVE SUBSTANCES 2

## CHAPTER OVERVIEW

'Pharmacology' is the term that is used to describe the action and effects of drugs on living organisms. Psychopharmacology is the branch of pharmacology that investigates the effects of drugs on the nervous system and behaviour. This chapter provides a brief overview of basic psychopharmacological principles and describes how some of the most commonly abused substances affect the mind and behaviour.

The drugs covered in this chapter include alcohol, tobacco, cocaine, amphetamines, opioids, benzodiazapines, cannabis and MDMA. Information regarding the legal classification of these drugs is provided in Chapter 9, and how some of these drugs are used therapeutically in the clinical treatment of addiction is described in Chapter 6, so will not be considered here.

This chapter will:

- Describe drug action
- Look at the importance of fast delivery of drugs

(Continued)

- Outline the pharmacology of addictive drugs:
    - alcohol
    - tobacco
    - cocaine
    - amphetamines
    - opioids
    - benzodiazapines
    - cannabis
    - MDMA

### LEARNING AIMS OF THE CHAPTER

- To understand the general action of drugs in the brain
- To understand the pharmacokinetics of drugs

# DRUG ACTION

Pharmacokinetics and pharmacodynamics are the two main factors that determine how a drug acts in the body. Pharmacokinetic factors are those that influence how biologically available a drug is within the body. Pharmacokinetic factors influence the absorption, distribution, metabolism, and elimination of a drug. Pharmacodynamic factors are concerned with how a drug interacts with its target receptors in the body to mediate the physiological effects of that drug within the body.

## PHARMACOKINETICS

Factors that determine how quickly and effectively a drug is absorbed and transported to the brain include the route by which it enters the body. Routes of administration include:

- oral, taken by mouth, e.g. swallowing a tablet
- rectal, administered in the rectum, such as a suppository (this is unusual for most drugs taken for recreational purposes, and is sometimes used medically if a drug cannot be taken by mouth)
- inhalation, via the lungs, e.g. tobacco smoking, vaping and, aerosol sprays
- transdermal, through the skin, e.g. nicotine patches
- transmucosal, which is absorption through topical application through the mucous membranes, e.g. snorting cocaine through the nose, or sublingual, under the tongue through the membranes in the mouth
- parenteral (by injection), which includes intravenous (IV) injection; other slower forms of injection include subcutaneous and intramuscular

In terms of addictive potential, it is the speed with which the drug reaches the brain that is important. This factor also influences the subjective experience of the drug-induced 'high' (see Box 2.1). Smoking and IV drug administration usually result in the drug reaching the brain within seconds. This is often associated with a 'rush' of pleasure, followed by a sharply contrasting decline, which further motivates the user to re-experience the drug-induced 'high'. These routes of administration are considered to be more problematic in terms of addictive potential. If a drug is taken orally it is transported to the gastrointestinal tract and the liver, where metabolism may reduce its activity considerably.

## BOX 2.1 PHARMACOKINETICS OF A DRUG-INDUCED 'HIGH'

Nearly all drugs that are addictive (not necessarily abused/misused) enter the body via a route that means they enter the brain rapidly. For example, intravenous drug use, as is frequently the case with heroin, ensures that the drug gets to the brain rapidly. It is not just what the drug does when it gets to the brain that is important,

(Continued)

the speed by which drugs enter the brain is also considered essential for their addiction liability.

The importance of the speed of entry was emphasised using cocaine and methylphenidate by Jim Swanson and Nora Volkow (Swanson & Volkow, 2003; Volkow & Swanson, 2003). Cocaine and methylphenidate both share near identical pharmacodynamic properties – they both block the dopamine transporter thereby increasing dopamine in the synapse. Methylphenidate is used for the treatment of Attention Deficit Hyperactivity Disorder (ADHD) and narcolepsy. It is prescribed orally, and its most common brand name is Ritalin. Cocaine and methylphenidate have different pharmacokinetic properties due to the way they are delivered: cocaine is snorted or smoked and leads to rapid increases within the brain, whereas methylphenidate is taken orally in which high concentrations take much longer to achieve.

In a laboratory setting intravenous methylphenidate produced a rapid rise in concentrations within the striatum, in comparison to oral administration that took approximately 60 minutes to reach the same levels. When looking at cocaine administration, the peak concentration of cocaine was near identical to the subjective self-reported high.

It was also demonstrated that intravenous methylphenidate elevated extracellular dopamine which was correlated with the self-reported high, and oral methylphenidate did not correlate with the self-reported high.

The speed of entry to the brain and the rate of metabolism are therefore important factors in methylphenidate's abuse potential (Volkow et al., 1995; Volkow et al., 2002; Volkow & Swanson, 2003).The therapeutic effects of methylphenidate can be differentiated from the abuse potential (Swanson & Volkow, 2003; Volkow & Swanson, 2003). Using immediate release methylphenidate and slow release methylphenidate (Spencer et al., 2006), it was found that participants were more sensitive to detecting an effect of the drug and liking the drug when they received the quick acting drug. Many preparations of methylphenidate are marketed with a clear statement of avoiding or minimising their addictive potential (Chandler, 2010).

Body membranes affect how a drug which is circulating through the blood is distributed in the body. These membranes include cell membranes, capillaries, the blood brain barrier (BBB), and in pregnancy, the placental barrier. Cell membranes are largely made up of phospholipids, so small lipid soluble drugs can readily penetrate these membranes, as can small polar molecules and gases. Larger molecules are transported via transporter proteins. The BBB is a specialised structural barrier which functions to protect the brain. The capillaries in the brain are packed tightly together, have no pores, and are surrounded by a fatty glial sheath extended from nearby astrocyte cells (a type of cell that functions to protect neurones). Therefore, in order to cross the BBB easily and quickly, a drug molecule has to be small and/or lipid soluble.

Drug action is generally terminated by chemical reactions that result in biological transformation, which facilitate excretion of the drug metabolite(s) through the urine, via the kidneys, or through other excretory routes, including the lungs, bile and skin. The 'drug elimination half-life' is a pharmacological term that is used to describe the time taken for the plasma concentration of a drug to fall by 50% when it has reached a state of being evenly distributed throughout the body. This is the initial or first half-life. The next ('second half-life') is the time taken for this concentration to fall by 50% again (so to 25%). Usually a single dose of drug is eliminated almost completely by the 'fifth half-life'. This concept allows scientific determination of the dose and timing needed in order to keep a steady and effective drug concentration in the body for clinical applications.

## PHARMACODYNAMICS

Pharmacodynamics is concerned with the interaction of the drug with its target tissue in the body. The basic types of drug action can be divided by their action at the neural synapse into agonists, antagonists, partial agonists and inverse agonists (see Figure 2.1).

Full agonists facilitate action at the synapse and produce a similar response to an endogenous neurotransmitter. A full agonist, in contrast to a partial agonist, produces the maximal response capability of the cell. Antagonists inhibit or block the activity of an endogenous neurotransmitter (or agonist) at the synapse by either physically blocking the actual receptor binding site, or by binding elsewhere, and affecting the conformation of the receptor site. Antagonists can therefore act in a competitive or non-competitive fashion.

A partial agonist has reduced response efficacy (reduced ability to generate a biological response) at the receptor, and its mode of operation can vary depending on the baseline levels of the endogenous neurotransmitter present in the system. A partial agonist is capable of acting as an agonist at low doses when no other agonist is present, and is capable of behaving as an antagonist when a full agonist is present. An inverse agonist produces a response which is opposite to the effects of the agonist, as opposed to simply blocking the actions of an agonist, as is the case with an antagonist.

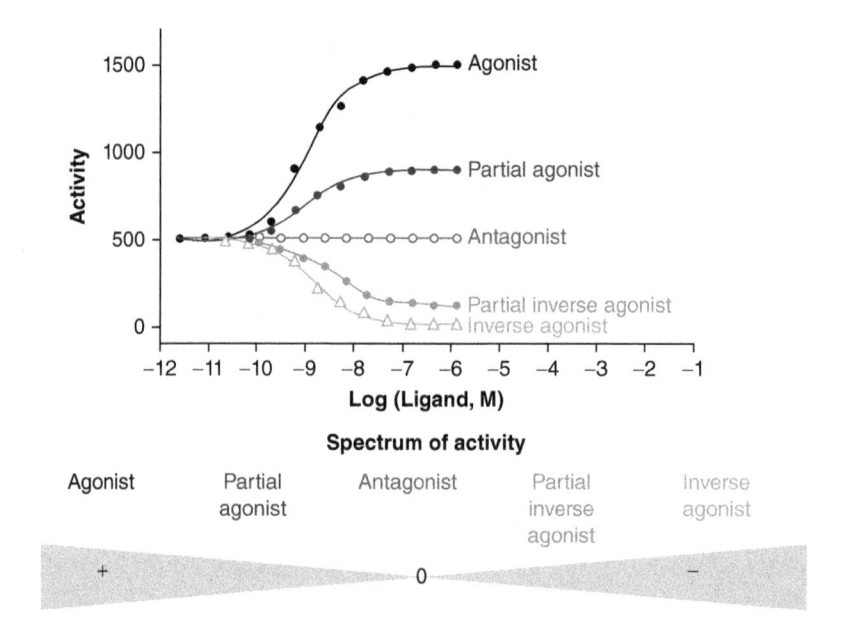

**Figure 2.1** Activity of agonists, partial agonists, antagonists and inverse agonists

Republished with permission of John Wiley & Sons Inc, from *Psychobiology* by Chris Chandler (2015); permission sourced through author and publisher

Psychoactive drugs are able to modulate neurotransmission through a number of different mechanisms which include the following (see Figure 2.2):

- Increasing the synthesis and turnover of a neurotransmitter by acting as a precursor molecule
- Inhibiting the synthesis of the neurotransmitter by inhibiting the action of synthetic enzymes
- Preventing effective storage of the neurotransmitter in storage vesicles
- Enhancing the release of the neurotransmitter from the presynaptic terminals
- Stimulating the postsynaptic receptor by receptor binding (agonist action)
- Blocking the action at the postsynaptic receptor (receptor antagonist action)

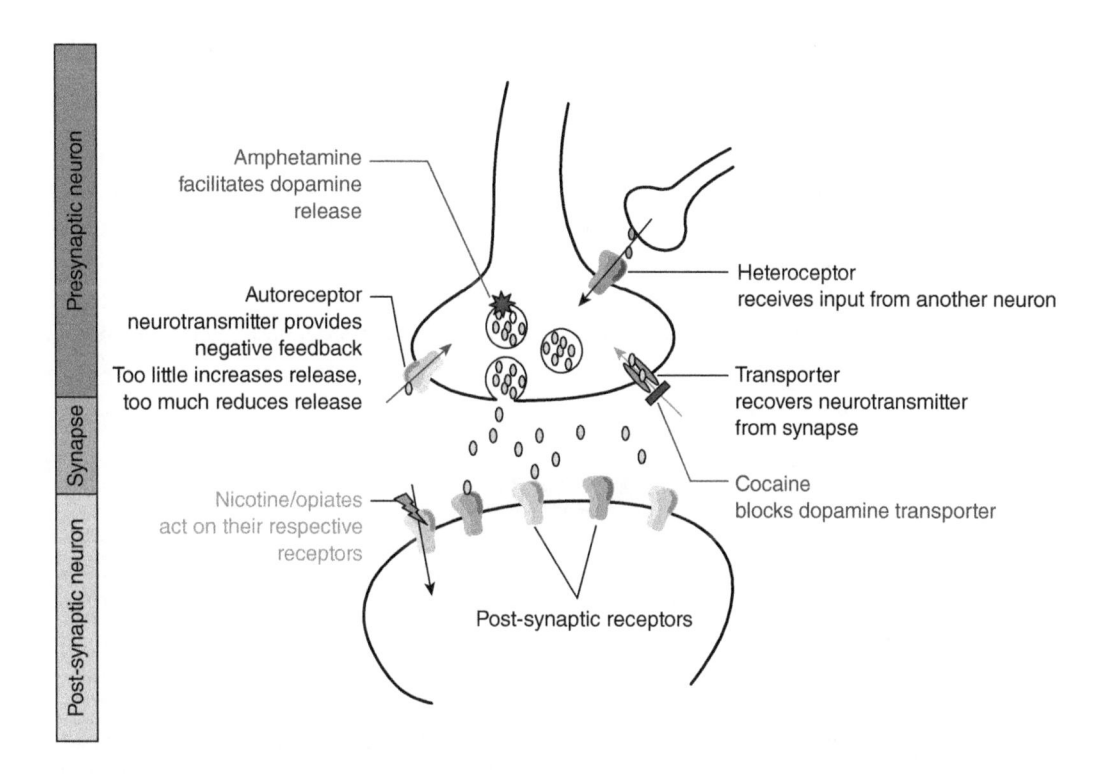

**Figure 2.2** A schematic representation of a general non-specific type of synapse (the process of neurotransmission at the synapse is an area where drugs of abuse act)

- Providing false feedback to the receptor and interfering with its normal biological response
- Blocking re-uptake of the receptor at the synapse causing an increase in neurotransmitter levels
- Inhibiting the metabolism of the neurotransmitter by inhibiting enzymes involved in its metabolic degradation

By testing incrementally increasing amounts of the drug, and determining the biological or behavioural effects for each dose, it is possible to generate dose response curves which can provide information on the therapeutic effects, the toxic effects, and the lethal effects (in pre-clinical studies on laboratory animals) of a particular drug. Another factor which can have an effect on the magnitude and type of response of a drug is its affinity for its receptor, which is a measure of how powerfully it binds to its receptor to generate a biological response. A higher affinity drug or ligand would be biologically active at a much lower concentration than a drug with low receptor affinity. Different types of drugs can vary in their receptor affinity and specificity of action depending on their chemical structure. Illustrative examples of some of these different mechanisms of action will be provided throughout this chapter in the sections below on the effects of different drugs. Further examples can be found in Chapter 6 on pharmacotherapy for addiction, and Chapter 4 on the genetics of addiction.

# ALCOHOL

Alcohol is formed from the fermentation of grains, vegetables or fruits. It has a long history of use in many societies, and is the most familiar, socially acceptable and widely used drug. Ethyl alcohol or ethanol (chemical formula $C_2\text{-}H_5\text{-}OH$) is a simple molecule present in all commonly consumed alcoholic drinks, in concentrations varying from approximately 5–15% in beers and wines to concentrations as high as 40–50% in distilled spirits.

Despite its familiarity and widespread use, alcohol has diverse and far-reaching detrimental effects on many different biological processes affecting the brain and behaviour. Alcohol has a wide spectrum of activity but the overall effect is depression of the central nervous system. The effects of alcohol are dose dependent, with disinhibition and euphoria common at low doses and impairment of numerous motor and cognitive functions at high doses. It is both fat soluble and water soluble, and is rapidly absorbed through the stomach and entire intestinal tract, evenly permeating all bodily fluids and tissues. It is able to rapidly cross the blood-brain barrier and the placental membrane, potentially impacting foetal development to varying degrees of severity, depending on the extent of alcohol consumed. The time taken to reach its maximum concentration in the blood (Blood Alcohol Concentration or BAC) typically varies between fifteen minutes to an hour, depending on the amount of food in the stomach, body size, body composition, and metabolic factors. Chronic long-term excessive consumption of alcohol can result in a wide spectrum of medical problems, including liver damage (including cirrhosis), stroke, heart disease, several types of cancer, respiratory problems, brain damage, impaired immunity, and damage to most systems of the body. Alcohol consumption whilst pregnant can result in foetal alcohol spectrum disorders (FASD) in the child. FASD has numerous detrimental effects on the child, including facial abnormalities and impaired social and cognitive functioning.

## ALCOHOL METABOLISM

Alcohol is metabolized mainly in the liver (85%) by the enzyme alcohol dehydrogenase (ADH), and also in the lining of the stomach (up to 15%) by a gastric ADH enzyme. The remaining is excreted unchanged through the lungs, skin, and urine. After correcting for differences in body weight, women generally have higher BAC levels for the equivalent amount of alcohol consumed than men, due to lower levels of gastric ADH and lower amounts of muscle compared to fat tissue (muscle tissue has a greater blood supply, thus diluting the BAC).

Ethanol is initially oxidised by the enzyme ADH to acetaldehyde, a toxic compound, using a co-enzyme called nicotinamide adenine dinucleotide (NAD). This is the rate-limiting step in the reaction, and is dependent on the availability of NAD. The next step is the oxidative conversion of acetaldehyde to acetic acid by an enzyme called aldehyde dehydrogenase (ALDH). The acetic acid is subsequently broken down into carbon dioxide and water. There are several distinct isoenzyme forms of both ADH and ALDH, which impact alcohol metabolism and may influence individual genetic susceptibility to alcoholism (see Chapter 4, 'Genetics of Addiction'). Chronic alcohol use leads to the induction of another pathway for oxidation called the microsomal ethanol-oxidising system (Lieber, 1987). Induction of this pathway can increase the rate of elimination of alcohol, and may be responsible for the increased metabolic tolerance seen in alcoholics for both alcohol and other sedative/hypnotic drugs.

Approximately one alcoholic drink containing 10 to 14 millilitres of ethanol is metabolized per hour by the average adult person. Amounts drunk in excess of the amount that can be metabolised will lead to an increase in BAC and a rise in the common symptoms of drunkenness. Understanding the pharmacokinetics of alcohol metabolism is important for understanding and establishing the legal limits for drinking and driving. Due to individual differences in alcohol metabolism and variations in factors that could affect the absorption of alcohol, the legal limit can only ever be an estimate for any particular individual's safe level, and it could be argued that the only completely safe level of alcohol consumption for driving is zero.

## PHARMACODYNAMICS OF ALCOHOL

Alcohol acts through multiple mechanisms, effecting various behavioural and biological changes. It causes disruption of the cell membrane, affecting associated proteins and cell signalling pathways. It has a general effect of psychomotor depression, and causes problems with memory, reasoning, sleep, and motor coordination. It additionally interacts with the brain reward system accounting for its addictive properties.

Alcohol acts on several central neurotransmission pathways causing both stimulatory and inhibitory effects. Pathways affected by alcohol consumption include GABAminergic, opioid, serotoninergic and cannabinoid systems.

Gamma-aminobutyric acid (GABA) is the main inhibitory neurotransmitter of the CNS. Alcohol enhances the inhibitory effects of GABA through its interaction with GABA receptors. These inhibitory effects include sedation, relaxation, and the inhibition of cognitive and motor skills. $GABA_A$, a subtype of the GABA receptor, is the target for alcohol, benzodiazepines, and barbiturates. Receptor binding causes chloride channels to open, resulting in hyperpolarization of the membrane and postsynaptic inhibition. Long-term use of alcohol results in impaired memory through its effect on signal transduction proteins involved in the formation of memories in the hippocampus. Down regulation (reduction in number) of receptors also occurs through chronic alcohol use, contributing to alcohol tolerance, and withdrawal effects if consumption is terminated.

Glutamate is the major excitatory neurotransmitter in the CNS. Ethanol, at high concentrations, is a powerful inhibitor of the N-methyl-D aspartate (NMDA) subtype of glutamate receptor, depressing its responsiveness to released glutamate in the hippocampus, amygdala, and striatum brain areas. This receptor is implicated in memory formation, neuronal excitability, and seizures. Up regulation of this receptor may occur with long-term alcohol use. This effect, coupled with the inhibitory effect of alcohol on GABAminergic neurotransmission, may contribute to the seizures experienced during alcohol withdrawal.

Alcohol also interacts with the brain reward system through its effects on the opioid and dopaminergic pathways. Alcohol can induce opioid release, which subsequently leads to the release of dopamine in several key brain reward areas, including the ventral tegmental area (VTA), nucleus accumbens (NAcc), and orbitofrontal cortex. Blocking of the inhibitory effect of the GABA system on dopamine release by opioid neurotransmitters also has the overall effect of increasing the potency and length of action of released dopamine, leading to an increase in the feelings of pleasure associated with dopamine release, and consequently increasing the addictive potential of alcohol. Serotonin (5-Hydroxytryptamine or 5-HT) is another neurotransmitter thought to play an important role in mediating some of the addictive potential of alcohol through its effects on particular serotonin receptor subtypes. There is also evidence for a role for the cannabinoid receptor in alcohol effects through its stimulation of anandamide, the endogenous neurotransmitter for these receptors. There appears to be a role for these receptors in the development of alcohol tolerance, and for the development of alcohol craving when consumption is ceased.

# PSYCHOSTIMULANTS: NICOTINE, CAFFEINE, COCAINE, AND AMPHETAMINE

## NICOTINE

Nicotine is a naturally occurring psychoactive alkaloid found in the leaves of the tobacco plant. Tobacco has a centuries old history of use, mainly in the form of pipe smoking and chewing, but the introduction of commercially produced cigarettes in the mid-nineteenth century greatly accelerated tobacco consumption. Due to its legality and availability, consumption of nicotine through tobacco use is widespread, with a consequently large toll of smoking-related illness, death, and other harms. There has been a worldwide rise in the use of electronic or e-cigarettes in recent years, particularly amongst teenagers, and these are thought to increase the likelihood of progression to adult smoking (Leventhal et al., 2015). In electronic smoking, a flavoured nicotine containing liquid is vaporised and inhaled. The long-term effects of this form of smoking are still under investigation.

### PHARMACOKINETICS

Nicotine is the main substance responsible for the addictive properties of tobacco. Over 4000 compounds are released from cigarette smoke, and many of these compounds are involved in the development of smoking-related diseases, including cancer, lung disease, and cardiovascular disease.

Nicotine is easily absorbed through multiple sites in the body, including the lungs, skin, gastrointestinal tract, and membranes of the nose and mouth. It enters the smoker's lungs in the form of tiny particles (tars) which are rapidly absorbed through the lungs into the bloodstream. A cigarette is a very effective delivery device for nicotine, and it can reach the brain in as little as 7 to 10 seconds after inhalation. The average cigarette contains about 8–10mg of nicotine, and roughly 20–25% of this is absorbed into the blood. Based on an average smoking rate of 10 puffs within 5 minutes it is estimated that roughly 1–2mg of nicotine will be absorbed, though absorption can range from 0.5–3mg. A typical smoker may absorb between 20–40mg of nicotine a day. The amount of nicotine absorbed into the bloodstream can be regulated by varying the length, depth and frequency of inhalation, as well as the number of cigarettes smoked. The elimination half-life of nicotine (amount of time for the dose to drop to half the original level) is roughly two to three hours, therefore smokers continue smoking regularly throughout the day to keep their blood levels constant. Overnight nicotine is cleared from the system and chronic smokers will eagerly anticipate the first cigarette on waking to restore their nicotine levels and avoid withdrawal symptoms.

These withdrawal symptoms include severe craving, irritability, anger, anxiety, attentional problems, and hunger.

Nicotine (roughly 70–80%) is metabolized primarily in the liver to cotinine, by a specific liver enzyme called cytochrome P450, family 2, subfamily A, polypeptide 6 (CYP-2A6). Cotinine and other nicotine metabolites are excreted mainly in the urine. Genetic variations, resulting in differences in enzymatic activity of CYP-2A6, are associated with differences in vulnerability to smoking, with less efficient metabolism associated with decreased cigarette consumption (Pan et al., 2015) (see Chapter 4).

## MECHANISM OF ACTION

Nicotine exerts most of its effects by activating nicotinic acetyl choline receptors (nAChRs). These are ligand gated ion channels composed of five subunits arranged around a central cation pore, and are expressed in the brain and in most tissues and organs throughout the body. The endogenous ligand for these receptors is the neurotransmitter acetyl choline. These receptors are distributed on presynaptic terminals, cell bodies, and dendrites of many neuronal subtypes. In the CNS, the nAChRs are widely distributed and may be located on the presynaptic nerve terminals of dopamine and serotonin secreting neurons. Dopaminergic activity is increased through these receptors. Activation of nAChRs can potentiate neurotransmitter release and neuronal excitability throughout the brain, influencing a diverse range of bodily processes. These include basic physiological functions such as pain sensation, sleep pattern and feeding, as well as more complex processes involved in learning, affect and reward. Nicotine acts as an agonist at these receptors at low doses, and an antagonist at high doses. Desensitisation to the effects of nicotine and acetylcholine occurs as a result of smoking, and tolerance develops as nicotine levels increase with continued smoking throughout the day. It is likely that the rewarding effects of nicotine involve intricate interactions between several different neurotransmitters, including glutamate, GABA, serotonin and acetylcholine, with a net result of increased dopamine levels in the mesocorticolimbic reward system.

# CAFFEINE

Caffeine is the most widely consumed drug in the world, and has many physiological effects, which are non-problematic for the majority of users. These effects include increased arousal, reduced fatigue, and enhanced psychomotor activity. Caffeine increases blood pressure, urine production, respiration rate, and catecholamine release. The main effects of caffeine are mediated by its effects on adenosine receptors, which are thought to be involved in inducing sleep. At high doses caffeine can cause unpleasant feelings of irritability, anxiety, and restlessness. There is growing concern about the increasing use of energy drinks containing caffeine, sometimes combined with alcohol, particularly by young children and adolescents, due to an increase in adverse reactions (including seizures) requiring medical attention after excessive consumption (Goldman, 2013). Stopping caffeine consumption after regular use leads to a variety of unpleasant withdrawal symptoms, including aches and pains and headaches. Inability to control intake despite recognised harmful effects is a problem for a minority of consumers. Caffeine Dependence Syndrome is recognised as a clinical condition in the ICD-10, and Caffeine Use Disorder has been identified as a condition requiring further research in the DSM-5.

## COCAINE

Cocaine is a stimulant alkaloid derived from the leaves of the *Erythroxylon coca* plant which is native to the high-altitude regions of the Peruvian and Bolivian Andes of South America. It has a long history of use amongst the indigenous people of this region, who chew the leaves in order to experience increased energy, elevated mood, and decreased hunger and tiredness. Before its addictive potential and harmful effects were fully realised, it was initially hailed as a wonder drug by some scientists and medical practitioners, including Sigmund Freud and the American surgeon William Halsted, both of whom experienced its euphoria, and later came to experience its addictive and harmful effects through personal experience (Markel, 2011). It is also an effective local anaesthetic and was used surgically, until it was superseded by later synthetic analogues such as lidocaine. In the nineteenth century it was an ingredient in a variety of widely sold tonic preparations, including the original recipe for Coca-Cola.

### PHARMACOKINETICS

Cocaine is available in several different forms, including coca paste, cocaine hydrochloride (cocaine HCL), and cocaine base or crack cocaine. Cocaine HCL is the common white crystalline powdered form, which is often diluted or 'cut' with other substances such as talc or flour. This form of cocaine is water soluble. Routes of administration for cocaine HCL are oral, intranasal through snorting, and intravenous injection. Cocaine base is made by processing the drug with an alkali, mixing this with a volatile solvent and then heating, creating a form of cocaine which can be smoked, making it particularly addictive. The term 'crack' refers to cocaine base, which has been made by mixing dissolved cocaine HCL with baking soda, heating it and then drying it. This form of cocaine makes a crackling sound when smoked.

Cocaine is absorbed from the stomach, lungs and mucous membranes, with absorption, onset of action, dose and duration of experienced 'high' varying with the route of administration and the chemical form of cocaine taken. Smoked coca paste, and free base or crack cocaine, are absorbed rapidly and completely within 8–10 seconds, with effects peaking within 5 minutes after the heated vapour is smoked. Absorption through the nasal mucosa is limited by the fact that cocaine causes constriction of the blood vessels in the nose. Injected cocaine reaches the brain rapidly within 30–60 seconds. Cocaine efficiently penetrates the brain after which it is redistributed to other tissues. It easily crosses the placental barrier, affecting the foetus according to dose and administration route.

Cocaine has a biological half-life of approximately 50 minutes. It is rapidly metabolized, mainly by an enzyme called butyrylcholinesterase present in the liver and in plasma, to an inactive compound called benzoylecgonine (BE). Removal from the brain is slower and can take up to 8 hours or more. Cocaine taken in combination with alcohol can lead to the formation of an ethyl ester of BE called cocaethylene. This compound has a longer half-life then cocaine, is more toxic, and can potentiate the effects of cocaine, making it particularly harmful.

## MECHANISM OF ACTION

Cocaine exerts its rewarding effects primarily through blocking the reuptake of all the monoamine neurotransmitters – dopamine, noradrenalin and serotonin. It binds to the membrane transporters of these neurotransmitters, inhibiting their function, resulting in increased levels of these neurotransmitters in the synaptic cleft, and increased neurotransmission. Dopamine is thought to be particularly important with regard to the stimulating, rewarding, and addictive effects of cocaine. There is a complex interplay amongst the neurotransmitter systems involved, with cocaine indirectly affecting the glutamate, GABA and opioid systems, as well as activating the stress response. At higher concentrations cocaine exerts its anaesthetic effects by inhibiting voltage gated sodium channels in nerve cells, thereby blocking nerve signals in sensory nerves.

As well as its potent stimulatory effects, which include euphoria, increased mental alertness and sensory awareness, cocaine is also a vasoconstrictor. Physiological effects of cocaine include increased heart rate, blood pressure and body temperature, loss of appetite, decreased need for sleep, restlessness, muscle twitches and agitation. High doses can cause psychosis, as well as bizarre and violent behaviour. Cocaine is commonly consumed in binges which can continue for a few days at a time. Users can also have the distressing feeling that insects are crawling underneath their skin (called formication). Severe medical consequences of excessive cocaine use include heart attack, stroke, seizures, and coma. Repeated use of cocaine can result in sensitisation to its psychomotor and toxic effects, and increased tolerance to its rewarding effects. A variety of health problems can manifest in chronic users, including depression, fatigue, irritation and damage to the nose if snorted, damage to the lungs if smoked, and increased risk of infectious diseases in IV users. Depletion of neurotransmitter levels, widespread organ damage, and reduced blood flow to the stomach and malnourishment, can also occur in chronic cocaine users.

## AMPHETAMINES

Amphetamines are a family of synthetic chemically-related psychostimulants that are structurally related to the neurotransmitter dopamine. They behave like cocaine in their sympathomimetic actions on the central and autonomic nervous systems, but they have a longer duration of action. They do not possess the anaesthetic properties of cocaine. Two naturally occurring compounds – cathinone (found in *Catha edulis* commonly known as *khat*) and ephedrine (found in the herb *Ephedra Vulgaris* commonly known as *ma huang*) – are similar in their structure and properties to amphetamine, and have a long history of use by people native to East Africa and Arabia, and China, respectively. Amphetamines have had various legitimate medical uses over the years, including as nasal decongestants and weight suppressants, and to maintain alertness in military personnel. Currently amphetamines are medically prescribed to treat ADHD in children (see Chandler, 2010) and narcolepsy.

Attaching an additional methyl group (CH3) to amphetamine increases the speed with which it reaches the brain, and hence its abuse potential. This form of amphetamine, called methamphetamine, has been on the increase globally in recent years. The current market includes the United States, Mexico, China and Thailand, and its use is increasing in countries in the Middle East and South Asia, posing significant health risks to individuals and their communities (Chomchai & Chomchai, 2015). Methamphetamine hydrochloride which has been purified for smoking forms large crystals referred to as 'ice' or 'glass'.

There has also been an upsurge in the synthesis and availability of mephedrone (4-methyl-methcathinone) and other chemically similar psychostimulant amphetamine-like drugs, which have been manufactured and sold as 'legal highs' labelled as 'not for human consumption' to circumvent the law. These substances have now been banned in the UK following a number of drug-related deaths. Users of such chemically tweaked synthetic substances sold in this way have no access to information on their safe use or their potential toxicity (see Chapter 9 for a further discussion of this issue).

### PHARMACOKINETICS

Amphetamines can be taken orally, injected, snorted or smoked. The pharmacological effects vary according to the dose, the chemical structure and form of the amphetamine taken, as well as the route of administration. A typical oral dose of 5–15mg usually takes effect after about 30 minutes, whereas the injection route is much faster, and provides a more intense 'high'. Amphetamines are slowly metabolized by the liver, and have an elimination half-life which ranges from between 7 hours to greater than 30 hours, with an average of around 10 hours for methamphetamine. This means their effects last longer than cocaine. Amphetamines readily cross the placental barrier and exert deleterious effects on the foetus, in addition to acting directly on the placenta itself (Ganapathy, 2011). Metabolites are excreted in the urine and can be detected for up to two days.

### PHARMACOLOGICAL EFFECTS

At low doses the effects include increased heart rate, increased blood pressure, increased temperature, relaxed bronchial muscles, feelings of increased alertness, dilated pupils, euphoria, restlessness, excitement, and decreased hunger. Amphetamines can also increase physical endurance and enhance physical performance, and have been misused by some to gain an unfair advantage in competitive sports, where they are included on the list of banned substances. Larger doses can cause fever, sweating, blurred vision, headaches, and dizziness. Chronic and excessive use can cause an irregular heartbeat, tremors, seizures, heart failure, and stroke. Other effects associated with chronic use include repetitive motor activity, feelings of aggression, irritability, mood swings, sleep disorders, cravings, paranoia, psychosis, violent behaviour, malnutrition, and depression. Toxicity related to amphetamine use can affect many organs, including the brain, heart, lungs, and skin. Both tolerance and sensitisation can occur to these effects, to varying degrees.

### MECHANISM OF ACTION

Amphetamines exert their effects through their indirect agonist actions on the catecholaminergic neurotransmitter systems, resulting in an increase in synaptic dopamine, noradrenaline, and serotonin. In addition to inhibiting reuptake through blocking the neurotransmitter transporters, amphetamines also cause neurotransmitter release from nerve terminals by interacting with the transporters in the synaptic vesicles, ultimately causing more neurotransmitter to be released into the cytoplasm of the nerve terminal, from where it is released into the synaptic cleft through a reversal of the transport process. Amphetamines are also able to bind to the enzyme monoamine oxidase in dopaminergic neurons. This inhibits the actions of monoamine oxidase, which prevents the degradation of dopamine and other monoamine neurotransmitters, leading to their increased levels in the nerve terminal.

## OPIOIDS

The opioids are a class of drugs that are all related in chemical structure to opium obtained from the sap of the opium poppy, *Papaver somniferum*. Opioids are best known for their analgesic (pain relieving) and euphoria-inducing effects. They have a long and interesting history of use dating back thousands of years, for both medicinal and recreational purposes. Morphine – a phenanthrene alkaloid – is the primary active ingredient found in opium. Deduction of the chemical formula of morphine and the introduction of the hypodermic needle in 1853, contributed to the subsequent widespread clinical use of morphine. Morphine and its acetylated chemical derivative heroin were both once widely available as ingredients in popular over-the-counter remedies, before awareness of the extent of their addictive potential was fully realised and their availability restricted.

In the last two decades there has been an escalation in the prevalence of prescription opioid abuse and misuse in the US, which has led to dramatic increases in overdose deaths and people seeking treatment for opioid use disorders. This escalation is thought to be related to a paradigm shift in the treatment of pain which occurred in the late 1990s, when physicians were encouraged to address and aggressively treat pain. Prior to this there had been criticism for undertreating pain (Brady et al., 2016). Unfortunately, physical dependence, tolerance and withdrawal are commonly experienced by those who are taking opioid medications. In recent years there have been efforts to create abuse deterrent and tamper resistant opioid formulations.

In addition to morphine, opium contains other naturally active compounds including codeine, thebaine and papaverine. Manipulation of the chemical structure of the naturally occurring compounds has led to the creation of a wide variety of clinically useful semi-synthetic and synthetic opioids. Small differences in the molecular structure of these compounds determine differences in their pharmacological properties. Morphine is still considered the most effective medication for severe pain when compared to other drugs. The challenge (so far unrealised) has been to formulate an equally effective opioid analgesic that does not have abuse potential.

One of the ways of classifying opioids is by their chemical structure and by their interaction with opiate receptors. Different opioid drugs act as agonists, partial agonists and antagonists at these receptors. There are three different types of G-protein coupled opioid receptors, *mu*, *delta* and *kappa*, also currently known as MOP, DOP and KOP, respectively. These receptors are distributed widely throughout the CNS, and to a lesser extent throughout peripheral tissues. The endogenous ligands for these receptors are the enkephalins, dynorphins beta-endorphin and endomorphins. A fourth receptor named the noiceptin receptor (NOP) has also been discovered that shares some similarities with the other opioid receptors. Stimulation of the different opioid receptors produces a range of effects which are often dependent on where the receptor is located. Binding of an opioid agonist leads to a series of intracellular events which result in reduced intracellular cyclic adenosine monophosphate (a molecule used to relay intracellular messages), a hyperpolarization of the cell (by activation of potassium conductance and inhibition of calcium conductance), and reduced neuronal neurotransmitter release (Pathan & Williams, 2012). Opiates act on various parts of the body, including different brain regions, on neurons located in the dorsal horn of the spinal cord, and on the peripheral tissues. In the spinal cord, opioid receptors are located on the presynaptic terminals of the nerves carrying sensory messages (primary afferents mediating pain signals). Opioid agonists work by blocking the release of pain-producing substances, including glutamate, substance P, and calcitonin gene related peptide, thereby reducing ascending pain signals to higher brain regions. Activation of *mu* receptors located in high densities in the brain stem and midbrain periaqueductal gray (PAG) region, are thought to mediate opioid analgesia. Indirect activation of the descending inhibitory input from these brain regions onto the pain processing neurones of the spinal cord by opiate agonists and release of serotonin, noradrenaline and encephalin by these pathways, all contribute to overall reduction of pain (Julien et al., 2014).

## OTHER PHARMACOLOGICAL EFFECTS

As discussed above, analgesia is the main clinically useful effect of opioids. This applies to both the experience of physical pain and the perception of emotional pain. Important to the addictive potential of opioids is the induction of a feeling of euphoria, which is mediated by increased dopamine release in the mesolimbic reward pathway. Additional effects include: depression of respiration, decreased blood pressure, hypothermia, suppression of cough, sedation, relaxation, relief from anxiety, nausea, vomiting, constipation, pupillary constriction, drying of secretions, alterations in endocrine and immune function, and itchy skin. Tolerance and dependence rapidly develop with chronic use of opioids, and typically withdrawal symptoms opposite to the above effects are experienced when drug use ceases. Tolerance and cross-tolerance occur to drugs in the same class. Tolerance occurs as a result of continuous occupation of receptor sites by opioid drugs. Withdrawal symptoms include: aches and pains, hyperventilation, low mood and depression, irritability, restlessness and insomnia, increased blood pressure, diarrhoea, pupillary dilation, hyperthermia, runny nose and chills. Respiratory suppression and loss of consciousness are the most common cause of opioid overdose fatalities. Symptoms can be reversed if an opioid antagonist drug such as naloxone or naltrexone is administered quickly enough.

## METABOLISM AND MECHANISM OF ACTION

The metabolism and mechanism of action of opioids vary with their chemical formulation and mode of administration. The majority of opioid analgesics are full mu agonists (e.g. morphine, oxycodone, hydrocodone) with some having additional activity at other opioid and non-opioid receptor sites, which accounts for many of their additional effects. Opioids can reach all tissues in the body, and can cross the placental barrier, potentially causing retarded growth and birth-related problems.

## MORPHINE AND OTHER OPIOID PAINKILLERS

Morphine can be taken by injection, orally, by inhalation, and rectally. Morphine penetrates the blood brain barrier slowly due to its low lipid solubility. It has a slow onset of action, even if taken through IV injection. If taken orally it takes effect even more slowly, with around 40–60% failing to reach the systemic circulation due to first pass metabolism in the liver and gut wall. Morphine is metabolised chiefly by glucuronidation to active metabolites which are excreted in the urine. These metabolites include morphine-6-glucoronide, which is more potent than morphine and is responsible for most of its analgesic effects. The half-lives of morphine and morphine-6-glucoronide are around 3 to 5 hours depending on age and kidney and liver function status.

Heroin (diacetylmorphine) is widely used illicitly and is produced from morphine. Heroin is more lipid soluble than morphine and therefore penetrates the blood-brain barrier more quickly, providing a powerful 'rush' of euphoria when smoked or injected. Heroin is metabolised to morphine and monoacetylmorphine before it is metabolised and excreted.

Codeine, a frequently prescribed short-acting orally-administered opioid painkiller (often taken in combination formulations with other types of painkillers), is metabolised by the enzyme CYP-2D6 in the liver to morphine, and this may account for some of its addictive potential. The duration of action and plasma half-life is around 3 to 4 hours, but genetic variation affecting codeine's metabolism can lead to dangerous unpredictability in its pharmacokinetics, resulting in high levels of accumulation of morphine in the body in some individuals.

Fentanyl, alfentanil, sufentanyl and remifentanil are all mu receptor agonists that are 80 to 500 times more potent than morphine. They are highly lipid soluble and therefore have a rapid onset of action. They are structurally related to the synthetic opioid meperidine. With the exception of remifentanil, they can accumulate in the fat depots of the body and take longer to clear from the system. Other commonly available opioids include hydromorphone, hydrocodone, and oxycodone.

Buprenorphine is a semi-synthetic partial mu receptor agonist which is associated with less risk of overdose and less severe withdrawal symptoms. It is sometimes used to clinically treat addiction. Methadone and levo-alpha acetylmethadol (LAAM) are both long-acting synthetic mu receptor agonists that are also used to treat heroin addiction (see Chapter 6). Naltrexone, naloxone and nalmefene are pure opioid receptor antagonists that are clinically useful to block or reverse the effects of opioids. The pharmacotherapeutic use of all these compounds in addiction treatment is considered in Chapter 6.

## BENZODIAZAPINES

Benzodiazapines belong to a chemically diverse group of drugs called sedative-hypnotics, anxiolytics (anxiety inhibiting drugs) or minor tranquillisers, which are known for their general non-selective depressant action on the nervous system. These drugs are commonly medically prescribed for short-term treatment of anxiety and sleep disorders due to their calming and relaxing effects. They are also used clinically to control seizures, relax muscles, induce short-term amnesia for surgical procedures, and as a prequel to surgical anaesthesia. Benzodiazepines include diazepam (Valium), lorazepam (Ativan), clonazepam (Klonopin), and alprazolam (Xanax).

Benzodiazapines became popular in the 1960s and replaced barbiturates due to their superior safety. Benzodiazepines, in comparison to barbiturates, are unlikely to produce surgical anaesthesia, coma or death, even if taken at high doses, unless they are taken with other drugs that cause respiratory depression. They are commonly abused alongside other drugs by people who have substance use disorders. Benzodiazapines are frequently taken by opioid, cocaine and metamphetamine users to help control withdrawal symptoms and unpleasant side effects. They are also used therapeutically to treat acute alcohol withdrawal, and in longer-term therapy to prevent relapse to alcohol addiction. Long-term use of benzodiazepines can cause cognitive and psychomotor impairment.

## PHARMACOKINETICS

Most of the benzodiazepines are taken orally, with some also available in injectable form. They are easily absorbed with maximum plasma concentrations being reached within an hour after oral dosage, although there are some variations in speed of absorption depending on drug type. Short-acting benzodiazepines are metabolised into inactive glucuronide conjugated compounds that are subsequently excreted in the urine. Other long-acting drug types (e.g. chlorodiazepoxide, trade name, Librium) form pharmacologically active intermediates that can have a prolonged half-life of around 60 hours or more, depending on age and speed of metabolism. The elderly have less ability to metabolise these long-acting active benzodiazepine metabolites, and are at risk of increased cognitive impairment from using these drugs. They freely cross the placenta and accumulate in the foetal circulation. They are associated with minimal risk to the developing baby, unless taken at high doses close to or at the time of delivery, which can result in dependency and withdrawal symptoms in the infant.

## PHARMACOLOGICAL EFFECTS AND MECHANISM OF ACTION

Benzodiazapines act by facilitating the binding of GABA, the main inhibitory neurotransmitter in the CNS, to its receptor. This occurs by the drug molecule binding to a modulatory site adjacent to the $GABA_A$ receptor sub-type, which causes a conformational change in the receptor's structure. This conformational change results in an increased affinity of GABA for its receptor. The inhibitory synaptic action of endogenous GABA is enhanced through facilitation of normal chloride ion influx as a result of this conformational change. This causes hyperpolarisation of the postsynaptic neuron, and further decreases its excitability, resulting in retarded neurotransmission. These inhibitory effects in the brain are thought to be responsible for the sedating and anxiety reducing effects of benzodiazepines. Benzodiazepines act on GABA receptors located in the amygdala, orbitofrontal cortex and insula to reduce anxiety, agitation and fear. GABA receptors located in the cerebral cortex and hippocampus are involved in mediating drug-induced amnesia and mental confusion. The muscle relaxant effects of these drugs are likely to be due to a combination of their anxiolytic properties and their action on receptors located in the spinal cord, cerebellum and brain stem, and receptors located in the cerebellum and hippocampus are involved in the antiepileptic actions of these drugs. Receptors influencing neurotransmission in the ventral tegmentum and nucleus accumbens regions of the brain's reward pathway, are likely to be involved in the positive rewarding effects and abuse potential of the benzodiazepines (Julien et al., 2014).

## CANNABIS

Cannabis (called marijuana/marihuana in the USA, Canada and Mexico) refers to the dried leaves and flowers of the hemp plant, *Cannabis sativa*, which contain many biologically active compounds with diverse physiological effects. This versatile plant has a long history of use for a variety of purposes in many cultures. Cannabis is commonly consumed by inhalation in the form of cigarettes, cigars, pipes, or water pipes. Hashish is a more potent derivative produced from the resin of cannabis flowers, and is usually smoked, but can also be eaten. It can also be brewed in drinks, and its oil-based extract (hash oil) can be added to tobacco and food.

Cannabis is estimated to be the illicit drug with the greatest levels of consumption and the highest reported lifetime prevalence levels in the world (see the review by De Luca et al., 2017). At the present time it is the subject of some interesting research regarding its potential for medicinal use. The pros and cons of legalising the medical and recreational use of cannabis are still being debated. However, there is a wealth of evidence regarding the negative consequences of non-medical recreational cannabis use, particularly during adolescence, which is a period of increased vulnerability due to the developing brain.

### MECHANISM OF ACTION

The cannabis plant contains around 400 different compounds, including the cannabinoids, which are a diverse group of chemicals that are active at cannabinoid receptors. Cannabinol (CBN) and cannabidiol (CBD) are abundant constituents of the plant with biological activity. The cannabinoid receptors CB1 and CB2 are G-protein coupled receptors, located throughout the CNS and the body. There are at least 85 different cannabinoids in the native plant. Delta-9-tetrahydrocannabinol (THC) has been identified as the primary active compound in cannabis. It is active predominantly at the CB1 cannabinoid receptor. CB1 receptors are abundant in the hippocampus, basal ganglia, cerebellum, and frontal cortex. The location of these receptors influences their physiological function. THC mediates many of the behavioural and physiological effects of cannabis, including analgesia, appetite control, and motor and cognitive impairments. CB2 receptors are found mostly outside the CNS in peripheral tissues, but they are abundant in immune cells, including the microglial immune cells of the CNS. These receptors may be involved in the anti-inflammatory actions of cannabinoids.

There are several endogenous ligands of the cannabinoid receptors, including 2-arachidonoylglycerol (2-AG) and arachidonoylethanolamine (AEA or anandamide). These endogenous compounds are produced as required, and function atypically compared to other neurotransmitters. They can inhibit synaptic transmission and have the overall effect of modulating neuronal excitability through activation of CB1 receptors. Endocannabinoids are thought to be involved in a wide range of physiological functions, including stress responsiveness, pain, memory, neuroprotection, and immune function.

## PHARMACOKINETICS

The amount of THC absorbed into the bloodstream through smoking is highly variable (between 5–60%) and depends on the amount of THC in the cannabis preparation, and the speed, length, and depth of the inhalation. THC is absorbed rapidly and completely and distributed throughout the body, especially in areas which have a higher concentration of fat such as the brain, the testes, and the placenta. The effects of the drug can be felt almost immediately after smoking, with peak plasma concentrations occurring within about 20 minutes. Levels decline after about 2 to 3 hours. If taken orally the effects are delayed, but can last for several hours longer than inhaled cannabis. However, the effects of orally consumed cannabis may be less potent due to acidic degradation, enzymatic action, and first pass metabolism. THC is metabolised in the liver by cytochrome P450 enzymes to its active metabolite, 11-hydroxy-delta-9-THC, which is then converted to an inactive metabolite, carboxy-THC (COOH-THC) before it is excreted in the urine. THC stored in body fat is slowly released, so small amounts can be detectable in the blood for up to several days, or even for up to several weeks in chronic users. The psychoactive effects of subsequently consumed drug may therefore be heightened by the presence of these low levels of THC already present in the body.

## PHARMACOLOGICAL EFFECTS

Cannabis has many interesting and diverse pharmacological effects, which can include both stimulatory and sedating actions. It causes a dose dependent increase in heart rate, and there is also a potential increased risk of heart attack and stroke in older users (although there may be confounding factors). Smoking cannabis is associated with arterial constriction in the brain, and, like tobacco smoking, cannabis smoking can cause inflammation and irritation of the respiratory system and is associated with symptoms of chronic bronchitis. The presence of CB2 receptors in cells of the immune system is suggestive of impaired immunity to infection in chronic cannabis users. Cannabis affects both male and female sex hormones and is associated with reduced levels of testosterone in males, decreased sperm count and viability, and an increased risk of testicular cancer. In females, cannabis can disrupt the menstrual cycle. It freely crosses the placental barrier in pregnancy and may have adverse effects, including decreased birth weight and increased risk of behavioural and cognitive impairment in the infant.

Cannabis is able to act as an analgesic pain killer and is particularly effective for inflammatory and neuropathic pain. This pain-relieving effect is referred to as an *opioid sparing action*, due to the reduction in opiate pain killer needed if cannabis is also taken. The development of a cannabis-based pain killer that does not also have the adverse effects of the drug is an area of active research exploration. Other potential medical uses of cannabinoids include treatment of glaucoma, nausea, epilepsy, and AIDS-related anorexia and wasting syndrome. At low doses the most commonly experienced psychoactive effects of cannabis are mild euphoria and relaxation. Altered perception of visual stimuli and time are also common effects. Cannabis is able to interact with the mesolimbic dopamine reward system in a similar manner to other addictive substances, and regular users are at high risk of addiction. At higher doses cannabis can cause delusions, hallucinations and psychosis. In chronic users there is an increased risk for the development of chronic psychotic disorders, including schizophrenia, in those with a biological vulnerability to psychosis. Additional psychoactive effects include impairments in memory, thinking and learning, and impaired body movement. Psychomotor impairment can last for many hours after drug consumption, and cannabis use is associated with an increased risk of road traffic accidents. Adverse health effects of cannabis use in adolescence include an increased risk for addiction to cannabis and other drugs, impaired neural connectivity, and a decline in IQ. Chronic cannabis use is associated with general apathy, lethargy, impaired judgement and a lack of motivation, with associated negative impacts on relationships, health, education and lifestyle (see the review by Volkow et al., 2014). Both tolerance and sensitisation can occur with chronic cannabis use. Withdrawal symptoms on cessation include craving, anxiety, irritability, disrupted and disturbed sleep, depression, anger, and decreased appetite. More recently there has been an increase in the availability and abuse of synthetic cannabinoid agonists such as 'spice' or 'K2' (amongst other names) labelled as 'not for human consumption'. These compounds can also cause addiction and adverse reactions, and they are particularly dangerous due to their unknown chemical composition (Julien et al., 2014).

## MDMA

MDMA (3,4-methylenedioxymethamphetamine, commonly known as 'ecstasy') is a synthetic derivative of amphetamine and belongs to the phenylethylamine family of chemicals. These chemicals are able to act as stimulants, hallucinogens, and/or entactogens (substances which increase feelings of openness and empathy). Their chemical structure is related to mescaline, a naturally occurring psychedelic substance found in the peyote cactus plant. MDMA became a popular recreational drug in the 1990s and is associated with the 'rave' subculture, which involves music, all night dancing, and flashing lights. Recreational MDMA users are often polydrug users, but as is the case with all street drugs, some MDMA users may also be unintentionally ingesting other drugs. The actual composition of tablets sold as MDMA has been found to vary widely.

### PHARMACOKINETICS

MDMA is usually taken in tablet form and exerts its effects in about 45 minutes, with peak effects experienced about 60 to 90 minutes after consumption. These effects last for about 3 to 4 hours. Recreational doses vary between 50 to 150 mg. The drug passes easily into body tissues and binds to the tissue constituents. It is metabolised in the liver, mainly by CYP2D6 and several other enzymes. The potentially toxic effects of the drug are enhanced by its inefficient degradation. The elimination half-life is about 8 hours and it takes about 40 hours to be cleared from the system completely. Some of the drug's metabolites are still pharmacologically active, and this can lead to persistent after-effects in some users.

### PHARMACOLOGICAL EFFECTS

The majority of users experience a feeling of loving connection to others and the universe whilst on the drug. This encompasses feelings of empathy and openness, which facilitate meaningful interpersonal communication. It is this aspect of the drug that is under scientific exploration as an adjunct to psychotherapy in conditions involving trauma such as PTSD.

The acute effects of MDMA taken in the context of a 'rave' can include an increase in heart rate, blood pressure, body temperature (hyperthermia), sweating, dehydration, psychomotor restlessness, involuntary jaw clenching, hot flashes, loss of appetite, and muscle fatigue. The ingestion of large quantities of fluid to try and offset some of these effects can also cause adverse reactions, including electrolyte imbalance and brain swelling due to water retention. It is possible that the simultaneous use of other substances including alcohol, and the adulteration of MDMA, may contribute to some of the acute adverse reactions. A potentially fatal condition called malignant hyperthermia can occur when MDMA is taken whilst engaging in extreme physical activity (such as non-stop dancing at a rave). As well as increased body temperature, this syndrome can cause a range of symptoms including convulsions, kidney failure, muscle breakdown, disorientation, and rapid heartbeat.

Long-term effects of regular MDMA use can result in multiple long-term psychobiological deficits in some users. These deficits adversely affect aspects of vision, memory, higher cognitive skill, neurohormonal functioning, cardiovascular functioning, foetal development, and sleep. MDMA is also associated with depression and anxiety in some users (see the review by Parrott et al., 2017). The dose and duration of drug use are likely to influence the degree of psychobiological impairment observed.

### MECHANISM OF ACTION

MDMA, like other amphetamines, acts by increasing the overall release of the monoamine neurotransmitters, serotonin, noradrenaline, and to a lesser extent, dopamine. Levels of these neurotransmitters are increased in the synaptic cleft through a combination of increased release and/or inhibition of reuptake. Increased levels of serotonin are thought to be responsible for the positive mood-enhancing effects of the drug. However, this greatly increased release of serotonin causes serotonin stores to be depleted and serotonin synthesis to be inhibited, which may mediate the feelings of depression experienced in the wake of the drug. Adaptations in the serotonin and dopamine systems that occur as a result of regular and long-term MDMA use may be associated with an increased risk of addiction, but this is thought to be less so than that for other drugs discussed in this chapter. This could be due to the development of tolerance to the positive effects of the drug with regular use.

## HALLUCINOGENS

Hallucinogens are a fascinating and diverse group of substances that are capable of producing unusual perceptual and cognitive experiences, which can be blissful, insightful and spiritually uplifting, and/or unpredictable, confusing, dissociative and frightening, depending on the drug type, dose taken and context of use. These types of experiences can encompass visual disturbances, hallucinations, synaesthesia, feelings of being out of the body, and other altered states of consciousness.

Naturally derived hallucinogenic substances include mescaline found in the peyote cactus, psilocybin found in certain types of mushrooms (commonly referred to as 'magic mushrooms'), and dimethyltryptamine (DMT) found in certain plants indigenous to South America. Lysergic acid diethylamide (LSD) is another hallucinogen which is synthesised from lysergic acid found in a fungus that grows on rye and other grains. These substances are structurally related to the neurotransmitter serotonin. In general, these types of hallucinogens are not reinforcing in the manner of other addictive substances, although in some cases tolerance can develop through repeated use.

Ketamine ('Special k') and phencyclidine (PCP or 'angel dust') have structural similarities to each other and are structurally unrelated to the above compounds. They are called 'dissociative anaesthetics' because they induce a state of memory loss and sensory distortion whilst the user remains conscious. Ketamine replaced PCP as a safer anaesthetic due to the potential for severe psychotic reactions induced by PCP. Ketamine is currently used medically as a veterinary and human anaesthetic, but both drugs are also used recreationally, and can be highly reinforcing, with significant abuse potential.

Ketamine acts as a non-competitive antagonist of the NMDA (N-methyl-D-aspartate) receptor, which results in an increase in the release of presynaptic glutamate, which may be responsible for some of its dissociative effects. An increase in dopamine release in the midbrain and prefrontal cortex, and other non-dopaminergic mechanisms, may mediate the reinforcing effects of these substances. Chronic ketamine or PCP use can have a number of adverse effects, including urological symptoms and cognitive deficits. Ketamine is also being explored as a potential therapeutic tool for the treatment of depression, and scientific investigation of its mechanism of action is providing insight into disorders involving glutamatergic dysfunction (Tyler et al., 2017).

# SUMMARY

This chapter has provided a brief overview of the psychopharmacology of commonly abused drugs. In addition to their other pharmacological effects, these drugs all share an ability to directly or indirectly influence neurotransmission in the brain's reward system to alter dopamine levels in the ventral tegmental area and nucleus accumbens regions of the brain (with the exception of some hallucinogens). This is thought to be an important factor in influencing their addictive potential. The dose of drug taken, the route of entry, and the speed with which it reaches the brain, are also important in how a drug is experienced. Different classes of drugs can vary in their actions at different doses, and can have overlapping pharmacological effects in some instances. An important factor in considering the effects of these different types of drugs on health is their availability and social acceptability, which influence the exposure and burden of drug-associated disease.

# QUESTIONS

- Discuss how the speed of entry to the brain is critical to the addiction process.
- Alcohol is a complex molecule with widespread neuropharmacological actions. Discuss.
- Compare the actions of cocaine and amphetamine.
- All drugs of abuse elevate dopamine levels. Discuss.
- Compare a hallucinogen with a psychostimulant.

# BIOLOGICAL THEORIES OF ADDICTION 3

## CHAPTER OVERVIEW

This chapter focuses on the biological theories of addiction, but should be read in conjunction with Chapter 5, 'Psychological Theories of Addiction'.

This chapter will:

- Outline the use of animals in the study of addiction
- Evaluate the key animal models of addiction
- Describe and evaluate theories of addiction
- Synthesise the theories of addiction
- Discuss the role of dopamine in learning

## LEARNING AIMS OF THE CHAPTER

- To understand the use of animal models of addiction in generating theoretical perspectives
- To understand the role of dopamine and the mesolimbic pathway in addiction
- To contextualise neurobiological mechanisms into the psychological accounts of addiction

# INTRODUCTION

The title of the chapter would lull the reader into thinking that finally there is a concrete account of addiction. In fact, the title of this chapter is a misnomer. The theories of addiction are really theories of a specific aspect of addiction and not the whole entity of addiction itself. The biological theories of addiction have focused on the role of the neurotransmitter dopamine (DA) in the addiction cycle. Moreover, the theories generally address the issue of addiction when it is fully entrenched, not the vulnerabilities that predispose the individual to addiction. The biological theories have taken advantage of the fact that drugs are biologically active agents, and that these agents can be followed on their journey to and through the brain. The drug that you use and the prototypical addictive agent can shape the view of addiction. Early theories focused on depressants such as heroin. More recently, the starting point for explanations has focused on stimulants, e.g. cocaine.

Many theories base much of their supporting evidence in the realm of animal studies. Such studies are open to debate on moral and ethical grounds. However, this chapter will look at their use in generating these theories. The debate will focus on the validity and reliability of the scientific use of animals.

# ANIMAL MODELS OF ADDICTION

Addiction is a human condition, but animals have been used to elucidate the neural mechanisms that potentially underlie it. The question that emerges in all animal experiments is how animals can tell us anything about humans. The simple answer is that they share common ancestors. We have evolved from the same origins as the rat; we share many similarities in brains, neurochemistry and genes. But we are different from the rat, and that is the greatest challenge of any animal model – that of extrapolation. From the evolutionary viewpoint humans diverged from the common ancestor a long time ago, but at the heart of survival of all mammalian species is a neurobiological system that serves all animals, and that system mediates motivation. That is motivation primarily for survival, but also for drugs of addiction.

The questions that attempt to unravel the neurobiological mechanisms of addiction cannot be answered purely by studying human behaviour and human brains. Ethical (and moral) principles ensure that we do not harm participants in a study – we cannot make someone addicted to cocaine for example, merely to view the neurobiological mechanisms. However, the laws of many nations permit such studies in non-humans, and there is of course an ethical and moral debate about the use of animals, but it is beyond the scope of this book to address such issues. However, if we accept that the law allows such experiments, then we must ensure that the use of animals is scientifically sound and of value: hence, the animal models of addiction.

Again, the title of this section is misleading. The animal models are not models of addiction, but of a facet of addiction, e.g. withdrawal, consumption or even impulsivity. A simulation of a behaviour such as addiction is an important tool for the scientist. According to Willner:

> ... models are tools. As such, they have no intrinsic value; the value of a tool derives entirely from the work one can do with it. Conclusions arising from the use of a simulation of abnormal behaviour are essentially hypotheses that must eventually be tested against the clinical state. An assessment of the validity of a simulation gives no more than an indication of the degree of confidence that we can place in the hypothesis arising from its use. (1991: 7)

The question is: *how can we be sure we are asking the right questions?* Using the concepts behind the development of psychometric testing and questionnaire design, Willner (1984) proposed that animal models should be validated. He developed the appraisal of an animal model for psychopharmacology, but it can be extended to other aspects of psychobiology. Three sets of validity are differentiated: predictive validity, face validity and construct validity. When assessing the utilisation of animals these criteria provide a useful structure.

- *Predictive validity* One should be able to predict how interventions manifest themselves in the animal model. All efficacious drugs for a condition should work in the animal model. It should not be limited to a specific chemical class or type of drug, e.g. just heroin. Furthermore, one should be able to exacerbate the symptoms in the animal in the same way you can in the human, e.g. stress. This gives symmetry to the interventions: can we make the condition better, but also can we make the condition worse?
- *Face validity* This is the degree to which there is a similarity between the model and the behaviour to be modelled. Additionally, with face validity new research findings need to be accounted for in the model. Thus, a model of behaviour may have face validity one day, but not the next, after new knowledge is assimilated. Perhaps the first place for assessing face validity is to look at the diagnostic criteria used. A considerable amount of research uses the American Psychiatric Association's guidelines, the *Diagnostic and Statistical Manual of the APA* (DSM), to characterise psychiatric disturbances. This provides a list from which one can extract behaviours to apply to

the animal model. There has been a substantial increase over the years of the DSM's existence in the size of the manuals. We now have DSM-5 and no doubt there will be revisions in the future. Looking at DSM-5 you will also note that the symptoms can be widespread across disorders. Given the overlap it is important to make sure that the symptoms being modelled are truly reflective of the disorder and are not secondary concerns.

- *Construct validity* A limitation with face validity is that the different species of animals have different overt behaviours. Willner (1991) uses the example of maternal behaviour to demonstrate this point. Maternal behaviour is evident across all species. However, it is expressed differently. A rat keeps her litter close and retrieves strays with her mouth. A rat mother does not change nappies, warm milk or go to rat playgroups, while a human mother, in general, performs some, if not all, of these behaviours.

The observable behaviours are different. However, they are regarded as homologous – arising from the same physiological substrate and theoretical construct. Construct validity refers to the theoretical rationale behind the behaviour. If experimentation supports the theory, then the model has a degree of construct validity. Construct validity is therefore the theoretical underpinning of the model that uses our current knowledge and view of a neuropsychiatric condition. When it comes to psychiatry and psychology, as we have already noted, aetiology is elusive, and we are therefore working in the realms of theoretical conjecture. A clear example of construct validity being harder to achieve can be seen for the animal models of addiction. People voluntarily consume drugs such as heroin and cocaine. However, because the theories behind drug misuse do not have a single theoretical rationale, it is hard to claim construct validity for the animal model. The most common animal model of addiction is drug self-administration in which the animal presses a lever to get a drug. Animals will readily do this; however, the reason they do so is open to conjecture. Some scientists argue that drug addiction is due to the positive actions of a drug, while others claim it is motivated by the urge to avoid unpleasant withdrawal symptoms (see Goudie, 1991). To have construct validity one must identify the variable being measured, and then assess the degree of homology and the significance of that variable to the clinical picture.

There is general agreement that there is a common mechanism in motivation and addiction. This view has been generated to a large extent by analysis of animal behaviour. Scientists have trained animals to consume drugs and studied the associations those animals make with drugs. The essence of such training is no different from how you would train any animal, such as a dog, to perform a task. Box 3.1 provides a brief description of learning theories central to understanding addiction and the biological mechanisms.

## BOX 3.1   LEARNING THEORIES

There are two theories of learning that are crucial for the understanding of addiction and the theories that have been generated to account for addiction.

### Classical conditioning

Classical conditioning is when a neutral stimulus becomes associated with a stimulus that is able to produce a reflex. The neutral stimulus, which previously had no effect, becomes able to produce the reflex. The work of Pavlov needs a little discussion. Pavlov and his students noticed that dogs would salivate to stimuli that were predictive of feeding time. When food was put into a dog's mouth, saliva was produced. Saliva contains enzymes that are used in the digestion of food. The saliva-producing response is a reflex to the orosensory stimulus of food in the mouth. In Pavlovian terms, the food is an *unconditioned stimulus* (UCS) and the production of saliva is an *unconditioned response* (UCR).

So far nothing had been learned by the dog in the experiment. During the next stage of the experiment a tone was introduced (a bell), which accompanied the presentation of food. Initially the tone was a neutral stimulus and did not produce a response. However, after a number of pairings of the tone and the food, when the tone was presented alone, it produced salivation in the dog. This tone is referred to as the *conditioned stimulus* (CS). The response to the tone is called the *conditioned response* (CR), in this case salivation.

Over successive pairings the CS gradually becomes associated with the UCS, producing a CR. The more pairings (or trials), the stronger the conditioning.

Once learned, presentation of the CS without the UCS would decrease the CR. Stop giving a dog food after it hears the tone and it will eventually stop salivating to the tone. This is called *extinction*. The CR is extinguished gradually as the animal experiences the CS without the UCS. After the extinction of the CR, and a period of rest without experimentation, the CR can appear again in response to the CS. This phenomenon is known as *spontaneous recovery* and may go some way to explaining the risk of relapse in addiction. If training is restarted, learning the CS–UCS pairing will be quicker than it was in the initial learning period. Spontaneous recovery can occur after a substantial rest period, indicating the permanence of learning. A person who successfully goes through detox still retains the learning of addiction. The drug

(Continued)

supplier knows this and will offer free drugs knowing that they will return and pay for them time and again.

An aspect of drug tolerance is also subject to the laws of conditioning. The body likes to maintain homeostasis. Opponent processes compensate for changes in the body to achieve homeostasis. If you take morphine for pain relief the body compensates for the drug by producing a reaction in the opposite direction e.g. more pain. After the drug has been given a number of times its effect weakens – tolerance. Tolerance could be seen as a pure biological activity in response to the drug, e.g. changes in the metabolism and brain structure. However, classical conditioning is very important in drug tolerance and can account for the overdose effect to a regular dose (Siegel et al., 1982; Siegel et al., 2000).

Most people take their drug in a particular environment. The very nature of heroin use means it has to be taken in a clandestine manner. All the cues in the environment provide the users with a CR. What happens if you take the drug user out of their environment, put them somewhere new, and give them their regular dose? They may well die from their regular dose in what looks like an overdose. In the new environment the cues are no longer there to provide the user with a CR. The absence of the compensatory CR means that the intake of their normal dose of heroin has a greater effect because it does not have to account for the CR.

This is an effect that has been systematically studied in the rat under controlled conditions. In this experiment one group of rats was exposed to heroin in the test environment and another group in a different environment. A third control group received neither. The group that received the heroin in a different environment showed the overdose effect, whereas the rats that received the same dose in the test environment did not.

## Operant conditioning

Operant conditioning (or instrumental conditioning) is about the organism operating in the environment to produce an outcome. If we do something and the outcome is good, then there is a greater chance we will do it again. This area of psychology is called behaviourism.

Skinner was instrumental in shaping behaviourism. Fundamental to operant conditioning is *reinforcement*. Reinforcement is when the consequences of a response increase the probability that the response will reoccur. If a rat presses a lever and gets food, it will be more likely to press the lever again. And here we can replace food with injections of drugs.

Using reinforcement, behaviours can be selected and strengthened. There are two types of reinforcement: positive and negative. *Positive reinforcement* is when a reinforcer is presented after a response and increases the likelihood of that response recurring.

In the animal experiments, food is a positive reinforcer. For humans, money and praise (particularly in children) are positive reinforcers. Basically, you get something you want after you have done something (e.g. wages for working).

*Negative reinforcement* also increases the probability of a particular response. However, in this case, it is the removal of an unpleasant event or circumstance that strengthens a response, e.g. a rat will press a bar or lever to escape an electric shock. When a stimulus is indicative of electric shock, the rat will press a lever and thus avoid the shock. Similarly, humans respond to negative reinforcement. The roles of positive and negative reinforcement have been used to account for drug addiction.

When a particular behaviour is reinforced every time, it is said to be on a continuous reinforcement (CRF) schedule. Behaviourists consider all our actions under the control of operant conditioning. Clearly, we are not on a CRF schedule for all our behaviours, so how is behaviour maintained in the absence of a CRF schedule?

The answer can be found when we consider partial reinforcement. With partial reinforcement the organism is not reinforced every time it responds. There are four schedules of reinforcement.

> With a *fixed ratio (FR) schedule* the rat is reinforced after a number of bar presses.
>
> A variable ratio (VR) schedule is similar to the FR schedule, except that reinforcement occurs after a variable amount of responses.
>
> A *fixed interval (FI) schedule* is when, after a specified period of time the rat receives reinforcement only if it has pressed the bar during that time.

(Continued)

A rat on *a variable interval (VI) schedule* receives reinforcement after an average period of time only if it has responded correctly.

Animals, like people, do not learn immediately. A number of learning trials have to be completed before a rat can respond to a stimulus reliably. Many of the experiments you will read about have involved long and sometimes complex training regimes. The more complex the task, the longer the training.

A complex piece of behaviour cannot be learned overnight. In order to train an animal, one must start with simple behaviours, which contribute to the overall goal behaviour. Once acquired, new behaviours can be worked on and refined. This process is called *shaping*. The shaping of the smaller subsets of behaviours is called 'shaping of successive approximations', – that is, one reinforces behaviours that are getting closer to the desired behaviour. Such procedures are used regularly in training animals (dogs in particular).

On a CRF the animal stops responding soon after reinforcement stops. Initially the rat presses the lever rapidly, but eventually this diminishes until it stops responding altogether. Partial reinforcement schedules make extinction of a response more difficult.

## Spontaneous recovery

As is the case with classical conditioning, spontaneous recovery can occur. After a period of absence from training, the rat, on re-acquaintance with the apparatus, will start responding again.

A number of methods are used to determine the reward pathways in the brain and the site of action of drugs in animals (see Stolerman, 1992).

- Intracranial self-stimulation (ICSS)
- Drug self-administration
- Conditioned place preference (CPP) (see Box 3.2)

# INTRACRANIAL SELF-STIMULATION (ICSS)

Classic experiments by Olds and Milner demonstrated that rats would press a lever to receive electrical stimulation, via an implanted electrode, in specific regions of the brain (Olds & Milner, 1954) (for a review see Wise, 2005). This paradigm (and many paradigms in addiction) take their lead from the early pioneering work on learning from Skinner and Pavlov (see Box 3.1), the rationale being that if the animal presses a lever to receive electrical stimulation, then it is doing so because it is motivated to do so, presumably because of a positive reinforcing effect. In terms of methodology it is important to extract motor behaviour from motivational behaviour. Electrical stimulation may just be stimulating motor neurons and therefore the animal lever presses because it cannot do anything else but lever press. It is not because it wants to lever press or is motivated to lever press. To subtract this confounding variable the use of two bars ascertains whether the animal is merely activated or motivated. If activated the animal will press on both bars with equal frequency, however if motivated the animal will focus its lever-pressing activity on the lever that delivers the electrical stimulation.

## BOX 3.2   CONDITIONED PLACE PREFERENCE (CPP)

Conditioned place preference (CPP) is a non-invasive method for assessing the reinforcing properties of a drug. CPP involves looking at drug-seeking behaviour. It does this by using secondary conditioning: a drug becomes associated with a specific environment (see Figure 3.1). Previously neutral stimuli become associated with the drug. The drug is the UCS that produces pleasurable effects (the UCR), and the environment in which it receives the drug becomes associated with the drug (CS). When tested drug-free, the rat seeks out the drug-associated environment if it is reinforcing (CR).

With CPP in its simplest form, a rat is exposed to one compartment of a chamber comprising at least two distinct chambers. The chambers can differ along a number of sensory dimensions that tap into visual, tactile and olfactory modalities (or indeed a mix of them). If the animal is exposed to the drug in environment A and placebo in

(Continued)

environment B, then the animal is more likely to spend time in environment A when tested drug free. Essentially the animal associates the environment with the drug, presumably the pleasurable effects. CPP has been used to assess DAergic drugs such as cocaine and amphetamine which both produce robust data showing a preference for the drug-associated environment (see Anderson & Pierce, 2005; Spyraki et al., 1982).

Clearly distinctive environments can trigger drug–taking behaviour, e.g. the bar and drinking. Embracing new technology, Astur, Carew, and Deaton (2014) used virtual reality to induce a conditioned place preference in humans (which is much easier than putting them in a box). In this study they used undergraduate students and put them in virtual environments. In one virtual environment they received the food reward and in a separate different virtual environment they did not receive the food reward. When they were given free access to the whole of the virtual reality world, those students that had received food reward spent more time in the environment where food had been associated.

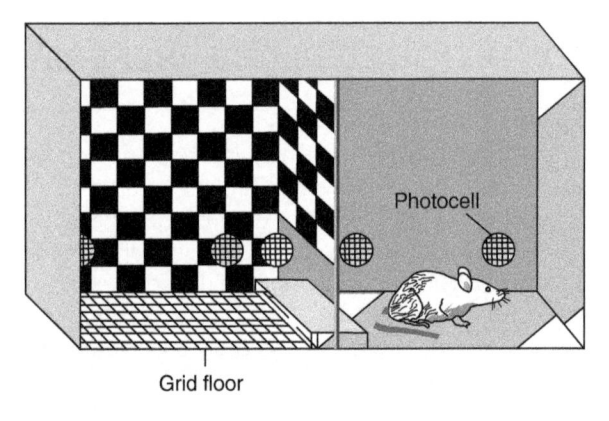

**Figure 3.1** The two distinctive sides of a typical CPP box

*Source*: reproduced with the permission of John Wiley & Sons Inc, from *Psychobiology* by Chris Chandler (2015); permission sourced through author and publisher

The areas of the brain that mediate electrical stimulation also contain high levels of DA (Corbett & Wise, 1980), in particular the *nucleus accumbens* (NAcc) (Phillips et al., 1975), the striatum (Phillips et al., 1976), and the prefrontal cortex (Mora et al., 1976).

This method of assessing the neural mechanisms of reward may seem a far cry from addiction, but it has been used to assess the addictive nature of drugs (see Kenny, 2007; Wise, 1996). The electrical stimulation produces neural activity in the brain regions where the electrode is placed; thus, action potentials and DA release occur. Using this method, the administration of cocaine and amphetamines has been shown to reduce responding for the electrical stimulation by presumably substituting for the rewarding effects of electrical stimulation (Leith & Barrett, 1981; Risner & Jones, 1975; Tyce, 1968).

The NAcc does not sit alone and has some very important connections. The area of the brain that has received most attention as the neural substrate of addiction is the *mesolimbic pathway* (see Figure 3.2). The mesolimbic pathway runs from the *ventral tegmental area* (VTA) to the NAcc. Destroying the mesolimbic pathway with a neurotoxin disrupts ICSS, especially if the electrodes are placed in the NAcc on the same side of the lesion (Fibiger et al., 1987; Phillips & Fibiger, 1978).

## DRUG SELF-ADMINISTRATION

Self-administration of drugs by animals is an important step in identifying their abuse potential (O'Connor et al., 2011). Drug self-administration is an operant task in which an animal receives an infusion of a drug after pressing a lever via an indwelling catheter in the jugular vein (but also into specific regions of the brain) (see Sanchis-Segura & Spanagel, 2006, for a review) .

The neurobiology of addiction has received extensive attention – after all there are now many tools (drugs) to probe this behaviour. Given that there are many addictive substances the question of common mechanisms remains.

The drugs that we choose to take, for whatever reason, differ considerably in their pharmacology: nicotine works at acetylcholine (ACh) receptors; heroin is converted into morphine and interacts with opiate receptors; diazepam operates at the benzodiazepine complex of the GABA receptors; cannabis works within the endocannabinoid system; and cocaine works within the DA system. Perhaps the hardest drug to account for is alcohol because it does so much that the identification of simple single neural systems is difficult. The different pharmacology of these drugs would at first lead one to assume that there are many different mechanisms that lead to reward and addiction. Despite differences in their pharmacology and subjective effects, most addictive drugs share a common neural substrate, which

(a) In the rat

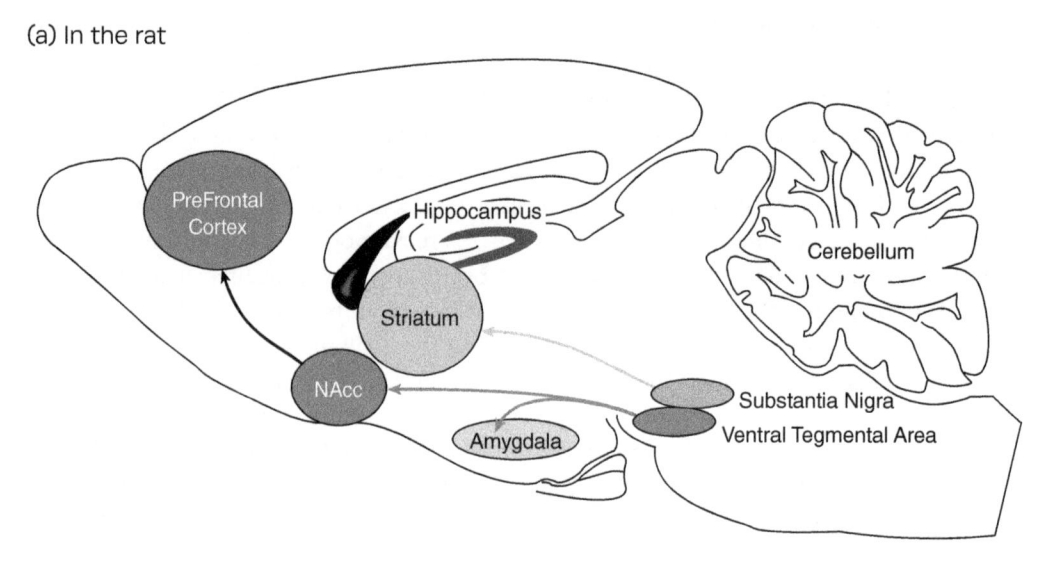

(b) In the human

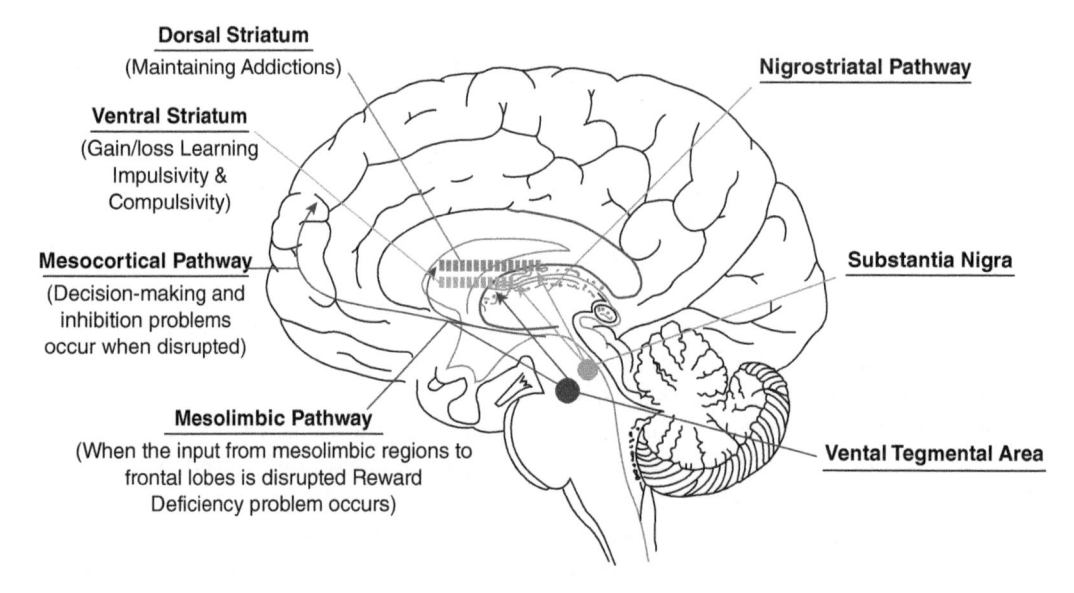

**Figure 3.2** Dopamine pathways in (a) the rat and (b) the human

*Source*: reproduced with permission from Davide Ferrazzoli, Adrian Carter, Fatma S. Ustun, Grazia Palamara, Paola Ortelli, Roberto Maestri, Murat Yücel, and Giuseppe Frazzitta (2016) Dopamine replacement therapy, learning and reward prediction in Parkinson's Disease: implications for rehabilitation. *Frontiers in Behavioral Neuroscience, 10*(121), doi:10.3389/fnbeh.2016.00121)

influences their motivational ability to produce compulsive drug seeking and drug consumption. Most drugs support self-administration, however the hallucinogenic drugs, e.g. LSD and mescaline, are exceptions (see Box 3.3).

## BOX 3.3   LSD AND SELF-ADMINISTRATION

LSD is the exception to the rule when it comes to drug abuse and self-administration.

It has been claimed that the common denominator of addictive drugs is the mesolimbic DA pathway; however, there is a group of drugs that are not addictive but misused – the psychedelics, typified by D-lysergic acid diethylamide (LSD). Animals do not self-administer LSD and other hallucinogens. In fact rhesus monkeys will press a lever to turn off a stimulus associated with LSD infusion (Hoffmeister & Wuttke, 1975). The reason for this is that LSD acts on serotonin and does not act in the mesolimbic pathway as does cocaine for example. However, MDMA (ecstasy), a mixed DA and 5-HT drug, is self-administered (Fantegrossi et al., 2002; Schenk et al., 2003), thus pointing to the role of DA in mediating these behaviours rather than serotonin.

In contrast to self-administration studies in CPP experiments, LSD produces a conditioned place preference in the rat (Meehan & Schechter, 1998; Parker, 1996). Thus, a CPP may be acquired without exclusive activation of the mesolimbic DA pathway.

Many experiments have verified that animals will self-administer cocaine and amphetamine (see Katz, 1989). Roberts and Ranaldi (1995) pointed out that DA antagonists increase responding for cocaine and amphetamine. This is a compensatory mechanism; the animal presses a lever even more to overcome the interruption of the drug effects (called an extinction burst; see Box 3.1 for a brief overview of conditioning). Cocaine and amphetamine are both DA agonists. Their powerful addictive properties appear to be mediated by DA in the mesolimbic pathway. But what about non-DAergic drugs? *Nicotine* acts at an ACh receptor and not at DA receptors, and provides an example of how a non-DAergic drug impacts upon DA.

Nicotine receptors can be found in the VTA and NAcc. A number of studies have shown that nicotine can also increase the levels of DA in the NAcc (e.g. Mirza et al., 1996). Imperato, Mulas, and Di Chiara (1986) found that nicotine increased DA in the NAcc by

100% and also increased the levels of the DA metabolites 3,4-Dihydroxyphenylacetic acid (DOPAC) and Homovanillic acid (HVA). Nicotine increases the levels of DA very quickly, but these then diminish. As the levels of DA diminish, the metabolites of DA increase. This is indicative of DA being used and eliminated by metabolic enzymes (e.g. MAO). Thus, the DA neurons in the NAcc have been extremely active following nicotine administration. Nicotine's ability to increase DA from the NAcc is something it shares with many other addictive drugs (e.g. the opiates, such as heroin; see Pontieri et al., 1996).

The use of drugs has pointed to the role of the DAergic mesolimbic system being a common denominator. Does this translate to non-drug reinforcers? Generally, the answer is yes. Using food as a reinforcer, rats were shown to have elevated dopamine levels in the NAcc when either food was presented or a signal associated with food was presented (Bassareo & Di Chiara, 1997, 1999). Similarly, dopamine is elevated in the NAcc when a male rat is exposed to a sexually receptive female rat (Damsma et al., 1992; Fiorino & Phillips, 1999). Dopamine would also appear to be behind the Coolidge effect in sexually satiated rats, in which the presence of a novel receptive female rat initiates rising dopamine and copulatory behaviour (Fiorino et al., 1997). The increasing dopamine is not restricted to male sexual behaviour, and is also evident within female rats (Pfaus et al., 1995) and in the human responses to sex-related stimuli (Sylva et al., 2013).

## BIOLOGICAL THEORIES OF ADDICTION

Having established that there is a physiological basis for addiction – mesolimbic DA – these physiological accounts can be placed within a theoretical framework to address the processes of addiction. The main theoretical positions are based on associative learning, those laws initially identified by Pavlov and Skinner (see Box 3.1). However, there is increasing evidence to suggest a genetic predisposition to addiction but as yet how this informs motivation needs to be determined (Uhl et al., 2002).

The theories of addiction fall into two main camps, positive reinforcement theories and negative reinforcement theories.

## POSITIVE REINFORCEMENT

Taking the position of explaining addiction from the perspective of the psychostimulants, Wise and Bozarth (1987) provided an account of addiction that focused on the psychomotor properties of drugs in which '*The crux of the theory is that the reinforcing effects of the drugs, and thus their addiction liability, can be predicted from their ability to induce psychomotor activation'* (Wise & Bozarth, 1987: 474). There are three major assertions of the theory:

1. All addictive drugs have psychomotor stimulant actions.
2. The stimulant actions of these drugs share a biological mechanism.
3. This mechanism is homologous with the mechanism for positive reinforcement.

The theory stems from an earlier account of reinforcement in which reinforcement is explained in terms of approach behaviours (Glickman & Schiff, 1967). If you want something then you have got to move to go and get it. Thus, drugs, like all positive reinforcers, should elicit forward locomotion. The neural basis of the psychomotor stimulant theory places emphasis on the two dopamine systems: (1) the mesolimbic system, in which low doses produce forward locomotion; and (2) the nigrostriatal system, in which high doses increase small localised movements, e.g. stereotypy.

The importance of these two systems is that they derive from the same embryological tissue. The ventral tegmental area is the equivalent of the substantia nigra and the NAcc with the nucleus caudate (striatum) (see Figure 3.2).

In their review of the evidence Wise and Bozarth account for numerous drugs including the depressants. They point out that even the CNS depressants have psychomotor activating effects depending upon time course and dose. For example, they state that the opiates have a biphasic effect on locomotor activation where low doses stimulate activity and high doses inhibit it. The time course of action of opiates psychomotor activation indicates an effect early on after drug administration, which may be partially down to the pharmacokinetics of absorption and distribution.

The psychomotor stimulant theory of addiction suggests locomotor activity is an important measure of reinforcement. However, whilst the theory provides a clear account of how drugs affect motor activity, it does not tell us about the adaptations that occur during the process of addiction. The neural adaptations following repetitive drug taking are currently central to many theories of addiction, and have been approached from many perspectives such as sensitisation and learning.

## SENSITISATION

In the search for a common denominator the sensitisation of locomotor behaviour has received considerable attention. Sensitisation is an increase in activity after repeated doses. Sensitisation as a psychopharmacological phenomenon has been incorporated into a theory of addiction and motivation.

# SENSITISATION OF INCENTIVE SALIENCE: A THEORY OF ADDICTION

With continuing exposure to a drug there is a heightened responsiveness to subsequent drug administrations – basically there is a bigger effect. This is an effect that mesolimbic DA may mediate (Kalivas & Weber, 1988; Kolta et al., 1989).

Wise and Bozarth (1987) presented a view that the common denominator of reinforcing drugs is their psychomotor stimulant properties, which are mediated via mesolimbic DA.

Robinson and Berridge's theory (Berridge & Robinson, 2003; Robinson & Berridge, 1993; Robinson & Berridge, 2000) has integrated learning and the physiological action of drugs: the incentive–sensitisation theory of addiction. The theory of incentive sensitisation has also been conceptualised as a computational model with successful predictions being made (Zhang et al., 2012).

In this theory there are three major features of addiction:

1. There is craving for the drug.
2. The drug craving is persistent and can reappear after abstinence.

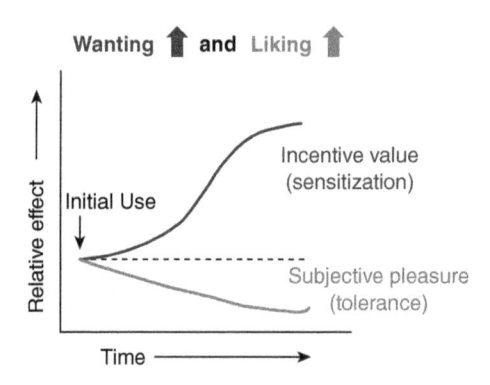

**Figure 3.3** The differentiation of wanting and liking of a drug according to Robinson and Berridge (1993). As the 'wanting' increases for a drug, the pleasure or 'liking' diminishes.

*Source*: reproduced with the permission of John Wiley & Sons Inc, from *Psychobiology* by Chris Chandler (2015); permission sourced through author and publisher. Original source Robinson, T. E., & Berridge, K. C. (1993). The neural basis of drug craving: An incentive-sensitization theory of addiction. *Brain Research Reviews, 18*(3), 247–291.

# BIOLOGICAL THEORIES OF ADDICTION

3. As the craving for the drug increases (the 'wanting' of the drug), the pleasure obtained from it decreases (the 'liking' of the drug) (see Figure 3.3).

The process of drug taking leads to sensitisation of physiological and behavioural measures. The neural system that is sensitised is hypothesised to mediate a psychological function involved in incentive motivation. In an addict, the drug becomes a highly motivating reinforcer and is given incentive salience – the wanting of the drug. Sensitisation, then, enhances incentive salience. Incentive salience is a motivational state, which turns stimuli into desired must-have objects (drugs or Gibson Les Paul Standard guitars [please take note Gibson USA]).

The theory continues to state that, via conditioning, the drug and associated stimuli become more salient (see Figure 3.4). Thus, the stimuli associated with the drug (e.g. drug paraphernalia, such as the syringe with intravenous heroin use) become able to control behaviour – that is, induce the wanting of the drug.

This increase in wanting the drug is due to the neural substrate, and the associative learning to it, becoming more sensitised. The bad news is that repeated exposure only sensitises the wanting, not the liking. The pleasure derived from the drug is mediated by another system, perhaps an opiate system (see the interview with Kent Berridge in Phillips, 2003), and is subject to tolerance. Robbins and Everitt (2007) suggest that wanting is linked to appetitive behaviour (drug seeking) and liking to consummatory behaviour

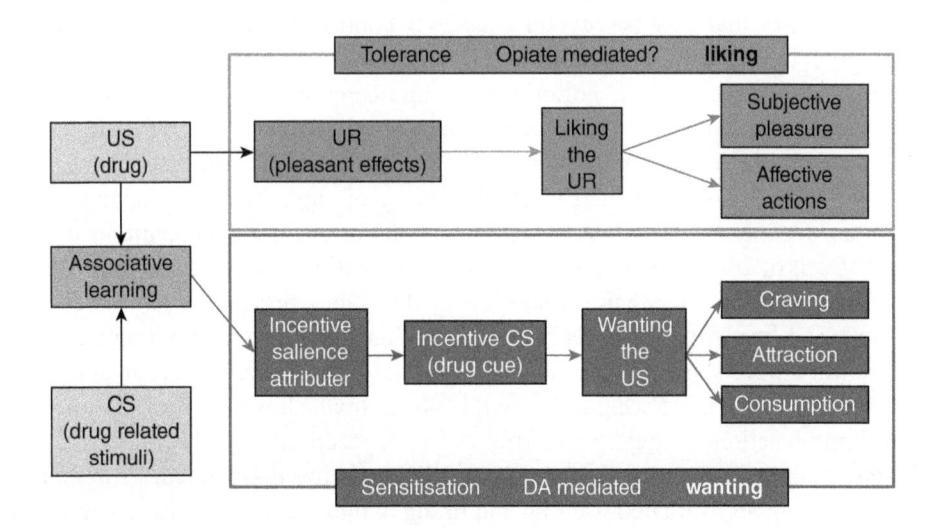

**Figure 3.4a** The mechanism of sensitisation

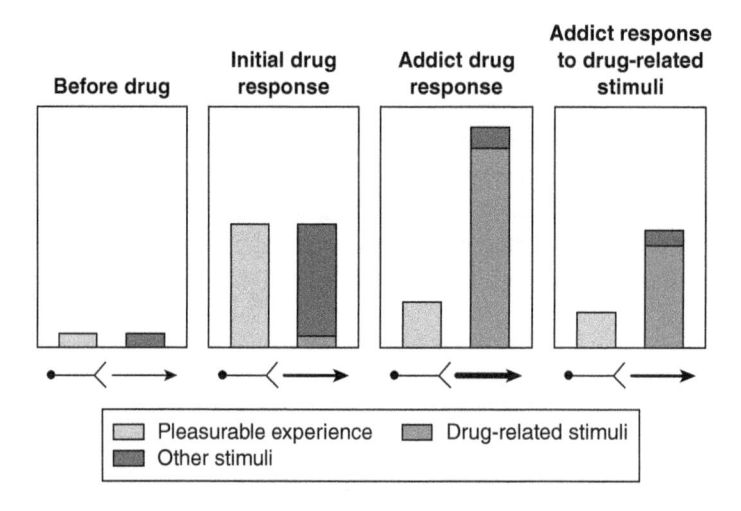

**Figure 3.4b** The effects of drug associated stimuli on craving: as the process of addiction progresses, drug-related stimuli have a greater influence on DA systems. From Chandler, C. (2015). *Psychobiology*. Chichester, UK.: John Wiley & Sons. Original source Robinson, T. E., & Berridge, K. C. (1993). The neural basis of drug craving: An incentive-sensitization theory of addiction. *Brain Research Reviews, 18*(3), 247–291.

(e.g. taking the drug). They continue to argue that wanting represents a stimulus-response processing circuitry that may be beyond conscious control. Liking may be mediated via opiate receptors in the nucleus accumbens (Berridge, 2000). A study by Lambert, McLeod, and Schenk (2006) supported the notion that liking decreases and wanting increases in a group of participants who had a previous history of stimulant medication and smoking (inducing sensitisation) when they were subsequently asked to rate cocaine. In dopamine deficient genetically modified mice, the liking of sugar was not dopamine mediated whereas the motor behaviour of licking to obtain sugar was dopamine mediated (Cannon & Bseikri, 2004). Mice that have been genetically modified to be hyperdopaminergic (which means that they have higher levels of synaptic dopamine) have been shown to have increased 'wanting' for sweet rewards, but this is not equated with increased 'liking'. These mice were shown to eat more food, drink more water, run faster in a runway to obtain food and gain more weight than wild-type animals, however they showed fewer orofacial liking reactions to sugar in an affective taste reactivity test (Pecina et al., 2003). Not all reports are consistent with wanting and liking being dissociated. Professor Paul Willner and colleagues evaluated wanting and liking in moderate to extreme alcohol drinkers (Willner et al., 2005). In their pseudo-dose response study wanting increased with the level of drinking, however in contrast to the predictions made by the incentive salience theory of addiction, liking also increased.

Sensitisation remains for a long period of time, even after the drug-taking has stopped; it may even be permanent. Persistent sensitisation has been demonstrated in human participants given amphetamine and tested a year later (Boileau et al., 2006).

It is this persistence that can lead to the reinstatement of drug taking (somewhat like spontaneous recovery). Because of the conditioning of drug-related stimuli to the drug, the drug-related stimuli can precipitate relapse. Anecdotal accounts from detoxified drug users have indicated that returning to the drug-taking environment can lead to a relapse.

Whilst the theory has generated a great deal of interest and debate, it does not hold out the prospect of an optimistic future for the drug addict. Cognitive behavioural therapy offers the greatest hope for reducing sensitisation to drugs and their associated stimuli (Robinson & Berridge, 2000).

# PHYSICAL DEPENDENCE THEORIES AND NEGATIVE REINFORCEMENT

Drugs clearly produce physiological effects. With positive reinforcement this may be the euphoric nature of getting high. However, drugs often produce withdrawal symptoms in their absence. Given the extremely unpleasant nature of withdrawal symptoms an addict is compelled to alleviate them by continuing to take the drug. Therefore, negative reinforcement maintains drug-taking behaviour: a response (drug taking) stops a negative consequence (withdrawal symptoms).

Withdrawal symptoms are an aversive state induced by the addiction process itself; however, another aspect of negative reinforcement that maintains drug consumption is that of self-medication. With self-medication the drug is consumed to avoid aversive states that exist prior to the drug-taking behaviour commencing, e.g. depression and/or anxiety (E. J. Khantzian, 1985). It is easy to see that a drink at the end of the day can help with all the stressors, or that diazepam can calm anxiety. The fact that comorbidity exists with addiction is a point highlighted by Professor Mike Gossop, who argues that treating the addiction and not the pre-existing comorbidities that can be revealed post detoxification is going to lead to limited treatment success (Gossop, 2003).

Perhaps the most influential theory focusing on negative reinforcement is that of Professor George Koob. Whilst Koob's theory focuses on negative reinforcement, the initial consumption of drugs leads to positive reinforcement (Koob, 1987). However, positive reinforcement diminishes and leads to negative motivational states in the chronic drug user

(Koob & Le Moal, 2005). This theory sees addiction as a dynamic process that moves from positive reinforcement into negative reinforcement, typified by positive reinforcement being a problem of impulse control developing later into a compulsive disorder, like OCD that is governed by negative reinforcement. During positive reinforcement there is pleasure relief and gratification, whereas in negative reinforcement it is the relief of anxiety and stress that is the goal position. The process of addiction is seen as a spiralling descent of preoccupation and anticipation leading to consumption and intoxication and then withdrawal, which then leads back to preoccupation and anticipation again (Koob & Le Moal, 1997).

The extended amygdala is composed of the central nucleus, bed nucleus of the stria terminalis, and the shell of the NAcc, and all of these are involved in negative reinforcement. Opioid and dopamine systems are concentrated in these regions (Koob, 2003).

Changes in the extended amygdala and brain stress systems provide the negative emotional state that drives addiction – in what Koob refers to as the *dark side* of motivation (Koob & Le Moal, 2005). Chronic drug use results in opponent processes in which there is a functional down regulation of the brain reward mechanisms through overexposure and that these reward systems do not reset themselves (Koob & Le Moal, 2001). The process by which the reward systems recalibrate themselves is not homoeostasis, but rather allostasis. 'Allostasis' was a term introduced by Sterling and Eyer (1988) as an alternative to homoeostasis, which is the ability to achieve 'stability through change' and in order 'to obtain stability, an organism must vary all of the parameters of its internal milieu and match them appropriately to environmental demands' (Sterling & Eyer, 1988: 636). The application of allostasis to addiction involves the stability of reward functioning being achieved by changes in the reward and stress neurocircuitry. These opponent processes are counter adaptive and lead to a deviation from the normal reward setpoints. Koob and Le Moal (2001) argue that there is a change in mood states associated with the transition to drug addiction. Elevated mood is countered by negative mood. GABA, opioids and dopamine mediate the positive mood, whereas the negative mood is a result of increased stress hormones. Due to the actions of drugs on the systems there is a shift from a homeostatic point to a new setpoint (allostatic setpoint) that is in opposition to normal reward processing (see Figure 3.5). According to this theory, addiction becomes a vicious circle in which drug consumption negates the negative affect, but it is that very drug consumption that changes the brain to potentiate the negative affect. Thus, negative reinforcement maintains addiction.

Neuroadaptations of the dopamine system have been revealed in imaging studies of human addicts. The general pharmacological principle is that stimulation of receptors leads to a functional down regulation in terms of number and affinity. Studies conducted by Nora Volkow (director of the National Institute on Drug Abuse [NIDA] in America) have shown reduced dopamine receptors in alcoholics and cocaine users (Volkow et al., 1993; Volkow et al., 1996; Volkow et al., 1997). Low levels of dopamine receptors have been linked with

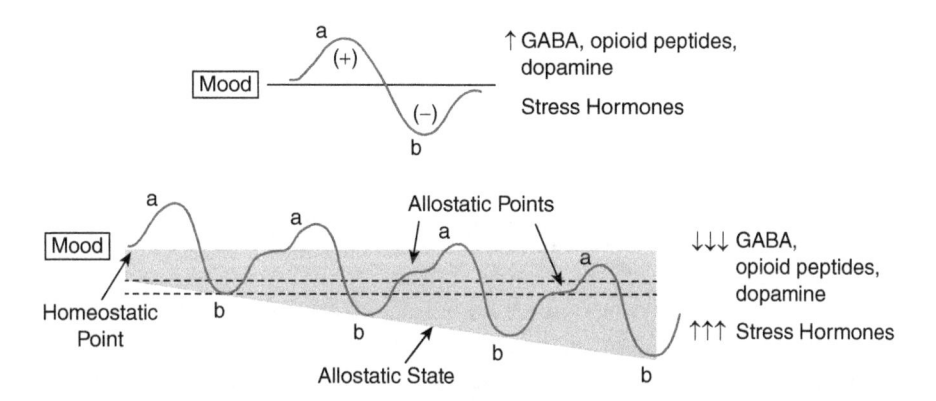

**Figure 3.5** The effects of stress and addiction on the equilibrium of the reward pathway. As the brain is bombarded with repetitive drug use it compensates by down-regulating via opponent processes. Eventually, the brain recalibrates to the new drug-infused environment via allostasis and a new lower level of DA activity becomes the norm.

*Source:* reproduced with the permission of John Wiley & Sons Inc, from *Psychobiology* by Chris Chandler (2015); permission sourced through author and publisher. Adpated from Original source Macmillan Publishers Ltd from Koob, G. F., & Le Moal, M. (2001). Drug addiction, dysregulation of reward, and allostasis. *Neuropsychopharmacology*, 24(2), 97–129 © 2001

increased liking of the drug (Volkow et al., 1999). Thus, it is conceivable that the drug user is consuming drugs in order to compensate for neural adaptations which have led to a reduction in dopamine receptors, which may consequently result in a hyperactive reward pathway. What is needed is a prospective study of humans to determine if low dopamine receptors are a risk factor for later drug abuse rather than an artefact of drug administration. A study using cynomolgus macaques sought to understand the influence of dopamine receptor number on subsequent cocaine self-administration. In this study by Morgan et al. (2002) dopamine receptors were measured using a PET scan. When the macaques were individually housed they all had a similar number of dopamine D2 receptors, but when they were put into group housing there was a difference between dominant and subordinate animals. Those that became dominant were not stressed and the number of dopamine receptors increased, whereas those that remained subordinate within the group enclosure did not have a corresponding elevation in dopamine receptors. When the animals were subsequently trained to self-administer cocaine, the significance of this finding became clearer. Those animals that were dominant were less likely to administer cocaine, whereas the subordinate animals readily pressed the lever to receive an infusion of cocaine. This study therefore suggests that environmental circumstances can lead to differences in dopamine receptor number which confers a vulnerability for drug addiction. Could the same extend to humans? The finding that social status has been shown to correlate with dopamine receptor levels in the striatum suggests this may be the case (Martinez et al., 2010).

## CONTROL MECHANISMS

If addiction is predominantly the by-product of a faulty reward system that is operating for positive and negative reinforcement, then the laws of associative learning would suggest that discontinuation of the drug would lead to extinction. When an animal trained to self-administer a drug has that drug removed, an extinction burst can be measured in which the animal rapidly responds to acquire the drug. As time goes by and the drug is no longer delivered extinction occurs. However, the laws of associative learning also tell us that there is spontaneous recovery. Priming doses of the drug, any conditioned stimuli associated with the drug, and life's stresses, can all precipitate drug self-administration.

Animal learning theories have told us some aspects of the addiction process, but according to W.R. Miller:

> Some years ago the eminent learning theorist, Frank Logan, gave the keynote address to the International Conference on Treatment of Addictive Behaviors. He offered a brilliant and encyclopedic review of research on animal self-administration of alcohol (including one ill-advised study of the effects of intoxication in elephants). He concluded that one needs nothing more than animal learning models to explain how people get trapped in addiction, but that there is no adequate animal model of recovery ... Animal learning principles describe the dilemma but not its resolution ... To understand how people escape from addiction – be it in treatment, in Alcoholics Anonymous, or in the natural course of life events – one must turn to that which is uniquely human, to the higher-order processes of the human mind. (2003: 63)

The behaviour of addiction and even some of the theories would suggest that all we have to do is say 'no' to drugs. The Just Say No campaign launched by Nancy Reagan wanted people to decline drugs. Similar views are all too often voiced in the letter pages of tabloid newspapers.

History indicates that this was easier said than done. Saying no requires the individual to override the neuroadaptations that have occurred in subcortical regions of the brain. The area of the brain that could potentially override the automatic processes of addiction is the frontal lobe. It is the frontal lobe that is able to inhibit our behaviour. It is the frontal lobe which

## BOX 3.4  BEHAVIOURAL INHIBITION

Behavioural inhibition is measured in the laboratory by two common methods, the Stop Signal Reaction Time Task and the Go/No-go task. Both require the individual to stop a simple hand movement. This sounds easy but it is not. And it is even harder for those with impulse control problems. The difficulty arises for two reasons: (1) there are more trials in which a response is required and therefore becomes well learned and automatic; and (2) the stimuli are presented very quickly.

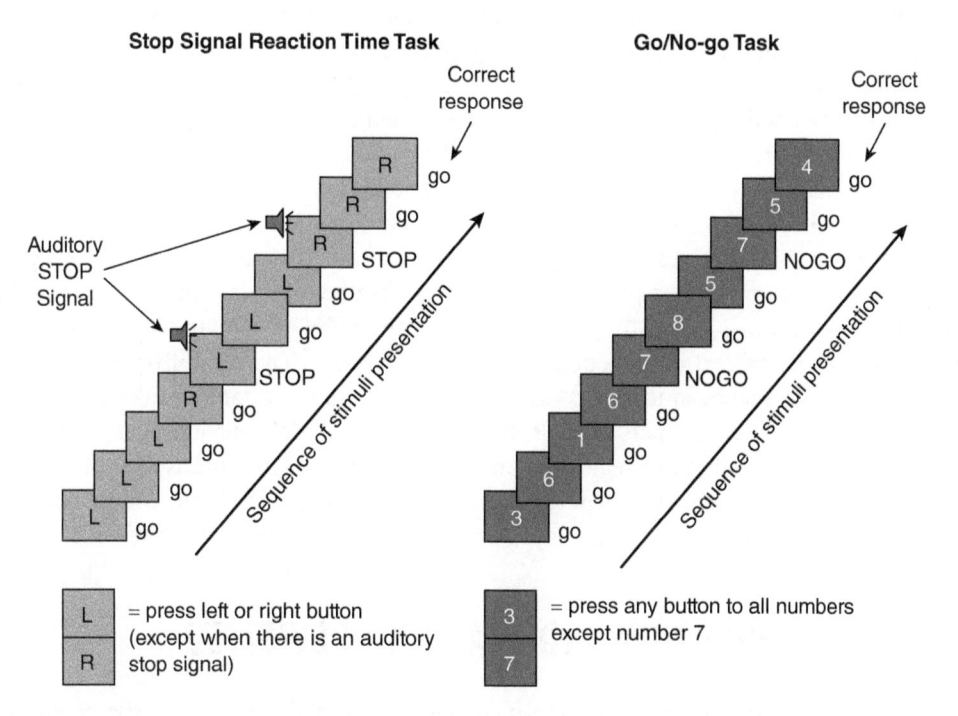

**Figure 3.6**  The Stop Signal Reaction Time Task and the Go/No-go Task. From Chandler, C. (2015). *Psychobiology*. Chichester, UK.: John Wiley & Sons. Original Souces Chandler, C. (2010). *The science of ADHD*. Wiley

enables us to say 'no'. However, the frontal lobe might not be fully operational and therefore cannot override the powerfully motivating effects of drugs on the mesolimbic system. Robbins states 'the notion that "pleasure" can be mediated by receptors in a sub-cortical nucleus is perhaps too simple. Activity in this circuitry is probably subject to further processing in cortical circuits' (Robbins et al., 2006: 22).

Drug users are often considered to be impulsive and lacking control. That impulsivity has been measured in the laboratory where drug users are unable to stop themselves on a test of behavioural inhibition, e.g. the Go/No-go Task (see Box 3.4). Behavioural inhibition is the ability to stop oneself doing something. Philosophers and neuroscientists argue that this is a characteristic of being human – that it is not a case of what we choose to do, but rather what we choose not to do (free will versus free won't).

Another facet of the failure to control behaviour is seen in the delay discounting task. This is a task in which participants in the study have a choice. They either take a small but immediate reward, or they can delay the receipt of the reward and get a bigger reward later. Essentially, do you want £5 now, or you can wait and get £20 at the end of the day? Typically, the average person will opt for the bigger reward later while a regular drug user would rather have the small reward now (Bickel & Marsch, 2001).

There are many neuropsychological accounts of addiction that describe the processes at a cognitive level. Cognitive models tend to talk about automatic processes which are effortless and beyond consciousness (Tiffany, 1990; Wiers et al., 2007; Wiers & Stacy, 2005). Being able to access conscious processes would therefore be important in mitigating addiction (Jentsch & Pennington, 2014). Thus the inability to inhibit drug taking has been considered by some to be critical in addiction (Volkow et al., 2004). The orbitofrontal cortex and the amygdala have also been identified as regions which are important in linking reward to hedonic experiences (Kringelbach, 2005; Rothkirch et al., 2012; Schoenbaum et al., 1998). The orbitofrontal cortex is therefore a region that may well be involved in some aspects of learning. In the preceding sections we have learned about the importance of dopamine in reward. The following section describes how dopamine is involved in how we learn about rewards.

## ADDICTION AND LEARNING REVISITED

The accumulated evidence supports a DA mediated reward pathway. The textbook case for mesolimbic dopamine being the reward pathway is appealing as the early data were supportive of such a position. However, science has moved the argument on further. The NAcc and other areas of the mesolimbic system are no longer considered to be the reward pathway per se. The evidence now points to these regions being involved in the learning of associations between stimuli and reward, and the probability of reward.

Much of the work that contributes to our new understanding of dopamine and reward has been conducted on the phasic dopamine response (for reviews see Schultz, 2006, 2007; Tobler et al., 2005). When an animal is presented with a primary reinforcer, e.g. food or water, dopamine cells respond with increased dopamine. The same is also true for stimuli that are associated with reward (Schultz, 1998; Schultz et al., 1997; Schultz et al., 1998). These DA neurons are depressed when a signalled reward is omitted and by stimuli predicting the absence of reward (Tobler et al., 2003). The changes in DA levels are argued to be a teaching signal involved in the learning of associations (Schultz, 2007). Dopamine neurons project to various brain regions including the dorsal and ventral striatum (NAcc) (which are now thought to have independent actions on learning with the transfer of new learning in the ventral regions to automated process in more dorsal regions; see Everitt et al., 2008) and to subregions of the prefrontal cortex. Haber, Fudge, and McFarland (2000: 2369) have identified cascading loops in which the striatal 'shell influences the core, the core influences the central striatum, and the central striatum influences the dorsolateral striatum. This anatomical arrangement creates a hierarchy of information flow and provides an anatomical basis for the limbic/cognitive/motor interface via the ventral midbrain'. In human participants the ventral striatum has been associated with learning and the dorsal striatum with the maintenance of information regarding reward outcomes (O'Doherty et al., 2004). Sensitisation by an increase in dopamine may strengthen the learning that takes place within the dorsal striatum (Nelson & Killcross, 2006). Within the wider theoretical context the learning that takes place under the auspices of dopamine leads to the capture of the habit, whereas the maintenance of the habit passes over to the automated processes of wider brain regions of the basal ganglia and the cognitive expectations of the orbitofrontal cortex (Newlin & Strubler, 2007).

The prefrontal neurons carry signals related to the preparation of movement and goal achievement (Matsumoto et al., 2003) and the motivational value of rewards (Shaw & Rolls, 1976). Imaging studies have indicated that there is dysfunction in cortical regions of the brain that are linked to drug compulsion and a lack of behavioural inhibition. In the case of addiction, this translates to not being able to stop taking the drug (Volkow et al., 2004).

An interesting feature of the phasic response to stimuli is that it occurs when rewards are different from predictions; this is called the *reward prediction error* (Schultz, 1998). The phasic dopamine response differs if a reward is unpredicted or not available or delayed (Hollerman & Schultz, 1998). Thus, the following dopamine codes are available to the organism:

1. An unpredicted reward elicits an activation – a positive prediction error.

2. A predicted reward elicits no response.

3. The omission or extended delay of a predicted reward induces a depression (Schultz, 2007).

According to Schultz, 'A "prediction error" message may constitute a powerful teaching signal for behavior and learning', and it 'may contribute to the self-organization of goal-directed behavior' (Schultz, 2001). Furthermore, the *reward prediction error* may act as an impulse to instigate neural changes that lead to subsequent changes in reward predictions and behavioral reactions, i.e. learning. The process continues until the behavioural outcomes match the reward predictions, and then there is no prediction error with no dopamine activity. A variation on the role of phasic dopamine states that negative DA signal would mean that behaviour would be suppressed, whereas positive signals increase repetition (Redgrave & Gurney, 2006; Redgrave et al., 2008).

This is fine for rats and monkeys, but does the reward prediction error occur in humans? It has been demonstrated that stimuli associated with drugs such as cocaine can in fact increase brain activation in their own right (Goldstein et al., 2007; Volkow et al., 2005; Volkow et al., 2006; Wong et al., 2006). Such studies clearly demonstrate that we humans learn that a previously neutral stimulus can become associated with the drug itself. Indeed, recent studies indicate that an increase in DA alone does not produce drug craving, but requires cues associated with the drug (Volkow et al., 2008), and in this study they used methylphenidate to increase DA levels. The use of neuroimaging techniques has revealed that there is also a case for the reward prediction error in humans (see Kelly et al., 2007 for a review). The concept of a reward prediction error has been incorporated into a computational model of learning about reward in which actions are evaluated through experience of a mismatch between expectancy and actual reward (Daw & Doya, 2006).

## WHICH THEORY IS CORRECT?

It is tempting to want to find one definitive theory of addiction and motivation. The theories above approach addiction from very specific starting points. The incentive salience theory presents a view of addiction that sees craving becoming unmanageable and leads to the motivation to consume drugs. The incentive value of drugs and drug-related stimuli becomes heightened which maintains the motivation to consume. The compulsive nature of addiction and the involvement of stress systems in maintaining it have been addressed by Koob. Continual drug-taking behaviour results in adaptive changes in the reward and stress circuitry of the brain. These changes provide a new set point that is lower than normal, and represents a shift from impulse control difficulties to more obsessive-compulsive like behaviour regarding the drug. Beyond the subcortical regions is the role of the cortex which has substantial effects on cognition and control within addiction. The orbitofrontal cortex and the dopaminergic regions of the ventral striatum have been shown to be particularly important in learning about reward rather than about reward itself. Once learnt the events are remembered, and in the case of addiction these memories are maladaptive (Milton & Everitt, 2012). Which theory is right?

Goldstein and Volkow (2002) acknowledge the extent of the neuroadaptations in addiction:

Saliency/reward     NAcc; Ventral Pallidum

Motivation/drive    orbitofrontal cortex

Memory/learning     amygdala, hippocampus, and basal ganglia

Control/inhibition  prefrontal cortex and anterior cingulate cortex

It is evident from the literature that the theories of addiction can all be a little right and a little wrong, in as much that they are addressing specific aspects of the addictive process rather than addiction as a fully defined and diagnosed entity. Furthermore, the drugs to which

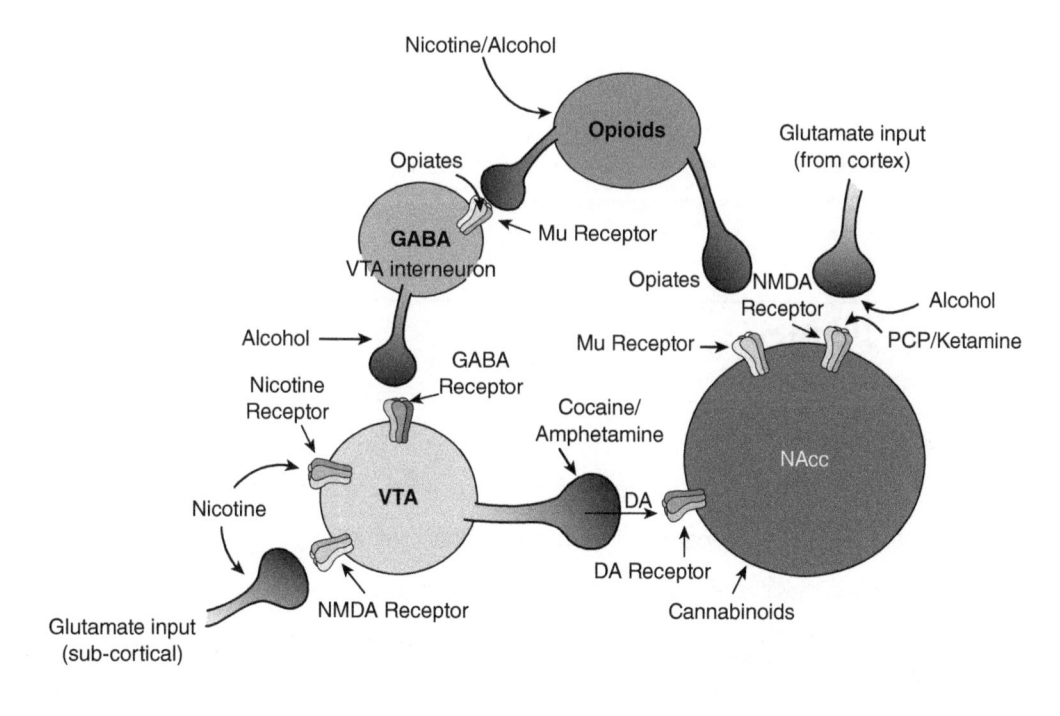

**Figure 3.7** The mesolimbic DA system and the impact of different classes of drugs illustrates a common mechanism of action in addiction

we become addicted have a varied pharmacology, e.g. cocaine is predominantly DAergic, whereas heroin is opiate mediated. Is there a common denominator for all these addictive drugs? The most parsimonious answer is that of the mesolimbic DA system. All the drugs impinge upon this system at some point, if not directly like cocaine, then indirectly like alcohol (see Figure 3.7).

# SUMMARY

- Animal models of addiction have been instrumental in probing the biological basis of addiction.
- The view that addiction is the result of aberrant dopaminergic activity has remained a strong contender in the explanations of addiction.
- The focus of many theories is the elevation of DA in the sub-cortical area: mesolimbic DA encompassing the ventral tegmental area and the nucleus accumbens.
- The simple view that DA levels increase as a result of receiving a reward or drug has been supplanted by complex theories of dopamine involvement in learning.
- The biological theories of addiction are not just theories of addiction, but also theories of motivation. Addiction just happens to be an extreme example of the triumph of motivation over that of reason.

# QUESTIONS

1. How can one be confident that the use of animal models helps us understand addiction?
2. To what extent are the theories of addiction elaborate theories of learning?
3. What is the role of dopamine in the addiction process?
4. Can the biological theories of addiction assist in the treatment of addiction?
5. What would you tell governments and policy makers about the biological basis of addiction?

# GENETICS OF ADDICTION 4

## CHAPTER OVERVIEW

This chapter will:

- Outline the process of genetic transmission in humans and define some of the key terms and processes involved
- Evaluate classical behavioural genetics research consisting of family, twin and adoption studies using alcohol addiction as an example
- Describe linkage studies and association studies, the two main molecular genetic approaches used to identify the genes involved in addiction
- Describe some of the findings of genetic research in the addiction field
- Consider the challenges facing genetic research in the addiction field

## LEARNING AIMS OF THE CHAPTER

- To understand the main principles of genetic transmission in humans
- To have a broad appreciation of behavioural genetic and molecular genetic research as applied to a complex behavioural trait such as addiction
- To be able to critically evaluate the advantages, future potential and limitations of genetic research in the addiction field

# INTRODUCTION

Genetics, the study of inherited biological and behavioural traits, is a complex, exciting and challenging area of research which has seen huge technological advances in recent decades. A thorough explanation of genetic transmission in humans is beyond the scope of this chapter. The following is a brief oversimplified account (see Chandler, 2015: 29–60, for a more detailed description).

# WHAT ARE GENES AND WHAT DO THEY DO?

In most cells (apart from bacteria) there is an inner membrane bound section called the nucleus, which is surrounded by an outer section called the cytoplasm. Located inside the nucleus are *chromosomes* which consist of tightly coiled rods of deoxyribonucleic acid (DNA) and structural support proteins called histones.

DNA is extremely important because it carries the hereditary information that is necessary for the perpetuation and maintenance of life. DNA directs the production of proteins that regulate the type and number of practically all types of cellular molecules. It is made up of many linked smaller building blocks called nucleotides, which consist of a phosphate group, a sugar moiety, and a pyrimidine or purine base. Segments of chromosomal DNA called *genes* carry specific instructions for making each specific protein required. There are different regions on each gene which deal with different functions. These regions consist of regulatory, coding, and non-coding sequences of nucleotides. The promoter region initiates the production of the gene product, the coding region carries the information that codes for the gene product, and a termination sequence signals when to stop production. DNA exists as a double stranded helix, with the complementary base pairs of each of the two polynucleotide strands bonded together by hydrogen bonds (see Figure 4.1).

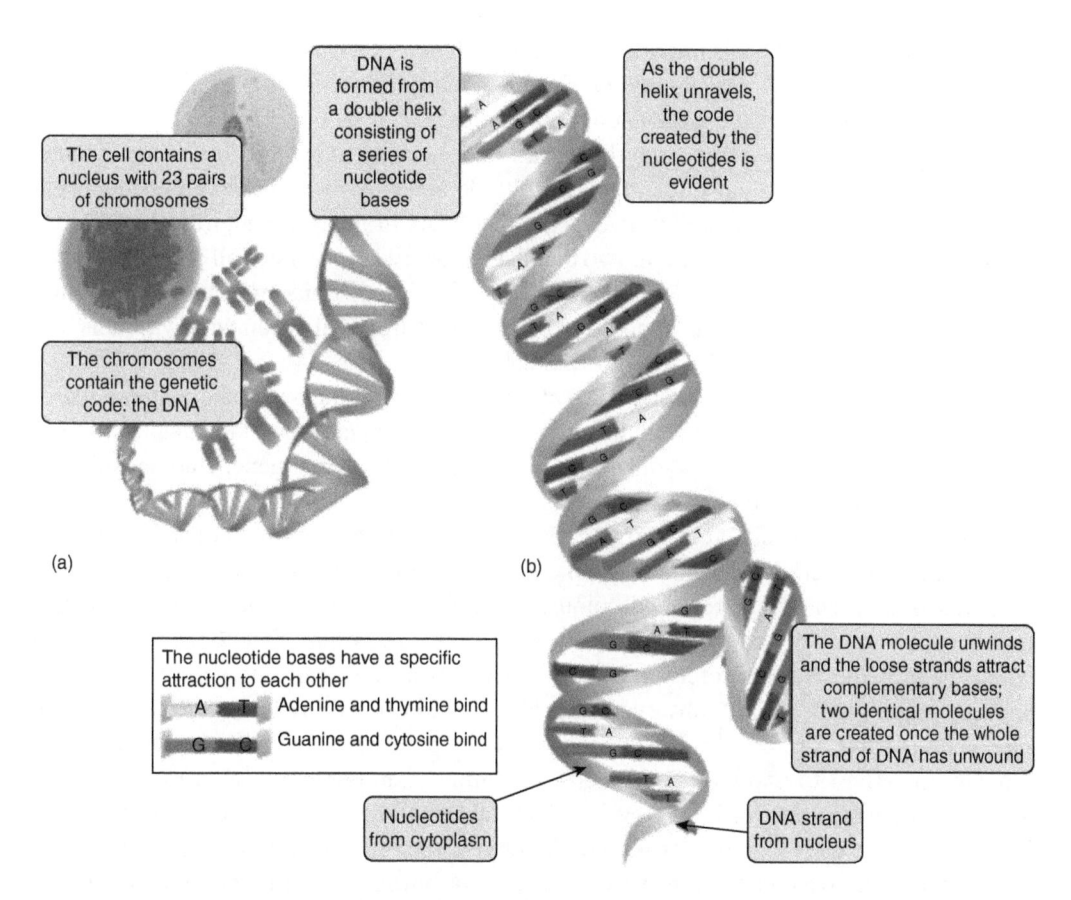

**Figure 4.1** DNA. (a) The chromosomes can be pulled apart to reveal the double helix. Strands of DNA are connected by the different nucleotide bases. (b) Replication: the strands of DNA unwind and the loose ends are joined by nucleotides from within the cytoplasm, thus making a copy.

Source: reproduced with permission of John Wiley & Sons Inc., from *Psychobiology* by Chris Chandler (2015); permission sourced through author and publisher

The nucleotide bases of DNA are adenine (A), guanine (G), cytosine (C) and thymine (T). They always pair up in a specific way, i.e. A with T and C with G. It is the sequencing of the bases along the DNA strand which form a specific code that determines which particular protein is made.

An important function of DNA is replication. During normal cell replication, known as *mitosis*, the DNA double helix unwinds and complementary nucleotide bases line up alongside each exposed nucleotide base of the original strands, such that an identical strand is recreated on each side. This is important because each new cell needs to have identical DNA to that of the original cell. During mitosis the cell doubles its chromosomes before division, which ensures new cells have a full set of chromosomes.

The study of genetics stems from the work of an Austrian monk called Gregor Mendel, who in the 1860s carried out numerous carefully documented breeding experiments using pea plants. His experiments led him to observe that many of the pea plant traits (e.g. colour and texture) were under the control of two distinct factors (what we now call genes) inherited from each parent plant. Mendel looked at simple dichotomous traits (which refers to either having or not having the trait, as opposed to a continuous trait which can vary within its category along a continuum, such as weight and height).

Particular patterns of inheritance were expressed in different types and generations of plant crosses. He also discovered that the outward physical appearance of the plant, currently referred to as its *phenotype*, was sometimes distinct from the actual genetic composition of the plant, which is referred to as its *genotype*.

Genes can exist in different forms called *alleles*, which control the same trait. For example, with reference to Mendel's pea plants, each plant could have two identical alleles inherited from each parent for seed colour, referred to as *homozygous*, or two different forms, which would be referred to as *heterozygous* for seed colour. Due to the yellow seed colour gene being what is referred to as *dominant*, if a plant had one yellow seed gene and one green seed gene, its observed phenotype would be yellow, not green. The green seed gene is what is referred to as *recessive*, and the plant would need to be homozygous (double recessive) to express green seeds. A similar example exists with eye colour in humans, where the gene for brown eyes is dominant over the recessive gene for blue eyes. In order for blue eyes to be the observed phenotype, the blue eyed individual would have to have inherited two copies of the recessive gene for blue eyes, either through having two genetically heterozygous phenotypically brown eyed parents (inheriting one recessive blue gene from each), two parents with blue eyes, or one heterozygous brown eyed parent and one blue eyed parent.

Every individual possesses two copies of each gene, one inherited from each parent. Chromosomes come in matched pairs and humans have 23 pairs of chromosomes. When the chromosome pairs are arranged by number and photographed together, this is referred to as a karyotype. Most cells of the body contain 46 chromosomes (diploid number), but sperm and egg cells contain only 23 single chromosomes (haploid number) so that when fertilisation occurs and the sex cells fuse, the offspring inherits an equal quantity (50%) of genetic material from each parent, making up the diploid number. The first 22 chromosomes, called autosomes, are the same in both sexes. The 23rd pair of chromosomes are the sex chromosomes and are labelled as X and Y. Females typically have two X chromosomes (XX) and males typically have one X chromosome and one Y chromosome (XY), although genetic variation can influence sexual differentiation such that things are not always so clear-cut.

Each chromosome has a constriction point called the centromere that divides it into two sections of different lengths, referred to as arms. These sections are referred to as 'p' for the shorter section and 'q' for the longer section (see Figure 4.2).

During the process of division of the sex cells, known as *meiosis*, sections of the chromosomal arms can cross over one another after duplication and break and recombine such that the information carried is no longer a faithful copy of the original genetic material of either parent cell. This is one way that genetic diversity is introduced into a species. Genes that are closely related on the same section of a chromosome are more likely to be inherited together (see the section below on linkage studies). Errors in the normal cell DNA replication process can also occur. These errors are called mutations. Some mutations which are harmful to life would be eliminated through natural selection. Other non-lethal mutations can be passed on to successive generations and also increase genetic diversity.

*Gene expression* refers to the process by which the gene is converted from DNA to a functional product in the cell, usually a protein (but also to ribonucleic acid, RNA). *Protein synthesis* involves several forms of RNA, which are involved in the process of transcribing or copying the DNA code (referred to as *transcription*), and then decoding or translating the code into the functional product (referred to as *translation*). RNA has a similar structure to DNA except that RNA has a ribose sugar group instead of a deoxyribose sugar group and RNA has a base called uracil in place of thymine. Three nucleotides, referred to as a codon, code for one particular amino acid in the protein. For example, the nucleotide sequence: Adenine, Uracil, Guanine (AUG), codes for the amino acid methionine. Amino acids are the building blocks of proteins and each protein is made up of a particular sequence of amino acids.

Gene expression is regulated in accordance with the genetic blueprint and needs of the organism, and in response to the environment. The body exists within an external environment which influences the biochemical processes that occur within the organism, including gene expression. The environment both within and outside of the organism is not static but is changing throughout the lifespan and from moment to moment. To suggest a strict dichotomy between genes and environment is both misleading and inaccurate.

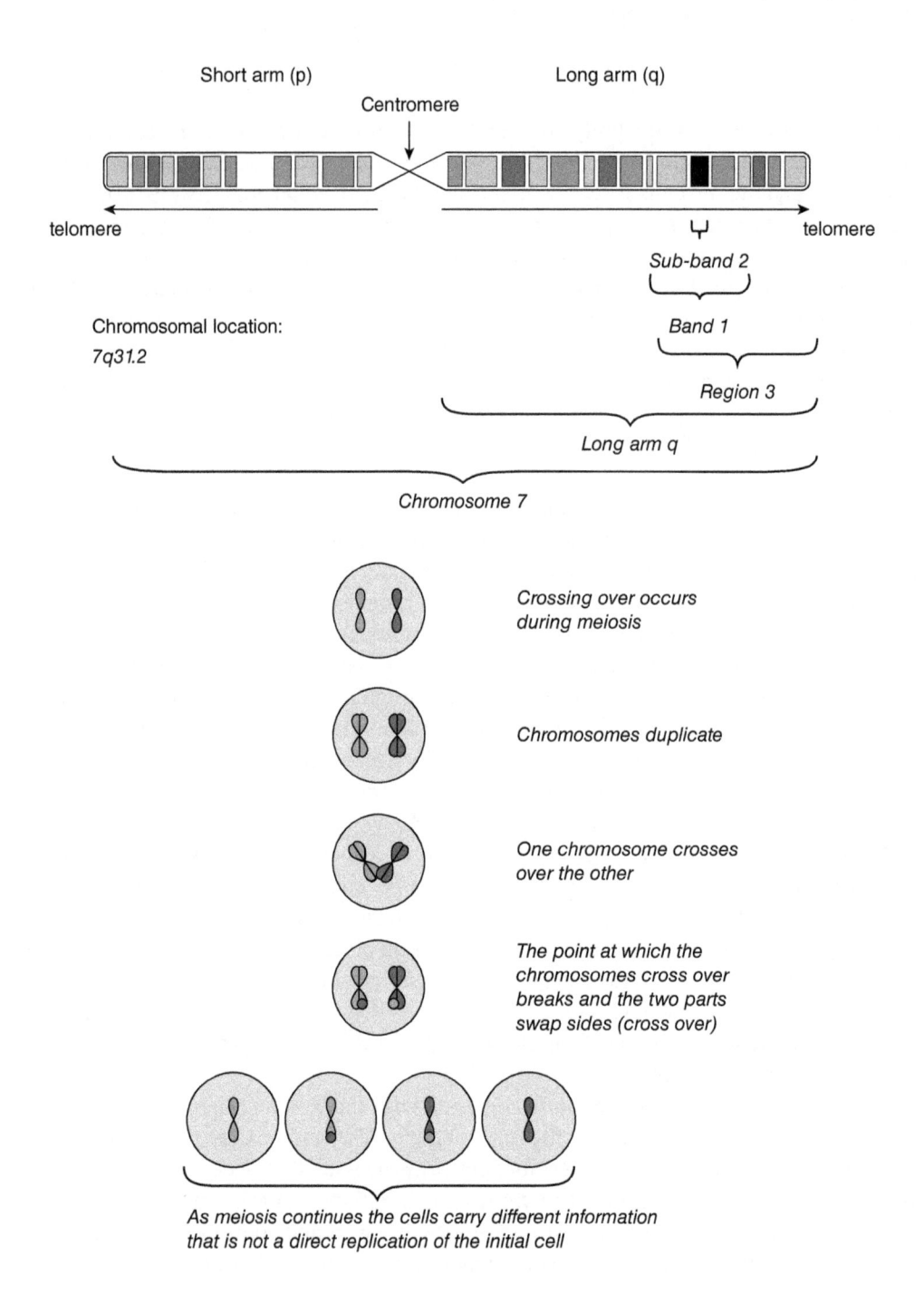

**Figure 4.2** (A) a single chromosome (chromosome 7 in this case), and (B) Crossing over and recombination of chromosomes during cell division

*Source*: reproduced with permission of John Wiley & Sons Inc., from *Psychobiology* by Chris Chandler (2015); permission sourced through author and publisher

# HOW DOES THIS APPLY TO THE GENETICS OF ADDICTION?

Geneticists readily admit that it is only possible to *estimate* the genetic contribution for any complex behavioural trait. This is particularly challenging for a complex trait such as addiction which encompasses such a large variety of both overlapping and distinct behaviours and substances, all of which are sensitive to environmental and developmental changes. A single gene for addiction is unlikely. Undoubtedly many genes conferring only a small degree of addiction risk or protection against addiction are involved. Also, it is not known how these risk conferring genes may interact with each other and the environment to influence a particular behavioural outcome.

Despite the different forms in which addictive behaviour shows itself, there are genetic, neurobiological and plausible evolutionary explanations to support an underlying behavioural/psychological trait supporting a common liability to addiction (CLA). CLA is associated with certain pre-disposing differences in mechanisms of socialisation and emotional and cognitive regulation in affected individuals, which subsequently influences their addiction risk (Vanyukov et al., 2012).

In addition to individualised genetic risk for each abused substance, the high incidence of multiple drug use and co-morbid psychiatric disorders may reflect the influence of genes in common. The risks for addiction to specific drugs are highly correlated with each other, and there is also commonality in the neurobiological systems underlying the effects of different drugs, reflecting broad dysfunction in reward related learning and memory pathways (e.g. Hyman et al., 2006). Mental disorders co-morbid with substance abuse include both externalising disorders such as attention-deficit/hyperactivity disorder (Biederman et al., 1998) and conduct disorder (Schubiner et al., 2000), and internalising disorders such as anxiety disorders (Zimmermann et al., 2003) and depression (Davis et al., 2008). The legal classification of drugs into licit/illicit (leading to use which reflects the behavioural response to societal norms) is proposed to underlie the genetic clustering of liabilities to dependence into two distinct, although correlated, groupings based on this licit/illicit division (Kendler et al., 2007). How addiction is defined and measured for research purposes will undoubtedly influence the genes and genetic pathways that will be subsequently identified.

Many molecular genetic studies have been conducted on addiction in recent decades due to the increase in available information and rapid technological advances in this field. This area of research encompasses multiple findings that often cannot be replicated (for reasons discussed below). A comprehensive overview is beyond the scope of this chapter, therefore only a few examples from molecular genetic research where robust evidence implicates particular gene variants in addiction will be discussed.

# CLASSICAL BEHAVIOURAL GENETICS RESEARCH: FAMILY, TWIN AND ADOPTION STUDIES

## FAMILY STUDIES

*Variability* is a term that is used to describe the differences that exist between members of the same species. The proportion of the total variability in a characteristic that is estimated to be caused by genetic differences compared with environmental differences in a *population* is called *heritability* ($h^2$). This is the proportion of genetic variation divided by the total variation, which is the sum of both genetic and environmental variation. Heritability can be represented on a scale of zero to one, with zero representing no variation due to genetic differences and one representing total variation due to genetic difference alone, with no environmental contribution.

Heritability estimates are often represented as percentages. For example, if height has an estimated heritability of 0.80 in a given population, we can say that the variation in height between different people in this given population is estimated as 80% due to genetic differences, with the remaining 20% attributable to environmental factors, e.g. nutrition.

Genetic variability cannot be measured directly and can only be inferred by examining the characteristic of interest in relatives with different degrees of genetic relatedness (for a review of terms used for estimating risk for a disorder, see Urbanoski & Kelly, 2012). The large variation (referred to as heterogeneity) of the addiction phenotype with the involvement of numerous risk conferring genes means that estimating genetic variability is extremely difficult. As many as 1500 risk conferring genes have been implicated in addiction (Kalant, 2010). Additionally, genetic variability also captures variance explained by *epigenetic mechanisms*. These are transmissible biological changes that influence gene expression without altering gene sequence and can result from gene-environment interactions. Due to the difficulty in untangling the relative contributions of genes and environment, it is clear that heritability in the context of a complex trait like addiction can only ever be a crude estimate.

Traditionally the genetic contribution towards a given characteristic is estimated by family, twin and adoption studies, which provide natural experiments in the inheritance of the characteristic under investigation. Family studies have historically demonstrated an increased incidence of alcoholism in the relatives of those with an addictive disorder (e.g. Cotton, 1979; Guze et al., 1986), but the reasons for this are also likely to be due to the impact of non-genetic influences. For example, in addition to their inherited genetic material, the children of alcoholics are exposed from conception onwards to adverse environmental influences that may potentially increase their risk of alcoholism. These influences include the maternal environment during pregnancy as well as exposure to the stress associated with growing up in an alcoholic home environment and potential consequent substance exposure.

In genetics, the term *proband* refers to the individual who is being used as the starting point of the study. A study on the familial transmission of alcohol, marijuana and cocaine dependence and habitual smoking (Bierut et al., 1998) found that the rates of dependence for all substances studied were increased in siblings of alcoholic probands compared with siblings of non-alcoholic controls. Up to 50% of brothers and 25% of sisters were alcohol dependent, but this elevated risk was not increased any further by co-morbid substance use. Siblings of marijuana or cocaine dependent probands, and probands who were habitual smokers, all had a substance specific elevated risk of developing each type of dependence, providing evidence for the involvement of both common and specific causative factors in the familial transmission of substance dependence.

## ADOPTION STUDIES

Adoption, in the context of addiction studies, generally represents a situation where the biologically vulnerable offspring of an affected parent is removed from their high-risk environment and placed in a different environment with their adoptive family. In this situation, the degree to which the offspring resembles their biological parent for the investigated phenotype is supposed to provide an estimate of the impact of genetic influence on the characteristic of interest because the environment is not shared.

For example, evidence from an early adoption study on alcohol dependence suggested that there is a strong genetic influence, with approximately equal rates of alcohol dependence in the biological children of affected individuals regardless of whether they were adopted (Goodwin et al., 1974). Additional studies have repeatedly demonstrated increased rates of alcoholism in adoptees with a positive family history of alcoholism compared to controls (Bohman et al., 1981; Cadoret et al., 1985; Cloninger et al., 1981; Sigvardsson et al., 1996). One such study (Cadoret et al., 1985) demonstrated an increase in alcohol abuse in both men and women who had first degree relatives with alcohol problems. Drinking was also increased in male adoptees if there were drinking problems in the adoptive home, also highlighting the importance of environmental factors.

This study also looked at the cross heritability of antisocial personality and alcoholism, and the results suggested specific inheritance and environmental effects for the alcohol and antisocial personality conditions.

Although adoption studies suggest an important genetic contribution to addiction risk, there are certain limitations to the conclusions that can be drawn from such studies. Adoption does not represent a normal situation. Both adoptive parents and adoptees are unlikely to be representative of the population in general. The adoptive family is usually matched as closely as possible to the birth family (called 'selective placement') which could potentially confound the assumption of dissimilar environments. However, in practice there are usually substantial differences in the psychosocial environment between adoptive and birth parents. An important potential confounding factor in these studies is that it is highly likely that any child that is given up for adoption has already experienced considerable stress, which could include: prenatal stress; in utero drug exposure; poor prenatal nutrition; postnatal stress; disrupted attachment; caregiver neglect; and poor or inconsistent care. The length of time prior to adoption is also variable, and can only be assessed if accurate adoption records are available. Exposure to high levels of the stress hormone cortisol both pre- and postnatally is just one of the potential ways in which neural development could be influenced in ways that could increase addiction risk through environmentally-driven epigenetic mechanisms (Anacker et al., 2014; Rovaris et al., 2015). Given these considerations, it is not possible to definitively attribute an increase in addiction risk in the adopted away biological offspring of addicted parents to a purely genetic component.

## TWIN STUDIES

Further information about the potential genetic contribution to addiction can be estimated through twin studies. Twins can either be monozygotic (identical) or dizygotic (fraternal). Monozygotic (MZ) twins are formed from the fertilisation of one egg that then splits to form two embryos. Monozygotic twins therefore share identical genetic material. Dizygotic (DZ) twins are formed by the fertilisation of two separate eggs which go on to form two separate embryos, and therefore share on average 50% of their genetic material like any other pair of siblings. Both MZ and DZ twins are assumed to be exposed to similar environmental conditions. If there is greater observed similarity (*co-occurrence* or *concordance*) in a given characteristic in MZ twins compared with DZ twins, this difference is attributed to their genetic similarity.

The heritability estimates from twin studies of alcoholism have reported greater concordance rates for MZ compared to DZ twins of alcoholics (Heath et al., 1997; Hrubec & Omenn, 1981; Kendler et al., 1997; Pickens et al., 1991). A recent meta-analysis of twin and adoption studies for the heritability of alcohol use disorders (AUDs) estimated heritability to be approximately 50% (Verhulst et al., 2015). These authors also found evidence for modest shared environmental effects, suggesting that environmental factors also contribute to the familial aggregation of AUDs, as would be expected. These authors argue that the validity of the magnitude of this estimate is strengthened by its consistency across different study designs. There were no significant differences in estimates derived from either twin or adoption studies, assessment procedures used for diagnosis of AUDs, information gathering across different studies, and sex differences, in the studies that were included in this meta-analysis.

Conclusions drawn from twin studies also need to be interpreted with caution because it is assumed in these studies that MZ and DZ twins do not differ in terms of their environment. This equal environment assumption has been subject to criticism (Guo, 2001; Pam et al., 1996). Although MZ twins are undoubtedly more genetically similar, they are also more environmentally similar than DZ twins. As a result of their similar appearance, it is proposed that MZ twins are often treated by others and their parents in a more similar manner than DZ twins. It is argued that this greater environmental similarity could theoretically result in higher concordance for a given phenotypic trait in MZ twins compared to DZ twins, in the absence of any genetic component.

Despite these criticisms there is converging evidence from different types of studies for a genetic component in the risk for alcoholism.

## METHODS FOR IDENTIFYING GENES

The two main approaches used to try to identify the genes involved in addiction are linkage studies and association studies. Information gained through the Human Genome Project, an international effort to map the entire sequence of the human genome, has greatly enabled advances in molecular genetic studies. There are also similar efforts to map the genome of several other species used in genetic and biological research such as rats and mice. The international HapMap project (completed in 2005), which catalogues the common genetic variants that occur in humans, has also provided a wealth of information on the human genome to inform molecular genetic research.

Linkage and association approaches can be complementary, with genetic linkage studies identifying a broad chromosomal region which can be further investigated using association studies. Drug response, withdrawal, tolerance, sensitisation, neuroadaptations and pharmacokinetics have been investigated in animal models of addiction. The findings from these types of experiments have been used to inform particular aspects of human genetic studies. Animal experiments allow researchers to tightly control environmental influences. Findings from animal models of addiction have influenced investigation of particular 'candidate gene' regions which may also be implicated in human addiction. Mouse strains that have been developed through selective breeding to be sensitive to alcohol and other drugs have been used in animal studies of addiction, and transgenic mouse models have been used to investigate the consequence of direct manipulation of particular genes and for elucidation of their roles in addiction relevant behavioural and physiological traits (see Crabbe et al., 2006; Crabbe et al., 2010; Hall et al., 2013, for reviews of animal studies in this field). Results from studies using animal models have been highly informative with regard to particular aspects of addiction, but need to be interpreted with caution due to their inability to capture the complexity of the multiple influences on genetic expression in human addiction.

# LINKAGE STUDIES

In the linkage approach the approximate location of the disease associated gene of interest is sought relative to another DNA sequence of known location on the chromosome called a genetic marker. These genetic markers are DNA sequences of high individual variability called *polymorphisms* and can be of different types. In terms of genetic variation, polymorphism refers to the different forms of a single gene that can exist in an individual or group. Polymorphisms are present at a frequency of greater than 1% of the population, and generally do not confer any genetic disadvantage or advantage, but in some cases can increase the risk for a disorder. If the frequency is less than 1%, the variation in DNA is referred to as a mutation. The most common type of polymorphism is what is called a single nucleotide polymorphism (SNP), which refers to a change in a single nucleotide base of the gene's DNA sequence, for example, cytosine is substituted for thymine.

As mentioned previously, sources of variation in a species include recombination, in which new combinations of genes in the offspring are produced that differ from that found in either parent. Linkage is based on the principle that if two DNA sequences are close together on a chromosome, genetic recombination is unlikely to occur between these sequences, whereas a greater distance between two DNA sequences will increase the likelihood of recombination. If the marker and the gene of interest are in close proximity to each other they can be described as being linked and will be more likely to be transmitted together.

In linkage analysis DNA samples from affected families can be systematically screened using a panel of different markers covering the entire human genome. The co-transmission of the condition and the marker in affected and unaffected family members can be compared and analysed using statistical programs, and a picture built up of the chromosomal regions implicated in transmission of the disorder. It is also possible to compare the genotypes of affected sibling pairs, and look for evidence of linkage through increased incidence of marker allele sharing above chance expectation in these affected pairs. One example, the large multi-centre Collaborative Study on the Genetics of Alcoholism (COGA) in the United States, has generated a dataset of 1,857 families consisting of 16,062 individuals (Foroud et al., 2010). Genetic analysis of a subset from the COGA sample of 105 families, and an additional replication sample of 157 families, found suggestive evidence of linkage on chromosomes 1 and 7 to alcoholism (Foroud et al., 2000).

The linkage approach suffers from several drawbacks. It lacks specificity because it only identifies broad chromosomal regions rather than any particular gene. It is an approach that is more suited to studying diseases of high genetic penetrance (which means if you have a particular gene variant you are more likely to express the particular disease), with genes of major effect, that run strongly within families. The number of markers used in linkage studies is relatively small, due to the small number of recombination events on each chromosome which are assumed to have occurred among relatives with shared phenotypes. It is therefore more suited to investigating rare dominant traits. It requires knowledge and identification of suitable numbers of affected families, and a clear definition of the phenotype under investigation. It is unlikely that the linkage approach, when used in isolation, will be able to identify genes involved in addiction. In practice, linkage and genetic association studies are often both performed and are complementary.

## GENETIC ASSOCIATION STUDIES

Genetic association studies compare the frequency of occurrence of particular gene variations (SNPs and other markers) in people with the disorder (cases) to people without the disorder (controls) in large groups of unrelated individuals. If the particular allele under investigation occurs at a higher frequency in cases than in controls, it is presumed to be potentially related in some way to the disorder under investigation. In comparison to linkage studies, association studies have greater power to detect common risk alleles with small effects which are more likely to be involved in most complex disorders (Risch & Merikangas, 1996). Association studies assume that many genetic recombination events have occurred in the lineage leading to unrelated individuals, and require analysis of large numbers of small genomic regions in comparison to linkage studies.

Current association studies are a trawl through the entire genome in a hypothesis-free manner with no prior assumptions. This has the advantage of allowing the potential identification of novel candidate genes which could lead to new avenues of investigation. These genome wide association studies (GWAS) involve scanning the genome for associations between genetic variants and the particular drug phenotype under investigation using high throughput microarray technology. This microarray technology allows the genotyping of up to five million SNPs simultaneously. Due to the large number of comparisons made in these analyses, there is an increased risk of detecting false positives. For this reason the accepted threshold for statistical significance has been set much lower than the usually accepted level of $5 \times 10^{-2}$ (at around $10^{-8}$). Due to the low statistical power to detect associations which involve multiple genes contributing small effects, extremely large samples are needed for these types of studies. There is also the possibility of misleading findings due to population stratification, in which differences in allele frequencies between the cases and controls is a result of differences in genetic ancestry in different subgroups of the population under study (e.g. differences caused by having a particular ethnic group overrepresented in a sample). Independent replication in different populations and the pooling of data through large meta- and mega-analysis based collaborations have been implemented, and replicable risk loci have been associated with particular alcohol and nicotine dependence phenotypes. In the majority of studies the risk loci identified through GWAS can only explain a small portion of the variance in the traits (Manolio et al., 2009).

# CANDIDATE GENES

The association approach was initially used for investigating 'candidate genes' thought to be involved in addiction based on existing biological data (functional candidate genes), and through identification of particular chromosomal regions by information gained through systematic analysis from linkage studies (positional candidate genes). Candidate genes include genes coding for drug metabolising enzymes and neurotransmitters and their receptors (reviewed by Dick & Agrawal, 2008; Ducci & Goldman, 2012). For example, a consistent association has been found between alcohol dependence and the gene encoding the alpha2 sub-unit of the gamma-aminobutyric acid neurotransmitter (GABAA) receptor (Covault et al., 2004; Fehr et al., 2006; Soyka et al., 2008). GABA is an inhibitory neurotransmitter thought to be involved in mediating many of the behavioural and physiological effects of alcohol. The association between alcohol dependence and the GABAA receptor is strongest in individuals who are also dependent on illicit drugs.

One of the most robust findings through complementary and convergent approaches in research into alcohol dependence has been the identification of polymorphisms in the genes involved in the metabolism of alcohol which confer risk for, and protection against, alcoholism in particular ethnic groups. Other candidate genes investigated include gene variants moderating the actions of monoamine neurotransmitters involved in regulating cognition, emotion and reward, including serotonin, noradrenalin and dopamine systems.

## GENES FOR ALCOHOL METABOLISING ENZYMES

The most common pathway for metabolising alcohol (ethanol) in the body involves the liver enzymes alcohol dehydrogenase (ADH) and aldehyde dehydrogenase (ALDH) which work sequentially. ADH converts ethanol into a toxic carcinogenic compound called acetaldehyde, which is then converted by ALDH into acetate, to be further metabolised into water and carbon dioxide and excreted.

There are several different variations of the ADH and ALDH enzymes resulting from polymorphisms in the genes coding for these enzymes, which affect how efficiently alcohol is metabolised (Edenberg, 2007). This influences how an individual experiences the biological and behavioural effects of alcohol and their subsequent risk for developing alcohol use disorders. A fast-acting ADH enzyme or slow-acting ALDH enzyme can cause the toxic build-up of acetaldehyde in the body. If acetaldehyde accumulates in the body it causes unpleasant symptoms, including facial flushing, headache, nausea and palpitations, which can be considered a significant deterrent to excess alcohol consumption. This biochemical consequence is exploited by the medication disulfiram, an ALDH enzyme inhibitor used for the treatment of alcoholism. Differences in alcohol sensitivity characterised by the flushing reaction observed in individuals of oriental descent compared to individuals of European descent (Wolff, 1972) were subsequently found to be the result of differences in a specific variant of ALDH, ALDH2 located on chromosome 12 (Goedde et al., 1980). The specific ALDH2 gene variant implicated, ALDH2*2, is the result of the substitution of the amino acid lysine for glutamate, leading to a nearly inactive form of the enzyme. This allele is not present in people of European and African descent, but is common in people of East Asian descent, conferring a protective effect against alcoholism in these populations (Oota et al., 2004). This protective effect can be further increased by an additive interaction with a gene variant for the ADH1 enzyme, ADH1B*1 (Chen et al., 1999). This finding has been been replicated in multiple studies (Chen et al., 1999; Luczak et al., 2006; Thomasson et al., 1991).

A high activity variant in the alcohol dehydrogenase enzyme ADH1B*2, *His48Arg*, in which the amino acid histidine is substituted for arginine, located on chromosome 4, also confers a protective effect against alcoholism by increasing the speed of conversion of ethanol to acetaldehyde, leading to the accumulation of acetaldehyde. This variant is more common in people of East Asian descent, but has also been demonstrated to be protective in European and

African populations (Bierut et al., 2012). Although protective against alcoholism risk, these gene variants increase the risk of upper gastrointestinal cancer (Brooks et al., 2009). More recent GWAS of alcohol dependence have consistently found associations with alcohol metabolising enzyme genes, replicating findings from candidate gene studies of alcohol dependence (for a recent review of GWAS and Post GWAS of alcohol dependence see Hart & Kranzler, 2015).

# SUSCEPTIBILITY GENES FOR NICOTINE ADDICTION

Converging evidence from various approaches used to study the genetics of nicotine addiction have identified a number of subunits of nicotinic acetylcholine receptors (nAChRs) that are critical for the ability of nicotine to activate the brain reward system (Mineur & Picciotto, 2008). These receptors are expressed in the brain and in most tissues and organs throughout the body. In the Central Nervous System, the nAChRs are widely distributed and have effects on both the dopamine and serotonin neurotransmitter systems. The endogenous ligand for these receptors is the neurotransmitter acetylcholine. Activation of nAChRs can potentiate neurotransmitter release and neuronal excitability throughout the brain, influencing a diverse range of bodily processes. These include basic physiological functions such as pain sensation, sleep pattern and feeding, as well as more complex processes involved in learning, emotional regulation and reward (Gotti & Clementi, 2004; Hogg et al., 2003; Picciotto et al., 2000; Wonnacott et al., 2000)

There are several different nicotinic receptor subunit proteins encoded by 16 different nicotinic receptor subunit genes. Recent research has focused on genes CHRNA5, CHRNA3 and CHRNB4, encoding the α5, α3 and β4 subunits. These genes are clustered on chromosome 15q24. Several gene variants in this locus have been shown to be associated with smoking behaviour, nicotine dependence phenotypes, and smoking-related diseases (Bierut, 2010; Bierut et al., 2007; N. L. Saccone et al., 2010; S. F. Saccone et al., 2007; Thorgeirsson et al., 2010; Wassenaar et al., 2011). A key α5 gene variant that changes aspartic acid (Asp) to asparagine (Asn) at codon 398, the *Asp398ASn* polymorphism is associated with a neurological brain circuit involved in emotional regulation and reward, and represents a trait-like biomarker that predicts addiction severity in smokers. This circuit is also impaired in individuals with co-morbid mental illness who have the highest rates of smoking (Hong et al., 2010). Variations in nicotinic cholinergic receptors, in particular polymorphisms in the CHRNA5 gene, have been shown in a recent meta-analysis to be implicated as an underlying common risk factor for drug addiction, with specific variants potentially acting differently depending on the form of addiction involved (Buhler et al., 2015).

Another gene implicated in smoking behaviour is the gene encoding the cytochrome P450, family 2, subfamily A, polypeptide 6 (CYP2A6) enzyme which is involved in nicotine metabolism in the liver. This enzyme converts nicotine to cotinine and accounts for 70% to 80% of inhaled initial nicotine metabolism (Hukkanen et al., 2005). Converging evidence suggests that inter-individual variability in expression of CYP2A6, and consequent variability in enzymatic activity and nicotine metabolism, are associated with differences in daily cigarette consumption. A recent meta-analysis performed to assess the association of CYP2A6 gene polymorphisms with cigarette consumption revealed that smokers possessing reduced activity alleles, slow metabolisers and reduced metabolisers smoked fewer cigarettes per day compared to normal metabolisers. There were also differences in age of initiation of smoking between normal and intermediate metabolisers, with delayed age of initiation in the intermediate group (Pan et al., 2015).

# GENE VARIANTS IN THE ANYKYRIN REPEAT AND KINASE DOMAIN CONTAINING 1 (ANKK1)- DOPAMINE RECEPTOR 2 (DRD2) GENES

The dopaminergic system has been extensively researched in addiction due to its involvement in reinforcement and reward. In particular, variants in the dopamine receptor 2 (DRD2) have been implicated in alcoholism, other addictions and neuropsychiatric disorders (Noble, 2003). The Taq 1 A restriction fragment length polymorphism (which is a particular type of genetic marker) was originally shown to be associated with severe alcoholism (Blum et al., 1990), but has since been shown to belong not to DRD2, but to a nearby gene called repeat and kinase domain containing 1 (ANKK1). This gene is a member of a serine/threonine kinase protein family involved in signal transduction pathways (Neville et al., 2004). Signal transduction is a process through which a substance interacts with its cellular receptor and instigates a chain of molecular events resulting in a cellular response, rather like passing a message to someone via a chain of intermediaries. Variants in ANKK1 have been associated with alcohol dependence (Dick et al., 2007; B. Z. Yang et al., 2007), nicotine dependence (Gelernter et al., 2006; Huang et al., 2009), co-morbid alcohol and drug dependence (Yang et al., 2008), and opioid dependence (Deng et al., 2015). The exact mechanisms involved in how this polymorphism influences dopaminergic neurotransmission are still being investigated.

A recent meta-analysis of 371 studies on common SNPs underlying drug addiction implicated SNPs in the alcohol metabolising genes, in the cholinergic gene cluster

CHRNA5-CHRNA3-CHRNAB4, and in the DRD2 and ANNK1 genes as the most replicated and significant gene variants associated with alcohol and nicotine-related phenotypes (Buhler et al., 2015).

## OTHER GENE VARIANTS ASSOCIATED WITH ADDICTION

The endogenous opioid system is involved in the modulation of the rewarding effects of several drugs of abuse in addition to the opiates, through its interaction with other neurotransmitter systems, including the dopamine neurotransmitter system. The mu opioid receptor is the main site of action of opiate drugs. Naltrexone, which is a mu opioid receptor antagonist, has been shown to block the rewarding effects of alcohol by preventing the stimulation of opioid receptors and reducing dopamine release in the ventral tegmental area of the mesocorticolimbic system (reviewed by Heilig et al, G 2011). There is evidence for individual differences in response to naltrexone treatment based on functional variations in the mu opioid receptor gene OPRM1. A common functional variant in the OPRM1 gene A118G SNP has been particularly implicated in the differential clinical response to naltrexone. The OPRM1-G variant has been shown to affect signal transduction and increase receptor binding of the endogenous opioid beta endorphin compared to the A variant (Bond et al., 1998). Several lines of evidence indicate that OPRM1-G carriers have a significantly improved outcome when treated with naltrexone for alcohol dependence, compared to OPRM1-A carriers. Significantly lower rates of relapse and longer time to return to heavy drinking after treatment with naltrexone, increased subjective effects of intravenous alcohol, and increased reports of a positive family history of alcohol abuse disorders, have all been reported by individuals carrying the OPRM1-G polymorphism (Oslin et al., 2003; Ray & Hutchison, 2004, 2007).

This differential response has important implications for selecting who may benefit from pharmacological treatment with naltrexone and highlights the clinical variation within alcohol dependence. Differential clinical response to a particular pharmacotherapy, based on specific differences in genetic variation, illustrates how the use of genetic markers offers hope for the future development of more personalised and effective treatments, based on the biological underpinnings of the disorder on an individual level.

Monoamine neurotransmitters, including serotonin (5-hydroxytryptamine, 5-HT), noradrenaline (NA) and dopamine (DA), are involved in the modulation of cognition, memory, emotion and reward. Considering how important these neurotransmitters are in brain function, it is understandable that functional variations in the genes encoding regulatory elements of these neurotransmitters are implicated in addiction, as well as in other psychiatric disorders such as depression, anxiety and schizophrenia. These genes act on common pathways in addiction to different substances, and are potentially involved in the shared genetic liability between addiction and other psychiatric illnesses, and interact with environmental factors such as stress.

The catechol-O-methyltransferase (COMT) gene encodes an enzyme (COMT) which is involved in the degradation of catecholamine neurotransmitters such as dopamine, adrenaline and noradrenaline. Different variants in the COMT gene have been shown to affect frontal lobe function, influence emotional state, and have been associated with personality traits which are more prevalent in drug addiction such as impulsivity and sensation seeking (for a review of COMT see Dickinson & Elvevag, 2009).

In addition to COMT, other gene variants implicated in the wider neurobiology of addiction and psychiatric illness include gene variants encoding monoamine oxidase A (MAO-A) and gene variants encoding the serotonin transporter (SERT or 5-HTT). MAO-A is a mitochondrial enzyme involved in the oxidative deactivation of monoamine neurotransmitters. The serotonin transporter (also known as the sodium-dependent serotonin transporter and solute carrier family 6 member 4), encoded by the SLC6A4 gene, is responsible for regulating the synaptic levels of serotonin.

Variable number tandem repeats (VNTRs) are large parts of non-coding DNA which are organised in repeated sequences. Although the repeated DNA sequences are the same, the number of these repeated sequences varies between different individuals and can be used for genetic fingerprinting. The SLC6A4 gene has a variable number tandem repeat (VNTR) in the promoter region, termed HTTLPR. Variations in the major alleles within this region are associated with differences in transcriptional efficiency which influence the regulation of emotion and stress. Variation in the HTTLPR region in relation to different stress-related phenotypes has been consistently observed in different populations. Such gene environment interactions may increase the risk for alcohol addiction and other neuropsychiatric illness (e.g. Rubens et al., 2015).

GWAS have also unexpectedly identified genes coding for cell adhesion molecules in relation to addiction vulnerability and other psychiatric disorders (Uhl et al., 2008). It is postulated that these genes may be involved in the way memories of habitual drug taking are formed.

## CHALLENGES FACING RESEARCH IN THIS FIELD

Unfortunately knowledge of an association between a given candidate gene and the addiction phenotype being investigated does not provide confirmatory evidence for a causal functional relationship between the gene and the disorder. One of the main challenges facing genetic research is relating any particular positive association finding to the underlying neurobiological mechanisms involved in conferring addiction risk. This is compounded by the wide variation within and between addiction phenotypes, their classification and measurement between studies, and their overlap with other neuropsychiatric disorders.

Many studies investigating particular gene variants and addiction phenotypes have yielded contradictory findings characterised by failure to replicate an initial positive association result. The failure to replicate positive association findings for candidate genes may be due to several factors. These include the possibility that the effects of any particular variant may be too small to be widely detectable, they may be distributed heterogeneously, and they may be specifically associated with a particular population or a particular characteristic of the drug. It is also extremely difficult to disentangle the contribution and influence of gene x gene (epistatic) interactions and gene x environment interactions to a given phenotype. These interactions will undoubtedly fluctuate throughout the lifespan in relation to developmental changes, substance exposure, and in response to a wide variety of fluctuating environmental signals which can dynamically influence gene expression.

The large number of statistical comparisons that are made in GWAS, and the stringently high statistical criteria used to identify positive results, may lead to false negative findings. Risk alleles identified by GWAS for complex traits such as addiction typically account for only a small percentage of the predicted genetic risk. It is possible that many other risk variants that fail to meet the statistical criteria for GWAS are involved in conferring risk, and when large sets of such variants are considered, a larger proportion of trait heritability could potentially be accounted for (Yang et al., 2011). In addition to the ethnic and geographical diversity that is observed in the underlying genetic pathways to addiction, variability also exists at the level of the individual (McClellan & King, 2010). To unravel these cumulative levels of complexity is extremely challenging.

Most investigations are based on the assumption that susceptibility to common diseases is caused by common genetic variants with small to moderate effects. This is called the common disease/common variant hypothesis. However, it is also possible that rare alleles with a frequency of <1% are important for the genetic vulnerability to some common traits including addiction. The rare-variants common disease model assumes that common diseases are the result of the additive effects of low-frequency dominantly and independently acting high-penetrance variants (Frazer et al., 2009; McClellan & King, 2010; et al., 2014). For example, a rare X-linked gene variant resulting in a deficiency of MAOA enzyme has been shown to be associated with impulsive aggression (a risk factor for substance dependence) in a Dutch pedigree of males (Brunner et al., 1993). A genetic variation in the serotonin receptor 2B gene (HTR2B), restricted to the Finnish population, has also been shown to be associated with severe impulsive aggression (Bevilacqua et al., 2010). Recent progress in gene sequencing technologies, coupled with investigation of family pedigrees, isolated founder populations, and behaviourally extreme phenotypes, may enable the future identification of other rare genetic variants implicated in addiction, which may be hard to detect in larger studies of ethnically diverse populations.

# THE INTERMEDIATE PHENOTYPE APPROACH TO THE STUDY OF THE GENETIC BASIS OF ADDICTION

'Phenotype' refers to any assessable characteristic, and the term 'intermediate phenotype' can be thought of as a subclass encompassed within this. Intermediate phenotypes can be defined as mechanism-related manifestations of a complex characteristic and include endophenotypes, which are heritable disease-associated phenotypes (Goldman & Ducci, 2007; Gottesman & Gould, 2003). The difficulties in identifying the specific genes involved in conferring risk for any complex psychiatric trait include the limitations inherent in the systems used to classify and diagnose psychiatric disorders. The same end diagnosis can be reached through many different combinations of descriptive (and subjectively judged) symptoms. The intermediate phenotype approach is a way to simplify this complexity by breaking it down into components which can be more easily measured, but which are still potentially related to the causal mechanisms by which the disorder arises, and its underlying genetic architecture.

An endophenotype can consist of specific measurements of neurophysiological, biochemical, endocrinological, neuroanatomical, cognitive, or neuropsychological processes. These processes should be able to be objectively and reliably measured and should also be state-independent; should co-segregate with the disorder and be found at a higher rate in non-affected family members than in the general population (Gottesman & Gould, 2003). The co-morbidity between different addictions and between addiction and other neuropsychiatric disorders, reflecting genes in common, may also be reflected in the contribution of the same intermediate phenotypes to a variety of different psychiatric disorders. These kinds of measures are considered more tractable and are proposed to be linked to particular disorders by common neurobiological pathways. They are considered to be less subjective and more homogeneous by virtue of their closer relationship to the neurobiological processes underpinning disease liability (for an in-depth account of the intermediate phenotype approach see MacKillop & Munafo, 2013).

An endophenotype can be specific to a particular disorder; for example, the biochemical endophenotypes of alcohol metabolism and acetaldehyde metabolism previously described, have been traced back to variations in the ADH1B and ALDH2 genes associated with risk for, or protection against, alcoholism. Examples of less specific endophenotypes include the character traits of impulsivity and sensation seeking. Both these traits are more common amongst chronic drug users, and are potentially associated with increased vulnerability to substance abuse. An investigation of these traits in chronic stimulant users identified impulsivity as a risk factor in mediating development of addiction, whereas sensation seeking appeared to be more of a consequence of substance exposure (Ersche et al., 2010).

# SUMMARY

- Genes are located on chromosomes which consist mainly of DNA, which is responsible for the perpetuation and maintenance of life.
- Evidence from family, twin and adoption studies supports an important role for genetic influences in the development of vulnerability to addiction.
- The molecular genetic techniques of linkage and association have been used to identify genes involved in addiction to specific substances, and genes influencing shared liability across different substances and co-morbid neuropsychiatric disorders.
- Single Nucleotide Polymorphisms in the alcohol metabolising genes, in the cholinergic gene cluster CHRNA5-CHRNA3-CHRNAB4, and in the DRD2 and ANNK1 genes, are the most replicated and significant gene variants associated with alcohol and nicotine addiction.
- Despite sophisticated technical advances, the problems inherent in studying a complex behavioural trait remain a fundamental challenge to genetic research on addiction.
- Converging evidence provided by research from different levels and types of analysis is a way to validate potential findings.
- A promising avenue of research in addiction genetics is the uncovering of individual genetic differences influencing less complex pharmacological traits, as has already occurred for particular alcohol and nicotine dependence endophenotypes. This offers the potential for identifying who may benefit from a particular type of treatment based on the results of genetic testing.

# QUESTIONS

1. How are genes transmitted from one generation to the next?
2. To what extent can we differentiate learned experiential influences on addiction from that of a pure genetic basis?
3. Why are twins so important to behavioural genetic research?
4. Genes can also be protective against addiction. Discuss.
5. What is an endophenotype?

# PSYCHOLOGICAL THEORIES OF ADDICTION

## 5

### CHAPTER OVERVIEW

This chapter will describe and evaluate some of the main theories and models which have been used to explain and understand addiction. Different theories and models emphasise different aspects of addictive behaviour to a greater or lesser degree, and offer different levels of explanation ranging from the biological to the societal. All the theories described are of value in contributing to our overall understanding, but no particular theory is able to comprehensively explain and capture all aspects of a condition which is influenced by so many interacting factors.

The theories in this chapter have been chosen as illustrative examples of particular approaches, but readers should be aware that there are many other theories, approaches and personal accounts, which attempt to explain and understand the driving forces behind addiction, which are not covered in this chapter.

This chapter will:

- Outline the disease or biomedical model of addiction, briefly tracing its history through alcohol and opioids to how it is currently conceptualised

ADDICTION

(Continued)

- Describe example theories which emphasise the role of choice and the influence of cognitive processes such as attention, perception and memory in driving addictive behaviour
- Outline two example theories which attempt to integrate diverse aspects of addiction into an overarching comprehensive framework

## LEARNING AIMS OF THE CHAPTER

- To have an awareness of the predominance of the disease model of addiction
- To gain an awareness of the factors which contribute to addictive behaviour and how some of these factors are linked to specific theories of addiction
- To be aware of the difficulties involved in limiting our understanding of a complex behaviour to any particular theoretical viewpoint
- To have an understanding of how different aspects of addictive behaviour can be integrated into broad theories which seek to synthesise different contributory components of addictive behaviour

# INTRODUCTION

A comprehensive theory of addiction should be able to account for the key features of addiction including: individual susceptibility; its development and maintenance; how it is experienced physically and psychologically (features such as tolerance, craving, impulsive and compulsive use); and be able to suggest possibilities for treatment. Ideally a good theory should generate testable hypotheses. This is extremely challenging because it is very difficult to design studies in this field which accurately represent experiences in the real world (ecologically valid experiments). This is because in addition to societal and cultural impacts, addiction is experienced on an individual level, as a personal conflict, in individually triggering and personal environments. As a result of this complexity, most theories of addiction help us to understand one part of the picture more clearly without necessarily adequately addressing the other parts.

Although the different theories in this chapter are organised under different subheadings for clarity, it will become evident that there is substantial overlap between theories and between attempts to explain observations. Different theories may incorporate widely applicable observations and offer distinct but mutually supportive explanations. It is difficult to experimentally evaluate all levels of analysis simultaneously.

The first section will provide a broad overview of the disease or biomedical model of addiction, briefly tracing its history through alcohol and opioids to the current conceptualisation of the 'disease'. The inclusion of the disease model in a chapter on psychological theories of addiction serves to illustrate the interrelationships between psychological processes and their biological underpinnings (see Chapter 3 for the neural systems involved). The next section will focus on theories which emphasise the role of choice and the influence of cognitive processes such as attention, perception and memory in driving addictive behaviour. The final section of this chapter will describe theories which attempt to integrate diverse aspects of addiction into an overarching comprehensive framework.

# THE DISEASE MODEL OF ADDICTION

The basic premise of the disease model of addiction is that addiction is comparable to other medically defined diseases (such as heart disease and cancer) in that it has a biological basis. Current conceptualisations of the disease model locate the disease in the brain circuitry of the affected individual. Addiction is viewed as a progressive chronic relapsing disorder, with a definable set of observable psychological symptoms through which the disease can be diagnosed. The addictive agent is viewed as able to disrupt brain circuits involved in normal reward processing, causing the addicted individual to become 'sick'. The labelling of addiction as a disease, which affects particular individuals who are genetically/developmentally/environmentally (or a combination of these factors) susceptible, has implications for how addicts are treated by professionals, how they understand and interpret their addictive behaviour, and how they are viewed by society. The general view of this model is that addictive drugs cause long-term progressive changes in the brain.

## ALCOHOL

The acceptance of addiction as a disease is thought to have gained increasing prominence from the late eighteenth century onwards, as can be illustrated by the history of alcohol use. Prior to this, habitual drunkenness was commonly perceived as an act of will. The habitual and excessive drinker was thought of as a morally flawed character. A shift to the perception of addiction as a disease, as opposed to a moral failing, historically coincided with the rise of the temperance movement, increased industrialisation, urbanisation, and the associated changes in living conditions and lifestyle. The widespread availability of alcohol, coupled with changing social conditions, created an environment where perceived problematic drinking was more common. Alcohol was increasingly depicted, particularly by certain members of the clergy, as an evil substance that could potentially affect large numbers of people without discrimination. The rise and influence of this view resulted in alcohol prohibition in America from 1919 until 1933.

After prohibition in America was repealed, there was an increasing level of scientific and medical collaborative research on alcohol and its effects. This resulted in the reformulation of alcoholism as a disease that affected only certain susceptible individuals. The formation of Alcoholics Anonymous (AA), and the research work of E.M. Jellinek, were influential in the widespread acceptance of this view. Jellinek had an important impact on the scientific study of alcoholism through his extensive academic research contributions, coupled with his ability to unite diverse groups interested in this newly emerging field. This included gaining both public and professional support for alcohol research and treatment, and the widespread dissemination of research findings. The publication of *The Disease Concept of Alcoholism* (Jellinek, 1960) consolidated acceptance of a disease model of alcoholism (Page, 1997). Jellinek broadly described alcoholism as any use of alcoholic beverages that caused damage to the individual, to society, or both. Components of the current diagnostic criteria for alcohol use disorder (see Chapter 1) also retain elements of the formulation of alcohol dependence and its provisional description as a clinical syndrome by Griffith Edwards and Milton Gross in 1976 (Edwards & Gross, 1976). They also speculated that the clinical syndrome involved both a biological component and aberrant learning.

## OPIOIDS

Widespread recreational use of opium in Asia occurred after the advent of tobacco smoking, and slowly spread to other countries. Opium smoking, as opposed to opium eating, increased its effect on the brain, and its addictive potential. The political and economic imperialism of

Western colonial powers influenced the addictive use of opium in various Asian countries, resulting in opium epidemics in those countries (Westermeyer, 2005).

The isolation of morphine, the major psychoactive component of opium and its subsequent commercialisation in the early 1800s, coupled with the invention of the hypodermic needle in 1856, led to a new route for drug administration with greater addictive potential. Until the early 1900s opium was legal and freely available in many countries including Europe and North America. Heroin, an opiate with a greater ability to cross the blood brain barrier, was synthesised in 1870, by the acetylation of morphine. The inclusion of opium, morphine and cocaine, but the omission of heroin, from the Harrison Narcotics Act passed in America in 1914, led to an upsurge in heroin use. Heroin was made illegal in 1924 in America. However, in general, punitive drug laws in America and elsewhere have not been successful in preventing illegal drug use, and have usually led to an increase in illegal supply and organised crime, and fuelled tabloid hysteria and public misperception. This is particularly evident when contrasted with the degree of harm and the number of people affected by legal addictions to gambling, alcohol and tobacco, and the insidious political reach of these industries in influencing policy and research (Fooks & Gilmore, 2013; Orford, 2013). The legal/illegal division has significance because of the stigma associated with the 'disease' of addiction, which must be the only disease in which the sufferer can be both simultaneously punished and treated.

Opioids are prescribed medically for the relief of pain, but also act on the brain's reward system and have significant addictive potential. They are important in a discussion of the disease model of addiction, because the neurobiological changes caused by opioid addiction provide strong support for the medical treatment of addiction using pharmacological therapy. Medications such as methadone, buprenorphine and naltrexone are used for the treatment of opioid addiction, with variable success. These drugs act on the same brain processes and pathways as opioids, but have some protective or normalising effects (Kosten & George, 2002). There is an acceptance in methadone maintenance therapy (MMT) that the individual has a chronic illness and is unable to abstain from drug use. This approach therefore seeks to reduce the harm caused by continued drug use by offering a less harmful alternative drug option, methadone, which reduces drug craving, tolerance and compulsion, due to its longer-lasting action on the mu opioid receptor. The aim of MMT (or other drug therapy) is to stabilise the individual enough to allow them to regain a degree of control over their lives, and reduce some of the problems associated with procuring and using illegal drugs (Gelkopf et al., 2002). It is the immediate physiological issues rather than the underlying socio-psychological issues leading to drug addiction which are initially addressed in MMT, but access to medical services at least opens the door to the potential for future improvement through ongoing counselling or psychotherapy. MMT can continue for months to years, and is continued for life in some individuals.

# ILLUSTRATIVE EXAMPLES OF THE DISEASE/MEDICAL MODEL

Evidence to support the idea that alcohol, tobacco, and other drug addictions are related through a common pathological action on the nervous system, which is changed through repeated drug use, has expanded through the technological developments and discoveries of the second half of the twentieth century (Courtwright, 2015). Discoveries in the fields of behavioural pharmacology, behavioural neuroscience, genetics, and more recently neuroimaging, have all contributed to this accumulating evidence.

The incentive sensitisation theory of addiction (Robinson & Berridge, 1993), the dysregulation of reward (allostasis) theory of addiction (Koob & Le Moal, 2001), and the Impaired response inhibition and salience attribution (I-RISA) syndrome of addiction (Goldstein & Volkow, 2002; Volkow et al., 2003) which are described in Chapter 3 on biological theories, can all be considered under the disease model of addiction, because drug-induced changes in the brain are at the heart of these theories. However, they could also be considered under a different subheading on the grounds that cognitive processes such as perception, attention and memory play a crucial explanatory role in these theories, and the underlying mechanisms are interrelated.

# AN EVALUATION OF THE DISEASE MODEL OF ADDICTION

The disease model has been influential within the addiction field and has had a significant impact on our understanding of some of the underlying neurobiological processes involved in addiction. Breaking down addiction into component processes which can be scientifically studied has provided a large body of neuroscientific evidence to support the view that addiction is a chronic illness with an underlying biological basis and a characteristic set of symptoms. This view of addiction has been useful because it has enabled objective identification of specific processes involved in addiction. By placing addiction within the medical arena, the disease model has partially reduced some of the guilt and stigma attached to addiction, and has provided a framework through which those who suffer can understand and interpret their behaviour and seek help and treatment. This biological level of understanding and analysis is critical for the development of pharmacological treatment of addiction, and places emphasis on the pharmacological properties of the abused substance as well as individual vulnerability factors which are intrinsic to the individual addict, or acquired through drug use. It also enables the identification and comparison of distinct and common neuroanatomical regions and neurotransmitters involved in different stages of the addictive process, between addiction and other mental disorders, and in addiction to different substances and activities. However, despite this knowledge, there is no specific or reliable biological marker available through which addiction can be diagnosed.

Although there are undoubted strengths to the conceptualisation of addiction as a disease there are also some fairly major criticisms. One of the main problems with the disease model is a failure to explain treatment-free recovery. People can and do decide to give up their addictions, even when those addictions have lasted for many years, without any medical intervention or formal treatment. The only way to understand spontaneous recovery from addiction is through understanding the factors and processes that influence behaviour change. This would include consideration of personal, interpersonal, developmental, cultural, and societal influences. Addicts are a diverse population, and it is possible that the brain disease model of addiction more appropriately describes a subset of addicts for whom recovery without some form of external intervention is less possible, and who represent the most severely affected individuals through a combination of the impact of genetic, developmental, and environmental/socioeconomic factors.

Another criticism of the disease model is that by placing emphasis on the faulty neurochemistry of the addicted individual, it has diverted resources and attention away from investigation of other important influences on addiction, particularly social, cultural and political factors. This has resulted in stunting exploration of potentially more successful alternative treatment approaches. Despite the good intentions of the medical model to reduce the stigma attached to addiction, it has failed to fully succeed, partly due to the variable success rate of current addiction treatments and to continued inconsistency in how drugs and alcohol are publically perceived and represented.

## CHOICE MODELS OF ADDICTION

In contrast to the disease model of addiction, other theories emphasise the role of personal choice, rational or otherwise, in the development and maintenance of addiction (see West & Brown, 2013: 41–94, for a comprehensive overview of choice theories of addiction). In the following section two such theories will be briefly described as illustrative examples of this view. The authors of these theories, John Booth Davies and Gene Heyman, have both published books describing their particular perspectives in detail, along with the supporting evidence.

*The Myth of Addiction* (Davies, 1997) puts forward the theoretical perspective that drug use is an entirely voluntary behaviour that serves a functional purpose for the person engaging in the behaviour. The response to this behaviour by other people and by treatment providers and society also serves a functional purpose in their understanding of the behaviour. This perspective is grounded in attribution theory, which seeks to understand human behaviour in terms of how people explain their own actions and the actions of others. These explanations do not necessarily have any objective scientific truth because they are based on social cognitions and vary according to the particular context of the social interaction taking place. Explanations for our own behaviour tend to be modified, particularly with regard to issues involving moral evaluation by others. Booth Davies postulates that the ideology behind the disease model of addiction is better explained by the common functions served by that type of explanation, rather than as a result of any underlying common cause or addictive process involved in addiction to different substances or activities. According to this view, explaining addictive behaviour in non-volitional terms such as malfunction or disease serves to abdicate personal responsibility for indulging in what the individual concerned and conventional society perceive as 'bad' behaviour. If this attribution was not made, punishment rather than treatment would be a more appropriate response, and drug use could be reasonably viewed as an adaptation to the environment in which the drug user or gambler lives. Booth Davies argues for a reconceptualisation of addiction as an activity which is under the voluntary control and management of the user, so that alternative and more helpful attributions can develop, rather than the widespread acceptance of the 'helpless addict' explanatory stereotype. This, he argues, could lead to implementation of more effective harm reduction approaches to treatment for those who want to continue to use drugs, and more effective, less punitive policies to control illicit drug use.

Although important observations are made by this theory, and compelling evidence is cited to support it, it fails to incorporate or adequately consider the large body of behavioural, pharmacological, physiological and experiential evidence which contradicts this view. For those individuals and their families who are suffering from the reality of the utter misery, despair and conflict created by addiction, and for those involved in their care, it is not helpful to refer to addiction as a 'myth'. Although functional attributions undoubtedly contribute to our understanding of how people talk about addiction, they are insufficient to provide a complete explanation of such a multi-faceted condition. Individual personal choice cannot arise independent of the influence of biology and environment, which calls into question how much of a truly volitional choice is ever actually being made.

This point is also relevant to the theory put forward by Heyman (2009, 2013) who also argues against the disease conception of addiction, and presents extensive evidence that addiction is a disorder of normal choice processes. Whilst acknowledging that addiction can be 'disease-like', Heyman questions the compulsive nature of addiction. He cites evidence from large epidemiological surveys (e.g. Lopez-Quintero et al., 2011; Warner et al., 1995) that most people who meet the diagnostic criteria for addiction quit using illegal drugs by approximately age 30. The majority of these people quit without professional treatment and the reasons that they give for quitting reflect the practical and moral concerns of their lives. These include reasons such as wanting approval and respect from family members, fear of legal sanctions, and practical and financial concerns. Those who remain chronic drug users and enter treatment facilities tend to be those with particular demographic characteristics such as poor educational achievement, disrupted work histories, extensive criminal records and additional psychiatric diagnoses. According to Heyman, this minority who enter formal treatment is not representative of the vast majority of addicts, and previous research based on this more extremely affected clinical minority has distorted our understanding of addiction.

Consistent with selfish and self-defeating addictive behaviour patterns, Heyman argues that quantitative empirical laws of choice derived from behavioural psychology and economics (e.g. Ainslie, 1992; Hernstein, 1990) are able to accurately predict the operation of stable but suboptimal choices under certain conditions. He refers to the 'matching law', 'melioration' and 'hyperbolic discounting'. Matching of competing choice options is achieved by the process of melioration, which in this context means that at any given time the choice that leads to the more immediately available reward will be chosen over a delayed reward. Hyperbolic discounting refers to the increase in tendency for choosing a smaller but more immediately available reward over a larger less tangible delayed reward. Rewards further into the future are discounted to a greater degree. This also applies to the motivational pull of behavioural consequences which steeply decline as a function of delay.

Since taking an addictive substance, or engaging in an addictive behaviour, usually involves an immediately perceptually pleasant effect coupled with delayed negative consequences, it becomes possible to see how suboptimal choices could be prioritised. This effect is exacerbated because the substance itself is able to interact with the neurochemistry of the individual in a manner which encourages future choices to re-experience these rewarding properties.

Heyman refers to the importance of how individual choices are framed in predicting addictive behaviour patterns. Addiction is more likely when choices are framed according to the best immediately available option using a local frame of reference. This is in contrast to global framing of choices, in which controlled drug use or abstinence can occur because the frame of reference is expanded to include long-term future costs and consequences.

According to this view, addiction is best combated by encouraging a focus on the long-term consequences of consumption coupled with decreasing the relative reward value of the substance or behaviour, as already occurs in successful treatment. This can potentially be achieved through using pharmacotherapy and/or behaviour change to reduce the relative reward value of the drug, encouraging adherence to societal norms regarding use and intake of substances, and considering how global framing can somehow be packaged to exert a greater effect on choice.

This theory of addiction is comprehensive and is consistent with a large body of existing empirical evidence, which Heyman has interpreted and re-evaluated to support his theory. Further research on how to implement reframing of choices may shed more light on potential future treatment applications based on these ideas. However, as previously stated, an addictive pattern of behaviour cannot develop independently of biological and environmental influences, including frequent exposure to advertising, other media and socio-cultural norms regarding drug use, substance availability and legality, and individual responses to these influences.

Environmental exposure to drugs and drug-related cues influence initiation, maintenance and relapse in addiction, and are the focus of cognitive bias theories of addiction, which are considered in the next section. Choice theories of addiction cannot explain addiction without considering the multiple factors, both conscious and unconscious, which influence choice.

## THEORIES OF ADDICTION WHICH EMPHASISE COGNITIVE BIAS

Cognitive psychology seeks to understand mental processes such as attention, perception and memory. Cognitive processes are considered to be central to addiction and cognitive control can be recruited to either support or inhibit drug use (Curtin et al., 2006). Outcome expectancies (Marlatt, 1985), or beliefs about the positive and negative consequences of drug use, can guide future drug use and also be open to influence by exposure to environmental drug cues. Placebo drinks have been shown to increase alcohol craving and subsequent consumption (Christiansen et al., 2013) and also to impair inhibitory control of alcohol consumption in accordance with participants' expectancies in relation to the effects of alcohol on cognitive impairment (Christiansen et al., 2016). The concept of self-efficacy, or the belief in the ability to control one's behaviour in particular situations (Bandura, 1977), is also important in the context of addictive behaviour, and such beliefs are important determinants of successful behavioural modulation (Job et al., 2010).

Cognitive bias can be thought of as a form of selective information processing directed towards the addictive substance or behaviour, and anything that through association has become linked to the drug or behaviour. This can include unconscious/implicit as well as conscious/explicit environmental and internal physiological triggers. This selective information processing influences drug use behaviour through the inseparable and interacting impacts of learning, physiology, emotion, attention, perception, and memory. The unconscious or automatic aspects of selective information processing can operate and influence behaviour outside of conscious control, and this can be experienced as the loss of control that arises in addiction. One of the commonalities of addictive drugs is their ability to invoke reactivity to environmental drug cues. Cue reactivity is the array of responses that are observed when drug users or former drug users are exposed to stimuli previously associated with drug effects (drug cues). These learned or conditioned responses (see Chapter 3) can produce effects in the body that are experienced as both similar to the effects of the drug itself, or opposite to the effects of the drug.

The cognitive model of drug urges and drug use behaviour (Tiffany, 1990), the affective processing model of addiction (Baker et al., 2004) and the attentional bias hypothesis for drug craving and addiction (Franken, 2003) will be described as illustrative examples of the many theories of addiction which incorporate a role for cognitive bias. Specific experimental methods have been developed to demonstrate the operation of cognitive biases, and some of these methods have been adapted to the study of addiction and will be described in the final part of this section.

# THE COGNITIVE MODEL OF DRUG URGES AND DRUG-USE BEHAVIOUR

The cognitive model of drug urges and drug use behaviour (Tiffany, 1990) incorporates findings from cognitive psychology about the properties of automatic and non-automatic behavioural processes, and applies these findings to explain drug use behaviour. Tiffany cites numerous lines of evidence from experimental cognitive psychology to support the theoretical framework for his theory. This theory proposes that behaviour associated with habitual drug use eventually becomes automatised. Automatic processes are characterised as:

- being relatively fast, with speed increasing as a result of increased practice;
- being initiated without conscious intention and triggered by particular stimulus conditions;
- lacking control, in that once elicited by triggering stimuli they are difficult to stop;
- being effortless, in that increased practice makes these processes cognitively undemanding;
- being carried out without conscious awareness.

With repeated practice, the skills required for obtaining and consuming drugs are hypothesised to become increasingly automatised. These skills are proposed to be stored in memory as automatised action plans, which once initiated, tend to run to completion. Tiffany proposes that these unitised memory structures will encode certain information about drug use behaviour. In contrast to automatic processes, non-automatic processes are slow, require effort, and conscious intention and attention. These non-automatic processes are activated in parallel with the drug use action plans, either in support of, or in opposition to, the drug use plan. Craving is proposed to result from the cognitively effortful, non-automatic interruption of these automatised action plans, for example when the individual tries to intentionally abstain from drugs or is somehow prevented from carrying out drug use behaviour. As initiation of these drug use action schemata is triggered by particular stimulus conditions, disruption of these triggering stimulus conditions would be the most effective means of inhibiting the associated automatic cognitive activity.

# THE AFFECTIVE PROCESSING MODEL OF ADDICTION

The affective processing model of addiction (Baker et al., 2004) argues that drugs are taken primarily to alleviate negative affect which occurs as a result of drug withdrawal. Addicted individuals are postulated as having an over-reliance on drug use as a way to influence how they are feeling, and experiencing severely negative emotional states is proposed to influence information processing in ways that lead to further drug use. Baker et al. suggest that negative affect increases levels of 'hot' information processing as opposed to 'cool' controlled information processing (Metcalfe & Mischel, 1999). Hot information processing is thought to be bottom up in nature, relatively uninformed by pre-existing declarative knowledge (Schwarz, 2000), and is able to override cognitive control and the application of more productive coping resources. This type of information processing causes attention to be focused on negative affect and its cause and relief. Since the drug user perceives drugs to have successfully relieved their negative feelings in the past, hot information processing leads to an attentional bias towards drugs and drug-associated stimuli. In support of this view of addiction, studies have shown that addicts rate coping with negative affect as the predominant motive for drug use (Goldman et al., 1987; Wetter et al., 1994).

# ATTENTIONAL BIAS HYPOTHESIS FOR DRUG CRAVING AND ADDICTION

This theory (Franken, 2003) integrates findings from psychological and neuropsychological approaches to understanding drug craving and addiction. The importance of attentional bias as the cognitive mediator between the drug stimulus and the behavioural response to this stimulus is emphasised. Drug craving is viewed as an emotional conditioned appetitive motivational state produced by stimuli associated with reward effects. Like Robinson and Berridge (see Chapter 3), Franken proposes that a conditioned drug stimulus produces an increase in corticostriatal dopamine levels, in particular in the anterior cingulate gyrus, amygdala and nucleus accumbens, which results in direction of attention towards drug stimuli. This is proposed to result in motor preparation and a hyperattentive state to drug stimuli, which enhances drug craving and promotes relapse.

# COGNITIVE METHODS FOR STUDYING DRUG USE BEHAVIOUR

Experiments derived from cognitive psychology have increased understanding of addictive behaviour. It is thought that experiments which assess biases in the processing of addiction-related stimuli are able to predict ongoing behaviour better than methods which rely on self-assessment (McCusker, 2001).

Introspective self-report methods which are used in research into addictive behaviour have shown inconsistencies in the self-reported beliefs and intentions of drug users compared with their actual drug use behaviour. A common feature of addictive behaviour is the continuation of the behaviour despite conscious intentions to abstain from it. This suggests that memory and attentional processes outside conscious awareness and voluntary control may be operating (McCusker & Gettings, 1997).

Methods for investigating cognitive biases in addiction which make inferences about cognitive processes and structures based on behavioural responses rather than potentially inaccurate written self-reported responses (e.g. self-reported questionnaires about drug use and positive and negative drug use expectancies) may therefore provide clearer insight into processes controlling actual drug use behaviour. These types of method, such as Stroop, memory priming, dot-probe and reaction time experiments, are thought to access processing which occurs at automatic, implicit and preconscious levels of awareness. These types of methods are also more demand free, since individuals are not asked to directly reflect about their behaviour or their reasons for engaging in it. Outside the field of addiction, there is strong evidence from neuropsychological studies, for the occurrence of selective dissociations between perceptual processes and conscious awareness, as well as evidence for semantic activation and learning outside consciousness (Styles, 1998). These processes may play a role in the transition from initial drug use to eventual drug addiction. In the following sections some of the methods for assessing cognitive biases in addiction will be considered because they have provided a large body of evidence to support the operation of selective information processing in addiction.

## THE EMOTIONAL STROOP TEST

In the classic Stroop test (Stroop, 1935) the participant is asked to name the colour of ink in which a series of colour words are written as quickly as possible. In order to name the ink colour quickly, attention is primarily focused on the perceptual characteristics of the word, whilst semantic processing (word meaning) is suppressed. However, reaction times to colour naming are longer if the colour of the word and its name are incongruent, for example, if the word 'red' is written in green ink. This interference effect is thought to result from failure to suppress semantic processing of the word.

The emotional Stroop task is a widely used experimental variation of the classic Stroop colour-naming task. This version of the Stroop task has been used to study cognitive-emotional processes in psychopathology. Participants with a particular psychopathology, generally show increased colour-naming times if words relevant to their disorder are used compared with neutral words. For example increased reaction times to disorder relevant words have been demonstrated for both depression and anxiety disorders (reviewed by Williams et al., 1996). Another variation on the classic Stroop task is the subliminal Stroop task. In this version of the task words are rapidly masked after their appearance so that they appear below the threshold of conscious recognition.

The version of the Stroop task mainly used in addiction research is referred to as the addiction-Stroop test. In the addiction-Stroop test latencies for colour naming addiction-related distracter words are compared with colour-naming times for neutral control words. Selective interference effects are observed in addicts when words which relate to their particular addiction are used. For example, gamblers show selectively elevated colour-naming times for gambling-related words (McCusker & Gettings, 1997), and an attentional bias for alcohol-related words in alcohol abusers has also been demonstrated in a number of studies (e.g. Lusher et al., 2004).

Variables related to stimulus selection, test format and mode of presentation all play an important role in the ability of these tests to detect a substance related attentional bias (Cox et al., 2006). Although it has been widely used in research into cognitive processes, the Stroop paradigm has also been subject to criticism. It is not clear which processes are responsible for the increased colour-naming latencies for disorder relevant words, and whether these increased reaction times truly reflect selective attention or some other process. Another criticism of the Stroop task is that it has little ecological validity. The serial presentation of single word stimuli is unlike most situations encountered in real life, where multiple stimuli compete for visual attention.

A role for dopamine in the processing of drug cues in heroin-dependent patients has been experimentally demonstrated (Franken et al., 2004). In this double blind, randomised crossover study, a D2 dopamine antagonist, haloperidol, or placebo, was administered to detoxified heroin-dependent patients. These patients performed an Emotional Stroop Task to assess their cognitive processing of drug cues under both conditions. The results showed that patients were faster to colour name heroin-dependent words in the haloperidol condition, suggesting decreased attentional focusing on drug cues mediated by decreased dopamine, and indirect evidence that the perception of drug cues results in an increase in dopamine activity (Di Chiara, 1999; Robinson & Berridge, 1993).

## THE DOT-PROBE TASK

Another task used to study attentional bias is the visual dot-probe task. This task is considered to be a more accurate indicator of attentional bias than the Stroop task. Unlike the Stroop task, the dot-probe measures shifts in attention between two co-present visual stimuli (Box 5.1). This task was adapted from earlier experiments in cognitive psychology which showed that spatial attention can be assessed from the speed of manual responses to visual probes (Posner et al., 1980).

In studies of addictive behaviour the dot-probe task has revealed an attentional bias for cocaine-related words in cocaine addicts (Franken et al., 2000), drug-related pictures in opiate addicts (e.g. Lubman et al., 2000), and for alcohol-related stimuli in alcohol abusers (e.g. Townshend & Duka, 2001). Studies using smokers have also indicated an attentional bias for smoking-related pictures in smokers (e.g. B. Bradley et al., 2004; B. P. Bradley et al., 2003; Ehrman et al., 2002). The dot-probe task has greater ecological validity than the Stroop because it more accurately reflects situations encountered in real life, where stimuli compete for the allocation of visual attention. Also, this task can use competing pictorial stimuli rather than the serial presentation of single words.

## BOX 5.1  THE DOT-PROBE TASK

This type of experiment works on the assumption that participants will respond faster to a visual probe stimulus (usually a small dot) that is presented to an attended rather than an unattended area of a visual display. Pairs of competing stimuli (either pictures or words) are briefly presented on a screen. The images then disappear and a small dot-probe stimulus appears in the location of one of the stimulus pairs. Participants are asked to manually respond to the position of the probe by pressing a button/key as quickly and accurately as possible. Experimental evidence indicates that participants are faster to respond to the location of the dot-probe if it appears to replace a concern-related stimulus, indicating that attention is preferentially deployed to such stimuli.

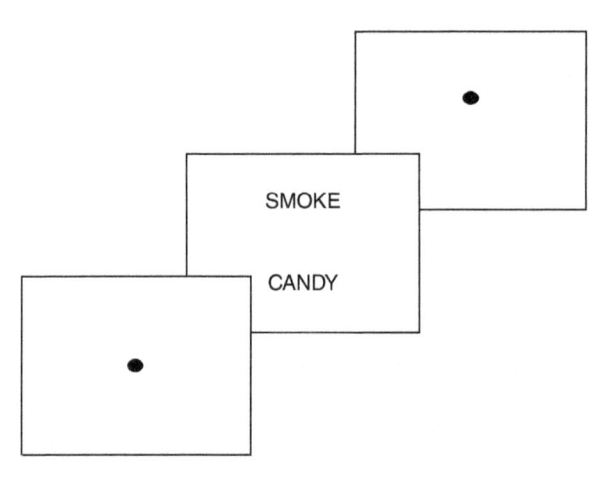

**Figure 5.1**

# OTHER COGNITIVE EXPERIMENTAL METHODS

Other methods used to study information-processing biases in addiction include tests which have their roots in the experimental study of memory. These tasks include memory priming, selective recall, and recognition memory tests. Such tasks have also been used to investigate information-processing biases in psychopathology, for example, generalised anxiety disorder (Hayes & Hirsch, 2007). Numerous studies using these types of experiments have demonstrated a selective information-processing bias in addiction (e.g. Glautier & Spencer, 1999; Hill & Paynter, 1992; Stacy et al., 1997). Increased processing of drug-related material, more spreading activation, and stronger associative links between drug-related concepts, is likely in those who indulge in using drugs more frequently.

The cognitive processing of drug-related stimuli necessarily involves the interaction of memory, motivation and attention as these are related and integrated processes. It is likely that multiple implicit and explicit memory and attentional functions are involved in the development and maintenance of addictive behaviour (Chiamulera, 2005; Weinstein & Cox, 2006).

The experimental study of information-processing biases in addiction holds promise for understanding and treating addictive behaviour. Recent work in the area of alcohol abuse highlights the potential of therapeutic interventions which make use of the measurement and alteration (retraining) of attentional biases in alcohol abusers (Cox et al., 2015; Wiers et al., 2006). These findings show that attentional retraining to ignore alcohol-related stimuli can be successfully used to reduce alcohol consumption in heavy drinkers. It is also likely that the magnitude of attentional bias for drug-related stimuli may be used to predict individuals who are most at risk of relapse after treatment. Attentional distraction for alcohol-related, concern-related, and neutral stimuli before and after treatment for alcohol abuse was investigated using the emotional Stroop task. Attentional bias for alcohol-related stimuli during the course of the treatment (four weeks) was significantly increased in those whose treatment outcome was unsuccessful (after a three month follow-up) compared to those who successfully completed treatment (Cox et al., 2002).

However, despite some encouraging findings, a recent review of the clinical relevance of attentional bias in addiction (Christiansen et al., 2015) questioned the validity of a causal role for attentional bias in substance use, and highlighted the widespread methodological and statistical limitations of empirical studies in this field. Criticisms of work in this field include: the absence of appropriate control groups; the use of small sample sizes; the variation in methodology between different experimental studies; and the inability to adequately address the relevance of findings outside of a laboratory setting.

## COMPREHENSIVE THEORIES OF ADDICTION

The final section of this chapter will describe two comprehensive motivational models of addiction which integrate information from the theoretical perspectives that have been considered. The first theory described is the broadly applicable excessive appetites model of addiction (Orford, 2001), plus a recent expansion of Orford's ideas to include the role of power and powerlessness in addiction (Orford, 2013). The second theory is PRIME theory, a synthetic theory of motivation for addictive behaviour (West & Brown, 2013). The acronym PRIME signifies: **p**lans, **r**esponses, **i**mpulses/inhibiting forces, **m**otives and **e**valuations. It should be evident from the preceding sections that although the theoretical perspectives differ in emphasis and level of analysis, they comprise multiple overlapping elements.

## THE EXCESSIVE APPETITE MODEL OF ADDICTION

The excessive appetite model of addiction is a comprehensive model of addiction which provides an explanatory framework for a broad range of behaviours which can become addictive. This includes both substance-related addictions and behavioural addictions such as excessive eating, sex, exercise, and gambling addictions. Elements from other theories are incorporated within this framework.

The central features of the model include what Orford defines as primary and secondary processes, which occur in diverse sociocultural contexts. He argues that these processes are sufficient to account for the strong attachment to an appetitive activity that constitutes addiction, resulting in a loss of control and 'disease-like' symptoms. Like Heyman, Orford also draws attention to the fact that evidence supports that most people recover from addiction without entering formal treatment. His theory considers the common features very different kinds of addictive behaviour share, and also what is common to successful recovery from these different kinds of appetitive behaviours.

The theory first draws attention to the fact that all appetitive behaviours that can lead to addiction are skewed towards the higher end of the population distribution curve. This means that whilst the majority of people conform to a moderate degree of consumption, smaller and smaller numbers of people display increasing consumption in excess of this statistical norm. One of the explanations given for this is that excessive behaviour is restrained in the majority by social conformity and other kinds of social forces and deterrents of different types. These controlling and restrictive factors include, for example, the restrictive role of adverse health consequences, personality variables, religious belief, influence of family members, and government policies.

Positive incentive learning mechanisms which highlight rapid emotional change and rewards, wide cue conditioning and complex memory schemata, are considered key primary processes which contribute to escalation of the excessive appetite. These processes are important and contribute to the development of cognitive biases in addiction. A wide variety of neurotransmitter systems in addition to the mesolimbic dopamine system are thought to be involved in mediating these appetitive reward mechanisms.

The additional secondary processes consist of what are described as 'acquired emotional regulation cycles' which encourage further increases in consumption. An example of this is the feeling of increased motivation towards further gambling that occurs as a result of the negative feelings associated with losing (Orford et al., 1996). Another secondary process which influences emotional regulation is the 'abstinence violation effect' (Cummings et al., 1980). This effect applies to relapse to both excessive drinking and excessive eating, and includes a variety of negative self-directed emotions resulting in feelings of helplessness and hopelessness which contribute to further uncontrolled consumption (Grilo & Shiffman, 1994; Hsu, 1990).

Additional processes which amplify excessive attachment to appetitive behaviour are what Orford describes as the *consequences of conflict*. These include dissonance or disharmony-reducing reactions. Cognitive dissonance is a way of thinking about conflicting attitudes, beliefs or behaviours in such a way as to reduce the internal conflict that is created by holding opposing views. This dissonance can manifest bodily as difficult emotional states such as tension, confusion and depression, which can escalate the appetitive behaviour in an attempt to reduce the uncomfortable feelings this internal state of conflict has created.

Orford argues that excessive appetites are non-pathological, and a natural consequence of the development of an excessive appetite is to eventually reduce or abstain from it. Common processes encompassing the social, moral and spiritual domains of experience appear to be important to successful recovery. This generally consists of leaving behind an old identity and reinventing oneself to an extent, and has been described as a form of symbolic death, surrender and re-education (Sarbin & Nucci, 1973). Self-liberation processes (Prochaska & DiClemente, 1992), the restructuring of interpersonal relationships, accountability to oneself and significant others, and the experience of some sort of humiliation (Premack, 1970), have also been considered important to successful recovery. Self-help groups based on the principles of Alcoholics Anonymous provide many with a framework for the kind of moral reform necessary for successful behaviour change (e.g. Miller, 1998). The proliferation of these groups to include many different types of excessive appetite adds weight to the importance of the common processes involved in the development and recovery from different addictions.

Orford's more recent work (Orford, 2013) has been on the psychosocial implications of the concepts of power and powerlessness in addiction. This excellent and much needed account is essential to fully understand the development and maintenance of addiction within the wider societal context. In this work Orford draws attention to how addiction erodes the personal power of the addict, and also creates powerlessness in others who are in social proximity to the addict to varying degrees. This web of influence includes close family members and extends out to friends, work colleagues and the wider community. Close family are particularly disempowered and represent a voiceless class who are confused about how to help, and who often assume a level of responsibility for the addict's behaviour. They often have to subordinate their own interests as the result of coping with the addicted family member. Orford draws an analogy with oppressed minorities to illustrate the loss of power of those who experience addiction second-hand.

To illustrate the effects of power and powerlessness in addiction Orford focuses on alcohol, illegal drugs and gambling. Evidence from multiple sources is used to illustrate how addiction is most prevalent amongst those who have the least power to resist, particularly the marginalised and the socially deprived. Those participating in the illegal drugs trade are often enmeshed through economic necessity and a lack of alternative opportunities.

The immense power exerted by the legal alcohol and gambling industries includes both overt and covert methods. This includes strategies such as extensive advertising, lobbying and influencing trade policies and the research agenda. These industries also promote their own interests by influencing the way people think and speak about addiction through the language which is used to discuss these issues. For example, commonly used phrases such as 'responsible gambling' and 'responsible drinking' carry the implication that most people are able to behave responsibly, apart from the problematic minority who cannot control themselves. Access to these 'harmless' products should therefore be unrestricted, allowing people the freedom to choose how they consume, and discussion of legitimate health concerns and genuine corporate social responsibility is avoided.

Orford also argues that the use of power is instrumental in overcoming addiction. This is evidenced by the successful use of techniques where power is manipulated by others to aid those in recovery, such as contingency management, motivational interviewing, and family drug and alcohol courts. Handing over personal power to a higher power through a religious belief system or self-help group and applying a variety of self-empowerment strategies (strengthening of 'willpower') are some of the other ways in which power can be used to help overcome addiction.

The excessive appetite model provides valuable insights into the common processes involved in the development, maintenance, recovery from and relapse to addiction. This theory incorporates findings from biological theories, learning theories, choice theories, social psychology and sociology to provide a comprehensive account of addiction. It would be helpful for future research studies to comparatively investigate these common processes across a range of different addictions as Orford suggests.

# PRIME THEORY

PRIME theory (Robert West & Brown, 2013) is a synthetic theory of motivation. It pulls together findings from a number of different aspects of motivation to form a broad coherent framework into which existing knowledge and future findings can be incorporated. An understanding of the dynamic operation of the human motivational system is seen as crucial to understanding addiction according to this theory.

From the perspective of PRIME theory, at any given moment in time behaviour is determined by what is most currently desired in that moment. The multiple component parts of the motivational system have been organised into five unifying themes: the structure of the motivational system; the focus on the moment; neural plasticity; the importance of identity; and the unstable mind.

The first theme is *the structure of the motivational system*. This operates at five levels of increasing complexity comprising responses at the lowest level, followed by impulses and inhibitory forces, motives, evaluations, and finally plans at the highest level. These levels influence and interact with each other to varying degrees. Responses refer to starting, stopping or modifying actions. Impulses and inhibitory forces act to drive or restrain actions and are influenced by external factors and internal states. Impulses can be experienced as urges when they are blocked from immediate fulfilment. Evaluations are beliefs which carry some form of judgement about the benefits or harm or rights and wrongs about particular behaviours or actions. These are hypothesised to work through motives and then impulses but do not influence actions directly. Impulses act over desires, and desires act over evaluations in the hierarchical control of dynamically changing behaviour. Plans operate at the final level of complexity and consist of conscious mental representations of future actions and require commitment. Plans can be adapted as needed and have to be kept in mind in order to influence behaviour.

The second unifying theme is the *focus on the moment*. This refers to the fact that our actions at any particular time are controlled by whatever forces are operating at that time. Motivation and behaviour are dynamic and fluid in nature. At any particular time the competing impulses and inhibitory forces acting on an individual will determine behavioural output. For example an urge may be triggered by an unexpected exposure to an environmental cue, which may result in the disruption of an intention or plan.

*Neural plasticity* is the third unifying theme in PRIME theory. This concerns the effects of experience on the neural pathways underlying the motivational system. This neural plasticity encompasses changes which occur as the result of habituation or sensitisation to a stimulus, explicit memory, and associative learning, which includes both classical and operant conditioning (see Chapter 3). Learning through imitation of others also occurs and can operate automatically to influence behaviour. The fourth unifying theme is the concept of *identity*, including self-awareness and the effect of these self-concepts on self-control. Identity and self-awareness are to do with how individuals perceive themselves and how this affects their behaviour. These mental representations constantly fluctuate according to current circumstance. A low self-evaluation, for example, may influence the self-perceived ability to formulate and carry out plans. Self-control is intrinsically linked to self-awareness.

The final theme in prime theory is that of *the unstable mind*. This crucial theme utilises ideas derived from a mathematical theory called 'chaos theory' to understand the instability inherent to the motivational system. Chaos theory is involved with the prediction over a period of time of what is unpredictable from moment to moment. The analogy of Waddington's 'epigenetic landscape' (Waddington, 1977) is used to illustrate how environmental factors influence behaviour through the motivational system, and how the system alters in response to experience to generate behaviour. Behaviour through life is likened to the movement of a ball across a landscape consisting of flat areas and grooves of various depths with multiple branches along the way. The ball is kept on a relatively stable course by constant balancing inputs, but a small change in the input, occurring, for example, at a critically shallow junction on the landscape, could easily send the ball in a different direction, down a different path. Another example is that of the ball travelling in a deep groove. In this case a strong external force has to be applied to shift it from this deeply ingrained groove. Removal or reduction of this force would result in the ball reverting back to its original position. It is easy to visualise how this analogy could apply to how behaviour interacts with and fluctuates in response to changes occurring throughout life.

West argues that addiction spreads through the whole motivational system because the system is linked at so many interacting levels. The complexity and situationally dependent fluidity of addictive behaviour suggest that successful addiction treatment should focus on each of the five unifying themes discussed and attempt to determine the level of disorder to each component part of the motivational system, so that appropriate multi-targeted treatment strategies can be formulated.

PRIME theory is a detailed, thoughtful and coherent synthetic theory which serves the essential function of drawing together the different motivational forces operating in addiction. The introduction of the idea of the 'unstable mind' constantly being kept relatively steady through balancing input, provides a useful way to understand the unpredictable and irrational nature of addiction. The role of motives arising from identity, drives, emotions and habit in the disruption of reasoned thinking is explored, and the different routes through which addiction may arise are also considered. Such a broad synthetic theory presents a practical challenge to experimental research and it is difficult to keep hold of so many ideas simultaneously and piece them together. Nevertheless, this complexity reflects the multi-faceted nature of addiction and is therefore unavoidable in any truly comprehensive theory of addiction.

## SUMMARY

- Consideration of the approaches and theories covered in this chapter should provide some insight into the shortcomings of attempting to understand addiction from one perspective alone.
- Addiction is driven by a multitude of interacting factors operating through biological, psychological and societal levels.
- To try and understand the processes operating in addiction it is pragmatic to formulate theories which focus on a particular level of analysis and from a particular theoretical perspective, in order to gain insight into the component processes involved.
- As experimental evidence accumulates, this information can be integrated to more fully inform a truly comprehensive theory of addiction.

## QUESTIONS

1. Critically evaluate the disease model of addiction.
2. 'People choose to be addicts'. To what extent do you agree with this statement?
3. To what extent is the addict primed by stimuli in the world to continue and maintain drug use?
4. Outline Orford's model of addiction.
5. Theories of addiction are theories of motivation. Discuss.

# PHARMACOTHERAPY FOR ADDICTION 6

## CHAPTER OVERVIEW

This chapter briefly outlines the scientific processes through which a potential pharmacological treatment for addiction is evaluated, before it can be licensed for therapeutic use in humans. Pharmacological treatments which are currently available for treating addictions to alcohol, opioids and nicotine will then be described. At the present time there are no medications available to treat addictions to cocaine, the amphetamines and cannabis, although some available medications can help to counter initial withdrawal symptoms experienced as a result of abstinence from these substances, or to treat co-occurring psychiatric disorders. The investigation of potential pharmacological treatments for addiction is an area of active research exploration.

This chapter will:

- Outline scientific principles of treatment
- Outline the process of clinical trials and licensing
- Provide an overview of common pharmacotherapies for several different drug dependencies, e.g. heroin and nicotine

ADDICTION

### LEARNING AIMS OF THE CHAPTER

- An appreciation of the processes through which a potential drug has to be evaluated before becoming available as a medication to treat addiction
- An awareness of the pharmacological compounds that are currently available to treat addiction to alcohol, opioids and nicotine and their limitations

# SCIENCE AND PROOF

When watching television advertisements for cosmetics, health products or the latest superfoods, the viewer is confronted with statements of authority such as '*clinically proven*' or '*scientifically proven*'. They present their product as having clinical powers that are real, that are indeed a FACT. The word *fact* is rarely used in behavioural sciences and psychiatry. A fact tends to lead the audience into assuming that the information is an irrefutable truth.

To obtain reliable information on human behaviour, groups of people are studied. In the case of addiction research, drug users may be compared with non-drug users; this comparison group is the control group. If we find a difference (and in behavioural studies that is a difference that is deemed significant after statistical verification), then we can discuss it as a real phenomenon. If many other studies find similar results then the confidence in that *fact* increases.

The use of the word *significantly* requires some clarification. In a statement such as 'drug users may be significantly different from non-drug users on a neuropsychological test', its use refers to a mathematically supported difference – a group of numbers are really different from another group of numbers. Lay use of the word 'significantly' means there is an *important* difference that sets those with an addiction apart from others.

The statistically significant effect is open to considerable confusion amongst not only the lay population and but also professionals. The ramifications of this 'statistical illiteracy' are seen in health care and policy making, which can be exacerbated by the media

(Monahan, 2007). Consider the effects of a press release to the media that starts off with a portrayal of information that maximises an effect. A journalist, who is also not adept at statistics, goes on to report this with their usual sensationalism. Suddenly something becomes a fact and not a tentative suggestion as originally published. The lack of transparency in a report can be seriously misleading. It has been argued that 'statistical literacy is a necessary precondition for an educated citizenship in a technological democracy. Understanding risks and asking critical questions can also shape the emotional climate in a society so that hopes and anxieties are no longer as easily manipulated from outside and citizens can develop a better-informed and more relaxed attitude toward their health' (Gigerenzer et al., 2007: 53).

Thus the understanding of statistical information is important, and to this end we will embark on a whistle-stop tour of some related features in addiction research.

In scientific and statistical terms *significance* refers to a measure of probability or chance. In an experiment or a study, we have a question or hypothesis that we are investigating, e.g. are those with an addiction more impulsive than others? The probability is the estimate of what is the likelihood of your finding an effect that is real and not down to a chance occurrence. The statistically significant effect is one in which there is a high probability that the finding is a result of addiction, and not a random chance finding that has nothing to do with addiction.

A statistically significant effect on a measure in addiction does not necessarily translate into a clinically significant or important difference in addiction, e.g. those with an addiction may have a tendency towards a cup of tea in the morning compared to non-addicts, but is this really an important difference then? We doubt it!

There are many mathematical tests that can be used on data to determine statistical significance. On the whole these tests give what is called a P value. The P value provides us with a percentage value that estimates if the result is down to chance. In gambling terms, it provides us with the odds of something being down to chance. In scientific literature the value of P that is held as a barrier between either a significant or a non-significant result/difference is $P<0.05$ – or the result is down to 5% chance (i.e. not much chance). Although 5% is used, and is now the gatekeeper of an effect within science, it does not necessarily have to be the case. As Everitt and Wessley (2004) state, the dichotomy of significance remains appealing to clinicians, students and scientists who are pleased when $p=0.049$, but are disappointed when $p=0.051$. With such a small difference the study will report either a positive effect or a negative effect.

With the arbitrary deployment of the 5% cut-off point for probability, an alternative, and some would argue superior, way of increasing the understanding of data is by looking at confidence intervals (CI) (Cumming, 2008). A confidence interval is a range of values within which our true value lies. CIs provide extra information on the upper and lower points of the range of effects, and tell us of how large or small the real effect might be. This additional information is very helpful in allowing us to interpret borderline significance and non-significance that is not captured by the dichotomous P value.

Remember that non-significance is also very different from insignificance (which is a common mistake students make when discussing their data). Non-significant data is as interesting and just as important as significant data, but due to a bias in publishing positive results they are harder to find in the literature. That is not to say the data, because it does not prove something, is insignificant – it is still important.

Significance has different meanings to different people, and we need to remember how statistics and significance can be used, misused and be misleading. The quote by Disraeli ('lies, damned lies, and statistics') springs to mind. In this book we use the word significant in the statistical sense – where a P value or CI indicates that the effect is real and not a chance occurrence.

More important than statistics is research methodology, which we will see when discussing clinical trials. Research methodology is all about the design of the study and is critical to answering questions correctly, and therefore critical in forwarding our understanding of addiction and treatments with any degree of confidence. There are numerous research methodologies that can be deployed, and interested readers are directed to Freeman and Tyrer (2006) if they want a more detailed account.

The media's portrayal of science is often misleading. It is true that most scientific papers are difficult to read, as the language they use is often turgid and technical. Scientific papers are often cautious accounts of what the data suggests and in the behavioural sciences rarely (if ever) prove anything as a fact. The media often cover science-related information, but the journalists who report on scientific publications have to turn the turgid and technical language into an interesting and entertaining story. Good journalism is valuable and informative, bringing complex ideas to a non-expert audience. Bad journalism is often ignorant and full of misinterpretation and prejudice – which in turn may appeal to a reader's own prejudices. Thus, the media can sometimes be guilty of sensationalising research in a non-critical and authoritative way. A recent example is the reporting of the MMR vaccine and its so-called link to autism, in which the poor science was broadcast via the media without critical awareness. The fact that it got published in the first place is worrying. Furthermore, the impartiality of the scientists had also been queried as they received funding that they failed to disclose. This is a problem as the companies have a financial interest in the direction of the results. It is commonplace for scientists to disclose information about potential conflicts of interest, e.g. a hypothetical cigarette company may not wish the results of a study they fund to link nicotine with addiction – this bias is not conducive to good science.

# GOOD SCIENCE AND TREATMENT DEVELOPMENT

Good science is critical for the understanding of addiction; it is also crucial for the development of new treatments. New drugs need to be tested to ensure they are safe and effective. Before drugs can be used in humans they have to go through a period of safety evaluation. This can be done in cells that are grown in laboratories and also in live animals.

Once a drug is considered safe enough in incubated cells and animals it goes to the next stage of development – the clinical trial.

There are many types of clinical trials, below are the most common:

1. *Treatment trials* seek to find out what new treatment approaches can help people who have an addiction or what is the most effective treatment for people with a particular addiction.

2. *Prevention trials* seek to find out what approaches can prevent an addiction from developing in people in the first place, e.g. inoculation against cocaine addiction.

3. *Early-detection/screening trials* seek to discover new ways of finding if people are vulnerable to an addiction before they display symptoms.

4. *Quality-of-life/supportive care trials* seek to find out what kinds of new approaches can improve the comfort and quality of life of people with addiction, e.g. harm reduction.

Clinical trials are divided into four phases. *Phase I* takes place in a small number of (paid) human volunteers. Small amounts of the novel drug are initially given and if all goes well the dose is then escalated, and again if all is well then repeated doses can be given. The drug is compared to a placebo, which is an inert substance that does not contain the active ingredients.

Why are placebos used and why are they so important? Placebo effects are complicated and a more detailed account can be obtained elsewhere (Benedetti, 2008; Crow et al., 1999; Klosterhalfen & Enck, 2006; Price et al., 2008), but essentially the whole experience of being in a study and receiving attention could have effects in its own right which are quite separate from the drug itself. People's expectations, experiences and emotions may be as big a determinant of an effect as a drug. Some people may get better over time and it may not be the drug at all. There is very little point in taking a drug that is no better than placebo. A further benefit of the placebo-controlled study is that it stops the experimenter having a bias in favour of the drug effect; especially if they do not know which patient has received the drug or which patient has received the placebo (such experiments are referred to as double blind – neither the experimenter nor the volunteer knows which they have had).

*Phase II* trials involve the new drug being given to a small number of the target patient population, e.g. naloxone for heroin overdose. These will be carefully controlled studies. This phase will help identify target populations.

*Phase III* occurs after the success of the previous Phase II trial, and whilst similar to the earlier trial, the Phase III trial involves many more patients randomly allocated to treatment groups, and within the context of how the drug is marketed in terms of efficacy and safety. The success with this trial feeds into the licensing of the new drug and is therefore very important.

*Phase IV* happens after a product has been licensed and placed on the market. Information gained from such large studies will permit a clearer picture to develop with regard to a drug or intervention. Despite the process of drug development taking around 12 years, the long-term safety is not immediately established in the human population.

Continuing the collection of drug information in the UK is the *Yellow Card system*, which is a process under the auspices of the Medicines and Healthcare products Regulatory Agency (MHRA) which operates a feedback system for drugs that are on the market. The Yellow Card is available for medics and patients to complete and send to the MHRA – and to this extent we are all part of a giant clinical trial if we take a particular drug. One of their aims is then to make more information on a particular drug available.

Clinical trials are in the interest of the public's safety. Given the financial interest of pharmaceutical companies, how can we trust clinical trials? The only way we can trust them is through publications demonstrating their good science and replicability. The International Conference on Harmonisation of Technical Requirements for Registration of Pharmaceuticals for Human Use (ICH) provides a consensus between European, Japanese and American regulatory authorities on the scientific and technical aspects of drug registration. The ICH lays out what is termed Good Clinical Practice. In a 59-page document, available from the ICH website,[1] details of international ethical and scientific quality standards for designing, conducting, recording, and reporting clinical trials that involve human subjects can be found. These guidelines include selection of investigators, trial protocols, ethics, and informed consent. Essentially adherence to the guidelines is a statement of the quality of the work, and ultimately the confidence one can place on the results. Studies with animals fall outside of the ICH remit, and are dealt with locally by host countries.

In academic studies, and by Phase II clinical trials, patients are selected for study alongside a control group or groups. The control group is the comparator group. Control groups do not have to be healthy-disorder-free people; they can be other patient groups, e.g. those with autism. In their studies scientists will compare substance abusers with control

---

[1] www.ich.org/cache/compo/276-254-1.html

groups, but they will also look at differences in response to a variable that they manipulate (e.g. giving a drug or a placebo). The decision of who gets placed in the experimental group and who gets placed in the control or placebo group is not done by careful selection on behalf of the experimenter; such decisions are done by the random allocation of the participants in the study. Hence, we have the Randomised Controlled Trial (RCT) that is operated to avoid contamination of experimenter effects of allocation bias, e.g. the most severe cases get the new drug. In Box 6.1 features of clinical trials are explained.

## BOX 6.1   COMMON TERMINOLOGY IN CLINICAL TRIALS

Below is a list of commonly used terms to describe clinical trials.

- *Protocol*: study design/instructions.
- *Cohort study*: participants with and without an addiction are followed over a period of time.
- *Prospective study*: in a prospective study the scientists conceive and design the study, recruit subjects, and collect initial data on all participants, *before* any of the participants have developed any addiction-related problems.
- *Retrospective study*: this is similar to prospective study but the features under study in participants are evaluated after they have become symptomatic.
- *Case Control study*: a study in which a person with an addiction is compared to those without an addiction.
- *Cross-sectional study*: presence or absence of exposure to possible risk factor measured at one point in time; the prevalence can be obtained.
- *Prevalence*: the number of new cases and existing cases during a specified time period.
- *Incidence*: the number of new cases in a population during a stated time period.

(Continued)

- *Randomised*: schemes used to assign participants to one group. If participants or health care providers choose a particular group based on what they think is best, then one of the groups would likely be very different from the other, making comparison between the groups difficult. Randomisation eliminates this bias because participants have an equal chance of being assigned to either group and the subgroups are as similar as possible. Comparing similar groups of people taking different treatments for the same disease (or class of disease) is a way to ensure that the study results are caused by the treatments rather than by chance or other factors.
- *Randomised/blinded trial*: participants are allocated to a group by chance and are not aware of what group they are in, e.g. the new drug group.
- *Randomised/double blinded trial*: participants are allocated to the group by chance, they are not aware of what group they are in and nor are the data collectors.
- *Non-randomised controlled trial*: an experimental study in which people are allocated to different interventions using methods that are not random.
- *Placebo trial*: a trial in which a new drug is compared to that of an inert 'dummy-drug'.
- *Historical controlled trial*: a study looking back in time that compares a group of participants receiving an intervention with a similar group from the past who did not.
- *Crossover trial*: in some crossover trials participants are randomly allocated to a study arm where each arm consists of a sequence of two or more treatments given consecutively. The simplest model is the AB/BA study. Participants are allocated to the AB study arm receive treatment A first, followed by treatment B, and vice versa in the BA arm.
- *Withdrawal trial*: refers to the withdrawal of treatment during one or more phases of a study to demonstrate the effects that it has on the target behaviour.

Scientists are only human and are open to bias, even when they think they are not. Certain methodological designs aim to minimise such biases. In a single-blind experiment, the individual participants do not know which group they are in; they have no prior knowledge or expectation that can influence the data. However, the experimenter is aware of the treatment the participant is to receive and such knowledge can influence the data, albeit unwittingly. In studies that use *good science*, the scientist in direct contact with the participant is unaware of the group that the participant is assigned. This is common in drug studies where the design of the experiment is said to be double-blind – neither the experimenter nor participant know which group they are in. This aspect of scientific work is crucial for the clinical trial or study to be credible.

Many studies are multi-centre trials which means they take place in many geographically separate locations and the data is pooled at the end, with a large number of people involved in such studies.

So far the clinical trials have only addressed new pharmacological interventions. However, the treatment of addiction is typically comprised of pharmacological and psychological interventions. How are those psychological interventions evaluated? The very nature of a therapeutic relationship requires that the therapist knows about the client, the therapist knows about the intervention, and the therapist and drug user know about the outcomes. Therefore, complex interventions such as psychological therapies cannot be blind as everyone has to be aware of what is going on in the therapeutic sessions.

Everitt and Wessley (2004) made an attempt to map the phases of the clinical trial onto that of a complex intervention. In the preclinical phase the theory is explored to determine the best choice of intervention, e.g. learning theory and cognitive behavioural therapy. In Phase I of the trial, the complex intervention is modelled in which component mechanisms are identified that should bring about a change in outcome. In Phase II, the pre-trial protocol is developed and compared against existing alternatives. Phase III is where a fully defined intervention is compared with an alternative, and this is akin to the randomised controlled trial. Finally, phase IV would look at the long-term implementation and whether or not the results can be replicated in other settings.

## OUTCOME MEASURES: THE MEASURES OF SUCCESS

An intervention in the addictions will often aim for complete abstinence as the end result. This is a noble goal, but not one that is always achievable. The interventions of the crime reduction agency and the title of the agency tell you what their outcome measure is (crime reduction, obviously!). In the disease model where we might look at heart disease or influenza, the outcome measures are relatively clear. For example, the use of flu vaccines should bring about a reduction in the incidence of influenza. However, when it comes to addiction the noble goal of abstinence may mean that the intervention is doomed to failure. What we measure will determine whether the intervention was successful or not, and therefore harm reduction, or controlled drinking, may be a more obtainable successful outcome than complete abstinence.

A large study was conducted in the UK called the National Treatment Outcome Research Study (NTORS) which looked at changes in substance use health and crime (Godfrey et al., 2004; Gossop, 2015; Gossop et al., 2000; Gossop et al., 2002, 2003; Stewart et al., 2002; Stewart et al., 2003). The outcome domains included substance use problems, health problems, crime and the economic costs.

Thus, the outcome domains can be divided into the following:

- Substance misuse behaviour – including substance type, frequency and quantity of use
- Health – psychological and physical health problems
- Social functioning – employment, accommodation and crime
- Harm – injecting and sharing injecting equipment

Within the domains outcome measures, e.g. reduced blood-borne viruses, less needle sharing etc. Figure 6.1 shows the translation of outcome domain and outcome measure into the realm of criminal activity.

Successful treatment may also imply that the addict has recovered. However, the term 'recovered' is rarely used. In Alcoholics Anonymous and other such organisations the term 'recovery' is used. It is an active word. If you are in recovery you are still working hard to minimise the impact of your addiction. It is important to note that abstinence and recovery are not one and the same thing. One can be abstinent, but there is always the very real chance of relapse (stress may precipitate the recommencement of drug taking).

## FROM TREATMENT TO THEORY

Practising *good science* is not only important for evaluating new drugs or treatments, it is also as important for evaluating theoretical accounts of addiction. Theories of behavioural disorders are designed to be thought provoking and have the power to explain the symptoms. A theory is not a fact. Addiction has many theoretical accounts. Experimentation can either support or refute theories. A publication bias in the literature often means that people will try

**Outcome domains, measures and recovery**

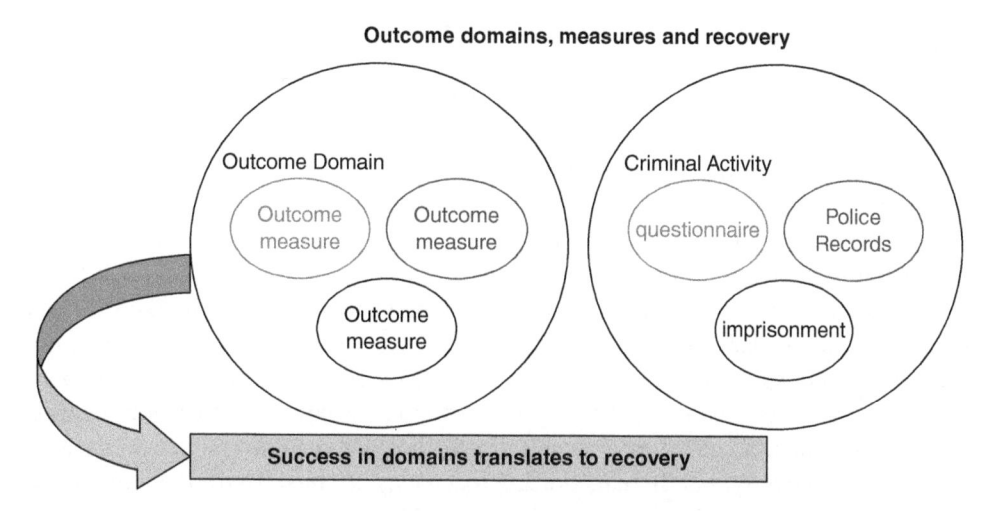

**Figure 6.1** Outcome domains and the measures of success may come from numerous metrics, e.g. criminal activity

to prove a theory or hypothesis is correct; the philosopher Karl Popper, who had a lot to say about science, states that one should try to refute the theory. If one fails to refute the theory then there may well be some credibility to it (see Popper, 2002). Unfortunately, there is a publication bias in favour of positive results, where the hypothesis is upheld.

Publishers, editors and funding bodies are not interested in experiments that do not show a difference, despite those studies being of equal importance if they are conducted correctly – perhaps editors etc. also have difficulty and misinterpret non-significant to mean insignificant! Scientists are like other members of society and are interested in extending old ideas to new subjects in what the philosopher Kuhn calls 'extending the paradigm'. Furthermore, a political agenda and cultural expectation exert an influence over what science is funded, which in turn can determine the results that are found and eventually published.

The large volume of literature on addiction can be daunting, but such an amount of work can be made into a single sensible account by using meta-analysis. Meta-analysis is a technique that has become more widely used in recent years, and consists of an analysis and evaluation of several original research reports: they are a study of the studies. Such meta-analyses use many separate research reports to determine if there is an overall effect or not. These are valuable additions on top of the original investigations, and make life so much easier in drawing conclusions from the data. Of course, a meta-analysis is only as good as the original studies themselves.

# PHARMACOTHERAPY FOR ALCOHOL, OPIOIDS AND SMOKING ADDICTIONS

The following sections will describe the pharmacological treatments which are currently available to treat alcohol, opioid and smoking addictions. When considering the use of medications to treat addiction, it is important to bear in mind that this approach is unlikely to be successful in the long-term unless it is coupled with psychological support and lifestyle changes. Addiction is complex, with many contributing factors, so it is more likely that medication will be particularly helpful to treat specific facets of addiction, for example, initial withdrawal symptoms and craving. For some individuals, social deprivation is an important factor which contributes to their addiction. If an individual is powerless to change contributing psychosocial factors such as poor health, unemployment, poor housing, low educational achievement and poverty, a harm reduction approach may be considered a more realistic and appropriate treatment goal than abstinence.

## ALCOHOL

The medical and social burdens of alcohol addiction are considerable in those countries where alcohol is legal and widely acceptable. In the UK, Europe, the USA and Australia, the recommended treatment for alcohol dependence generally consists of psychosocial treatment tailored to the severity of the problem. Pharmacotherapy is used as an additional treatment (sometimes referred to as adjuvant) and is rarely used in isolation. Pharmacotherapy is advised for:

- individuals with moderate to severe dependence after successful withdrawal from alcohol;
- people with mild dependence who have specifically requested pharmacotherapy, or people who have not responded to initial attempts to abstain.

Specialist agencies concerned with alcohol addiction all advocate the use of adjuvant pharmacotherapy coupled with behavioural intervention or addiction-focused counselling for the treatment of alcohol dependence (Goh & Morgan, 2017). Pharmacotherapy can be potentially useful for the following therapeutic goals (Julien et al., 2014):

- Treating and preventing withdrawal effects
- Reducing alcohol cravings

- Reducing alcohol consumption
- Helping to prevent relapse to drinking
- Helping to address complications associated with reducing or stopping alcohol
- Helping to manage and treat co-morbid psychiatric problems

Alcohol has multiple biological effects and influences several neurotransmitter systems in the brain, including gamma aminobutyric acid (GABA), dopamine, serotonin, noradrenaline, opioid, glutamate, and the endocannabinoid system. Additionally, alcohol influences the hypothalamic-pituitary-adrenal axis, which is involved in regulating the stress response. At present there are only a few medications available to treat alcohol use disorders and these are Disulfiram, Acamprosate, naltrexone and nalmefene, which are discussed in the sections below. Additionally benzodiazepines are used in the management of alcohol withdrawal.

Compounds which have been developed for the treatment of other neuropsychiatric disorders may also be helpful for some people. These include topiramate, gabapentin and varenicline, which may help some individuals with co-occurring nicotine dependence. Baclofen, a selective GABA-B receptor agonist, approved for the treatment of spasticity, has also received temporary approval in France for the treatment of alcohol dependence (Soyka & Muller, 2017). A new and promising exploratory approach for treating alcohol addiction includes using psychedelic/hallucinogenic drugs in low doses and controlled settings to assist psychotherapy. The experiences facilitated by these types of drugs can sometimes lead to ego reduction, shifts in personal feelings and values, and feelings of increased spirituality, that are incompatible with addictive behaviour (Sessa, 2017a). Psychedelics which have been explored as adjuvants to psychotherapy to treat alcohol addiction include ketamine (Krupitsky & Grinenko, 1997) and psilocybin (Bogenschutz et al., 2015). MDMA assisted psychotherapy is also under investigation as a potential new therapeutic option to treat alcohol use disorder (Sessa, 2017a). These ideas stem from earlier experimental work on LSD in the 50s and 60s which showed some promise for the use of psychedelics to treat alcoholism, before they became mired in controversy, and this line of research was impeded (see meta-analysis by Krebs & Johansen, 2012).

## BENZODIAZEPINES

Benzodiazepines are useful for the first step in the treatment of alcohol dependence, which is to assist in preventing and treating the effects of alcohol withdrawal in patients who are severely dependent on alcohol. Typically these patients need medical supervision in a residential or hospital setting. When alcohol consumption ceases, there is the potential for uncontrolled excitatory activity in the nervous system, which can cause a number of problems including neuronal damage, cognitive deficits and seizures. This is due to the removal of the increase in GABA activity and inhibition of glutamate activity that is the result of long-term alcohol consumption. As a response to this, a reduction in GABA activity and increased glutamate activity occurs. Benzodiazapines help to counter this reaction by acting to increase GABA activity. The longer duration of action of benzodiazepines such as chlordiazepoxide (Librium) and diazepam (Valium) helps to counter the withdrawal symptoms that begin within hours of ceasing to drink. The longer-acting benzodiazepine drug is usually prescribed for a limited time period at a low dose and is gradually tapered down. Shorter acting benzodiazepines (e.g.lorazepam) can be used to control acute seizures. Caution must be used when using benzodiazepines to manage alcohol withdrawal due to their potential for abuse, coupled with other adverse effects including additive interactions with alcohol, psychomotor damage and sedative effects. Other drugs used to help control withdrawal are discussed in later sections.

## DISULFIRAM

Disulfiram has been used in clinical practice for over sixty years and is available in many countries to prevent relapse. The logic behind its use is the highly unpleasant physical reaction it creates if alcohol is ingested. Disulfiram works by inhibiting the enzyme acetaldehyde dehydrogenase (ALDH) which is involved in alcohol metabolism. It additionally inhibits other enzymes, including dopamine β hydroxylase which converts dopamine to noradrenaline, and has also been used to treat cocaine addiction, particularly in people who have co-occurring alcohol dependence.

When alcohol is consumed it is converted to acetaldehyde by alcohol dehydrogenase. The acetaldehyde produced is then further metabolised into acetate by ALDH. Disulfiram is an irreversible inhibitor of ALDH. If alcohol is consumed in the presence of disulfiram a toxic accumulation of acetaldehyde occurs, which causes a host of unpleasant deterrent symptoms, including nausea, vomiting, flushing, tachycardia (rapid heartbeat), hypotension, difficulty breathing, dizziness and headache. These symptoms start after around 5–15 minutes after alcohol consumption and can last for many hours. The severity of the symptoms varies with the dose of disulfiram and the amount of alcohol consumed. The efficacy of disulfiram rests largely on compliance with supervised treatment. It has been demonstrated to have greater efficacy compared to other currently available treatments in suitable patients (Brewer et al., 2017; Skinner et al., 2014). Disulfiram has a number of side effects and is contra-indicated in patients with cardiovascular disease, high blood pressure and severe mental health problems. In some cases there have been serious adverse reactions, including fatalities, and therefore the use of supervised disulfiram remains a second line treatment option, unless it is specifically requested.

## ACAMPROSATE

Acamprosate is approved in many countries to help maintain abstinence after detoxification from alcohol. It is the calcium salt of N-acetyl-homotaurine. The exact mechanism of action of Acamprosate is unclear at present, but it is thought to modulate glutamatergic neurotransmission by normalising hyperglutamatergic states precipitated after alcohol withdrawal. It is also thought to exert an agonistic action at GABA receptors. The drug is difficult to absorb orally and therefore has to be taken at high doses. It is considered to be relatively safe because it is not metabolised by the liver and is excreted unchanged by the kidneys. Recent pre-clinical research suggests that the therapeutic effects of acamprosate may be due to the calcium component of the drug (Spanagel et al., 2014). However, a study in human alcoholics did not confirm these pre-clinical findings (Mann et al., 2016). Further experimentation in humans is needed to elucidate the role of calcium in the mechanism of action of acamprosate (Spanagel et al., 2016). A number of clinical studies and meta-analyses support modest efficacy of acamprosate in maintaining abstinence (e.g. Donoghue et al., 2015). Other studies demonstrate no efficacy of acamprosate either given alone or given in combination with naltrexone (Anton et al., 2006). Acamprosate has been shown to be a beneficial and safe treatment for a number of outcome measures other than complete abstinence, such as an increase in number of abstinent days, a reduction in return to drinking and a reduction in the risk of drinking (reviewed by Rosner, Hackl-Herrwerth, Leucht, Lehert, et al., 2010).

## NALTREXONE

Naltrexone is an opioid receptor antagonist that has been used in the treatment of opioid dependence since 1984. Oral naltrexone has subsequently (since 1994) been licensed in many countries as a treatment to reduce alcohol craving. It is thought to act by reducing the rewarding properties of alcohol which may be mediated through the endogenous opioid system. The endogenous opioids are involved in regulating various physiological processes including pain, mood, the response to stress, and reward. Several lines of evidence from pre-clinical and human studies implicate the opioid system in modulating the rewarding effects of alcohol. In a sub-population of alcohol dependent individuals, blockade of the µ-opioid receptor (MOR) reduces the risk of relapse (see Chapter 4 for the genetics of addiction). Positron-emission tomography (PET), using a radio-labelled ligand for the MOR, has demonstrated increased MOR availability in the ventral striatum, including the nucleus accumbens region, in abstinent alcoholics, which was correlated with the severity of their craving for alcohol, suggesting a neural correlate of alcohol urges (Heinz et al., 2005). A more recent study sought to clarify if increased radio-labelled ligand MOR binding in PET studies is due to increased MOR availability, or lower concentrations of endogenous opioids (for details see Hermann et al., 2017). The findings of this interesting study identified low MOR status in alcohol dependent individuals using a combination of post-mortem brain analysis and PET. The authors of this study suggest that reduced MOR may be a neuroadaptation to an alcohol-induced release of endogenous opioids in patients with severe alcoholism. Also, low MOR availability may help explain the ineffectiveness of naltrexone treatment in this population. These authors propose that low MOR binding sites may be a molecular marker for a worse disease prognosis. Overall, cumulative data from a number of reviews and meta-analyses of RCTs of naltrexone show that it has a modest effect on reducing relapse rates and alcohol intake. A large systematic review of naltrexone showed it reduced the risk of heavy drinking by 17%, reduced the number of drinking days by 4%, and the number of heavy drinking days by 3%. It did not have a significant effect on abstinence (Rosner et al., 2010). The most common side-effects reported are headaches, drowsiness, nausea, vomiting, abdominal pain, dizziness, and reduced appetite. Naltrexone is metabolised by the liver, and is reasonably safe when taken at the standard daily oral dose of 50mg, though there is a dose-dependent increase in liver toxicity. Due to its antagonistic opioid blocking effect, opioid painkillers will be ineffective if taking naltrexone, and it will precipitate opioid withdrawal effects if opioids are present in the system.

## NALMEFENE

Nalmefene is a naltrexone derivative. It is an opioid receptor antagonist at the mu and delta opioid receptors, and a partial agonist at the kappa opioid receptor. It is approved for treating alcohol use disorders in most of Europe, but its use is still controversial. Relative to naltrexone, nalmefene has a number of potential benefits including reduced hepatotoxicity, more effective binding to central opioid receptors, and increased bioavailability. It has a slower onset of action and longer duration of action than naltrexone (see the review by Soyka, 2016). It has been approved as a treatment for the reduction of alcohol consumption in people who are drinking at high-risk levels who do not need medical detoxification. It can be taken 'as needed' at a daily oral dose of 18mg. The harm-reduction approach to alcohol treatment remains controversial. The findings from clinical trials have been mixed. A recent literature review and meta-analysis of published studies on the risks and benefits of nalmefene found some evidence for a reduction in the number of drinking days per month and total alcohol consumption, but the findings were not robust, and there were more withdrawals for reasons of safety in the nalmefene-treated groups (Palpacuer et al., 2015). Firm conclusions await further research.

## OPIOIDS

Opioid use disorder (OUD), which encompasses use of both heroin and prescription opioids, is a significant worldwide health concern. Opioid use is associated with particular risks including both fatal and non-fatal overdose, and the acquisition of infectious diseases such as HIV and hepatitis B/C through unsafe injecting practices. Additionally, criminal behaviour and low educational and occupational achievement are increased amongst those with OUD. In the USA, a combination of misuse of pharmaceutical opioids together with an increase in heroin and fentanyl use has led to a combined and interrelated opioid epidemic, with an increase in opioid-related illness and death.

Pharmacotherapy for treating opioid dependence can be an effective treatment option, and is important in controlling opioid withdrawal symptoms, drug craving, and regaining some form of physiological and psychological stability. Pharmacological treatments for OUD include opioid agonist medications (e.g. methadone), opioid partial agonist medications (e.g. buprenorphine), and opioid antagonists (e.g. naltrexone). These medications and the rationale for their use are considered in the following sections.

Additionally, alpha-2 adrenergic agonist drugs (e.g. Clonidine and Lofexidine), which are widely used to treat high blood pressure, are also used to manage some of the discomfort caused by opioid withdrawal symptoms. These drugs reduce opioid withdrawal mediated hyperactivity within the noradrenergic system.

## OPIOID AGONIST TREATMENT

### METHADONE

Methadone is a full agonist at the mu opioid receptor, and is useful for both detoxification from opioids and for preventing relapse to illicit opioid use through long-term methadone maintenance therapy (MMT). Oral methadone has been used for the treatment of opioid dependence since 1965, and has demonstrated effectiveness for reducing some of the harms caused by illicit opioid use. Compared to non-pharmacological approaches to treatment, methadone has been found to be more effective in reducing heroin use and keeping patients engaged in treatment (Mattick et al., 2009).

In contrast to heroin, methadone has a slow initial onset of action of roughly 30 minutes, and a long elimination half-life (24–36 hours). The rationale for its use is that as a long-acting opioid, it can occupy the receptor and provide relief from withdrawal symptoms and craving, and counteract the euphoria associated with the use of illicit opioids. Initially, tapered methadone doses are given over a period of time for detoxification purposes. For MMT a target daily dose of methadone is reached by incrementally increasing the dose to approximately 80–120mg. This optimised dose is administered daily for an extended period of time, which can be weeks, months or many years. The idea is to provide a degree of physiological stability and psychosocial rehabilitation, leading to disengagement from unsafe practices associated with illicit drug use and drug-related criminal activity. The most important predictor of success of MMT is the dose of methadone used, with higher drug doses resulting in higher retention rates in MMT programmes. Deaths associated with methadone dosing can occur as a result of unforeseen drug–drug interactions, and unintentional overdose can occur in the initial stages of treatment. The side effects of methadone include nausea, vomiting, constipation, sweating, decreased libido, sedation, and reductions in levels of testosterone and luteinising hormone in men and women respectively. Methadone can also have effects on the heart, causing an abnormal heart rhythm that can result in sudden cardiac death. There has been a degree of stigma surrounding the use of methadone, with some holding the view that addiction to one substance is being replaced by addiction to another. Alternatively, long-term pharmacotherapeutic use of methadone can be thought of in the same way as other long-term medications given to control chronic disease states such as cardiovascular disease and diabetes. MMT can have a beneficial impact on stress responsiveness and other neurobiological processes that contribute to relapse in vulnerable people (Bart, 2012).

### LEVO-ALPHA-ACETYLMETHADOL (LAAM)

Levo-alpha-acetylmethadol, or LAAM, is another compound with full agonist activity at the mu-opioid receptor. It has an even longer duration of action than methadone (approximately 72 hours) and so daily dosing is not necessary. It is of comparable efficacy to methadone for treating OUD. It was approved in 1993 and initially showed promise, but was withdrawn several years later due to concerns over its cardiac side effects and relative safety.

### HEROIN

The provision of clinically supervised heroin with access to clean injecting equipment is another form of treatment, which although controversial, may be helpful for IV heroin users who are unresponsive to other forms of therapy (Strang et al., 2015). This form of treatment is offered in some European countries including Switzerland, the UK and Germany, but not currently the USA.

### PARTIAL AGONIST TREATMENT: BUPRENORPHINE

Buprenorphine is a semi-synthetic, high affinity, partial mu opioid receptor agonist that has become an important treatment for both detox and maintenance therapy for OUD.

The ceiling effect on its agonist actions means the risk of respiratory depression is considerably reduced and its use is less restricted than methadone. Its high affinity and low efficacy at the mu-opioid receptor mean that it dissociates slowly, which contributes to its long-lasting clinical actions (approximately 24 hours). It also has antagonist actions at the kappa opioid receptor and is an effective analgesic.

Its partial agonist activity enables it to produce less subjective euphoria than full opioid agonists. It can also block opioid mediated euphoria, reduce craving, and reduce the severity of withdrawal symptoms. Due to its high first-pass metabolism by the liver, it has limited oral activity and is usually administered as a sublingual tablet (Subutex). To counteract potential misuse of the tablets by crushing and subsequent snorting or injecting, buprenorphine can be given in a combined formulation with naloxone, an opioid antagonist drug. In this combined formulation (Suboxone) the effect of buprenorphine is predominant and the naloxone effect minimal. However, if the tablet is crushed, any rewarding effect that might be experienced from snorting or injecting is negated by the antagonistic effects of naloxone. Buprenorphine is also available as a buccal/sublingual film. The frequent dosing requirements, potential for misuse, accidental ingestion by minors, and drug diversion, may be avoided by the recent development and approval of a long-acting (six months) subdermal implant which provides a constant low dose of buprenorphine in patients already stabilised on low doses of the drug (Chavoustie et al., 2017). Side effects of buprenorphine include nausea, vomiting, constipation, and dizziness. A systematic review of buprenorphine maintenance therapy compared to placebo and methadone maintenance found buprenorphine to be equally effective as methadone at fixed medium to high dosing, but not as effective as methadone when given with low or flexible dosing (Mattick et al., 2014). Its success as a treatment option may be dependent on patient characteristics and addiction severity.

## OPIOID ANTAGONIST TREATMENT: NALTREXONE, NALOXONE AND NALMEFENE

### NALTREXONE

Naltrexone is a long-acting semi-synthetic opioid receptor antagonist, with high affinity for the mu opioid receptor. Naltrexone, naloxone and nalmefene are structurally related to oxymorphone, which is a pure opioid agonist. Naltrexone is able to produce a dose-dependent blockade of opiate effects (for 24 hours at low doses and up to 72 hours at high doses) and can precipitate withdrawal symptoms in opioid-dependent individuals. It is considered to be well tolerated, relatively safe, and is not known to interact with other drugs or cause tolerance or dependence (Bart, 2012). Orally-administered naltrexone is rapidly absorbed and undergoes substantial first-pass metabolism by the liver. It is mainly metabolised to a weak active opiate antagonist, 6-beta-naltrexol, which has a longer plasma half-life (approximately 13 hours compared to 4 hours for naltrexone) which contributes to its prolonged activity. Side effects for naltrexone include gastrointestinal discomfort, headache and nausea.

The effectiveness of naltrexone hinges on high patient motivation and adherence, due to the absence of any intrinsic rewarding effects of the drug. When oral naltrexone is given without additional incentives or adequate supervision and strong psychological support, adherence to the medication is low (Dunn et al., 2015; Minozzi et al., 2011). The problem of adherence has led to the more recent development of extended release long-acting depot formulations of naltrexone. An extended release intramuscular injection (XR-NTX; Vivitrol) and a subdermal implant (SBM NTX) both hold considerable potential for the effective treatment of OUD. Exploration of treatment protocols which combine initial stabilisation of the patient on opioid agonist therapy, followed by transition to depot or implant antagonist therapy, is a promising area of active research into the future effective treatment of OUD (Ayanga et al., 2016).

## NALOXONE (NARCAN)

Naloxone is a pure competitive opioid receptor antagonist with high affinity for the mu-opioid receptor. It is used primarily to reverse the effects of acute opioid toxicity, in particular the respiratory depression that occurs as a result of accidental or intentional overdose. Naloxone is used to treat overdose caused by misuse of heroin, methadone, fentanyl (a highly potent post-surgical pain killer), carfentanil (diverted from veterinary practice), hydrocodone and oxycodone (prescription pain killers) amongst others. There has been a rise in fentanyl-related accidental overdose deaths caused by the use of illicitly manufactured fentanyl and other counterfeit narcotic and benzodiazepine pills containing opioids, particularly in parts of the USA (Jordan & Morrisonponce, 2017). It is also used to reverse opioid-induced respiratory depression in newborn babies of opioid-dependant women. Naloxone is not absorbed from the gastrointestinal tract or oral mucosa, so is usually given through intravenous injection. Its onset of action is fast (within minutes), and its duration of action is brief (approximately 15–30 minutes), so it has to be frequently readministered in order to maintain antagonism of the longer-acting opioid agonist actions that it is blocking. Naloxone does not have many side effects and does not have abuse potential.

## NALMEFENE

Nalmefene acts as an opioid antagonist at mu and delta receptors and a partial agonist at the kappa opioid receptor (see the information above in the section on alcohol pharmacotherapy). It is used to treat acute opioid overdose-induced respiratory depression.

# PHARMACOTHERAPY FOR SMOKING CESSATION

The tobacco epidemic is one of the biggest public health threats, killing more than 7 million people a year through diseases such as cancer, respiratory disease, and cardiovascular disease. National comprehensive smoking cessation services with full and partial cost coverage are available to help smokers to quit in 24 countries, which represents 15% of the world's population. There is no help available of any kind in one quarter of low-income countries (WHO, 2017). Although many smokers want to quit and make attempts to do so, the available evidence suggests that the number of people who are successful remains low, even with the help of psychological and pharmacological cessation interventions.

Pharmacotherapy for nicotine dependence aims to reduce the rewarding aspects of smoking and to prevent the manifestation of unpleasant withdrawal symptoms which may prompt relapse. The three first line smoking cessation treatments are: nicotine replacement therapy (NRT); bupropion, an antidepressant shown to have a benefit in smoking cessation; and varenicline, which acts as partial nicotine receptor agonist.

## NICOTINE REPLACEMENT THERAPY

The principle of NRT is to deliver nicotine to the person trying to stop smoking in a less harmful way, in order to decrease the unpleasant physiological and psychomotor withdrawal symptoms that are generally experienced as a result of stopping smoking. Since smoking is a learned habitual behaviour as well as a physiological dependence, the use of NRT can help to break the smoking habit whilst alleviating some of the distress, which could contribute to relapse. Nicotine can be absorbed from nicotine replacement products through several types of non-tobacco delivery systems. Nicotine is not suitable to be taken in pill form due to the reduction in bioavailability that occurs as a result of poor absorption from the stomach and first pass metabolism in the liver. The dose of nicotine that would be needed to produce CNS effects would potentially cause unpleasant gastrointestinal symptoms if taken through this route. Nicotine replacement products are therefore formulated for absorption through the skin, or through the oral or nasal mucosa.

These products are available in various forms, including chewing gum, nicotine transdermal patch, inhaler, sublingual tablet, lozenge, and nasal spray. The gum, patches and lozenges are available over the counter. The inhaler and nasal spray are available through prescription only. Nicotine patches deliver nicotine slowly, can be worn for 16 hours or 24 hours, and are available in different doses which deliver between 5mg and 52.5mg of nicotine over the course of 24 hours. This is a similar concentration to the lowest levels of plasma nicotine experienced by heavy smokers (Fiore et al., 1992).

The other forms of NRT deliver nicotine at a faster rate and offer flexible dosing and can therefore be combined with the nicotine patch if higher acute dosing is required to combat withdrawal symptoms and craving. The gum, patch and lozenge formulations are available in different doses, with higher dosing and combination therapy recommended for greater addiction severity. Nicotine gum is available in 2mg and 4mg doses and nicotine lozenges are available in 1.5, 2 and 4mg strengths. The patch is usually used for around six to eight weeks. The amount of nicotine actually absorbed varies both within and between different people and is influenced by multiple factors. The nasal spray delivers nicotine at a faster rate (though not as fast as smoking) and therefore may have some abuse liability. Adverse effects of NRT are related to the type of product and include local irritation at the site of delivery, for example skin irritation for the patch, and mouth and nose irritation for the products that deliver through these routes. There is also an increased risk of insomnia with overnight use of the patch.

A review (of 150 trials including 50,000 people) on the effect of different types and doses of NRT compared to placebo, on abstinence at six months or longer, found that all available forms of NRT can be helpful, and increase the chances of stopping smoking by 50 to 70%, with no additional benefit gained through a clinical setting or counselling support (Stead et al., 2012).

Attention should also be given to the use of electronic nicotine delivery systems or e-cigarettes as a potentially reduced nicotine exposure product or harm reduction strategy. Many people use these products and they are more appealing to smokers because they simulate the motor actions of smoking to a greater degree. At the present time there are still outstanding questions regarding the long-term safety of electronic nicotine delivery systems, particularly with regard to adolescent use. However, the majority of evidence suggests that compared to combustible tobacco products such as conventional cigarettes, e-cigarettes are demonstrably less harmful in several ways, including lower levels of exposure to toxic and carcinogenic compounds (Drope et al., 2017).

## BUPROPION (ZYBAN)

Antidepressants may be helpful for smoking cessation for a number of reasons. These include alleviating both withdrawal and the depressive symptoms experienced during smoking cessation, and also potentially substituting for the antidepressant actions of nicotine. Bupropion is a dual inhibitor of noradrenaline and dopamine reuptake, which was approved as a treatment for depression before it was recognised and approved as an aid for smoking cessation. Its use as an aid for smoking cessation resulted from the observation that smokers treated with this drug for depression reported decreased craving for cigarettes and were able to quit smoking without additional intervention. It has the advantage of being a non-nicotine-containing therapy, so may be helpful for those people who have been unsuccessful on NRT, or who do not want to take nicotine-containing medication. Although bupropion is useful for individuals with co-morbid depression, it is also equally effective in non-depressed people.

The mechanism of action of bupropion is not fully understood. It is known to increase both noradrenergic and dopaminergic neurotransmission through inhibition of reuptake of their transporters. Its mechanism of action may also involve the presynaptic release of noradrenaline and dopamine. Bupropion additionally has an affinity for nicotinic receptors and is a non-competitive antagonist of nicotinic acetylcholine receptors, which is thought to contribute to its effectiveness as a smoking cessation medication as well as its effectiveness as an antidepressant (Stahl et al., 2004; Warner & Shoaib, 2005).

Bupropion, in a sustained release formulation, is usually initially taken at a daily dose of 150mg/day for 3 days, increasing to twice a day (300mg total) for 7–12 weeks, and can be started whilst an individual is still smoking. The lower dose is equally effective, and may cause fewer side effects. Adverse effects of the drug include insomnia, a dry mouth and nausea, and there is a rare risk of seizures. A Cochrane review, which examined the effect and safety of different types of antidepressants for smoking cessation, found that bupropion, when used as the sole medication, was an effective aid to smoking cessation and significantly increased long-term abstinence (six months or longer). It was found to be as effective as nicotine replacement therapy. In this review another antidepressant, nortriptyline, a tricyclic antidepressant, was also found to aid smoking cessation. However, antidepressants which are selective serotonin reuptake inhibitors, or monoamine oxidase inhibitors, were found to be ineffective for smoking cessation (Hughes et al., 2014).

## VARENICLINE (CHANTIX)

Varenicline and cytisine are pharmacologically-related compounds developed to aid smoking cessation. Varenicline is widely available worldwide, whereas cytisine (Tabex) is available in some central and eastern European countries and is also available over the internet. Varenicline acts as a nicotine receptor partial agonist, with high specificity for the $\alpha 4\beta 2$ nicotinic acetyl choline receptor (nAChR) subtype. Nicotine's agonist activity at $\alpha 4\beta 2$ nAChR stimulates the release of mesolimbic dopamine, which contributes to its addictive properties (Coe et al., 2005). Varenicline mimics some of the effects of nicotine through its partial agonist activity at these receptors (see Figure 6.2), which results in moderate levels of sustained dopamine release, rather than the large, rapid dopamine increase evoked by nicotine itself. Varenicline's agonist activity acts to relieve craving and withdrawal symptoms which are experienced as a result of quitting smoking. In the presence of nicotine, varenicline has the potential to act as an antagonist at nAChRs, which results in the ability to reduce the rewarding effects of nicotine if the smoker has a relapse. Varenicline is usually started one to two weeks prior to quitting and then taken at a low dose, which is increased gradually to 1mg twice a day for 12 weeks, with a further 12-weeks treatment recommended to prevent relapse. The main adverse effects of varenicline are nausea, abnormal dreams and insomnia, which usually recede over time as tolerance develops. The drug has also been associated with particular safety concerns, including an increased risk of cardiovascular events in susceptible people, and also an increased risk of psychiatric and neurological adverse effects in people who may have a past or current psychiatric disorder. Further research may shed more light on these concerns. The results of a review of studies on nicotine partial receptor agonists for smoking cessation concluded that varenicline increased the chances of quitting for six months or longer, between two- and three-fold, compared to no pharmacologically assisted treatment. Additionally, a larger number of people quit smoking successfully with varenicline compared to bupropion and NRT (Cahill et al., 2016).

A network meta-analysis of data from 12 Cochrane reviews of the three first line pharmacological treatments for smoking cessation (abstinent for six months or longer) showed higher rates of abstinence for NTR (17.6%) and bupropion (19.1%) compared with a placebo (10.6%). However, varenicline (27.6%) and combination NRT (31%) were found to be the most effective smoking cessation treatments. None of the therapies was associated with a higher risk of serious adverse events (Cahill et al., 2014).

## PHARMACOTHERAPY FOR PSYCHOSTIMULANTS: COCAINE

There are no pharmacological treatments currently available to treat addiction to cocaine and the amphetamines, although it is possible to treat some of the symptoms experienced as a result of abuse of these drugs, e.g. depression. There are many potentially promising pre-clinical research studies and some clinical trials on human participants, but so far no pharmacological treatment has been found to be both safe and effective in large-scale clinical trials in humans. However, some of these putative pharmacological treatments are the subject of continued active research, development and clinical investigation.

The neurochemical complexity of addiction and the interrelationships between the different neurotransmitter systems involved make it extremely challenging to target a specific receptor or enzyme to treat addiction to psychostimulants. Dopaminergic, glutamatergic and GABAergic dysregulation are implicated in cocaine addiction, and cocaine is a dopamine and noradrenaline reuptake inhibitor. It is more likely that one particular aspect of addiction

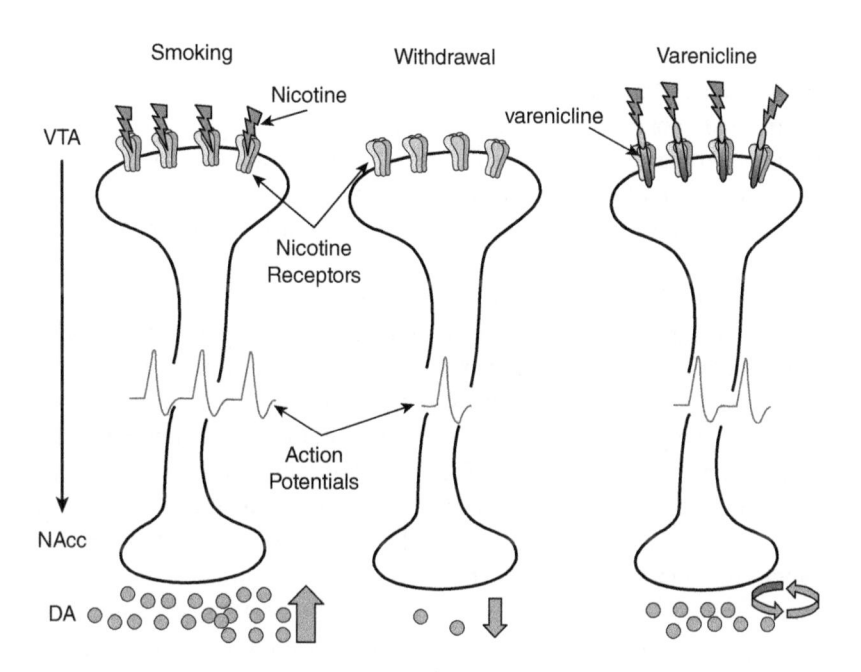

**Figure 6.2** The role of Verenicline on the nicotine receptor. Verenicline is a partial agonist that stimulates the nicotine receptor submaximally whist blocking nicotine from exerting an effect at the receptor.

is affected by the particular treatment being investigated, and/or the treatment is only effective in a subset of people, due to variations in individual neurochemistry. A few examples of some of these approaches are briefly outlined below.

The importance of dopamine in the rewarding effects of cocaine and the amphetamines has led to the investigation of various dopaminergic agonists, antagonists and uptake inhibitors as potential therapeutic agents to treat cocaine addiction. No clear evidence in support of these agents has been obtained so far. One approach has been to investigate antipsychotic drugs to treat cocaine addiction because of cocaine's ability to induce psychotic symptoms such as paranoia and hallucinations. The authors of a recent Cochrane review of the antipsychotic medications risperidone, olanzapine, quetiapine, lamotrigine, aripiprazole, haloperidol and reserpine, concluded that at the present time there is no evidence to support the use of these agents to treat cocaine dependence, although the included studies were few in number, with small sample sizes and moderate to low quality evidence (Indave et al., 2016).

A different approach has been to test the efficacy of cocaine-like psychostimulant drugs as a replacement therapy for cocaine addiction. The logic used is similar to nicotine replacement therapy or methadone maintenance treatment for heroin addiction. The replacement drug used as pharmacotherapy has a similar mode of action and behavioural effect as the one it is replacing, but it is administered orally, has a longer half-life, helps to ameliorate some of the symptoms of cocaine craving and withdrawal, and has less potential for addiction. A recent Cochrane review to assess this form of treatment on cocaine abstinence and retention in treatment showed some encouraging findings. The included studies assessed nine drugs: bupropion, dexamphetamine, lisdexamfetamine, methylphenidate, modafinil, mazindol, methamphetamine, mixed amphetamine salts, and selegiline. Although results were mixed and the drop-out rate was high, psychostimulants appeared to increase the proportion of patients achieving sustained cocaine and heroin abstinence amongst a subgroup of methadone-maintained dual heroin-cocaine addicts. Bupropion and dexamphetamine appeared to increase the proportion of patients achieving sustained cocaine abstinence when type of drug was included as a moderating variable. The authors concluded that this approach warrants further investigation (Castells et al., 2016).

A systematic review of N-acetylcysteine (NAC) for treating cocaine addiction also reported encouraging findings for the potential use of this compound as a relapse prevention agent in already abstinent individuals (Nocito Echevarria et al., 2017). NAC is an established, safe and well-tolerated glutamatergic agent that is used to treat paracetamol overdose and thin mucous in cystic fibrosis and chronic obstructive lung disease. NAC reverses the disruption of glutamate homeostasis that occurs as a result of long-term cocaine use. It may also be effective for treating other substance use disorders, including cannabis use disorder (Gray et al., 2012). Disulfiram, an inhibitor of aldehyde dehydrogenase, which has a history of use for treating alcohol use disorder, has also been shown to reduce cocaine consumption in dual cocaine and alcohol addiction, as well as cocaine addiction alone. This is thought to be due to the ability of disulfiram to additionally inhibit the enzyme dopamine β-hydroxylase that synthesises noradrenaline from dopamine, leading to a reduction in the levels of noradrenaline in relation to dopamine (Gaval-Cruz & Weinshenker, 2009). Disulfiram also inhibits enzymes involved in the metabolism of cocaine. Clinical investigation of disulfiram has revealed that its effects on cocaine use are highly dependent on the dose given relative to the body weight of the consumer, with both decreased and increased cocaine consumption observed at higher and lower doses/kg body weight, respectively. This finding may help to explain conflicting data obtained in previous research studies (Haile et al., 2012). Another area of active investigation is the development of vaccines against cocaine. The antibodies produced can reduce the amount of drug reaching the brain, either through binding to the drug to prevent it crossing the blood-brain barrier, or by breaking down the drug in the bloodstream through catalytic action by cocaine metabolizing enzymes (Julien et al., 2014).

# CHAPTER SUMMARY

- Good science demands research studies that are carefully designed using appropriate numbers of the target group(s) and control group(s), as well as comparison treatments and/or placebo treatments.

- Before a drug can be licensed for human use it has to undergo several levels of testing. This includes testing in cell culture and laboratory animals before progressing to phased clinical trials in humans.

- Optimal clinical trials are designed to limit or reduce experimenter bias and research participant bias through random allocation of active treatment or placebo treatment in a way that excludes knowledge of who receives which treatment from both parties (the experimenter and the participant). These trials are referred to as double blind placebo controlled experimental trials.

- Pharmacological treatments are available to treat addiction to alcohol, opioids and nicotine. In some cases a harm reduction approach through drug replacement is a more realistic treatment goal than abstinence, particularly when social deprivation is a powerful factor in maintaining addiction.

- Alcohol affects a number of neurotransmitter systems. Treatments for alcohol use disorders include: benzodiazepines to help with initial alcohol withdrawal symptoms; disulfiram, an inhibitor of acetaldehyde dehydrogenase, an enzyme involved in alcohol metabolism; acomprosate, a potential modulator of glutamatergic neurotransmission; and naltrexone, an opioid receptor antagonist, which may blunt the rewarding effects of alcohol.

- Pharmacological treatments for opioid use disorder can be effective in controlling opioid withdrawal symptoms, drug craving, gaining physiological and psychological stability, and keeping patients engaged in treatment. These treatments include opioid agonist medications such as methadone, opioid partial agonist medications such as buprenorphine, and opioid antagonists such as naltrexone.

- Pharmacotherapy for smoking cessation aims to reduce the rewarding aspects of smoking and to prevent the manifestation of unpleasant withdrawal symptoms which may prompt relapse. The three first line smoking cessation treatments currently available are nicotine replacement therapy, bupropion, an antidepressant, and varenicline, which is a partial nicotine receptor agonist.

- Pharmacological treatments used alone, without additional psychological support and lifestyle changes, are unlikely to be successful in the long-term treatment of

# ADDICTION

addiction. Treatment success is linked to treatment compliance, which is associated with individual patient characteristics.

## QUESTIONS

1. What are the different phases of clinical trials and how do they differ from each other?
2. What are the treatment options for nicotine dependence?
3. Describe a partial agonist and how they have been used for the treatment of addiction.
4. What is the rationale for replacement therapies?
5. Explain the rationale for the treatment options that are currently available for alcoholism.

# PSYCHOLOGICAL TREATMENTS 7

## CHAPTER OVERVIEW

Ideally, treating addiction requires an individualised approach, reflecting the multi-faceted nature of the problem and its variability between and within individuals. Psychological treatments can also be combined with pharmacological treatments, where this is appropriate. The psychological treatments covered in this chapter are illustrative examples, and there are other approaches not covered here. All successful psychological treatments incorporate many common elements, as illustrated by the treatment approaches which are discussed in this chapter.

This chapter will:

- Outline some psychological methods for treating addictive behaviour
- Describe different treatment approaches and the common elements that they share

# ADDICTION

> **LEARNING AIMS OF THE CHAPTER**

- To have an awareness of different psychological approaches to addiction treatment and the contexts for their use
- To understand the rationale behind different treatment approaches and how they can be effectively combined
- To have an awareness of the common factors shared by successful treatment approaches
- To have an awareness of the limitations of different approaches

# INTRODUCTION

Since behaviour change is fundamental to recovery from addiction, a general framework for understanding an individual's readiness, or motivation to change, is presented at the beginning of this chapter. This model, the transtheoretical model (TTM) of change, has been influential in guiding clinical practice, although it has also generated criticism.

The psychological treatments considered in this chapter recognise the importance of learning, cognition, context and interpersonal interaction, in addiction development, maintenance, relapse and recovery. The first treatment approach to be considered is Motivational Interviewing (MI). MI evolved from clinical observation and research in the field of addiction, but has now become more broadly applicable to other types of behaviour change. This approach is often successfully paired with other treatment approaches, including Behavioural Therapy, Cognitive Behavioural Therapy and Relapse Prevention techniques, which will be detailed in subsequent sections of this chapter. The final section of this chapter will consider the power of group therapy, in particular the twelve-step community of Alcoholics Anonymous, and a more recently developed group approach called SMART Recovery.

# THE TRANSTHEORETICAL MODEL OF BEHAVIOUR CHANGE

The transtheoretical model (TTM) of behaviour change (also called the stages of change model) gained prominence in the 1980s (e.g. Prochaska & DiClemente, 1982), and has continued to expand, develop and influence clinical practice. Ideas relevant to behaviour change derived from studying many different theoretical perspectives are integrated within this comprehensive model, which has received both experimental support and criticism.

Recovery from chronic behavioural patterns is classified by the TTM into different *stages* of change. These stages are integrated with different *processes* of change derived from several theories of psychotherapy (hence the term 'transtheoretical'). These characteristics are thought to be common to successful behaviour change, including recovery from addiction. Recovery is proposed to result from an individual progressing through these five different stages of change, which are: pre-contemplation; contemplation; preparation; action; and maintenance. The complete cycle may be repeated numerous times with back and forth movement between the successive stages, before the behaviour is finally terminated. Different change processes are activated in the progression from one stage to the next. Change is recognised in this model as a process that occurs over time, rather than as a specific event in time. Other key principles of change important to this model are decisional balance (Janis & Mann, 1977) and self-efficacy (Bandura, 1977). The premise of this model is that particular principles and processes of change work best at each stage to reduce opposition to change, facilitate forward progression to the next stage in the sequence, and prevent relapse. These stages, principles and processes are outlined below with a brief explanation.

# STAGES OF CHANGE

## PRE-CONTEMPLATION STAGE

At this stage the individual is not seriously considering change (within a defined period of six months). They may have some limited knowledge of the adverse health effects of their behaviour. It is possible to influence an individual to progress from this stage to the next by increasing their knowledge and awareness of the negative consequences of continuing, coupled with the rewards of discontinuing the behaviour.

## CONTEMPLATION STAGE

This is defined as having the intention to change in the future (within a defined period of six months). At this stage the individual has an increased awareness of the costs and benefits of the behaviour but they are still not ready to change. This ambivalence can cause an individual to remain stuck in this stage for extended periods of time. They can move from this stage to the next by altering the balance between the costs and benefits of the behaviour such that the benefits of changing become more evident, and by increasing their belief in their capacity to change.

## PREPARATION STAGE

At this stage an individual is ready to change and has made plans to take action in the immediate future (within the next months), or has already taken significant action within the past year.

## ACTION STAGE

The change plans which have been formulated are implemented in the action stage (for up to six months). This stage is identified more easily because observable behaviour modification has occurred.

## MAINTENANCE STAGE

In this stage the specific overt behaviour modifications implemented in the action stage are sustained over a longer period of time and require less intensity and effort. As this time period increases, the likelihood of relapse decreases, and confidence to maintain the behaviour change grows.

## THE PROCESSES OF CHANGE

The TTM identifies ten specific processes of change which facilitate movement from one stage to the next. These fall into two groups, cognitive and affective experiential processes and behavioural processes:

*Cognitive and Affective Experiential Processes*

1. Consciousness Raising
2. Dramatic Relief
3. Environmental Re-evaluation
4. Self-re-evaluation
5. Social Liberation

*Behavioural Processes*

6. Self-liberation
7. Counter Conditioning
8. Helping Relationships
9. Reinforcement Management
10. Stimulus Control

# PSYCHOLOGICAL TREATMENTS

For each process within the TTM there are numerous techniques which can be used to help an individual progress to the next stage, therefore within this framework matching of stage and process is important and provides direction and structure to treatment interventions. However, there is also flexibility within this framework. Some of the early stage processes are comparatively distinct whilst later stage processes, for example, stimulus control, counter conditioning and reinforcement management, often work together.

## DECISIONAL BALANCE

Decision making can be thought of as a 'balance sheet' of potential gains and losses (Janis & Mann, 1977). The pros (advantages) and cons (disadvantages) of changing behaviour are

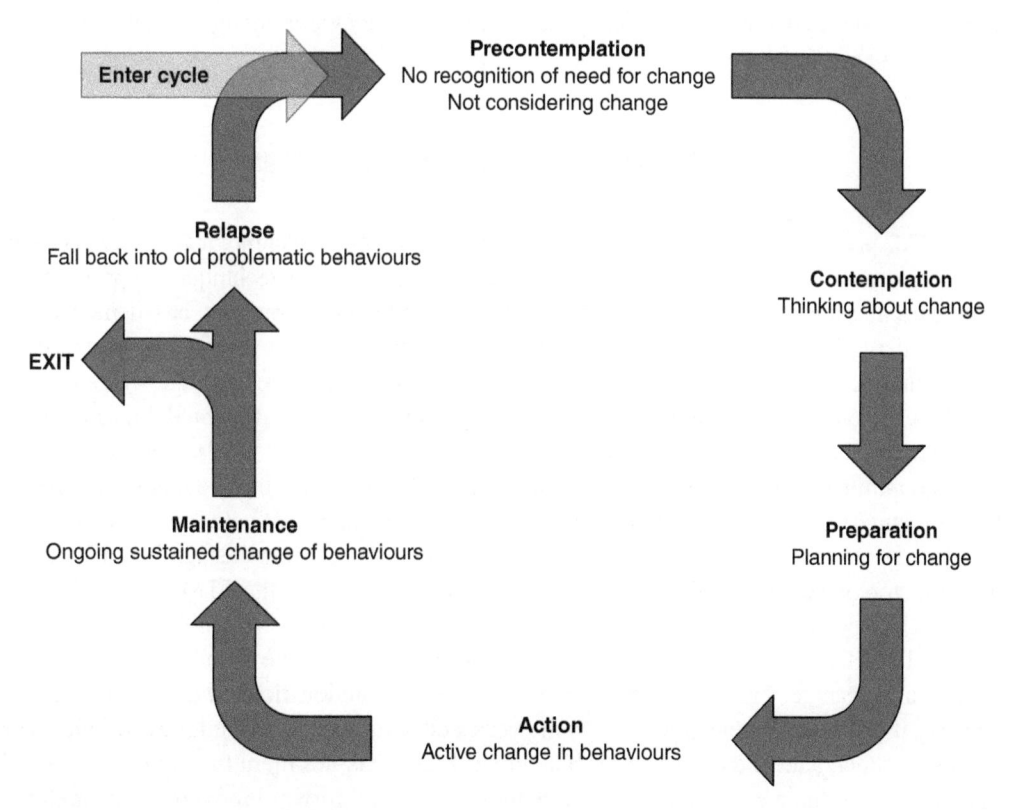

**Figure 7.1** The stages of change

important in the TTM. Decisional balance shifts as an individual moves through the stages of change. Initially, the cons outweigh the pros for behaviour change in the pre-contemplation stage. In the contemplation stage the pros and cons are roughly equal, resulting in ambivalence towards change. When the decisional balance is tipped in favour of change, an individual will move towards the preparation and action stages of change, and this balance in favour of change continues in the maintenance stage if relapse is avoided.

## SELF-EFFICACY

Self-efficacy (Bandura, 1977) or the belief an individual has about their own capability to succeed in achieving their aims in the face of challenges, is a key factor in the TTM. This applies to the ability to implement and maintain behaviour change in the face of obstacles and situations which might trigger relapse. Self-efficacy beliefs can change as progression through the stages occurs. Self-efficacy can increase as behaviour change is maintained and can decrease in the face of relapse.

## BRIEF EVALUATION OF THE TTM

The TTM provides a broad framework in which different psychological treatments can be used to direct an individual through the various stages, using techniques appropriate to their current stage. Research using stage-matched intervention strategies has demonstrated improvements in treatment recruitment, retention and progress, and consistent patterns have been found between the pros and cons of changing and the stages of change across distinct health behaviours (Prochaska & Velicer, 1997). The development of this model encompasses a large body of research within the area of addiction (Prochaska et al., 1992). However, despite its broad intuitive appeal, the overall evidence that TTM stage-based interventions are superior to control interventions remains equivocal, with numerous examples of both supportive and critical data. For example, a comparative investigation of the effectiveness of stage-based interventions for smoking cessation (the dominant area of research output for the TTM (West & Brown, 2013: 82) found no clear advantage for using stage-based interventions (Cahill et al., 2010).

The TTM has been widely accepted in healthcare settings as the dominant paradigm for behavioural change. Frontline support workers in the addiction field find the TTM useful because it provides a clear practical framework and a toolbox of techniques to help their clients to understand and change their behaviour. It also enables them to help clients to feel that they are within a cyclical process of change, where any forward movement through the stages is seen as encouraging. Even if they relapse, this is seen as part of the process of eventual permanent change, rather than as an outright failure to change.

The main criticisms of the model are directed at the theoretical definitions of the actual stages and the arbitrary nature of the time periods used to define each stage. It has been argued that evidence for important stage transition determinants, decisional balance, self-efficacy and other processes of change, is largely based on cross-sectional data that does not address the predictive power of the model for longer-term behavioural outcomes. The TTM has also been criticised for failing to capture the complexity of human functioning by its overly simplistic categorisation of behaviour change into discrete stages (Bandura, 1997). It also places emphasis on factors determining individual motivation whilst underplaying societal influences on behaviour.

# MOTIVATIONAL INTERVIEWING

Motivational Interviewing (MI) fits conceptually well within the framework of the TTM, providing a practical method to work with individuals who are less ready to change: those in the precontemplation, contemplation, and preparation stages of change.

## THE METHOD OF MI

MI has its roots in the empathic person-centred counselling style of Carl Rogers (Rogers, 1959, 1980). MI initially developed from the clinical observations of its founder, Bill Miller, whilst counselling problem drinkers (Miller, 1983). Miller observed that behaviour change was more likely to succeed if individuals were first listened to empathically, enabling active engagement with the therapist, who could then guide them to identify and articulate their own reasons for making positive changes. Drinking outcomes were found to be correlated with therapists' skilfulness in client-centred counselling. Higher relapse rates were found to be associated with counsellors who were less skilled in interacting with clients in this way Miller & Baca, 1983; Miller et al., 1980; Valle, 1981). This style of empathic engagement with the client was in contrast to the more directive and confrontational style of interaction which was prevalent in addiction treatment settings at the time. This style of interaction assumes that ambivalence is a natural part of preparing for change, and the individual already has in their own mind arguments both for and against making positive changes. A directing or confrontational style of counselling can be counterproductive, in that it activates the individual's arguments against change in reaction to what they are being told they should do. In contrast, MI aims to encourage the individual to voice both sides of the argument through empathic engagement. This consists of a collaborative partnership founded on acceptance, compassion and evocation. This helps the MI practitioner to understand the individual's internal frame of reference. Once a therapeutic interaction is established, subtle use of psycholinguistics helps to guide the individual into voicing their own arguments for positive change, and then helps them to formulate a workable plan to succeed. Five key communication skills used throughout MI are as follows:

1. Asking open questions (questions that elicit further information)
2. Affirming what the individual has said
3. Reflecting back the salient information gathered from the interaction
4. Summarising the salient information gathered from the interaction
5. Providing information and advice with permission

During the interaction the individual's core personal values and goals are discussed and explored. This highlights any discrepancy between their current behaviour and their core values and goals. This self-exploration and self-confrontation, coupled with subtle yet skilful guidance and focus, is thought to be a powerful motivational force to drive subsequent behaviour change. The MI practitioner places particular emphasis on those parts of the conversation that focus on behaviour change, thereby strengthening the belief that it is possible. Once this belief is instilled, the practitioner can help with formulating specific plans to implement the change and handle obstacles.

## HOW EFFECTIVE IS MI?

Early research using MI on problem drinkers who were not in formal treatment demonstrated the utility of MI delivered as a brief intervention to reduce drinking in this group. Miller and colleagues developed and tested a brief intervention called the Drinker's Checkup (Miller et al., 1988). This consisted of a detailed initial assessment of alcohol consumption and related problems, coupled with a return visit to receive personalised feedback delivered in an MI consistent style. The effectiveness of MI delivered as a prelude to formal treatment has also been demonstrated in both alcohol outpatients (Bien et al., 1993) and residential alcohol treatment settings (Brown & Miller, 1993).

A review of 32 controlled trials found brief interventions to be superior to no treatment and often as effective as more intensive treatments (Bien et al., 1993). Interest in the effectiveness of brief interventions and their potential utility, compared with longer and more intensive treatments, resulted in the inclusion of a form of MI labelled Motivational Enhancement Therapy (MET) (Miller et al., 1992) in a large multi-site study conducted by the National Institute of Alcohol Abuse and Alcoholism (NIAAA). This study, called Project MATCH, compared different treatment approaches with different kinds of people, aiming to discover if certain treatments were better suited to people with particular needs and characteristics than others. The two other treatment approaches tested were Cognitive Behavioural Therapy and Twelve-Step Facilitation. MET was found to be as effective as these other two types of treatment, despite being less intensive. The study also found angrier people derived greater benefit from MET, and people who lacked social support for remaining abstinent benefited more from Twelve-Step treatment due to its greater levels of social support (see Babor & Del Boca, 2003, for a description and critique of Project MATCH).

Over time the theory and practice of MI have been standardised, developed and refined, and it has diffused into many other fields of practice. In general, meta-analyses show that MI is associated with small to medium effect sizes across a range of behaviours, with the strongest supportive evidence showing a beneficial effect on addictive behaviours. The high degree of variability in MI effects which are observed across different studies, is thought to be due to the significant influence of therapist and contextual aspects of delivery (Miller & Rollnick, 2013). These factors are also important in the types of treatment considered in the next two sections of this chapter; Behavioural Therapy and Cognitive Behavioural Therapy.

# BEHAVIOUR THERAPY

Behaviour therapy developed from research into normal learning processes and is theoretically grounded in the two main types of conditioning studied in the experimental analysis of behaviour: classical conditioning and instrumental conditioning (see Chapter 3 for a more detailed description of these learning mechanisms). Behaviour therapy focuses on changing overt behaviour, rather than trying to understand the underlying causes. Addiction is viewed as maladaptive learning and the focus of treatment is to unlearn these maladaptive behaviour patterns.

Classical conditioning hypothesises that cues associated with drug use act as conditioned stimuli due to their repeated association with the drug effect, the unconditioned stimulus. Stimuli associated with taking the drug, such as the place, the preliminaries, other people, objects, moods, and any drug-associated behaviour, can elicit powerful neurophysiological effects in the absence of the drug itself, resulting in the experience of craving, and potential relapse during drug abstinence.

By identifying drug-associated stimuli, it is possible to learn to avoid or alter these drug-associated triggers as much as possible, and to learn different associations and consequences for drug use and drug abstinence. There are a wide variety of behavioural techniques which have evolved through experimental research, including behavioural skills training and modelling, which arose from the influence of Albert Bandura's work on social cognitive processes on behavioural therapy (Bandura, 1969). The forms of behaviour therapy considered in this section are aversion therapy and contingency management therapy. Additionally two experimental techniques, cue exposure therapy (CET), a behaviouristic psychological approach, and cognitive bias modification training (CBM), a method of targeting and retraining attentional and approach biases to drug-related stimuli, will also be described.

## AVERSION THERAPY

Aversion therapy was more commonly used from the 1940s and 50s onwards (Cannon & Baker, 1981; Lemere & Voegtlin, 1940; Smith, 1982) but is no longer considered an appropriate choice of therapy by most treatment providers, due to the more recent development and implementation of greater or equally effective, less ethically questionable forms of treatment.

Aversion therapy involves pairing the problem behaviour to be controlled or eliminated with aversive highly unpleasant experiences. The aim is to counter-condition or replace the pleasurable thoughts, feelings and sensations associated with the problem behaviour with negative and unpleasant associative experiences. These aversive experiences include pairing the behaviour, for example alcohol consumption or drug use, with chemically-induced nausea or the delivery of electrical shocks. Chemical aversion treatment for alcohol dependence involves pairing alcohol consumption with emetine, apomorphine or disulfiram administration.

Aversion therapy has also been used to treat nicotine addiction. This type of treatment can induce aversion to smoking by directing smokers to smoke in ways that make it an unpleasant and nausea-inducing experience. One example, rapid smoking, involves taking a puff of smoke every six to ten seconds, smoking for three minutes, smoking three cigarettes, or smoking until it feels intolerable. This process is then repeated a further two or three times interspersed with rest intervals. Other techniques include: rapid puffing whilst avoiding inhalation (Erickson et al., 1983); holding smoke in the mouth for 30 seconds whilst breathing through the nose (Becoña & García, 1993); and steeply increasing cigarette consumption above the levels usually smoked (see the review of aversive smoking for smoking cessation in Hajek & Stead, 2001).

Covert sensitisation or symbolic aversion is another less controversial form of aversive conditioning, which involves pairing the problematic behaviour with imagined negative sensations or consequences. The efficacy of this type of aversive conditioning is uncertain.

## CUE EXPOSURE THERAPY

There is a large body of experimental research which supports the operation of selective attention (termed 'attentional bias') to addiction relevant cues in perpetuating addictive behaviour. Cue reactivity consists of the different types of physiological responses which occur when users or ex-users are exposed to conditioned stimuli associated with their addiction. These cues can include people, places and things, as well as triggering emotional states. Cue exposure therapy (CET) is based on the idea that this reactivity to addiction-related cues, which contributes to craving and relapse, can be extinguished through repeated deliberate exposure to these cues, usually in a clinical setting (Conklin & Tiffany, 2002). It is assumed that systematic desensitisation to addiction-relevant cues, in the absence of reward, whilst learning effective coping strategies, will translate into reduced cue reactivity in the real world, with a consequent reduction in craving and uncontrolled behaviour.

Evidence for the potential clinical utility of measures of cue reactivity has been demonstrated in a number of experimental studies. For example, greater attentional bias for addiction-relevant cues has been associated with increased relapse in studies with smokers (Waters et al., 2003), alcohol users (Cox et al., 2002), and opiate users (Marissen et al., 2006). A reduction in cue reactivity using cue exposure delivered in virtual reality (VR) environments has also been shown for gambling (Park et al., 2015), cannabis, cigarettes and alcohol (Bordnick et al., 2005; Bordnick et al., 2008; Bordnick et al., 2009). However, despite some encouraging findings, the evidence for the effectiveness of CET for the treatment of substance use disorders is inconsistent. A recent meta-analytic review of CET for the treatment of alcohol use disorders concluded that improved experimental studies are needed before firm conclusions can be made. The quality of experimental evidence available was judged to be poor, inconsistent and imprecise, with a suspected publication bias (Mellentin et al., 2017).

## COGNITIVE BIAS MODIFICATION

An example of another potential clinical application of targeting attentional and approach biases to addiction-related stimuli is the development of the Alcohol Attention Control Training Program (AACTP) (Fadardi & Cox, 2009). In this programme a computerised intervention is used to train drinkers to overcome their automatic distraction by alcohol stimuli. The training uses personally relevant, individualised, simultaneously competing alcoholic and non-alcoholic visually-presented beverage cues, presented on coloured backgrounds or with coloured outlines around the pictured beverages. Over a series of increasingly challenging trials (an hour a week for four weeks), the individual learns to preferentially respond to the coloured backgrounds, and then the coloured outlines of non-alcohol cues whilst ignoring the alcohol cues. This training has been associated with a reduction in alcohol attentional bias in problem drinkers, accompanied by a reduction in alcohol consumption, which was sustained at a follow-up after three months. Further novel methods for attentional retraining using gaming technology on mobile devices are also being developed and experimentally investigated. This type of delivery would increase the potential for use and the practical utility of the methodology (Cox et al., 2014).

CET and CBM are not widely used in clinical settings for treating addictive behaviour. This is due to the absence of long-term follow-up, adequately controlled, sufficiently powered, clinical outcome studies demonstrating their efficacy compared to other therapies. Based on current knowledge, CET and CBM techniques show some promise for the effective treatment of addictive behaviour when combined with other treatment approaches. It is unlikely that these techniques alone would constitute effective treatment for addictive behaviour, due to the fact that they are only targeting one aspect of a complex behavioural disorder. It is also unlikely that desensitisation to particular cues would generalise to encompass all potential triggers to craving and relapse in the real world. The higher rate of relapse observed in individuals who show increased cue reactivity, offers potential for the future use of this measure as a clinical marker to target individuals who may be more vulnerable to relapse, and who may require more intensive treatment.

## CONTINGENCY MANAGEMENT

Contingency management (CM) treatment techniques are theoretically based on the principles of instrumental or operant conditioning. The basic idea is that behaviour can be controlled through its consequent outcome. Behaviour which results in positive consequences is more likely to be repeated, whereas negative consequences will discourage the behaviours that preceded them. CM treatment was initially developed in the 1960s and was used to modify the behaviour of institutionalised psychiatric patients, who were otherwise difficult to control, using rewards such as therapist attention and cigarettes for compliant behaviour, and withdrawal of attention, as a behavioural disincentive (Gossop, 2003: 144). Further development of CM techniques led to the use of vouchers or tokens, which could be given out contingent on performance of the target behaviour. These representative tokens could later be exchanged for other desirable rewards and privileges. This type of system became known as a 'token economy' (Ayllon & Azrin, 1968). These token economies were used to manage behaviour in a variety of settings, including with children in classrooms and with mentally impaired and schizophrenic patients in psychiatric wards (Kazdin & Bootzin, 1972).

A large body of work supports the effectiveness of CM techniques, particularly when used with opioid-dependent populations, including polydrug users, who are on methadone maintenance programmes. CM treatment in these programmes usually involves the reward (clinic privilege) of being permitted to take home methadone doses, or receive an increase in methadone dose, contingent on providing opioid- (and other drug-) free urine samples (Stitzer & Higgins, 1995; Stitzer et al., 1986; Stitzer et al., 1992).

CM treatment has developed to include other types of incentives and disincentives. Another more cost-effective CM technique is the 'variable magnitude of reinforcement procedure' which enables or withholds from individuals permission to participate in prize draws, with the variable chance of winning large, small, or zero value prizes, contingent on providing a drug-free biological specimen (Petry et al., 2000). The use of vouchers which can be exchanged for goods and other financial incentives has been effectively used to sustain abstinence in cocaine dependence (Higgins et al., 1993), and has also been shown to reduce frequency of marijuana use (Budney et al., 2007).

A series of three systematic reviews on the use of voucher and related monetary-based CM interventions for a variety of substance use disorders, covering the time period from 1991 up until 2014, found a large proportion of the included studies (86%) supported the efficacy of CM interventions (Davis et al., 2016; Higgins, 2011; Lussier et al., 2006). These treatment effects were stronger whilst the incentives were in place compared to the follow-up period after discontinuation of the incentives. The use of CM techniques has been shown to be particularly effective in challenging and special populations when compared to other interventions. For example, meta-analyses of smoking cessation interventions for pregnant women showed larger treatment effects for CM compared to other treatment interventions tested (Higgins & Solomon, 2016), and CM has been shown to be effective in reducing marijuana use in patients with serious mental illness (Sigmon & Higgins, 2006).

Important factors which increase CM treatment efficacy and effect size include longer duration of treatment, higher value incentives, and a shorter delay time between carrying out the target behaviour and earning the reward. The main drawbacks and barriers to the widespread clinical adoption of CM treatments are their cost effectiveness, the uncertainty surrounding their long-term durability, and the practicalities involved in the implementation of CM, such as staff training and repeated collection, monitoring and testing of biological samples. Employment-based workplace contingencies, or other cost-effective community-based contingencies, which reinforce abstinence through the gradual transfer of CM using extrinsic rewards to more self-generated intrinsically rewarding incentives, may help to sustain the initial effectiveness of this form of treatment. Based on current evidence, CM may be a particularly useful treatment to use in the early initial phase of treatment, particularly to retain individuals who are at high risk of dropping out of treatment.

# COGNITIVE BEHAVIOURAL THERAPY

Cognitive Behaviour Therapy (CBT) integrates the methods and processes of behaviour therapy, whilst incorporating and more fully addressing the mental processes and direct experience of the individual being treated. The term 'cognitive' widely covers mental processes like perception, attention, memory, and thinking. A link is drawn between these mental processes and their interrelationship and reciprocal influence on emotional experience and behavioural output. CBT is a problem-focused therapy approach which can be carried out in both group and individual settings. It is usually implemented in a set time frame, varying between five and twenty 30- to 60-minute weekly sessions.

Important influences on the evolution of CBT were the 'cognitive revolution' in experimental psychology, the personal construct psychology of George Kelly, and the work of psychologists Albert Ellis and Aaron Beck (Thoma et al., 2015).

Ellis's approach, Rational Emotive Therapy (Ellis, 1962), challenged individuals' irrational beliefs and their 'should statements', encouraging them to develop a more rational perspective on their problems in order to change their behaviour to achieve desired goals. Beck sought to encourage individuals to become scientific observers of their own experience. This involved training people to challenge their negative automatic thoughts by identifying and drawing attention to their distorted thinking, and restructuring those thoughts, through the use of homework and collaboration with the therapist (Beck, 1993).

CBT is a highly integrative therapy and has expanded to incorporate elements from other approaches. These newer approaches encompass Mindfulness-Based Stress Reduction, Mindfulness-Based Cognitive Therapy, Acceptance and Commitment Therapy and Dialectical Behaviour Therapy (Thoma et al., 2015). These more recent approaches are referred to as the 'third wave' of CBT in the context of the 'first wave' of behaviour therapy and the 'second wave' of conventional CBT methods. These 'third wave' techniques focus on 'mindfulness' and emphasise the importance of awareness in the present moment, and the compassionate, non-judgemental acceptance and observation of thoughts and feelings. Cultivation of this awareness through regular practice, enables development of a level of detachment, affording the mental space to access greater emotional and behavioural control.

## SOME METHODS USED IN CBT

A main concept in CBT is that how you think influences how you feel and how you behave. The idea is to change the learned maladaptive patterns of thinking and behaving by the use of practical tools to break down, interrupt and analyse in a logical evidence-based way the cyclical links between events, thoughts, emotions (including physical sensations) and behaviours. This can involve the use of personal diaries, charts and maps in order to identify, organise, analyse and challenge these cognitions. These tools can be adapted to the specific behavioural problem for which help is being sought.

One example of the type of tool available is the ABC form. The ABC form is a chart in which the activating event (A) is linked to the emotions and beliefs (B) generated by the activating event, the associated thinking errors identified, and the consequent feelings and actions (C) recorded. Types of thinking error can include: catastrophising, inflexible thinking, overgeneralising, making assumptions, positive or negative perception bias, personalising, and low frustration tolerance. By systematic evaluation of the activating event, the feelings generated and the behavioural consequences (e.g. using alcohol or drugs to avoid or escape uncomfortable feelings), it is possible to challenge those thoughts and formulate potential alternative behavioural strategies. These alternatives can then be tested through further experimentation.

Another CBT-based treatment approach used in the addiction field is called Node-Link Mapping. This approach originated from research in psychology and communication suggesting that using visual displays enhances communication in the therapeutic setting (Dansereau & Simpson, 2009). The use of simple box-line (node-link) visual charts provides a way to focus on the problem behaviour and helps to identify causes, consequences and potential solutions during the therapeutic session. This type of tool can be particularly useful for clarifying communication with those who may find it hard to verbally express their thoughts. For example, node-link maps can be used for exploring areas such as personal characteristics, relationships and decision making. The interrelationships between ideas, emotions and behaviour can be grasped more easily using these types of visual displays, compared with verbal communication alone. The tools discussed above are useful for identifying, analysing and preventing situations which may increase the risk of relapse. This important aspect of treatment is discussed below.

## RELAPSE PREVENTION

The Relapse Prevention (RP) model (Marlatt & Gordon, 1985) is an important and widely implemented social cognitive behavioural approach to treating and preventing relapse. This model is both practically and conceptually useful given the chronically relapsing nature of addictive disorders. Relapse prevention is the ultimate goal of all treatment approaches.

Relapse is posited to be influenced by both covert and immediate determinants. Covert influences include factors such as stress exposure and urges and cravings caused by lifestyle imbalance and maladaptive coping strategies. Immediate determinants include exposure to high-risk situations, and the ability to cope in such situations. This model teaches individuals how to identify all the potential factors that influence the likelihood of relapse, and also teaches effective cognitive and behavioural skills which can be used to reduce the risk of relapse. Factors that are known to influence relapse include environmental cues, both negative and positive emotional states, interpersonal conflict, and social pressure. It is how an individual responds to these types of trigger situations which is important, and this is influenced by their self-efficacy beliefs and their positive expectancies about the anticipated relief they will gain from their problem behaviour (e.g. excessive alcohol use). RP techniques include having a lifestyle management plan in place, and learning how to tolerate uncomfortable feelings and find alternative ways to cope with stress. These techniques encompass: stimulus control (e.g. removing environmental cues); urge management (e.g. learning imagery techniques to cope with managing urges); coping skills training (e.g. relaxation training, stress management techniques, assertiveness training, relapse rehearsal); and cognitive restructuring. Cognitive restructuring involves learning to reconceptualise a lapse as a mistake rather than as a global personal failure, which helps to avoid the abstinence violation effect, whereby the distressing feelings associated with an initial lapse precipitate a full-blown relapse.

A more recent evolution of RP for substance use disorders involves incorporating mindfulness meditation techniques with cognitive behavioural RP strategies (Bowen et al., 2010). This treatment approach, called Mindfulness–Based Relapse Prevention, involves additionally learning to be mindfully aware in the present moment, so that automatic, habitual and destructive ways of reacting can be more easily identified and controlled. This approach has been shown to be superior to standard RP in reducing drug use and heavy drinking at one year follow-up (Bowen et al., 2014).

There is a large body of research evidence to support the overall efficacy of CBT for the treatment of substance use disorders, including both alcohol and other addictive drugs (e.g. Carroll & Onken, 2005; Irvin et al., 1999; Jhanjee, 2014; McHugh et al, 2010; Miller & Wilbourne, 2002). These CBT interventions encompass a variety of different techniques and approaches, as outlined in the preceding sections, and also include group-, couples- and family-based treatment approaches.

Despite the differences in the treatment approaches considered, there are commonalities based on the fact that SUDs are characterised by learning processes coupled with the reinforcing effects of substances (McHugh et al., 2010). A recent systematic review of psychosocial interventions for cannabis use disorder (CUD) found that an intensive intervention provided over more than four sessions based on a combination of Motivational Enhancement Therapy (MET) and CBT, with abstinence-based incentives, was the most consistently supported treatment for CUD at short-term follow-up of approximately four months, although this effect was not supported at the longer-term nine month follow-up (Gates et al., 2016). A systematic review on the efficacy of psychosocial interventions in inducing and maintaining alcohol abstinence in patients with chronic liver disease, found that an integrated therapy approach combining CBT and MET with comprehensive medical care was effective in increasing alcohol abstinence by 26% in those patients compared to a control group, and an integrated therapy combining CBT with medical care successfully reduced recidivism by 42.3 % in this group, compared to a control group, over the two year follow-up period (Khan et al., 2016). Addition of computer-assisted delivery of CBT treatments to standard drug counselling treatment has also been shown to be effective in increasing abstinence for up to six months, and holds promise as a method to increase the availability of this technique (Carroll et al., 2008; Carroll et al., 2009).

Another important factor in successful recovery from addiction is consistent social support in a substance free context. This is the focus of the group approaches considered in the following sections.

# TWELVE-STEP APPROACHES

Attending a self-help or mutual aid group based on a twelve-step programme is perhaps the most widely known treatment for addiction. The twelve-step approach established by Alcoholics Anonymous (AA) has spread worldwide, entered public consciousness, and expanded to include anonymous groups for other substance and behavioural addictions. These groups include, for example, Narcotics Anonymous, Sex Addicts Anonymous, Overeaters Anonymous and Gamblers Anonymous, to name just a few. This approach has also led to the creation of related support groups for those affected by someone else's addiction, such as Al-Anon and Al-Ateen for family and friends and teenage children of alcoholics respectively, and Gam-Anon, for people affected by someone else's gambling addiction.

AA was founded in Akron, Ohio, in the USA in 1935 by two former alcoholics, Bill Wilson, a broker, and Bob Smith, a physician. Wilson had experienced some kind of spiritual insight whilst in hospital recovering from a severe drinking episode. In the wake of this insight he subsequently abstained from alcohol and remained sober. The two men recognised similarities in relation to their struggle with trying and repeatedly failing to control their alcohol use, and decided to help each other and others suffering with this problem. Both men were influenced by the teachings of the Oxford Group, a popular evangelical Christian movement of the time, and by psychologists Carl Jung and William James. These influences were significant in their development of the Twelve Steps and Traditions of AA.

AA is not just a programme to help addicts deal with their specific addiction. It is an organisation that teaches people how to live a different kind of life with a different identity and different values. Working through the twelve steps is seen as the means to achieving an abstinent and fulfilling life. The twelve steps of AA are given below and are essentially the same for all other twelve-step programmes, apart from the substance or behaviour specified in Step 1.

## THE TWELVE STEPS OF AA

1. We admitted we were powerless over alcohol – that our lives had become unmanageable.
2. Came to believe that a Power greater than ourselves could restore us to sanity.
3. Made a decision to turn our will and our lives over to the care of God as we understood him.
4. Made a searching fearless moral inventory of ourselves.
5. Admitted to God, to ourselves, and to another human being the exact nature of our wrongs.
6. Were entirely ready to have God remove all these defects in character.
7. Humbly asked Him to remove our shortcomings.
8. Made a list of people we had harmed and became willing to make amends to them all.
9. Made direct amends to such people wherever possible, except where to do so would injure them or others.
10. Continued to take personal inventory and when we were wrong promptly admitted it.
11. Sought through prayer and meditation to improve our conscious contact with God as we understood Him, praying only for knowledge of his will for us and the power to carry that out.
12. Having had a spiritual awakening as a result of these steps, we tried to carry this message to alcoholics, and to practise these principles in all our affairs.

AA has been criticised on the basis of its religious overtones, historical origins (including the ideology of the temperance movement), widespread influence in addiction treatment, and the absence of any place for critical analysis of its methods (e.g. Bufe, 1998). However, despite its evangelical Christian origins, AA is non-dogmatic in how an individual may wish to interpret God/a higher power (e.g. the higher power can be interpreted as the power of the group), and there is evidence that AA is equally beneficial for those who are atheist/agnostic, as it is for those who consider themselves to have more spiritual or religious beliefs (Kelly et al., 2006). Power within the organisation is decentralised and there is a non-hierarchical structure to meetings. The universal spirituality, which is fundamental to AA, is fully inclusive. The only requirement for attendance of AA, as stated by the organisation, is an honest desire to stop drinking. The disease model of addiction, along with the concepts of craving and loss of control are implicit within the AA view of alcoholism, and complete abstinence is the only acceptable goal, which has also led to criticism of the organisation. People are encouraged to attend AA meetings for life on a regular basis, and to label themselves as recovering addicts. This could be viewed as replacing one dependency with another. The basic idea is to keep things structured and simple and to follow the rules without question. This is not a suitable treatment option for those who wish to simply reduce their problem drinking. Individuals would probably not be able to tolerate attending meetings and working through the twelve steps unless they felt it resonated with their personal truth, as reflected in their personal experience of loss of control, and its attendant, sometimes catastrophic consequences. In light of these types of serious life consequences (e.g. hospitalisations, failed relationships, unemployment, legal convictions) a substitute dependency on AA can be viewed in a positive light. Just like all the other treatments discussed in this chapter, the twelve-step approach is not going to be helpful for everyone. An individual's perception of twelve-step treatment may also vary widely, depending on the composition of the group they attend and the interaction with their sponsor.

Apart from severity of dependence, four critical factors have been identified to be important to recovery from alcoholism: engaging in a substitute behaviour; compulsory supervision; forming new relationships; and engaging in spiritual practices. It has been suggested that because AA combines all four of these factors, it is highly effective. Men who achieved stable abstinence in a sixty-year long-term follow-up study were found to have attended approximately 20 times the number of AA meetings as those who did not (Vaillant, 2003).

Many studies have found a positive relationship between alcohol use outcomes and AA attendance, and this has been attributed to therapeutic elements common to other theories of behaviour change and also to AA specific mechanisms. Common psychological processes include many of the cognitive, affective and behavioural processes of behaviour change identified by the TTM. AA specific processes include increased frequency of attending meetings, doing step work, helping other alcoholics, and having a sponsor (see the references in the review by Tusa & Burgholzer, 2013). AA has the advantage of being widely accessible and practically cost free (voluntary donation), with members being able to attend as many meetings as they feel they need to.

There is undoubtable therapeutic power in a group of individuals coming together with shared problems, a shared understanding, and a shared common purpose. This is particularly so when addiction may have led to prior feelings of guilt, shame and isolation. Fortunately, there are other more recently developed therapeutic mutual aid group approaches available for those who cannot relate to AA. One such approach, SMART Recovery, is considered in the next section. Moderation Management is another mutual aid organisation which offers help, advice and information to those who want to reduce their problematic drinking, as well as those who want to achieve abstinence.

## SMART RECOVERY

SMART stands for **S**elf-**Ma**nagement and **R**ecovery **T**raining. SMART Recovery was developed in 1994 in the United States, and operates as a non-profit secular organisation in many countries including Canada, Australia and the UK (where it is a registered charity). SMART Recovery organises mutual aid meetings both online and in person to help people recovering from any type of substance or behavioural addiction. There are many resources available on the SMART Recovery website, and the information imparted and methods used in SMART Recovery are established evidence-based psychological techniques. There is a continuing commitment to expand and evolve the methods offered as new information becomes available.

SMART recovery meetings are set up and run by trained Facilitators, who can be either trained professionals who operate in partnership with the organisation, or members of the recovery community who have completed the online facilitator training course. This volunteer facilitator training is encouraged by the organisation and is important in the sense of building an ethos of 'giving back'. Participants can attend meetings for as long as they find it useful, but there is no lifetime commitment required, and labels such as 'addict' are avoided and considered disparaging and unhelpful to recovery. The organisation has the support of an International Board of Advisors consisting of professional psychologists and scientists active within the addiction treatment field.

The SMART recovery four-point programme, as detailed on their website, consists of: building and maintaining motivation; coping with urges; managing thoughts, feelings and behaviours; and living a balanced life.

The methods used to deliver this programme incorporate ideas and methods from Motivational Interviewing and Motivational Enhancement Therapy, Rational Emotive Behaviour Therapy, Relapse Prevention, and other cognitive and behavioural techniques previously described in this chapter.

Recent evidence from a clinical trial comparing a SMART Recovery-based online treatment intervention with face-to-face meetings, showed the web-based application (called Overcoming Addictions) to be just as effective at reducing drinking overall as attending face-to-face SMART Recovery meetings, at three month and six month follow-up, with no additional benefit gained from combining both approaches (Campbell et al., 2016; Hester et al., 2013). As the number of people that can be potentially reached and helped by online resources is far greater than conventional resources, this is an encouraging finding.

# SUMMARY

- Treatments which engage individuals regularly and consistently for a sufficient period of time to help effect permanent identity and lifestyle changes are likely to be successful aids to overcoming an addiction.
- This encompasses treatments which increase self-efficacy; change expectancies around substance use or addictive behaviour; teach relapse prevention; and encourage an individual to learn new habits, skills, and ways of thinking and coping.
- The period of time and treatment intensity needed will vary with the severity of the problem and the interaction of the substance with individual biological and social factors.
- Different types of psychological treatment appear to be equally effective as long as they are skilfully and empathically delivered, regardless of their theoretical basis (Imel et al., 2008).
- The sense of understanding, companionship, safety, shared experience and support, coupled with the self-worth gained from helping others in the same situation, suggest that attending a mutual aid group is a valuable treatment in itself as well as a helpful adjunct to other forms of treatment.
- Online interventions and resources can also increase the cost effectiveness, practical delivery and reach of some forms of treatment, such as CBT-based interventions.
- There is no universally successful treatment approach, and all approaches are valuable if they help some people to achieve and maintain control or abstinence from addictive substances and behaviour.

# QUESTIONS

1. Describe the stages of change.
2. What is motivational interviewing and how can it be deployed?
3. Should we use aversion therapy for addiction?
4. Describe the relapse prevention model.
5. How can CBT be used in addiction treatment?

# NON-SUBSTANCE ADDICTIONS 8

## CHAPTER OVERVIEW

This chapter will review the evidence for two non-substance or 'behavioural addictions'. The non-substance addictions considered in this chapter are gambling disorder and internet gaming disorder, although there are many more potential behavioural addictions, for example compulsive shopping and sex addiction. Gambling has been investigated more thoroughly and for a longer period of time then other non-substance addictions, which is why it is the main focus of this chapter. This chapter will:

- Describe how the disordered behaviour in gambling addiction can be differentiated from substance addictions
- Describe the commonalities between gambling and substance addictions
- Describe the unique features of gambling addiction which differentiate it from other non-substance and substance addictions
- Describe internet gaming disorder

# ADDICTION

## LEARNING AIMS OF THE CHAPTER

- Understand the similarities and differences between substance addictions and behavioural addictions
- Understand the common and distinct features of substance addictions and gambling addiction
- Have an awareness of the problems involved in the classification and diagnosis of non-substance addictions and the need for further research

# INTRODUCTION

## WHAT CONSTITUTES A NON-SUBSTANCE OR BEHAVIOURAL ADDICTION?

There are overlaps in the development, underlying neurobiology and learning of substance and behavioural addictions, although the evidence base is more speculative and less extensive for non-substance addictions. There is also overlap in the methods used to treat non-substance and substance addictions.

Behavioural addictions have been previously conceived as lying along an impulsive-compulsive behavioural spectrum, with some classified as impulse control disorders and others as leaning more towards the obsessive-compulsive end of the spectrum (see the review by Grant et al., 2010). Where these excessive behaviours produce short-term reward that may precipitate persistence in the face of knowledge of adverse consequences and increasing loss of control, it may be more appropriate to classify them with substance addictions, although the line is not always clear-cut. The reclassification of Gambling Disorder in the 'Substance-Related and Addictive Disorders' section of the DSM-5 (American Psychiatric Association, 2013) has been seen as an important step in recognising the commonalities between these conditions. This may pave the way towards the future incorporation of other behavioural disorders in this section, if supportive evidence becomes available. Internet gaming disorder is a potential future addition to this section and has been highlighted for further study.

Other disorders which may share some features in common with substance use disorders and gambling, such as loss of control and compulsivity, are currently classified under different sections of the DSM-5. These disorders include, for example, trichotillomania (hair-pulling disorder) and excoriation disorder (skin picking disorder), which are classified within 'Obsessive-Compulsive and Related Disorders', and kleptomania (stealing disorder), which is classified within 'Disruptive, Impulse-Control, and Conduct Disorders' (Chamberlain et al., 2016). Other disorders characterised by impulsivity, such as intermittent explosive disorder, have little in common with behavioural addictions (Grant et al., 2010). Importantly, unlike substance addictions, non-substance addictions do not have direct neurotoxic effects resulting in cognitive impairment and other directly deleterious impacts on health (Robbins & Clark, 2015). However, the adverse consequences caused by excessive engagement in any activity may result in indirect effects on health, through the effects of stress and neglected self-care.

On a theoretical level the study of non-substance addictions is highly relevant to understanding the biological, psychological and social commonalities underlying excessive engagement in an activity in the absence of the confounding influence of the physiological effects of substances.

It has been powerfully argued that the term 'addiction' has been overly identified with substance dependence, and this has hampered interdisciplinary research and a broader understanding of excessive behaviour. According to this view, addiction may be better understood more broadly as an 'excessive appetite' encompassing non-substance addictions, as has been argued for many years by Jim Orford (Orford, 2001) whose theoretical approach is explained in more detail in Chapter 5. Quite often these excessive appetites are applicable to ordinary commonplace behaviours such as eating, shopping, sex and exercise, which can become compulsive for a small minority of people. The labelling of a behaviour as an addiction, confined to particular individuals, also has implications for relevant societal and political issues. For example, changing social norms regarding what is an acceptable level of a particular behaviour may exert an influence on patterns of that behaviour (e.g. decreased smoking in response to increased awareness of smoking-related harms and changes in legislation in recent times). Other contributory factors may include technological innovation and increased usage, and exposure to multi-media advertising.

The entire field of psychiatric classification of behaviour is controversial due to the difficulty of defining where the lines between what is considered normal and disordered behaviour should be drawn, and the degree of subjective judgement involved in these types of decisions. If future research evidence further illuminates the commonalities between non-substance and substance addictions, and impulse control and compulsive disorders, the future DSM classification of these disorders may shift to reflect this evidence.

It has been suggested that the potential overpathologising of a plethora of everyday life activities as putative behavioural addictions may lead to a dismissive appraisal of behavioural addiction research (Billieux et al., 2015). A recent large-scale five-year longitudinal study (Konkoly Thege et al., 2015) found that self-identified excessive shopping, exercising, eating, video gaming, online chatting and sexual behaviour, were context dependent and transient for the majority of people who at one time reported a problematic involvement with one of these activities. This is inconsistent with the conceptualisation that these addictions are progressive unless treated. This transience has also been observed in non-clinical samples of substance addictions (Lopez-Quintero et al., 2011) and gambling addiction (Slutske, 2006). Some consider that the group of symptoms and impairments in functioning seen in behavioural addictions are symptoms of other disorders, and do not have enough in common to deserve either group or individual disorder categorisation in their own right (Karim & Chaudhri, 2012).

The public perception of behavioural versus substance-related addictions has also been shown to differ, with perceived addiction liability being more associated with substance addictions, and character flaws being more associated with behavioural addictions (Konkoly Thege, Colman, et al., 2015). The authors of this large Canadian population-based survey (which compared social judgements of four substance addictions and six behavioural addictions) speculate that these public attitudes may influence the extent to which people believed to manifest behavioural addictions feel stigmatised, seek treatment, or initiate self-directed behaviour change. Ultimately a substantial body of converging evidence from a number of research domains will be needed (as has been the case for gambling) before other behavioural addictions are classified alongside substance use disorders. Beliefs and attitudes towards behavioural addictions may well lag behind research findings and take time to infiltrate public consciousness.

## FEATURES OF BOTH SUBSTANCE AND NON-SUBSTANCE ADDICTIONS

The failure to repeatedly resist an impulse to engage in a particular act that is harmful to oneself and/or others is an essential feature of both non-substance and substance addictions. In general, the behaviour under consideration is initially motivated by pleasure (positive reinforcement), and becomes increasingly motivated by relief from discomfort (negative reinforcement), and transitions from greater impulsivity to increased compulsivity and loss of control. This ultimately results in impaired functioning in other life domains such as interpersonal relationships, finances and health. Some of the shared features between substance and behavioural addictions include the following:

NON-SUBSTANCE ADDICTIONS

1. Higher rates of adolescent onset and higher incidence and frequency in adolescents and young adults.
2. Similar progression with frequent attempts to control the activity followed by relapse (chronicity). Natural recovery in a proportion of people.
3. Subjectively experienced feelings of craving, manifested as tension or arousal before committing the act, satisfaction whilst engaging in the activity (subjective 'high') and increasing tolerance to the behaviour, experienced as a need for increasing the intensity or frequency of the behaviour to achieve the same effect.
4. The behaviour is used to regulate mood.
5. Shared neurobiological mechanisms including involvement of opiate, serotonergic, glutamatergic and dopaminergic neurotransmitter systems.
6. Co-morbidity with other psychiatric disorders and with substance use disorders.
7. Shared response to treatment.

There are also important differences between non-substance and substance addictions, particularly the absence of physiological or medically serious withdrawal states when the behaviour is stopped (see the review by Grant et al., 2010). It should be kept in mind that there is a large degree of individual variation within a particular addiction, regardless of whether it is a substance or non-substance addiction. This is illustrated by gambling disorder, the most thoroughly researched non-substance addiction, which will be considered in the next section.

# GAMBLING DISORDER

## DIAGNOSTIC CRITERIA

Gambling is basically an activity in which something valuable is risked on the outcome of an event when the probability of gaining or losing is uncertain.

As previously stated, Gambling Addiction was moved to the substance disorders chapter in the DSM-5 and renamed Gambling Disorder (GD). Pathological gambling in the DSM-IV was formerly categorised under the section 'Impulse-Control Disorders Not Elsewhere Classified'. This reclassification under the 'Substance-related and Addictive Disorders' section reflects recognition of the numerous commonalities between GD and alcohol and drug use disorders. This includes similar neurobiological effects, analogous diagnostic criteria, shared genetic liability, high comorbidity rates, and shared treatment approaches (Rash et al., 2016). Gambling is the only formally acknowledged non-substance behavioural addiction in this chapter. At the time of writing there is an ongoing debate over whether Pathological Gambling should be reclassified in the 'Substance-related and Addictive Disorders' category in the upcoming eleventh edition of the *International Classification of Diseases* (ICD-11) in line with its reclassification in the DSM-5. It is currently classified with Impulse Control Disorders in ICD-10.

## PREVALENCE AND SOCIO-DEMOGRAPHIC VARIABLES

A recent systematic review of empirical research on problem gambling worldwide covering the timespan from 2000 up to 2015 (Calado & Griffiths, 2016) found wide variations in past-year problem gambling rates across different countries in the world (0.12 to 5.8%). Within Europe prevalence rates varied between 0.12 to 3.4%. The authors highlight the difficulty involved in trying to compare gambling prevalence rates obtained from different studies (even within the same country) due to the variation in the methodological procedures used. This includes differences in the gambling screening instruments, cut-off values and time frames used between studies. In spite of these differences consistent results emerged for socio-demographic characteristics obtained across studies. Problem gambling was more common amongst males, divorced or single people, and younger people. It was additionally associated with being unemployed, having a low income, belonging to an ethnic minority or having been born abroad, and having a lower level of education.

The most common gambling activities found across most countries were lotteries, scratch cards, sports betting and gambling machines. The addictive potential of certain gambling activities may be exacerbated because they are easy to access, can be played continuously, and involve paying out rewards quickly and frequently. The most frequent activities played by problem gamblers were slot machines and internet gambling games, confirming previous research on the addictive potential of these types of activities (Parke & Griffiths, 2006).

The prevalence of problem gambling in adolescents has also been systematically reviewed for the same fifteen-year time period (Calado et al., 2016). The findings from included studies showed youth prevalence rates varied between 0.2% and 12.3% worldwide. As observed in the studies with adults, comparison between studies using adolescents were hampered by the differences among assessment instruments, cut-off periods and time frames used. Despite the wide variation between studies, consistent demographic characteristics associated with adolescent gambling were: being male; belonging to an ethnic minority group; parental gambling; parental separation; and being older.

Internet gambling was found to be particularly popular amongst adolescents. Previous research has shown that increased availability of opportunities to gamble is associated with higher levels of gambling and problem gambling (e.g. Room et al., 1999; Welte et al., 2016), and also helps to explain the differences in prevalence rates within different regions of the same country and across different countries. Internet gambling is particularly easy to access, affordable, and can be played anonymously by adolescents without age verification and parental supervision. This may make adolescents particularly vulnerable to this mode of gambling. As with adult gambling, this review noted that gambling activities that were the most problematic amongst adolescents were those that involved high event frequencies and a short interval between stake and payout, such as slot machines. These types of gambling machines are ubiquitous in popular locations such as bars, restaurants and amusement arcades, and can be played with small amounts of money. The authors note that the higher rates of past year gambling in adolescents compared to adults may be due to the increased risk taking observed in adolescence due to a developmental lack of maturity and absence of adult responsibilities. An important point raised in this review is that the current generation of adolescents are the first to grow up in a society where gambling is widely accepted, available and promoted, and this may increase the risk for problematic gambling in this vulnerable age group.

In the UK, a report from the Institute of Public Policy Research (IPPR) in 2016 estimated that the costs to the government associated with gambling problems were somewhere between £260 million and £1.16 billion for one year. Even at the lowest end of this estimated range, these costs are huge. As well as the unaccountable emotional costs in terms of mental health and disrupted relationships from problem gambling, there are also the practical costs associated with incarceration, loss of tax revenue, homelessness and hospitalisations. Additionally, the finding that gambling is more common amongst the socio-economically disadvantaged and particular ethnic minority groups, coupled with the fact that there are a greater number of gambling outlets in socially deprived areas, illustrates the insidious hold this addiction takes where there is the least power to resist (Orford, 2013). The report recommends that problem gambling is tackled from a public health perspective in the UK. At the time of writing, gambling in the UK is regulated by the Gambling Commission, a branch of the Department of Culture, Media and Sport, rather than by the Department of Health. It has been argued that UK gambling research and policy decisions are not entirely independent and are subject to covert influence by the gambling industry (Orford, 2013).

A large-scale research study which looked at associations between national gambling policies and disordered gambling prevalence rates across Europe, surprisingly found only one statistically significant relationship between policy and disordered gambling prevalence (Planzer et al., 2014). This study collected data from key informants for each European jurisdiction studied. The only statistically significant finding was that rates of subclinical gambling were lower where there were greater restrictions on advertising for online games. These results suggest that regulatory restrictions on advertising may be effective for reducing gambling, particularly for vulnerable groups such as adolescents and disordered gamblers.

The authors of this study emphasise that the absence of finding a statistically significant relationship between policies and gambling disorders in general does not mean the absence of such relationships, and may well have been due to the methodological limitations of the study, such as small effects and limited sample sizes.

## CO-MORBIDITY

Research studies have consistently found problem and pathological gambling to co-occur with several psychiatric disorders, including substance abuse disorders, mood and anxiety disorders and other impulse control disorders (Crockford & el-Guebaly, 1998; Lorains et al., 2011; Petry et al., 2005). Findings from both population-based studies, and studies using clinical samples, support high prevalence rates for co-morbid psychiatric conditions in those who experience gambling problems.

A recent systematic review and meta-analysis of population surveys (Lorains et al., 2011) found the highest mean prevalence rates for nicotine dependence (60.1%), followed by a substance use disorder (57.5%), any mood disorder (37.9%), and any type of anxiety disorder (37.4%).

Another systematic review and meta-analysis carried out on studies using treatment-seeking problem gamblers, rather than studies using community samples, also found high prevalence rates for both current and lifetime co-occurring psychiatric disorders (Dowling et al., 2015). The results from 36 included studies estimated that roughly 75% of treatment-seeking problem gamblers have both current and lifetime co-morbid psychiatric disorders. The prevalence estimates across studies were highly variable, but were generally consistent with the findings from previous research in both treatment seeking and community samples. The most common lifetime disorders were major depressive disorder and alcohol and substance use disorders. The most frequently occurring current disorders were: nicotine dependence; major depressive disorder; alcohol abuse and dependence; social phobia; generalised anxiety disorder; post-traumatic stress disorder; cannabis use disorder; attention deficit hyperactivity disorder; adjustment disorder; bipolar disorder; and obsessive compulsive disorder.

There is supportive evidence to suggest that gambling disorder can precede and be a risk factor for the development and maintenance of other psychiatric conditions, or it can be a form of maladaptive coping to manage an underlying pre-existing disorder. The presence of multiple co-occurring disorders is also common (Chou & Afifi, 2011; Kessler et al., 2008; Parhami et al., 2014). Regardless of the temporal sequence of events, it is evident that there is a necessity for routine assessment and screening for other co-morbid psychiatric disorders, so that appropriately tailored treatment can be given.

# WHO DEVELOPS GAMBLING PROBLEMS?

An influential and comprehensive model that accounts for the multiple influences on the development of disordered gambling behaviour is the Three Pathways Model of Pathological Gambling (Blaszczynski & Nower, 2002). The pathways model is an attempt to integrate the contributory biological, psychological and ecological factors into a coherent conceptual framework. This model acknowledges the existence of different subtypes of gamblers. Although the outcome is similar in terms of observed gambling problems, the factors that contribute to the development of the behaviour vary in different subtypes of gambler and this has implications for how the disorder is subsequently treated.

Each of the three proposed pathways share common processes and symptoms, but are also distinguishable from each other. The first group is influenced by maladaptive learning and distorted cognitions, but lacks psychiatric pathology. The second group is additionally emotionally and biologically vulnerable, and often presents with mood disorders such as anxiety and depression. The third group, in addition to this biological and emotional vulnerability, also posesses impulsivist personality traits, and typically also suffers from antisocial behaviour and substance abuse.

The starting point essential to all three pathways is the availability, accessibility and acceptibility of gambling. This is influenced by factors such as public policy and regulatory legislation. Also common to all three pathways are the influences of learning and cognition. These include classical and instrumental conditioning to gambling, and also by associative learning, to gambling-related cues. These cues can be both external environmental cues or mood states. Faulty cognitions about the probability of winning result in a habitual pattern of gambling, which results in chasing wins and losses and ultimately losing more than expected. The three pathways are briefly outlined below.

## PATHWAY 1: BEHAVIOURALLY CONDITIONED PROBLEM GAMBLERS

These gamblers generally do not have existing psychological problems. They are the people who end up with a problem due to the nature of gambling itself. They lose control over their gambling as a result of conditioned learning and the cognitive distortions that occur as a result of habitual engagment in the behaviour. In general these gamblers have the most promising outlook in terms of recovery. They are more likely to recover without external intervention and require less intensive treatment.

## PATHWAY 2: EMOTIONALLY VULNERABLE PROBLEM GAMBLERS

These gamblers are characterised by their emotional and biological vulnerability. They are more likely to have experienced childhood adversity and suffer from maladaptive coping skills and affective instability as a result of both biological and psychosocial factors. This group uses gambling behaviour to escape uncomfortable emotions through dissociation and to regulate mood states such as depression and anxiety. These gamblers can also use gambling to regulate states of both hyper- and hypo-physiological arousal.

## PATHWAY 3: ANTISOCIAL IMPULSIVIST PROBLEM GAMBLERS

In addition to the biological and psychosocial vulnerabilities of pathway 2 gamblers, pathway 3 gamblers are those that manifest impulsive behaviour, an anti-social personality and attentional deficits. This group is more likely to be easily bored, emotionally unstable and difficult to treat, having a greater severity of gambling problems. The impulsivist traits of pathway 3 are thought to be a result of dysregulated neurotransmitter systems and dysfunctional neurological structures.

A recent study (Valleur et al., 2016) provided validation for the existence of the three pathways model by identifying these three subgroups of gamblers amongst a sample of 372 pathological gamblers meeting DSM-4 (2000) criteria. Additionally, this study demonstrated differences in the choice of gambling activity by these different subgroups. Impulsivist gamblers preferred semi-skilful gambling games (e.g. horse racing and sports betting), whereas emotionally vulnerable gamblers preferred to play games of chance, such as slot machines and scratch cards. These differences in choice of activity are proposed to reflect differences in the underlying pathology in the subgroups, with Group 3 seeking stimulation and novelty, and group 2 seeking avoidance, self-medication and escape. These subgroups may not always be clearly separable as discrete entities, because the underlying pathologies are dimensional in nature and may vary depending on the diagnostic instruments used to determine categorisation. A stronger validation for the existence of the three pathways has been demonstrated using a longitudinal prospective study design in which adolescents were followed up until early adulthood (Allami et al., 2017). In this study a statistical profiling analysis technique identified three profiles that were consistent with the three groups described in the Pathways Model. An additional fourth profile that was a combination of the emotionally vulnerable and biologically vulnerable (Impulsivist/antisocial) types was also identified.

In the next section some of the underlying neurobiology of gambling behaviour will be considered, and the distorted cognitions that arise as a result of maladaptive learning in those with gambling problems will be described. These cognitive distortions help to escalate gambling behaviour in susceptible individuals.

# NEUROBIOLOGY OF GAMBLING

## IMPULSIVITY

Neuroadaptive changes are thought to occur as a result of all learning, including the maladaptive learning which occurs in disordered gambling behaviour. Neuropsychological studies have identified impulsivity as an important marker that is shared across a range of substance and behavioural addictions including gambling (Clark, 2014).

Impulsivity refers to behaviour that is hasty, unplanned, potentially risky, and generally involves a lack of self-control. There is some evidence to suggest that this trait is evident from an early age and predicts an elevated risk for the development of later gambling problems as well as problematic substance use (Slutske et al., 2005; Slutske et al., 2012; Vitaro et al., 1999). In the study by Slutske (2012) behavioural undercontrol observed at age 3 was found to be associated with a greater likelihood of experiencing gambling problems at ages 21 and 32, highlighting the potential importance of pre-existing vulnerability factors in the development of gambling disorder. The antisocial impulsivist subtype of gambler identified in the pathways model (Blaszczynski & Nower, 2002) are those thought to have the worst clinical prognosis.

Impulsivity is considered to be a multi-dimensional construct. Two of the core components of impulsivity which have been experimentally investigated are choice impulsivity and response impulsivity. Choice impulsivity (decision making) refers to the selection of sooner, smaller rewards in preference to delayed, larger rewards, and is experimentally asessed by exploiting this particular aspect of decision making, using tasks such as the Iowa Gambling Task and the Cambridge Gambling Task. Response impulsivity refers to motor action and can be thought of as an inability to inhibit a motor response, which typically occurs without consideration of the consequences. Behavioural inhibition is usually measured using either observer or self-report, or via behavioural performance on tasks requiring inhibitory control. The tasks most commonly used are Go/No-Go tasks, continuous performance tasks and Stop-Signal Reaction Time tasks (SSRT) (Fauth-Bühler et al., 2016).

A recent meta-analysis which examined impairments in inhibitory control in substance abuse and addiction using results from 97 studies, found that inhibitory control deficits were apparent for heavy use/dependence on cocaine, MDMA, metamphetamine, tobacco and alcohol (including heavy drinkers) and also in pathological gambling (Smith et al., 2014). This meta-analysis found no evidence of performance deficits for pathological gamblers in studies using two types of Go/No-Go task, but found a medium to large effect for studies using the Stop Signal Reaction Time task. These two tasks are thought to measure different aspects of behavioural inhibition: cancellation of an initiated response (SSRT), or witholding a planned but unitiated response (Go/NoGo). The SSRT task may therefore be a more sensitive indicator of deficits in pathological gambling.

Conflicting findings from different individual studies are complicated by the influence of confounding factors, including poly-drug use and co-morbid psychological disorders which also have an effect on inhibitory control (Grant & Chamberlain, 2014). Many studies have used small sample sizes and are unable to consider the different subtypes of individuals with gambling disorder and their level of gambling severity, and this may also impact on the ability to detect differences in response inhibition. It is possible that different tasks differ in their sensitivity to detect facets of motor impulsivity and choice impulsivity, and/or individual differences exist in the developmental trajectory of gambling disorder with regard to these different facets of impulsivity. Impairments in impulsive action (using a Stop Signal task) have been shown to be associated with greater gambling severity in pathological gamblers compared to problem gamblers and controls, whereas abnormal choice impulsivity (using a delay discounting task) was characteristic of both gambling groups regardless of level of gambling severity (Brevers et al., 2012).

Several studies have demonstrated impulsive choice in problem gamblers. For example neuropsychological impairments in reflection impulsivity (using the Information Sampling Test) and risky decision making (using the Cambridge Gambling Task) have been observed in problem gamblers and alcohol-dependent individuals compared to healthy controls, potentially reflecting pre-existing shared addiction vulnerability in these groups. Additional deficits in working memory and decision-making deliberation times were specific to the alcohol group. The shared deficits in impulsive decision making are thought to be indicative of dysfunction of the ventral prefrontal cortex, whereas deficits specific to the alcohol-dependent group are hypothesised to be indicative of impairment of the dorsolateral prefrontal cortex as a result of chronic alcohol use (Lawrence et al., 2009).

Impaired decision making in gambling disorder has also been demonstrated using the Iowa Gambling Task (IGT) (Bechara et al., 1994). Performing well on this task requires participants to forego short-term benefits for long-term benefits. Findings from a review of studies investigating IGT performance in pathological gambling, are consistent with the idea that poor performance in this task may result from a hyperactive automatic attentional and memory system for signalling the presence of addiction-related cues (short-term high value and uncertain rewards), and attributing pleasure and excitement to those cues. It is speculated that the high incentive-salience associated with gambling-related choice in pathological gamblers could influence executive functions involved in emotional self-regulation, such that powerful impulsive motivational automatic processes are activated and influence the disadvantageous deck selection observed during this task (see the review of IGT in gambling disorder by Brevers et al., 2013). Poor performance in the IGT is also observed in substance use disorders, potentially reflecting a common influence on the shared neurobiological systems underlying these disorders (Leeman & Potenza, 2012). A study comparing cognitive measures, including impulsive choice on a delay discounting task, in pathological gamblers, cocaine users and healthy controls, found that the pathological gamblers showed steeper delay discounting than the cocaine-using group. The cocaine group showed greater problems with working memory, consistent with the potential neurotoxicity associated with cocaine exposure (Albein-Urios et al., 2012).

The neural basis of impulsivity in gambling disorder has been investigated in a number of studies using fMRI. For example, a comparison of pathological gamblers and controls in an event-related fMRI study of impulsive decision making revealed differences in brain activation patterns between the two groups (Miedl et al., 2015). In this study pathological gamblers recruited an executive control network to a greater extent than controls, when presented with larger delayed rewards, suggesting that they had to work harder to overcome an inclination to choose the smaller immediate reward. This study adds to accumulating evidence that pathological gambling is associated with a shift in the balance between brain networks involved in immediate reward consumption and brain networks involved in pre-frontal-parietal control.

Disrupted reward processing is characteristic of addictive behaviours, but overall there have been conflicting findings from fMRI studies of reward processing and decision making in gambling disorder. Both hyper and hypo activation of key regions involved in the processing of rewards in gambling disorder have been observed. These regions include the striatum, medial PFC, amygdala and insula (Clark, 2014). Interestingly, a differential sensitivity to the type of reward presented has also been shown in pathological gamblers compared to healthy controls (Sescousse et al., 2013). This study compared behavioural and brain responses to monetary and sexual rewards (in the form of erotic images) in gamblers and controls, and found a blunted response in the ventral striatum to erotic cues, compared to the monetary rewards, in gamblers. This decreased response correlated with severity of gambling symptoms, and was accompanied by decreased behavioural motivation for erotic compared to monetary rewards.

A recent meta-analysis of fMRI studies investigating reward processing in addiction to substances and gambling found evidence to support both reward deficiency and learning deficit theories in addiction (Luijten et al., 2017). This meta-analysis also found both similarities and differences between substance and gambling addiction in the processing of rewards. The results from 25 studies (representing 643 individuals with addiction and 609 controls) found that during reward anticipation individuals with substance and gambling addictions showed decreased striatal activation compared with controls. However, during reward outcome, differences were observed between substance and gambling addiction, with increased activation in the ventral striatum in substance addiction and decreased activation in the dorsal striatum in gambling addiction, compared to controls. The picture is complicated by various issues in fMRI experiments. Reward anticipation and reward outcome are different aspects of reward, and reflect distinct processes (Miller et al., 2014). Reward anticipation is more associated with incentive motivation as a result of exposure to appetitive cues and associated learning of positive outcomes, whereas reward outcome has greater relevance for learning about new stimuli and their potential importance. Results can vary depending on which phase of the addiction cycle an individual is engaged in, and if they have one or more co-occurring psychiatric disorders (including poly-substance use), which may also influence reward processing.

The authors of this meta-analysis interpret their findings with reference to temporal difference reinforcement learning theories (Redish, 2004; Schultz, 2013). In this theoretical framework increased activation is observed in response to unexpected rewards, reflecting what are called 'reward prediction errors'. Research evidence supports the existence of these reward prediction error signals, which reflect the dopamine response, in brain reward neurocircuitry, including the ventral striatum (O'Doherty et al., 2003). These striatal responses gradually transfer to cues predicting rewards as learning occurs. Reward prediction errors represent the difference between the reward obtained and the reward that was predicted, which can be better than, equal to, or worse, than its prediction. The difference experienced between the reward and its prediction shapes future behaviour (Lak et al., 2016). The finding of reduced anticipatory striatal activation in substance use and gambling disorder may reflect impaired reinforcement learning processes, which subsequently contribute to impaired decision making in these addictive behaviours.

Different patterns of brain activation observed in the processing of reward outcome in gamblers compared to substance users, may reflect the fact that the monetary rewards used in these experiments mean different things to individuals with gambling disorder, compared to individuals with substance use disorders, and controls. Money is the reward itself in gambling, whereas in substance use money is the means to obtain the desired reward. Experimental findings suggest that activation of the dorsal striatum has a greater association with arousal, rather than reward (Miller et al., 2014). It is therefore possible that the decreased activation in the dorsal striatum in gamblers may reflect a lack of arousal in these types of experimental situation. The monetary wins in the contrived context of an fMRI experiment may well be less arousing for individuals with gambling disorder, than for the healthy controls. The real-life experience of actual gambling play, with its attendant stimulatory cues (e.g. venue atmosphere, anticipation, competitors, flashing lights, noise, spinning wheels, colours etc.), is likely to generate more excitement and physiological arousal from a monetary win, than a monetary win in a non-naturalistic experimental situation. This lack of ecological validity in gambling research is a drawback which may potentially result in misleading findings in some experiments.

Dopamine dysregulation in gambling disorder is also implicated by the observation that problem gambling and other impulse control and addictive disorders, such as compulsive shopping, hypersexuality and binge eating, develop as a side effect in some Parkinsons disease patients, who escalate their prescribed dopamine agonist medication over that required for managing motor control (Katzenschlager, 2011). Current research suggests that differences exist in dopamine neurotransmission in drug addiction compared to gambling addiction. Using positron emission tomography (PET) imaging, the reduced dopamine D2/D3 receptor availability in the striatum that has been observed in substance abuse disorders has not been replicated in gambling disorder (see the review by Clark, 2014). Further clarification on the comparative neurobiology of substance use and gambling will hopefully be obtained from future research.

## COGNITIVE DISTORTIONS IN GAMBLING DISORDER

The view that faulty learning occurs in individuals who develop gambling disorder is supported by experiments which show that some of these individuals have experienced a 'big win' in their early involvement with gambling (Turner et al., 2006). It is thought that these early large unexpected financial gains represent positive prediction errors which result in reinforcement learning. Additionally, although wins are experienced as positive prediction errors which promote learning acquisition, financial losses, experienced as negative prediction errors, do not result in unlearning. Instead they have been attributed to promote a belief in the ability to win at some future timepoint, whilst minimising the experience of losing, an effect referred to as 'hindsight bias' (Gilovich & Douglas, 1986). Decisions made under conditions of uncertainty, with the potential for both gains and losses, have been hypothesised to be important factors in the development of gambling addiction (Redish et al., 2008).

Two of the cognitive distortions or faulty beliefs that occur in gambling disorder are referred to as the 'illusion of control' and the 'gambler's fallacy'. The increased vulnerability of some individuals to develop these cognitive distortions is exploited by the very nature and design of some gambling games. The illusion of control is a false belief that an uncontrollable outcome is somehow under the control of the individual holding this belief. This can be a belief that a level of skill is being used in a gambling game that operates entirely through chance. A study which used a gambling unrelated associative learning task to examine this belief in pathological gamblers compared to undiagnosed controls, found the illusion of control to be significantly stronger in the gambling group. This finding suggests that in pathological gamblers the illusion of control may be higher than usual in general day-to-day life, and is not only applicable to gambling contexts (Orgaz et al., 2013). The gambler's fallacy is a belief that if something occurs more frequently in a given time period, it will occur less frequently in the immediate future, when in fact the outcome is controlled entirely by random chance (Tversky & Kahneman, 1974). For example, a belief that if a coin is tossed and lands on heads numerous times in a row, it will be more likely to land on tails next time. This effect has been shown to influence gambling decisions in roulette (Croson & Sundali, 2005) and in choosing lottery numbers (Clotfelter & Cook, 1993).

Slot machines and other forms of electronic gaming machines incorporate features that may exploit inherent or situation-specific individual vulnerabilities to encourage continuous play. Two such features of these machines are 'near misses' and 'losses disguised as wins' (LDWs). An example of a near miss event is when two identical jackpot symbols appear on the payline and a third stops visibly just above or below the payline, in the type of game where three symbols are needed to line up for a win. These type of events potentially generate feelings of excitement, frustration and arousal. The fact that a near miss is often associated with increased talent, practice and skill in many real-life sporting activities, may foster and promote the faulty belief that skill is somehow involved in the 'near misses' which occur in gambling play, when in reality skill is irrelevant (with the exception of certain gambling games such as poker which requires some skill). The visual and auditory feedback that is programmed to coincide with an actual win on gambling machines, increases the physiological arousal inherent to winning, and acts as cues, resulting in classical conditioning. This may increase the desire to keep playing to re-experience these physiological effects. LDWs occur when a certain amount of money is won, but it is less than the amount that has been spent to obtain it. These smaller wins are often celebrated (e.g. excitement generating auditory and visual cues) by the gambling machine as though they are true wins.

There is some evidence to suggest that electronic gaming machines are a particularly addictive form of gambling (Breen & Zimmerman, 2002). A systematic review of the psychological, behavioural and psychobiological effects of near misses and LDWs in electronic gaming games across 51 studies, covering the years between 1991 and 2015 (Barton et al., 2017), found that near misses reliably motivate continued play but have variable effects on the player's emotional state and betting behaviour. Near misses were found to be associated with elevated physiological arousal as measured by skin conductance responses, and with diffuse activity across the brain, most consistently in brain areas processing reinforcement and reward. Analysis of near misses in relation to game feedback revealed that near miss events promote continued play as a result of their actual experience, rather than as a response to the type of machine feedback delivered when they occur. However, LDWs were found to consistently elicit player excitement, an overestimation of the amount actually won, and were always viewed as a positive event. In contrast to near misses, results suggested that the effect of LDWs were mediated by the presence of sights and sounds that were most often associated with a real win. These effects, coupled with the delivery of rewards on a variable ratio schedule of reinforcement (Skinner, 1953), lead to particularly persistent reward seeking in this type of gambling behaviour.

Evidence suggests that the insula may be a key brain region involved in the processing of cognitive distortions in gambling. This region of the brain is involved in interoception, which is the processing, representation and perception of bodily signals (Craig, 2009; Herbert & Pollatos, 2012). Selective neurological damage to the insula has been associated with selective abolition of cognitive distortions associated with gambling in an experimental study of simulated gambling involving near misses and the gambler's fallacy (Clark et al., 2014). Compared to neurological cases with damage to the ventromedial PFC and the amygdala and healthy controls, cases with insula damage failed to be motivated to continue gambling play by experiencing near misses in a slot machine game, and also failed to show the gambler's fallacy in a roulette game chosen to examine choice behaviour following red/black runs of varying lengths. It is speculated that overrecruitment of the insula region in problem gamblers may render them more vulnerable to gambling-related cognitive distortions. These types of cognitive distortions may be linked to the interoceptive processing of the physiological arousal which is experienced during gambling. In the wider context of addiction, the insula has been shown to be activated by exposure to multi-sensory drug cues and drug craving (Yalachkov et al., 2012). Damage to this region in smokers has been associated with spontaneous cessation of smoking and abolition of smoking urges (Naqvi et al., 2007). It is thought that the insula plays a role in how individuals feel and remember the experience of drug taking, and influences future decision making with regard to re-experiencing these effects (Naqvi & Bechara, 2010; Naqvi et al., 2014).

## INTERNET GAMING DISORDER: THE NEXT BEHAVIOURAL ADDICTION TO BE CLINICALLY RECOGNISED?

Aside from gambling, Internet Gaming Disorder (IGD) is the only other behavioural addiction to be seriously considered in the DSM-5. IGD is listed in section III of the DSM-5, for further research. There is already a substantial body of research on video gaming from the 1990s onwards, but the gaming research field is hampered by confusion and a lack of clarity surrounding the terminology and diagnosis of IGD. IGD has emerged as a specific behavioural manifestation from the broader syndrome of 'Internet Addiction' which refers to non-specific internet use (Young, 1998) and many of the research studies on internet gaming use this term to describe the disorder. Internet Addiction as a concept in itself is considered too heterogeneous by some researchers, and the confusion around diagnosis has led to a wide variety of measurement instuments and a lack of international consensus (Griffiths et al., 2016; Kuss et al., 2014; Kuss et al., 2016; Starcevic & Aboujaoude, 2017). As gaming can additionally occur offline, it has been argued that the terminology of IGD should also reflect this distinction (King & Delfabbro, 2013).

There is currently still a need to establish clear diagnostic criteria and definitions around 'Internet Addiction' and the multiple potentially addictive behaviours which can be accessed using the internet as a delivery mechanism. Gaming and erotica were found to be particularly important internet applications in relation to future development of compulsive internet use, in a study which compared the predictive power of various internet applications on the subsequent development of compulsive internet use after a one year follow-up (Meerkerk et al. 2006). Online social networking is also another potentially addictive behaviour for some individuals (Kuss & Griffiths, 2011).

The current DSM-5 classification of IGD bears similarities to that for gambling disorder (and therefore substance use disorders) on which it is based. A diagnosis of IGD requires the presence of five or more of the following criteria in the past 12 months:

a. Preoccupation with internet games (individual thinks about previous gaming activity or anticipates playing the next game; internet gaming becomes the predominant activity in daily life)
b. Withdrawal symptoms when the internet is taken away (typically irritability, anxiety, sadness)
c. Tolerance (the need to spend increasing amounts of time in internet games to achieve the same 'high')
d. Unsuccessful attempts to control or cut down the participation in internet games
e. Loss of interest in previously enjoyable activities with the exception of internet gaming
f. Continued excessive use despite knowledge of negative psychosocial problems
g. Has deceived family members, therapists, or others regarding time spent on gaming
h. Use of internet games to escape or improve dysphoric mood
i. Jeopardised or lost relationships, jobs, educational opportunities because of internet use

Based on a large multinational European survey of 12,938 adolescents aged between 14–17 years, prevalence rates have been estimated at around 1.6% for adolescents meeting full criteria for IGD, with a further 5.1% meeting criteria for being at risk for later development of IGD. Prevalence rates as high as 17.7% have been reported using a broader age range of 13 to 40 years in a study conducted on a sample of 1251 participants in Singapore (Subramaniam et al., 2016). In general IGD has been found to be more prevalent in some Asian countries (Zhang et al., 2008), and this increased prevalence has been partly attributed to the different sociocultural pressures facing adolescents and young people in these countries (Yen et al., 2010). A two-year prospective study on adolescents in Taiwan found that depression, ADHD, social phobia and hostility were signifiicant predictors for later development of IGD at a two year follow-up (Ko et al., 2009). Massively Multiplayer Online Role Player Games (MMORPGs) such as World of Warcraft are thought to be particularly risky for the development of IGD. These types of games provide a degree of social support for players, which poses particular problems for a minority who play excessively and who lack social support in real life (Longman et al., 2009).

Internet gaming shares certain features in common with gambling, including physiological arousal (Borusiak et al., 2008), potential for both losses and gains during play, and unpredictability of outcome. Although a level of skill is required in gaming, there is a potential risk for gamers who also gamble to start to believe that skill is being used in random outcome gambling games, and they may be prone to the same cognitive distortions described above for gamblers (Robbins & Clark, 2015). Attentional bias for gaming cues and diminished gaming-related response inhibition have also been demonstrated in adolescent problem gamers, which indicates that problem gaming potentially shares similarities with substance use disorders and gambling disorder with regard to the underlying cognitive motivational mechanisms that influence addictive behaviour (van Holst et al., 2012).

There is evidence to show striatal dopamine release occurs during video game play (Koepp et al., 1998), and individuals with internet addiction have been shown to have reduced dopamine receptor availability in the striatum compared to controls (Kim et al., 2011). Further evidence for the potential classification of IGD as a behavioural addiction is provided by a meta-analysis of ten fMRI studies of individuals with IGD compared to healthy controls, which revealed prefrontal dysfunctions in brain regions associated with reward and self-regulation, as has been similiarly observed in substance use and gambling disorder (Meng et al., 2015).

All too often the phrase 'I am addicted to the internet/my phone' is used. Technology is often blamed for a new generation of problems. What will be interesting in the future will be to see what the speed of delivery of information via fast phone signals and broadband technology brings. In Chapter 2 we saw that the speed that a drug gets to the brain is as important

# ADDICTION

as what it does when it gets there. To feel the high from cocaine means it is delivered quickly. Similarly, technology has permitted the delivery of information and interactions with others and websites to be almost instantaneous. No longer is there the wait for a slow conection. This speed of delivery may well be as important as the content (whether it is gambling, pornography, shopping or gaming).

## SUMMARY

- This chapter has reveiwed gambling disorder as the prototypical behavioural addiction and presented evidence for the commonalities that it shares with substance use disorders.
- What is clear is that learning processes are critically important in the development of both substance and non-substance addictions.
- A large body of cumulative evidence highlights the shared psychological and biological underpinnings of substance use and gambling addictions.
- Gambling also has particular features not shared with substance use disorders, including gambling-related cognitive distortions and the unique features of gambling games that help to drive continued play, such as near misses, and losses disguised as wins.
- Future research will clarify which other behavioural addictions may be classified alongside gambling and substance use as addictive disorders, with evidence accumulating for internet gaming to be classified as a behavioural addiction.
- What may be perceived as pathological internet use varies with historical and cultural context, and the rapid expansion and development of digital technology in recent times is bound to have an impact on human behaviour in ways that are currently poorly understood.
- As internet use has become so prevalent and necessary in the lives of the vast majority of people, it will become increasingly important to continue to carry out research to clarify what constitutes 'internet addiction' and addictions to various behaviours accessed through the internet as a portal, such as gambling and internet gaming, as well as other potential behavioural addictions such as pornography and shopping.

## QUESTIONS

1. What similarities are there between gambling and drug addiction?
2. Is problematic gambling an addiction?
3. Can one become addicted to the internet?
4. What are the risk factors for gambling problems?
5. What is the impact of problematic gambling on cognitive processes?

# SOCIETY, POLICY, LAW AND ETHICS

# 9

## CHAPTER OVERVIEW

This chapter places addiction in the difficult and opiniated world of policy, law and society. As a society we adhere (or not) to the common rules of the land. However, rules can change, and the war on drugs that has been waged for over four decades has still not been won. And, as with military wars, the war on drugs has cost billions in its lifetime.

This chapter will:

- Provide a description of the legislation in place in the UK
- Look at alternative methods of managing the drug trade
- Place drug taking in the big context of societies and politics

ADDICTION

> **LEARNING AIMS OF THE CHAPTER**

- To gain an overview of current drug policy in the UK
- To understand the complexity associated with ensuring a workable drug policy
- To appreciate how some countries are choosing to tackle their drug problems

# INTRODUCTION

In the past century there has been a dramatic shift towards viewing drug taking as a legal and moral issue and thus the worlds of drugs and crime have become inexplicably tied together on a global scale. It is therefore easy to forget that, relatively speaking, the prohibition of drugs is a new phenomenon. As long as there have been humans, there has existed a desire within humans to experiment with chemically induced states of mind (Pryce, 2012). The motives for this are diverse; in many ancient cultures substances were used in the context of a spiritual ceremony – Native Americans' use of peyote, and the Aztecs' use of psychedelic mushrooms to give two examples (Clark, 1968). In fact even in Western civilisation, reference can be found to a drug that sounds a lot like LSD in Plato's *The Laws* (Clark, 1968).

For some, however, substances have always been used to anesthetise or escape. Aldous Huxley writes of how 'most men and women lead lives at the worst so painful, at the best so monotonous, poor and limited that the urge to escape, the longing to transcend themselves if only for a few moments, is and has always been one of the principal appetites of the soul' (Huxley, 1954). In a chronic addict we see this behaviour repeated over and over again. Despite the often destructive effects of the substance on the user, they are often prepared to 'jeopardize their lives for the sake of making the moment liveable' (Maté, 2008, p. 28).

The logic of jeopardising one's life for the sake of momentary relief does not stand up very well to a cost benefit analysis, and this point is at the very heart of why tackling drug addiction is so very difficult. Addicts often do not act in a rational, self-interested manner, or at least not a manner that appears to be. There is a logic at work but it is a logic that is warped by the insidious hold that addiction has; Orford talks of 'the ability of addiction to blur the picture, hide its real intentions and mask its power' (Orford, 2013: p. 52). Thus, behavioural theories such as control theory struggle to explain the behaviour of an addict – such a logic would expect that legal sanctions imposed upon a drug user would deter them from future use (Orford, 2013). Yet one only need look at the prison population of the UK (85,975 at the time of writing), full to capacity with addicts and people involved in drug-related crime, to know that when it comes to addiction this does not work.

The link between certain crimes and drugs is evident, but there are many crimes driven by drugs where the link is less obvious. For example, it is rather obvious that repeated offences for drug possession are being driven by addiction. But a huge proportion of acquisitive crime such as theft, burglary and robbery is also being driven by addiction. Then there are the crimes committed by people under the influence of drugs, which account for many violent and sexual crimes, although here correlation does not signify causation necessarily. Then, of course, there are the crimes that are not driven by addiction to drugs but are tied to drug distribution. Possession of drugs with intent to supply, conspiracy to supply drugs and importation offences are the obvious, but drug feuds are the fuel for many violent crimes, gang violence and firearm offences. Basic market principles of supply and demand dictate that as long as there is a demand for drugs there will be a supply, and as the demand for drugs from populations has never abated, neither has the supply and neither have these offences. Thus, prison populations continue to rise.

Whilst there are intrinsic harms associated with drug use from a mental and physical health perspective, it is important to recognise that the social harms caused by drugs largely stem from our legal and societal construction of drugs. Such harms stem from the big business opportunity that drugs represent due to the aforementioned large-scale demand for them, and in turn how governments have chosen to tackle the issue. Despite this being the case there is a deeply pervasive notion that runs through our population that 'drugs are bad'. This will be explored further below, but if we are to develop an evidence-based, rational drug policy, it is vital to shed such abstract notions and look purely at facts.

The global drugs market is a very complex web involving a huge number of individuals, syndicates, governments and motives at work. This 'colossal illicit market' has numerous players, some who have much to gain and many who have much to lose (Orford, 2013: 157). Richard Nixon famously declared a war on drugs in 1971 (Nixon, 1971), and this approach has continued to be adopted in countries such as the UK and USA since. As it is often accepted that 'drugs are bad' and that 'bad should be criminalised', it is therefore also accepted that 'drugs should be criminalised'. But we need to question whether this is a winnable war, and who exactly the war is being fought against. For invariably, as in all wars, it is the foot soldiers not the generals who are the primary victims (Maté, 2008).

It is important to bear in mind that the legal issues surrounding drugs and addiction cannot be seen in isolation; a number of authors have contended that these problems are part of a wider picture. Orford describes a 'broader system of noxious social conditions that spread along vectors of disadvantage' (Orford, 2013: 127). Meanwhile Bruce Alexander's research has elucidated that dislocation is a major factor (Alexander, 2010). Gabor Maté has described addiction as being inherent across society, the drug addicts he worked with simply being the most severe representation. Maté poses the question 'why do we despise, ostracize and punish the drug addict when as a social collective we share the same blindness and engage in the same rationalizations?' (Maté, 2008).

We would argue that the modern approach of prohibition of drugs has been an abject failure. This is a view that is supported by much evidence, along with a growing amount of academic opinion, which sees our present drug laws as somewhat arbitrary and based on very little evidence (Nutt et al., 2007). Drug policy is a hugely nuanced and complicated issue however, and there are myriad considerations to take into account when looking at what a rational drug policy in the UK would look like.

This section will begin by exploring what the present system is, and some of the ways in which it is unfit for purpose. Some recent events – such as the sacking of David Nutt and the epidemic of New Psychoactive Substances or 'legal highs' – will be focused on as examples of ways in which the law is deeply flawed as a way of maintaining order or protecting the public. The implications of taking a different path will be subsequently addressed, e.g. decriminalisation and legalisation. Furthermore, the potential medical uses for certain illegal drugs requires careful consideration and is fraught with political input. Finally, drawing on all of the above, an attempt to suggest what a rational drug policy might look like, whilst acknowledging that any answer to this question will be incomplete and flawed, will be addressed.

# THE PRESENT UK DRUG LAWS: UNFIT FOR PURPOSE?

## A GLOBAL PERSPECTIVE

Far from being confined to the UK, the prevailing attitude towards drugs as something that can be fought and defeated by criminal sanctions is almost worldwide. On a global scale UK drug laws can be found to be somewhere in between the more liberal and more hardline attitudes.

There are countries in which drug traffickers, and at times even those in possession of narcotics, receive draconian prison sentences or are even executed (Greenwald, 2009). These countries often do have lower rates of drug use, but at the huge cost of losing human rights and essentially living in a police state. Whilst it is popular amongst certain commentators to state that the war on drugs has only failed because we haven't been tough enough, we are sceptical about how many of these commentators would actually like to live in a society which infringed on civil liberties to that extreme.

At the opposite end of the spectrum in terms of drug laws is Portugal, which has since 2001 decriminalised all drugs and taken an approach that prioritises public health concerns (Greenwald, 2009). To date the present evidence indicates this policy has been successful. Some countries in South America have also taken similar steps, with Uruguay legalising cannabis and Brazil and Argentina increasingly moving towards a framework of decriminalisation. The argument has been postulated that it is in the countries where the negative effects of the war on drugs have been felt most acutely that there has been a drive for reform, because it becomes blatantly obvious to the public that the war is failing, and thus there is no choice but to look for other solutions.[1] This has certainly been the case with regard to all of the above countries.

But in the UK, where the bleakest consequences of the war on drugs can be pushed underground to some extent,[2] we are a long way from such a change. A marked double standard exists in the minds of many people in our society between drugs that are legal such as alcohol and tobacco and drugs that are illegal; some might argue that whilst certain drugs such as alcohol are almost socially encouraged, certain drugs are demonised (Orford, 2013). There is an idea that certain drugs are morally bad, and thus accordingly those who use them are *'bad people'*. This perhaps goes some way to explaining why legislators are not following where the evidence is pointing. For politicians to suggest decriminalisation or legalisation of drugs is risky in terms of securing votes in the UK.

## UK DRUG LAWS AT PRESENT

Present drug laws in the UK draw upon three primary pieces of legislation; the *Medicines Act 1968*, the *Misuse of Drugs Act 1971*, and most recently, the *New Psychoactive Substances Act 2016*. It is largely the latter two that are relevant to our present discussion.

The Misuse of Drugs Act divides drugs into three categories of harmfulness, A–C, with A being the drugs that parliament believes are most harmful and C the least.

> Class A drugs include Heroin, Cocaine, MDMA (ecstasy), LSD, Psilocybin and Methamphetamine.

---

[1] www.theguardian.com/commentisfree/2009/sep/03/drugs-prohibition-latin-america

[2] www.theguardian.com/commentisfree/2009/sep/03/drugs-prohibition-latin-america

Class B drugs include Amphetamines, Ketamine, Cannabis and Codeine

Class C drugs include Benzodiazepines, GHB and Anabolic Steroids

There are numerous offences surrounding drugs outlined in the Misuse of Drugs Act such as:

- possession of a controlled drug
- possession with intent to supply another person
- production, cultivation or manufacture of controlled drugs
- supplying another person with a controlled drug
- offering to supply another person with a controlled drug
- import or export of controlled drugs
- allowing premises you occupy or manage to be used for the consumption of certain controlled drugs (smoking of cannabis or opium but not use of other controlled drugs) or supply or production of any controlled drug

We will not go through the sentencing guidelines for each of these, but we will focus on the first two offences on that list: possession of a controlled drug, and possession with intent to supply another person.

For possession the guidelines are as follows:

**Table 9.1** Sentencing guidelines for possession

| | |
|---|---|
| CLASS A | Maximum: 7 years custody |
| | Range: Fine – 51 weeks custody |
| CLASS B | Maximum: 5 years custody |
| | Range: Discharge – 26 weeks custody |
| CLASS C | Maximum: 2 years custody |
| | Range: Discharge – Community order |

For possession with intent to supply the guidelines are as follows:

**Table 9.2** Sentencing guidelines for possession with intent to supply

| CLASS A | Maximum: Life imprisonment |
| --- | --- |
|  | Range: Community order – 16 years custody |
| CLASS B | Maximum: 14 years custody and/or unlimited fine |
|  | Range: Fine – 10 years custody |
| CLASS C | Maximum: 14 years custody and/or unlimited fine |
|  | Range: Fine – 8 years custody |

It can be seen from the above tables that these offences have an extremely wide range. There are a number of steps judges take to determine the culpability of an offender. Firstly, they will determine the offence category; they will then look at the aggravating and mitigating factors of any given offender. Finally, there may be reductions for guilty pleas and time spent on remand. In practice, the maximum sentences for these offences are rarely passed. It would be extremely unlikely that someone would ever be sentenced to seven years in custody for possessing a Class A drug.[3] Whilst the UK is certainly a long way from decriminalisation it could be said that in terms of policing there has been a move towards depenalisation for possession of drugs, certainly those of the lower categories. It could be argued that the very fact the law is often not put into practice goes some way to suggest that it is flawed. Why would judges not sentence according to guidelines otherwise?

## THE CASE OF DAVID NUTT

As stated above, drug classification is supposed to be based on the level of harm caused. However, the law's current categorisation bears little correlation with how experts have scored the relative harm caused by different drugs, and in fact seems to have a level of disregard for expert opinion on the subject. One of the clearest indications of this is the treatment of David Nutt, formerly the Chairperson of the Advisory Council on the Misuse of drugs, more informally known as the 'drugs czar'.

David Nutt was consistently critical of drug laws in the UK, and was sacked for his criticisms of the government toughening its stance on cannabis, as well as claims that MDMA and LSD are less harmful than alcohol.

---

[3] The same cannot be said in the USA; see www.huffingtonpost.com/entry/bernard-noble-marijuana_us_55b6b838e4b0074ba5a5e160

David Nutt and colleagues conducted an extensive study which attempted to rank drugs by their harmfulness (Nutt, King, Phillips, & Independent Scientific Committee on Drugs, 2010). Of course, this is not an easy task, since drugs can cause myriad types of harm. For example, nicotine has a proven destructive effect on physical health but limited psychoactive effects. LSD, on the other hand, is physically almost harmless but could have psychological effects so great as to cause a user extreme psychological distress. Because of this complexity ranking drugs by level of harm will always be difficult, but this study took into account the wide range of harms listed below:

*Drug-specific mortality*: how intrinsically lethal the drug is, in terms of the ratio between lethal dose and recreational dose

*Drug-related mortality*: how likely the drug is to shorten a user's life in other ways, such as long-term illness or road traffic accidents

*Drug-specific damage*: damage to physical health

*Drug-related damage*: consequences such as STIs and damage from cutting agents

*Dependence*: how addictive the drug is

*Drug specific impairment of mental functioning*: impairment of mental functioning

*Loss of Tangibles*: how likely the drug is to cause loss of home, employment etc.

*Loss of relationships*: the drug causing damage to relationships (friendships, romantic, family etc.)

*Injury*: likelihood of causing serious injury

*How much the drug leads users into crime*: how likely the drug is to lead the user into the world of crimes other than the drug taking itself, such as acquisitive crime

*Environmental damage*: extent to which the drug causes damage to the local environment, e.g. heroin needles ending up littered around a neighbourhood

*Family adversity*: extent to which the drug can lead to family problems such as child neglect

*International Damage*: extent to which use of the drug in the UK has ripple effects internationally

*Damage to Community*: the extent to which the drug creates a decline in social cohesion

The scores of the drugs are calculated such that a drug with a harm rating of 100 is classified as doubly as harmful as a drug with a rating of 50. A discussion of the methodology used in the study can be found in Nutt et al.'s (2010) paper.

## SOCIETY, POLICY, LAW AND ETHICS

The results of the study can be seen in Figure 9.1. Perhaps the most striking aspect of this figure is that alcohol was found to be the most harmful drug, despite its legality, with a score of 72. This should not necessarily lead us to jump to the conclusion that alcohol is categorically the most dangerous drug; factors relating to its legality and place in our society may have an effect on the level of harmfulness suggested here. Even factoring this in, however, its position certainly highlights a double standard in policies for different drugs.

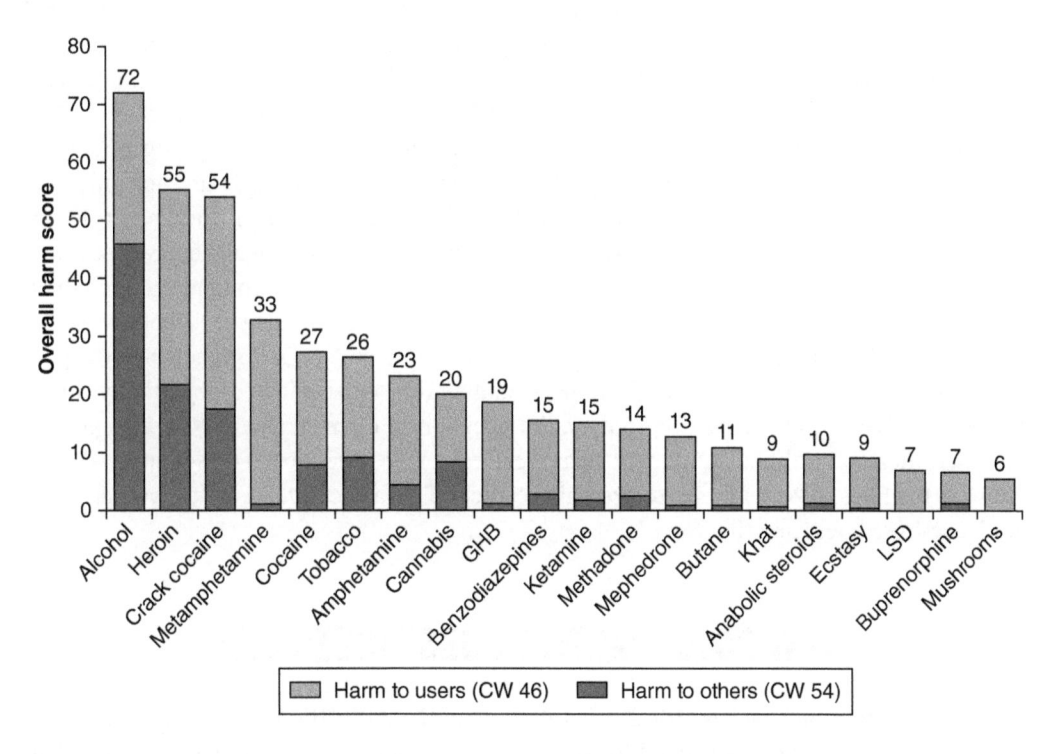

**Figure 9.1** Drugs ordered by their overall harm scores, showing the separate contributions to the overall scores of harms to users and harm to others The weights after normalisation (0–100) are shown in the key (cumulative in the sense of the sum of all the normalised weights for all the criteria to users, 46; and for all the criteria to others, 54). CW=cumulative weight. GHB=γ hydroxybutyric acid. LSD=lysergic acid diethylamide. From Nutt, D. J., King, L. A., Phillips, L. D., & Independent Scientific Committee on, D. (2010). Drug harms in the UK: a multicriteria decision analysis. *Lancet*, 376(9752), 1558–1565. doi:10.1016/S0140-6736(10)61462-6

The same double standard is also evident for tobacco, which is ranked just behind heroin, crack cocaine, methamphetamine and cocaine. The Class A drugs ecstasy (MDMA), LSD and Magic Mushrooms (psilocybin mushroom) make up three of the lowest four, scoring 9, 7 and 6 respectively. According to this system of categorisation, alcohol poses 12 times the level of harm that Magic Mushrooms do, and eight times the level of harm over that of ecstasy (MDMA).

It is hard not to be somewhat surprised by aspects of these results, and it should be noted that theory does not always correlate to practice. There can be no doubt that taking a dose of LSD or Magic Mushrooms could have more dangerous knock-on effects than having a pint of beer. This is arguably because we live in a society which is not designed for LSD use but has fully integrated alcohol. Assessing drug harms becomes even more complex when context begins to be factored in. But looking specifically at the actual harms caused by drugs, these findings were not a revelation and echo much previous research, including research conducted by UK experts and the Dutch addiction medicine expert group (Nutt et al., 2010). Having said this it is important to state that Nutt's views are not universal amongst experts and have been critiqued at times by other academics such as Professor Andy Parrott, who has published extensively on the psychobiological harms associated with MDMA use (e.g. Parrott, 2013a, 2013b). As has been stated throughout the chapter, this is an issue too complex to suggest there is a right or wrong answer. When taken out of context and sensationalised by the popular press, some of Nutt's statements can appear to be irresponsible, whereas they do remain challenging when viewed objectively. From the perspective of improving drug policy, the decision to dismiss David Nutt appeared to be based more on political sentiment than clear scientific evidence. The scientific debate between the likes of Nutt and Parrott remains critical if, as a society, we are to progress with evidence-based best practice.

## NEW PSYCHOACTIVE SUBSTANCES BILL

The Psychoactive Substances Bill 2015–16 was introduced in the House of Commons on 21 July 2015. It received its Second Reading on 19 October 2015 to introduce a blanket ban on the production, supply, and possession with the intent to supply, and import and export of, psychoactive substances. Alcohol and nicotine were excluded, despite the fact that the death toll these drugs account for far exceeds all deaths from the new psychoactive substances (NPS) combined.

This bill followed approximately ten years of chaos where new drugs were constantly springing up with a chemical formula which circumvented existing drug laws, but created effects as powerful and at times even more powerful than their illegal counterparts. This would be followed by attempts to ban the drug, which would eventually be successful. But by that time a new drug would have hit the market, and so the cycle went on.

'Legal highs' have been around for a long time. Walking around the stalls in London's Camden Market in the early 2000s one was greeted with a wide range of different herbal mixtures in clear plastic bags promising to be powerful alternatives to cannabis. There as an array of colourful pills and powders too, promising to replicate the effects of drugs like MDMA, cocaine and LSD. But no one took much notice of them, other than perhaps tourists or teenagers unable to access illegal drugs. They were largely considered a joke.

It was mephedrone which kick-started the modern era of legal highs which eventually ended in the New Psychoactive Substances Bill. Far from being regarded as a joke, mephedrone became the drug of choice for many, and a media-driven moral panic ensued.

To understand why mephedrone captured a market and took off in the way it did, it is important to see the bigger picture of what was going on in the War on Drugs at this time. In 2008, 33 tonnes of Safrole were seized and destroyed by Cambodian authorities. Safrole is a vital precursor involved in the production of MDMA, and thus it is estimated that this one seizure prevented the synthesis of what would have been the equivalent of $8 billion worth of MDMA. This had a huge impact on the quality of MDMA being sold around the world and together with at around the same time a large decrease in cocaine purity. For several periods in time MDMA was only a small ingredient, or not present at all, in ecstasy (Parrott, 2004), and in 2010 most 'MDMA' seized by authorities didn't actually contain any MDMA at all. The correlation between established drugs becoming increasingly impure and of poor quality and the rise of the purer legal highs would seem obvious. The effects of mephedrone are usually described as being somewhere in between the loving, empathogenic serotonin rush of MDMA and the dopamine-based pleasure and drive that cocaine bestows on a user (Winstock et al., 2011). Even more grave a consequence of the Safrole seizure was a spike in PMA use. This is a drug with similar effects to MDMA, but it is far more dangerous in terms of the dose needed to have fatal consequences.

David Nutt (2011) has put forth the interesting viewpoint that whilst there were deaths related to mephedrone use, there would have been far more deaths if the drug was not popular at the time because people would have used the more dangerous drugs of amphetamines or cocaine instead. Nutt estimated that mephedrone may have prevented more than 300 deaths from cocaine and amphetamine while it was legal. Since it has been banned the fall in cocaine-related deaths has reversed. Amphetamine-related deaths have also risen, and there has been a *resurgence* in MDMA use. This may also be linked to an increase in the purity of these drugs, but it is an interesting perspective that the 'success' that banning a particular drug brings truly needs to be viewed in the context of a broader picture.

Following the banning of mephedrone a range of other legal highs sprung up to take its place. In terms of the stimulants, many contained Methiopropamine (MPA), a structural analogue of Methamphetamine, and/or Ethylphenidate, a dopamine reuptake inhibitor closely resembling Methylphenidate (e.g. Ritalin). These chemicals would be sold in a range of colourful packets, with names such as 'China White', 'Chalk' and 'Gogaine'. Meanwhile synthetic cannabinoids were also on the rise, sold under names such as 'Spice' and 'Black Mamba'. These drugs were sold in *head shops*. They contained labels stating 'Not for human consumption', and vendors would refuse to give out any information about how to take the drug or what a safe dose was. Thus, what was going on was the diametric opposite of a harm reduction policy.

In *Blueprint for Regulation*, a publication by Transform, the possibility of a 'pharmacy model' of legalisation is discussed, where drugs could be acquired from a pharmacist (Rolles & McClure, 2009). Some drugs might need a prescription, and others would require that the purchaser be informed of the risks of the drug and advised how to take it safely. This is in fact the model already being used for cannabis in Uruguay (Walsh & Ramsey, 2016). Such a model can be contrasted with the incredibly dangerous model operated by the head shops. This is the danger that comes with pushing drugs underground and not regulating them. The demand does not change, but the risks increase.

Whilst the 'legal high' stimulants were generally regarded to be weaker and inferior to their illegal counterparts, the same was not true of the synthetic cannabinoids, which were significantly stronger and more addictive than cannabis. These drugs became particularly popular in prisons and amongst homeless people, and use has not abated since the New Psychoactive Substances Bill came in. In many UK prisons at present 'spice attacks', where users lose consciousness entirely and need to be rushed to hospital, are a frequent occurrence.

Going back to basic principles of supply and demand, stimulant 'legal highs' have largely ceased to exist since the NPS Bill, but the only change that appears to have occurred with spice is that it has become even more dangerous as producers try to find ever more ingenious ways of getting it into prisons.

Afron Jones, the Police and Crime Commissioner for Wrexham, a UK town heavily affected by legal highs, said of the problem: 'Personally, I think the situation has got worse. The psychoactive substances act has had unintended consequences in sending the problem underground. I am not saying everything was hunky dory when we had head shops selling on the high street, but the government missed a trick in not regulating the head shops, rather than prohibiting the psychoactive substances'.[4]

---

[4]www.theguardian.com/uk-news/2017/aug/06/spice-ban-prisoners-homeless-at-risk-drug-goes-underground

# A PHILOSOPHICAL REFLECTION ON OUR PRESENT DRUG LAWS

The concept of natural law is based on the idea of distinguishing what is intrinsically right from what is intrinsically wrong and is thus rooted in an a priori morality. In a Hobbesian model of social contract theory, the people governed under any jurisdiction have collectively agreed to give up a level of autonomy in order to follow such laws and escape from the 'war of all against all'. It should be the case theoretically that it is the law that sets out what is right and wrong and the people then derive their ideas of morality from this. At present, however, there is the curious situation where the law derives its morality from public sentiment; it is reactive rather than instructive.

If the law is being derived from public views on morality and not vice versa, we then have to consider where people are deriving their sense of morality from? What is the driving force behind this hugely powerful and pervasive idea that does not question whether the criminalisation of drugs is working?

Some might argue that religious views influence attitudes towards drugs, for historically along with law, this has been the second pillar from where people derive their sense of morality. But the power of religion in the modern age is waning. Furthermore, there is little to be found in the way of outlawing drugs in religious texts, and in fact going back to the roots of many religions, there is evidence of drugs being used in a spiritual context. Many anti-drug crusaders in the modern age are religious and do base their stance on their religious belief, but it can be argued that this is a moral interpretation that is a posteriori to religion itself. It is not within religion that this idea of drugs as immoral has its roots.

This conflation of drugs as a moral issue, and drug users as inherently morally wrong, also may have a problematic knock-on effect. In his famous work *Outsiders: Studies on the Sociology of Deviance*, sociologist Howard Becker demonstrated that deviance is the 'product of a process which involves other people's responses to the behaviour' (Becker, 1963: 9) rather than it being an inherent quality. Becker attaches much significance to the way in which labelling can amplify deviance, using an example very relevant to our present discussion – that of a heroin addict. The act of using heroin is generally harmful only to the user themself, but because of the social condemnation surrounding such a habit, they would be likely to lose their employment if exposed. It is highly likely that, if unemployed, they would end up involved in other areas of crime in order to fund their habit, and possibly end up incarcerated. But it was the social condemnation rather than the original habit that directly led to this outcome (Becker, 1963: 34), and thus it was the process of condemnation that actualised the deviance.

Furthermore, if we take the idea that drug users are often the 'hungry ghosts' that Gabor Maté (2008) talks of, people who already experience a feeling of being othered and isolated, the fact that they are then labelled deviant may only serve to further amplify such feelings, thus increasing their desire to use drugs and thus increasing their 'deviance', and so the cycle goes on.

Stanley Cohen coined the term 'moral panic' and defined this as 'a condition, episode, person or group of persons emerges to become defined as a threat to societal values and interests' (Cohen, 2011: 9). Moral panics perhaps represent this process of othering on a large scale. We used the phrase to describe the media's attitude towards the rise of mephedrone, but this is just the most recent in a long line of moral panics about different drugs. Cohen has pointed out that since 'values and interests' is a matter of politics and economics in itself, the determination of what constitutes moral panic is also determined by these factors. Thus, complex as the issues at stake here are, we perhaps begin to see some kind of answer as to why the government continues to blindly follow a drug strategy unfit for purpose.

## NEW WAYS FORWARD: DECRIMINALISE OR LEGALISE?

To anyone who spends some time examining the evidence, it is rather clear that the war on drugs is failing. What is not so obvious is what exactly the way forward should be. As previously mentioned, some countries in South America have moved towards decriminalisation, and in some cases even the legalisation of '*softer*' drugs such as cannabis. As these are relatively recent developments, however, there is not a plethora of research on the results and it is difficult to measure what the long-term results will be.

It is also important to consider that different approaches may yield different results in different countries, given the widely different cultures. For example, we are about to examine Portugal in more depth, which is arguably the case closest to a success that exists. However, one must consider that the culture of the UK differs radically from Portuguese culture. One difference is the fact that family and community play a far greater role in Mediterranean culture than they do in UK or US culture.

It is unwise to jump to conclusions about what will and will not work; there is no clear-cut solution to this question. Having said that, it is prudent to follow where the evidence points, rather than continue to pursue the same arbitrary policies which guarantee failure. One should note what Albert Einstein is often quoted as saying: 'The definition of insanity is doing the same thing over and over again, but expecting different results'.

## PORTUGAL: A CASE STUDY OF DECRIMINALISATION

On July 1, 2001, the decriminalisation of all drugs became enshrined into Portuguese law.[5] This meant that drug possession for personal use remained illegal, but violations of those prohibitions were now to be 'deemed to be exclusively administrative violations and are removed completely from the criminal realm' (Greenwald, 2009: 1). Drug trafficking continues to be prosecuted as a criminal offense (Greenwald, 2009).

As was mentioned above, the political impetus for decriminalisation was far from a desire to be 'soft on drugs' or downplay their dangers. The decision to decriminalise was driven by the fact that drug abuse and all the social problems that accompany it were becoming destructive to an uncontrollable extent, and a growing view that 'the principal obstacles to effective government policies to manage the problems were the treatment barriers and resource drain imposed by the criminalization regime' (Greenwald, 2009: 6). Criminalisation was seen as hindering efforts to tackle drugs rather than aiding them, and recommendations to decriminalise were made in a 1998 report on the subject. Stated simply, the point of decriminalisation was to reduce drug use and abuse (Orford, 2013).

This shift in the law has been almost universally lauded as a success, with only a small number of politicians entertaining a debate about whether the 2001 law should be repealed. None of 'the nightmare scenarios touted by pre-enactment decriminalization opponents' have occurred, such as 'rampant increases in drug usage among the young' and 'the transformation of Lisbon into a haven for drug tourists' (Greenwald, 2009: 1). In reality, 'decriminalization has had no adverse effect on drug usage rates in Portugal, which, in numerous categories, are now among the lowest in the EU', and 'drug-related pathologies—such as sexually transmitted diseases and deaths due to drug usage—have decreased dramatically' (Greenwald, 2009: 1).

This shift in the law has not occurred in isolation, it is important to note. It has been accompanied by an increase in treatment offered to addicts, and a broader shift towards viewing drugs as a public health issue. In practical terms, decriminalisation 'freed up resources that could be channelled into treatment and other harm reduction programs' (Greenwald, 2009: 9). It is also noteworthy that one of the reasons cited for the change in law's success is that far more addicts are now seeking treatment because the stigma of being a drug addict has dramatically lessened since the change in law, and addicts no longer fear being criminalised. In the previous section we looked theoretically at how the stigmatising and othering of addicts can be destructive; in Portugal we can see an actual example of the opposite occurring. The closeness of community in a country such as Portugal may have been a contributing factor as to why this stigma represented a major barrier; under decriminalisation that can be turned into a positive, with people more likely to reach out to the support networks around them.

---

[5]Article 2(1), Constitution of Portugal

Around the world it is clear that criminalisation is having destructive effects in terms of public health; in the present day, injecting drug use accounts for 30% of HIV infections outside sub-Saharan Africa (Rolles & McClure, 2009). It is often the unsafe conditions drugs are taken in that account for the health issues they create, and thus Maté (2008) has called the idea of regulating these conditions and keeping them safe as 'the indispensable foundation of a rational stance toward drug addiction'; this can only be done by decriminalisation.

As can be seen from Portugal there are direct and indirect reasons why this would have such a positive impact on the health of addicts. There would be reduced infection and disease transmission, less risk of overdose and more regular access to medical care, which addicts would be more likely to make use of due to less fear of stigmatisation, and thus improved health. If addicts did not have to purchase drugs at inflated prices then there would be less likelihood of their turning to crime, violence or prostitution to fund their habit (Maté, 2008). This would benefit the whole of society, as well as drastically reducing the number of inmates in the currently overflowing prison system. Rather than further isolating a group of people who often already feel othered, such a step would also help addicts reintegrate into the community, which is essential for their rehabilitation.

The decriminalisation of drugs can bring about a number of positive effects and drastically reduce harm; however, there are problems that decriminalisation would not solve. Decriminalisation legitimises drug use itself, but it still keeps drugs on the black market. As long as drugs are still on the black market the global implications remain similar. Furthermore, power is still ultimately in the hands of actors on the black market. For example, a contradiction that in part prompted Uruguay's shift from decriminalisation to legalisation was that whilst possession of a small amount of the drug was not punishable, cultivation was still illegal. Thus, rather than being able to grow their own plants, Uruguayans had to purchase their drugs from criminal actors who were often also involved in the cocaine trade.[6]

## LEGALISATION

Though it is true that some legal corporations exploit workers in third world countries and make extortionate profits, there at least theoretically exists some level of regulation regarding treatment of workers. Even where this does not exist there is some framework in place

---

[6]John Walsh and Geoff Ramsey, *Uruguay's Drug Policy: Major Innovations, Major Challenges*, Center for 21st Century Security and Intelligence Latin America Initiative, p. 3 www.brookings.edu/wp-content/uploads/2016/07/Walsh-Uruguay-final.pdf

that would allow for its implementation. Only by bringing drugs entirely above board and regulating them would such global problems be circumvented. The total lack of any regulation whatsoever under criminalisation means that extreme brutality can occur. As Orford (2013: 158) puts it, 'the exercise of power is more naked'.

Legalisation can broadly be divided into a state monopoly model and a free market deregulation model. An example of a state monopoly is present day Uruguay, where cannabis is now legalised but regulated and controlled by the state. Full free market deregulation can be seen most clearly with regard to alcohol and tobacco around the majority of the world. Legalised cannabis in Colorado and Washington in the USA is also far less regulated than in Uruguay, and perhaps represents the clearest example of a usually illegal drug on the free market.[7]

State regulated legalisation would appear the safer of the two options, however one could argue that the government has a duty to legislate in some protective way on drugs since research shows the issue of addiction has a greater impact on those who struggle socio-economically. This is a major flaw with the idea of a state regulated market (Orford, 2013: 99), particularly for the most harmful of drugs such as methamphetamine, cocaine and heroin. To have a government who pass the laws and are theoretically supposed to be arbiters of morality making money from taxing drugs which cause massive socio-economic problems would arguably cause them to be seriously delegitimised. Perhaps a bigger obstacle to this model of legalisation is the neoliberal ideology of every successive UK and US government since the late 1970s. Since we are now living in an age where everything from railways to prisons to hospitals is moving towards the private sector, it is difficult to imagine drugs would not also be in the hands of the private sector.

Free market legalisation brings with it a far greater array of problems, though; we need look no further than the alcohol, tobacco and gambling industries to see this. The way that black market drug dealers operate, and the way that some legitimate corporations operate, are in fact incredibly similar. Both are driven entirely by a desire for profit and are prepared to do whatever is necessary to obtain this end. They differ in how they do so, but both are morally dubious. The problem with legalising drugs is that since the law and morality are often seen as synonymous by the public, it will be easy for the public to be duped by corporations into harmful use of drugs. Corporations would be free to 'aggressively promote consumption' (Rolles & McClure, 2009: 19), and if it were in the interests of big business to promote drug addiction, then there might well eventually be a paradigm shift from the moralistic stances on drugs that run through society today to an attitude towards all drugs that resembles our attitude to alcohol and, in the past, tobacco. One must always remember that

---

[7]Ibid., p. 9.

a corporation, although bound to abide by legislation, is by the very nature of its structure bound to prioritise maximising profits for shareholders. And thus, in some respects at least, free market legalisation of drugs has the potential to perhaps be even more dangerous than criminal markets if our end goal is harm reduction.

The best way to illustrate the potential dangers of full-scale free market legalisation is to explore how toxic the alcohol industry has been in setting its desired agenda. Its power is extremely far reaching. Taking a Gramscian view on what it is to wield power, power is most effectively exercised not through brute force but in a way which is invisible. By setting the agenda, by controlling the discussions that are had, and by becoming so insidious and omnipresent you are no longer seen to wield power; it simply becomes the status quo. In Gramsci's image of the 'power centaur', this is the human face that obtains the consent of the victim to be controlled, all the while backed up by the animal body of force. In the criminalised drug industry, the animal body is the dominating feature; arguably in legal industries, this is hidden by the cloak of legitimacy, the human face.

The alcohol industry has not been afraid to use this force in the past where necessary. In 1840 Father Matthew was making considerable progress with alcoholics in Ireland, advocating abstinence-based recovery and encouraging the people he was working with to take pledges, in what could be seen as an early forerunner of the model which eventually became Alcoholics Anonymous and twelve-step programmes. When he tried to extend his work to England, however, the meetings he organised were broken up by representatives. In the present day, though, the tactics employed are often far subtler. Orford (2013) writes about five key narratives that industries such as the alcohol and gambling industries use to influence public opinion. These are:

*The Harmless Entertainment discourse*: Somewhat self-explanatory, this is the discourse which promotes the idea that activities such as gambling, drinking or smoking are in fact innocuous and largely harmless. Implicit in this discourse can be seen the messages that if someone chooses to abuse such an activity then the blame lies solely with them, and that if you oppose such activities you are opposing people's right to have fun.

*The Ordinary Business discourse*: This is the discourse promoting the idea that these activities are businesses no different to any other and therefore it is wrong for governments to intrude on their freedom. Implicit here is the idea that by having an oppositional view you are seeking to make ordinary business owners trying to make an honest living suffer.

*The Cultural and Economic Capital argument*: The argument that these industries enrich the culture of a nation and attract increased tourism, thus making a positive contribution to the economy. Implicit here is the idea that by opposing these industries you oppose culture and do not want to see your country prosper.

*The Freedom to Choose argument*: The idea that people should be free to make their own decisions about issues such us these, free of intervention from the 'nanny state'. Such an argument of course ignores any debate on what exactly real freedom constitutes. Can you make an informed choice if your opinions are being constantly swayed by marketing? Implicit here is the idea that opposing these industries is showing support for a nanny state.

*The Personal Responsibility discourse*: The idea that almost all negative consequences that befall anyone who gets addicted are their own responsibility. This is closely linked to the 'harmless entertainment' discourse. Implicit here is the othering of the addict, positioning them outside the realms of the norms. The message is 'if you can't handle this harmless fun there is something intrinsically wrong with you'.

The implicit messages in these five discourses/arguments are highlighted because it is here where they have the greatest power. Fed into the public consciousness from many sources every single day, members of the public ultimately grow to hold these opinions as their own. They genuinely believe they have come to these conclusions themselves, and that to hold any other opinion is ridiculous, when in fact the agenda has been set by those who stand to make vast amounts of money from them. As Plato once wrote, 'the *highest* reach of *injustice* is: to be deemed *just when you are not*'.

Much of what applies to the gambling and alcohol industries has in the past applied to the tobacco industry also. But times have changed, in the Western world at least, and now tobacco is regulated far more heavily. And in terms of cutting the population of smokers, this regulation has largely worked. But the more extensive regulation has not occurred in isolation. This increased market control and reining in of the 'rampant commercial marketing that fuelled the explosion of tobacco use in the first half of the last century' (Rolles & McClure, 2009: 107) has occurred in conjunction with education and a public health-based approach. In the present day the major health risks that are associated with smoking are now far more widely understood. Clearly, this does not deter some people from choosing to take up smoking, and many people are still dying of smoking-related illness. Similarly, no framework of new drugs policy will eliminate the problems caused by other drugs. We can only seek to improve and minimise harm.

Arguably what has been done with smoking in recent years provides a good blueprint for how other drugs might be controlled. Education and health policies have to run alongside policies on legality. This connects back to the roots of what addiction is and why people turn to drugs in the first place.

# MEDICAL USES

There are a number of currently illegal drugs which have potential medical uses; more so than at any other time since the 1960s the debate about their use in a medical context has been reignited. Furthermore, the legal status of some drugs has impeded research into possible benefits of their use (Nutt et al., 2013). There are an increasing number of findings that cannabis could have a variety of medical uses, and in some states of the USA it can be acquired on prescription. Meanwhile MDMA is currently being trialled as a potential treatment for Post-Traumatic Stress Disorder. Psychedelic drugs such as psilocybin and LSD have long since been looked at as potentially having scope for use in a therapeutic context (Rolles & McClure, 2009). Some experiments in the 1960s yielded interesting results (Clark, 1968), but further research has been scarce since media hysteria broke out. Meanwhile ketamine is currently being trialled as a potential antidepressant (Malhi et al., 2016).

In the following sections we will explore and critically analyse some of the recent research on these drugs.

## CANNABIS

Cannabis is widely considered the 'softest' recreational drug, and thus openness to its use in either recreational or medical contexts has been far greater than other drugs, such as the ones that will be discussed below. It is also widely acknowledged that there are some medical benefits; what is disputed is whether these benefits are outweighed by its risks to mental health (Borowicz et al., 2014).

Research has elucidated that cannabis can be beneficial for a number of conditions. These include cancers such as lung cancer, where cannabis has been shown both to reduce tumour growth and the spreading of metastases. In addition, it has also been shown to reduce nausea during chemotherapy more effectively and with fewer side effects than traditional anti-vomiting medication (Borowicz et al., 2014). Cannabis has also been shown to have positive effects on glaucoma and multiple sclerosis (Alexander, 2016). It can be an effective anti-inflammatory, and this has led to it being applied to conditions such as inflammatory bowel disease (Ahmed & Katz, 2016). Meanwhile research from Harvard found that cannabis can help protect the brains of HIV sufferers from deterioration caused by neurotoxin Gp120 (Costantino et al., 2012).

In the USA cannabis has been legalised for medical use in a number of states. As recreational use has also been legalised in two states, there has been a cultural shift towards its acceptance. One study found that in states where medical use of cannabis has been legalised, there was a higher prevalence of adolescents using the drug recreationally (Wall et al., 2011).

Advocates of cannabis use for medical purposes are still cautious of its side effects however. Certainly, for those with pre-existing mental health issues the side effects can be concerning, causing an increased incidence of conditions such as schizophrenia. Thus, a sensible conclusion regarding cannabis's medical use is perhaps that it should be used but with a degree of caution.

## MDMA

MDMA (sometimes known as ecstasy) is best known as a drug taken at raves and clubs, but it also has a number of effects that potentially lend it to psychotherapeutic use. MDMA promotes feelings of relaxation, thoughtfulness, insight and contemplation, as well as 'a loosening of the ego' (Sessa, 2007: 220). Such traits have the potential to be very useful in providing an improved ability to explore painful memories which might ordinarily be repressed. Greer and Tolbert have put this down to the inhibiting of 'the subjective fear response to an emotional threat' (Sessa, 2007: 220). Thus, MDMA has the potential to be particularly beneficial to those suffering from Post-Traumatic Stress Disorder (PTSD). In addition to this, its empathogenic effects mean that it can help build a trusting, close relationship between patient and therapist at a faster rate than might ordinarily be possible (Sessa, 2007).

There has been exploration of the potential medical uses of MDMA for a number of decades, with various studies being conducted in the 1970s and early 1980s which showed promise. But, much like previous research with LSD, when the harmful effects of MDMA broke out into the mainstream, a media moral panic followed, which hindered legitimate research on its therapeutic potential. Concerns over MDMA's harmfulness are not without any basis; there have been a number of studies which have elucidated the neurotoxicity of MDMA, e.g. impairment of memory following its use (Curran & Travill, 1997) and a long-term risk of affective disorders (Taurah & Chandler, 2003; Taurah et al., 2014). Andy Parrott's research has suggested that negative interactions and experiences can also stem from MDMA use, even in experienced users (see Parrott, 2013b, for a review). However, such studies on MDMA have sometimes been conducted using samples of people who are polydrug users, and almost all studies have been on people who take MDMA in a club setting, in doses far higher than what would be used in a clinical setting (Sessa, 2007).

There is still controversy around the idea, but it is gaining increasing traction, and in August 2017 the FDA in the USA deemed it a 'breakthrough therapy' which set it on the fast track for review and approval. At present it is looking like it could be approved by 2021. Sessa (2007) has argued that whilst many currently used medications for problems such as depression and anxiety or sleep disorder only mask the symptom, MDMA has the potential to get to the core of the problem and actually help the patient work through the initial trauma (Sessa, 2017a). Viewed from this angle, it could be rather promising.

## KETAMINE AND HALLUCINOGENS

The deeply spiritual or transcendental effects that hallucinogens and ketamine can produce (Pahnke et al., 1970) make them distinct from any other class of drugs. Despite very different mechanisms of action, ketamine and psychedelic hallucinogens such as LSD and psilocybin can have the effect of seeming to hit a reset button in the brain. Rather than just producing an alteration in mood or profound thoughts, these drugs can induce a profoundly altered state of reality; thus, the medical implications are not around the drugs' physical effect, but rather the lasting impact of the psychological effects.

There have now been a number of studies which have suggested that ketamine may be an effective treatment for major depressive disorder which is resistant to other treatments. A study showed that 71% of participants had a greater than 50% reduction in depressive symptoms within 24 hours of ketamine administration, whereas the same participants showed almost no change in symptoms after a placebo injection of saline (Singh et al., 2017). This response was also sustained for one week of follow-up in around a third of the participants (Singh et al., 2017). Another study demonstrated reductions in suicidal ideation in patients with depression who received ketamine (Ballard et al., 2014).

There are concerns, however, about using ketamine in a medical context, including concerns about its long-term toxicity. Another key concern is that there is no evidence that the positive effects described above are lasting, and therefore there is a risk that 'patients who achieve a dramatic beneficial response to ketamine might face a serious fall in morale after rapid relapse', or, if suicidal, they 'might be harmed by the false reassurance of an abrupt, but potentially brief, reduction in suicidality' (Singh et al., 2017).

Research regarding promising effects of hallucinogens in a psychotherapeutic context dates back thousands of years; in a number of cultures and tribes, hallucinogens have been used for their benefits, and would be administered by a shaman or professional healer in a ceremonial context (Grinspoon & Doblin, 2001). In the 1950s there was a lot of research conducted regarding the powerful impact hallucinogens, particularly LSD, could have on a number of conditions as varied as sociopathy, addiction, and easing the acceptance of dying in mentally ill patients (Grinspoon & Doblin, 2001).

It is difficult to statistically quantify the changes to people's lives brought about by these drugs. It has been noted that 'authentic emotional power is not a guarantee against backsliding when the old frustrations, limitations, and emotional distress have to be faced in everyday life' (Grinspoon & Doblin, 2001: 136). It is difficult to know how lasting these kinds of changes are, even if they are instantaneously profound. It is possible that in some instances these drugs may have an impact where other drugs have failed. Whilst hailing them as wonder drugs would be dangerous, keeping the door open to further research on their therapeutic benefits and their toxicity can only increase our understanding of their potential benefits and harms.

## DANGERS OF MEDICALISATION

We are living in an age of increased medicalisation. More and more problems are becoming pathologised and medication is being touted as the answer. There are obvious benefits and uses of medications, but there is little doubt that there is a darker side to the production and the producers of these drugs. The simple reason is that there is money to be made.

We have explored above the many actors who stand to profit from drugs, both legal and illegal. What they all have in common is the employment of ethically dubious tactics in order to make profits. The pharmaceutical companies who produce medical drugs are no different in this respect. And like other manufacturers of drugs who are operating within the law as companies, the requirement to maximise profits for their shareholders is built into their legal structure.

In the USA particularly, the wealth of large pharmaceutical companies has enabled them to buy large-scale influence in politics, law and in the media, and thus ultimately in public perceptions. Here we see an even more disturbing manifestation of some of the problems discussed earlier with regard to free market deregulation. With pharmaceutical companies, not only can manufacturers sell the message that the drug is not harmful, they can in fact also sell the message that the drug is actively beneficial.

Pushing the drug industry underground has created an unregulated and unchecked market where human suffering is rife. One potential solution might be cautious legalisation of drugs, implementing a pharmacy model in the manner of Uruguay. Similar tactics could be employed as have been used to reduce smoking, such as higher taxes, bans on advertising, and use only being allowed in certain locations.

One fears that in the present day, even if governments intended to implement legalisation in this manner, corporations could potentially exert influence, shift norms, and set the agenda. Thus in all probability full legalisation could only work in a world where the values mentioned above do not reign supreme. In such a world we might well not have so many addicts desperately trying to escape, nor corporations trying to ruthlessly exploit them and push products on them, nor governments passing self-interested laws. Such a world is a long way off though, and quite possibly will never come to pass. But it is something for us to keep in mind. Until then the best that can be done is to try and shift our approach to drugs to an approach that is more humane, compassionate, evidence based, and less rhetorical and reactionary.

## SUMMARY

- Legislating on drugs is a complex issue. Whether you believe in a punitive stance towards drugs or a harm reduction stance, it is not clear that an evidence-based approach is currently being followed. Largely this would seem to be because there are such huge amounts of money and power at stake, and how laws are made ultimately influences where that money and power will fall.

- Drugs themselves are not inherently problematic. It is human interaction with drugs that creates problems. The same drug that can be highly destructive in one context can be potentially beneficial in another.

- The reason drug policies are not dictated by evidence is that an entire economy exists around drugs in the present day. Were illegal drugs to be made legal all around the world, a whole new economy would potentially spring up. Power would be redistributed.

- There is no simple solution to what drug policy should look like moving forward, and as things currently stand any solution is likely to have both drawbacks and benefits.

- Perhaps a workable drug policy can only come into effect in a society where care, compassion and public health are prioritised over profit and consumerism.

## QUESTIONS

1. Describe the legislation controlling drugs.
2. How has Portugal faced its drug problems?
3. What are the differences between decriminalisation and legalisation?

# REFERENCES

Ahmed, W., & Katz, S. (2016). Therapeutic use of cannabis in inflammatory bowel disease. *Gastroenterol Hepatol (N Y)*, *12*(11), 668–679.

Ainslie, G. (1992). *Picoeconomics: The Strategic Interaction of Successive Motivational States within the Person*. Cambridge: Cambridge University Press.

Albein-Urios, N., Martinez-González, J. M., Lozano, Ó., Clark, L., & Verdejo-García, A. (2012). Comparison of impulsivity and working memory in cocaine addiction and pathological gambling: implications for cocaine-induced neurotoxicity. *Drug and Alcohol Dependence*, *126*(1), 1–6.

Alexander, B. K. (2008). *The Globalisation of Addiction*. New York: Oxford University Press.

Alexander, B. K. (2010). *The Globalization of Addiction: A Study in Poverty of the Spirit*: Oxford: Oxford University Press.

Alexander, B. K., Coambs, R. B., & Hadaway, P. F. (1978). Effect of housing and gender on morphine self-administration in rats. *Psychopharmacology*, *58*(2), 175–179. doi:10.1007/bf00426903

Alexander, S. P. (2016). Therapeutic potential of cannabis-related drugs. *Prog Neuropsychopharmacol Biol Psychiatry*, *64*, 157–166. doi:10.1016/j.pnpbp.2015.07.001

Allami, Y., Vitaro, F., Brendgen, M., Carbonneau, R., Lacourse, É., & Tremblay, R. E. (2017). A longitudinal empirical investigation of the Pathways Model of problem gambling. *Journal of Gambling Studies*, 1–15. doi:10.1007/s10899-017-9682-6

American Psychiatric Association (APA) (2013). *Diagnostic and Statistical Manual of Mental Disorders* (5th edn). Washington, DC: APA.

Anacker, C., O'Donnell, K. J., & Meaney, M. J. (2014). Early life adversity and the epigenetic programming of hypothalamic-pituitary-adrenal function. *Dialogues in Clinical Neuroscience*, *16*(3), 321–333.

Anderson, S. M., & Pierce, R. C. (2005). Cocaine-induced alterations in dopamine receptor signaling: implications for reinforcement and reinstatement. *Pharmacol Ther*, *106*(3), 389–403.

Anton, R. F., O'Malley, S. S., Ciraulo, D. A., Cisler, R. A., Couper, D., Donovan, D. M., ... Zweben, A. (2006). Combined pharmacotherapies and behavioral interventions for alcohol dependence: the COMBINE study: a randomized controlled trial. *Jama*, *295*(17), 2003–2017. doi:10.1001/jama.295.17.2003

Astur, R. S., Carew, A. W., & Deaton, B. E. (2014). Conditioned place preferences in humans using virtual reality. *Behav Brain Res*, *267*, 173–177. doi:10.1016/j.bbr.2014.03.018

Ayanga, D., Shorter, D., & Kosten, T. R. (2016). Update on pharmacotherapy for treatment of opioid use disorder. *Expert Opin Pharmacother*, *17*(17), 2307–2318. doi:10.1080/14656566.2016.1244529

# REFERENCES

Ayllon, T., & Azrin, N. (1968). *The Token Economy: A Motivation System for Therapy and Rehabilitation*. New York: Appleton-Century-Crofts, Educational Division, Meredith Corporation.

Babor, T. F., & Del Boca, F. K. (2003). *Treatment Matching in Alcoholism*. Cambridge: Cambridge University Press.

Baker, T. B., Piper, M. E., McCarthy, D. E., Majeskie, M. R., & Fiore, M. C. (2004). Addiction motivation reformulated: an affective processing model of negative reinforcement. *Psychological Review, 111*(1), 33–51. doi:10.1037/0033-295x.111.1.33

Ballard, E. D., Ionescu, D. F., Vande Voort, J. L., Niciu, M. J., Richards, E. M., Luckenbaugh, D. A., ... Zarate, C. A., Jr. (2014). Improvement in suicidal ideation after ketamine infusion: relationship to reductions in depression and anxiety. *J Psychiatr Res, 58*, 161–166. doi:10.1016/j.jpsychires.2014.07.027

Bandura, A. (1969). *Principles of Behavior Modification*. New York: Holt, Rinehart and Winston.

Bandura, A. (1977). Self-efficacy: toward a unifying theory of behavioral change. *Psychological Review, 84*(2), 191–215.

Bandura, A. (1997). Editorial. *American Journal of Health Promotion, 12*(1), 8–10.

Bart, G. (2012). Maintenance medication for opiate addiction: the foundation of recovery. *J Addict Dis, 31*(3), 207–225. doi:10.1080/10550887.2012.694598

Barton, K. R., Yazdani, Y., Ayer, N., Kalvapalle, S., Brown, S., Stapleton, J., ... Harrigan, K. A. (2017). The effect of losses disguised as wins and near misses in electronic gaming machines: a systematic review. *J Gambl Stud*. doi:10.1007/s10899-017-9688-0

Baskin-Sommers, A. R., & Foti, D. (2015). Abnormal reward functioning across substance use disorders and major depressive disorder: considering reward as a transdiagnostic mechanism. *Int J Psychophysiol*. doi:10.1016/j.ijpsycho.2015.01.011

Bassareo, V., & Di Chiara, G. (1997). Differential influence of associative and nonassociative learning mechanisms on the responsiveness of prefrontal and accumbal dopamine transmission to food stimuli in rats fed ad libitum. *J Neurosci, 17*(2), 851–861.

Bassareo, V., & Di Chiara, G. (1999). Differential responsiveness of dopamine transmission to food-stimuli in nucleus accumbens shell/core compartments. *Neuroscience, 89*(3), 637–641. doi:http://dx.doi.org/10.1016/S0306-4522(98)00583-1

Bechara, A. (2005). Decision making, impulse control and loss of willpower to resist drugs: a neurocognitive perspective. *Nature Neuroscience, 8*(11), 1458–1463. doi:10.1038/nn1584

Bechara, A., Damasio, A. R., Damasio, H., & Anderson, S. W. (1994). Insensitivity to future consequences following damage to human prefrontal cortex. *Cognition, 50*(1–3), 7–15.

Beck, A. T. (1993). Cognitive therapy: past, present, and future. *Journal of Consulting and Clinical Psychology, 61*(2), 194–198. doi:10.1037/0022-006X.61.2.194

Becker, H. S. (1963). *Outsiders: Studies in the Sociology of Deviance*. New York, NY: The Free Press.

Becoña, E., & García, M. P. (1993). Nicotine fading and smokeholding methods to smoking cessation. *Psychological Reports, 73*(3, Pt 1),779–786.

Benedetti, F. (2008). *Placebo Effects: Understanding the Mechanisms in Health and Disease*. Oxford: Oxford University Press.

Berridge, K. C. (2000). Measuring hedonic impact in animals and infants: microstructure of affective taste reactivity patterns. *Neurosci Biobehav Rev, 24*(2), 173–198.

Berridge, K. C., & Robinson, T. E. (2003). Parsing reward. *Trends Neurosci, 26*(9), 507–513.

Bevilacqua, L., Doly, S., Kaprio, J., Yuan, Q., Tikkanen, R., Paunio, T., ... Goldman, D. (2010). A population-specific HTR2B stop codon predisposes to severe impulsivity. *Nature, 468*(7327), 1061–1066. doi:10.1038/nature09629

Bickel, W. K., & Marsch, L. A. (2001). Toward a behavioral economic understanding of drug dependence: delay discounting processes. *Addiction, 96*(1), 73–86. doi:10.1080/09652140020016978

Biederman, J., Wilens, T. E., Mick, E., Faraone, S. V., & Spencer, T. (1998). Does attention-deficit hyperactivity disorder impact the developmental course of drug and alcohol abuse and dependence? *Biol Psychiatry, 44*(4), 269–273. doi:10.1016/s0006-3223(97)00406-x

Bien, T. H., Miller, W. R., & Boroughs, J. M. (1993). Motivational interviewing with alcohol outpatients. *Behavioural and Cognitive Psychotherapy, 21*(04), 347–356.

Bien, T. H., Miller, W. R., & Tonigan, J. S. (1993). Brief interventions for alcohol problems: a review. *Addiction, 88*(3), 315–335.

Bierut, L. J. (2010). Convergence of genetic findings for nicotine dependence and smoking related diseases with chromosome 15q24-25. *Trends Pharmacol Sci, 31*(1), 46–51. doi:10.1016/j.tips.2009.10.004

Bierut, L. J., Dinwiddie, S. H., Begleiter, H., Crowe, R. R., Hesselbrock, V., Nurnberger, J. I., ... Reich, T. (1998). Familial transmission of substance dependence: alcohol, marijuana, cocaine, and habitual smoking – a report from the collaborative study on the genetics of alcoholism. *Arch Gen Psychiatry, 55*(11), 982–988. doi:10.1001/archpsyc.55.11.982

Bierut, L. J., Goate, A. M., Breslau, N., Johnson, E. O., Bertelsen, S., Fox, L., ... Edenberg, H. J. (2012). ADH1B is associated with alcohol dependence and alcohol consumption in populations of European and African ancestry. *Molecular Psychiatry, 17*(4), 445–450. doi:10.1038/mp.2011.124

Bierut, L. J., Madden, P. A., Breslau, N., Johnson, E. O., Hatsukami, D., Pomerleau, O. F., ... Ballinger, D. G. (2007). Novel genes identified in a high-density genome wide association study for nicotine dependence. *Hum Mol Genet, 16*(1), 24–35. doi:10.1093/hmg/ddl441

Billieux, J., Schimmenti, A., Khazaal, Y., Maurage, P., & Heeren, A. (2015). Are we overpathologizing everyday life? A tenable blueprint for behavioral addiction research. *J Behav Addict, 4*(3), 119–123. doi:10.1556/2006.4.2015.009

Blaszczynski, A., & Nower, L. (2002). A pathways model of problem and pathological gambling. *Addiction, 97*(5), 487–499.

Blum, K., Noble, E. P., Sheridan, P. J., Montgomery, A., Ritchie, T., Jagadeeswaran, P., ... Cohn, J. B. (1990). Allelic association of human dopamine D2 receptor gene in alcoholism. *Jama, 263*(15), 2055–2060.

Bogenschutz, M. P., Forcehimes, A. A., Pommy, J. A., Wilcox, C. E., Barbosa, P. C., & Strassman, R. J. (2015). Psilocybin-assisted treatment for alcohol dependence: a proof-of-concept study. *J Psychopharmacol, 29*(3), 289–299. doi:10.1177/0269881114565144

# REFERENCES

Bohman, M., Sigvardsson, S., & Cloninger, C. R. (1981). Maternal inheritance of alcohol abuse: cross-fostering analysis of adopted women. *Arch Gen Psychiatry, 38*(9), 965–969.

Boileau, I., Dagher, A., Leyton, M., Gunn, R. N., Baker, G. B., Diksic, M., & Benkelfat, C. (2006). Modeling sensitization to stimulants in humans: an [11C] raclopride/positron emission tomography study in healthy men. *Arch Gen Psychiatry, 63*(12), 1386–1395.

Bond, C., LaForge, K. S., Tian, M., Melia, D., Zhang, S., Borg, L., … Yu, L. (1998). Single-nucleotide polymorphism in the human mu opioid receptor gene alters beta-endorphin binding and activity: possible implications for opiate addiction. *Proc Natl Acad Sci U S A, 95*(16), 9608–9613.

Booth Davis, J. (1997). *The Myth of Addiction*. Amsterdam: Harwood Academic Publishers.

Bordnick, P. S., Copp, H. L., Traylor, A., Graap, K. M., Carter, B. L., Walton, A., & Ferrer, M. (2009). Reactivity to cannabis cues in virtual reality environments. *Journal of Psychoactive Drugs, 41*(2), 105–112. doi:10.1080/02791072.2009.10399903

Bordnick, P. S., Graap, K. M., Copp, H. L., Brooks, J., & Ferrer, M. (2005). Virtual reality cue reactivity assessment in cigarette smokers. *CyberPsychology & Behavior, 8*(5), 487–492.

Bordnick, P. S., Traylor, A., Copp, H. L., Graap, K. M., Carter, B., Ferrer, M., & Walton, A. P. (2008). Assessing reactivity to virtual reality alcohol based cues. *Addictive Behaviors, 33*(6), 743–756. doi:http://dx.doi.org/10.1016/j.addbeh.2007.12.010

Borowicz, K. K., Kaczmarska, P., & Barbara, S. (2014). Medical use of marijuana. *Archives of Physiotherapy & Global Researches, 18*(4).

Borusiak, P., Bouikidis, A., Liersch, R., & Russell, J. B. (2008). Cardiovascular effects in adolescents while they are playing video games: a potential health risk factor? *Psychophysiology, 45*(2), 327–332. doi:10.1111/j.1469-8986.2007.00622.x

Bowen, S., Chawla, N., & Marlatt, G. (2010). *Mindfulness-based Relapse Prevention for Substance Use Disorders: A Clinician's Guide*. New York: Guilford Press.

Bowen, S., Witkiewitz, K., Clifasefi, S. L., & et al. (2014). Relative efficacy of mindfulness-based relapse prevention, standard relapse prevention, and treatment as usual for substance use disorders: a randomized clinical trial. *JAMA Psychiatry, 71*(5), 547–556. doi:10.1001/jamapsychiatry.2013.4546

Bozarth, M. A., Murray, A., & Wise, R. A. (1989). Influence of housing conditions on the acquisition of intravenous heroin and cocaine self-administration in rats. *Pharmacology Biochemistry and Behavior, 33*(4), 903–907. doi:10.1016/0091-3057(89)90490-5

Bracken, P., Thomas, P., Timimi, S., Asen, E., Behr, G., Beuster, C., … Yeomans, D. (2012). Psychiatry beyond the current paradigm. *Br J Psychiatry, 201*(6), 430–434. doi:10.1192/bjp.bp.112.109447

Bradley, B., Field, M., Mogg, K., & De Houwer, J. (2004). Attentional and evaluative biases for smoking cues in nicotine dependence: component processes of biases in visual orienting. *Behavioural Pharmacology, 15*(1), 29–36.

Bradley, B. P., Mogg, K., Wright, T., & Field, M. (2003). Attentional bias in drug dependence: vigilance for cigarette-related cues in smokers. *Psychology of Addictive Behaviors, 17*(1), 66.

Bradley, K. A., & Rubinsky, A. D. (2013). Why not add consumption measures to current definitions of substance use disorders? Commentary on Rehm et al. 'Defining Substance Use Disorders: Do We Really Need More Than Heavy Use?'. *Alcohol and Alcoholism, 48*(6), 642–643. doi:10.1093/alcalc/agt132

Brady, K. T., McCauley, J. L., & Back, S. E. (2016). Prescription opioid misuse, abuse, and treatment in the United States: an update. *American Journal of Psychiatry*, *173*(1), 18–26. doi:10.1176/appi.ajp.2015.15020262

Breen, R. B., & Zimmerman, M. (2002). Rapid onset of pathological gambling in machine gamblers. *Journal of Gambling Studies*, *18*(1), 31–43.

Brevers, D., Bechara, A., Cleeremans, A., & Noel, X. (2013). Iowa Gambling Task (IGT): twenty years after – gambling disorder and IGT. *Front Psychol*, *4*, 665. doi:10.3389/fpsyg.2013.00665

Brevers, D., Cleeremans, A., Verbruggen, F., Bechara, A., Kornreich, C., Verbanck, P., & Noel, X. (2012). Impulsive action but not impulsive choice determines problem gambling severity. *PLoS One*, *7*(11), e50647. doi:10.1371/journal.pone.0050647

Brewer, C., Streel, E., & Skinner, M. (2017). Supervised Disulfiram's superior effectiveness in alcoholism treatment: ethical, methodological, and psychological aspects. *Alcohol and Alcoholism*, *52*(2), 213–219. doi:10.1093/alcalc/agw093

Brooks, P. J., Enoch, M. A., Goldman, D., Li, T. K., & Yokoyama, A. (2009). The alcohol flushing response: an unrecognized risk factor for esophageal cancer from alcohol consumption. *PLoS Med*, *6*(3). doi:10.1371/journal.pmed.1000050

Brown, J. M., & Miller, W. R. (1993). Impact of motivational interviewing on participation and outcome in residential alcoholism treatment. *Psychology of Addictive Behaviors*, *7*(4), 211.

Brunner, H. G., Nelen, M., Breakefield, X. O., Ropers, H. H., & van Oost, B. A. (1993). Abnormal behavior associated with a point mutation in the structural gene for monoamine oxidase A. *Science*, *262*(5133), 578–580.

Budney, A. J., Roffman, R., Stephens, R. S., & Walker, D. (2007). Marijuana dependence and its treatment. *Addiction Science & Clinical Practice*, *4*(1), 4–16.

Bufe, C. (1998). *Alcoholics Anonymous: Cult or Cure?* San Francisco, CA: Sharp Press.

Buhler, K. M., Gine, E., Echeverry-Alzate, V., Calleja-Conde, J., de Fonseca, F. R., & Lopez-Moreno, J. A. (2015). Common single nucleotide variants underlying drug addiction: more than a decade of research. *Addict Biol*, *20*(5), 845–871. doi:10.1111/adb.12204

Cadoret, R. J., O'Gorman, T. W., Troughton, E., & Heywood, E. (1985). Alcoholism and antisocial personality: interrelationships, genetic and environmental factors. *Arch Gen Psychiatry*, *42*(2), 161–167.

Cahill, K., Lancaster, T., & Green, N. (2010). Stage-based interventions for smoking cessation. *Cochrane Database Syst Rev* (11), Cd004492. doi:10.1002/14651858.CD004492.pub4

Cahill, K., Lindson-Hawley, N., Thomas, K. H., Fanshawe, T. R., & Lancaster, T. (2016). Nicotine receptor partial agonists for smoking cessation. *Cochrane Database Syst Rev* (5), Cd006103. doi:10.1002/14651858.CD006103.pub7

Cahill, K., Stevens, S., & Lancaster, T. (2014). Pharmacological treatments for smoking cessation. *Jama*, *311*(2), 193–194. doi:10.1001/jama.2013.283787

Calado, F., Alexandre, J., & Griffiths, M. D. (2016). Prevalence of adolescent problem gambling: a systematic review of recent research. *Journal of Gambling Studies*, 1–28. doi:10.1007/s10899-016-9627-5

Calado, F., & Griffiths, M. D. (2016). Problem gambling worldwide: an update and systematic review of empirical research (2000–2015). *J Behav Addict*, *5*(4), 592–613. doi:10.1556/2006.5.2016.073

# REFERENCES

Campbell, W., Hester, R. K., Lenberg, K. L., & Delaney, H. D. (2016). Overcoming addictions, a web-based application, and SMART recovery, an online and in-person mutual help group for problem drinkers, Part 2: Six-month outcomes of a randomized controlled trial and qualitative feedback from participants. *J Med Internet Res, 18*(10), e262. doi:10.2196/jmir.5508

Cannon, C. M., & Bseikri, M. R. (2004). Is dopamine required for natural reward? *Physiol Behav, 81*(5), 741–748. doi:10.1016/j.physbeh.2004.04.020

Cannon, D. S., & Baker, T. B. (1981). Emetic and electric shock alcohol aversion therapy: assessment of conditioning. *J Consult Clin Psychol, 49*(1), 20–33.

Carroll, K. M., Ball, S. A., Martino, S., Nich, C., Babuscio, T. A., Nuro, K. F., … Rounsaville, B. J. (2008). Computer-assisted delivery of cognitive-behavioral therapy for addiction: a randomized trial of CBT4CBT. *American Journal of Psychiatry, 165*, 179–187.

Carroll, K. M., Ball, S. A., Martino, S., Nich, C., Babuscio, T. A., & Rounsaville, B. J. (2009). Enduring effects of a computer-assisted training program for cognitive behavioral therapy: a 6-month follow-up of CBT4CBT. *Drug and Alcohol Dependence, 100*(1), 178–181.

Carroll, K. M., & Onken, L. S. (2005). Behavioral therapies for drug abuse. *American Journal of Psychiatry, 162*(8), 1452–1460. doi:10.1176/appi.ajp.162.8.1452

Casey, K. F., Benkelfat, C., Cherkasova, M. V., Baker, G. B., Dagher, A., & Leyton, M. (2014). Reduced dopamine response to amphetamine in subjects at ultra-high risk for addiction. *Biological Psychiatry, 76*(1), 23–30. doi:10.1016/j.biopsych.2013.08.033

Castells, X., Cunill, R., Perez-Mana, C., Vidal, X., & Capella, D. (2016). Psychostimulant drugs for cocaine dependence. *Cochrane Database Syst Rev, 9*, Cd007380. doi:10.1002/14651858.CD007380.pub4

Chamberlain, S. R., Lochner, C., Stein, D. J., Goudriaan, A. E., van Holst, R. J., Zohar, J., & Grant, J. E. (2016). Behavioural addiction – a rising tide? *Eur Neuropsychopharmacol, 26*(5), 841–855. doi:10.1016/j.euroneuro.2015.08.013

Chandler, C. (2010). *The Science of ADHD: A Guide for Parents and Professionals*. Oxford: Wiley Blackwell.

Chandler, C. (2015). *Psychobiology*. Chichester, UK: John Wiley & Sons.

Chavoustie, S., Frost, M., Snyder, O., Owen, J., Darwish, M., Dammerman, R., & Sanjurjo, V. (2017). Buprenorphine implants in medical treatment of opioid addiction. *Expert Rev Clin Pharmacol, 10*(8), 799–807. doi:10.1080/17512433.2017.1336434

Chen, C. C., Lu, R. B., Chen, Y. C., Wang, M. F., Chang, Y. C., Li, T. K., & Yin, S. J. (1999). Interaction between the functional polymorphisms of the alcohol-metabolism genes in protection against alcoholism. *American Journal of Human Genetics, 65*(3), 795–807. doi:10.1086/302540

Chiamulera, C. (2005). Cue reactivity in nicotine and tobacco dependence: a 'multiple-action' model of nicotine as a primary reinforcement and as an enhancer of the effects of smoking-associated stimuli. *Brain Research Reviews, 48*(1), 74–97.

Chomchai, C., & Chomchai, S. (2015). Global patterns of methamphetamine use. *Curr Opin Psychiatry, 28*(4), 269–274. doi:10.1097/yco.0000000000000168

Chou, K. L., & Afifi, T. O. (2011). Disordered (pathologic or problem) gambling and axis I psychiatric disorders: results from the National Epidemiologic Survey on Alcohol and Related Conditions. *Am J Epidemiol, 173*(11), 1289–1297. doi:10.1093/aje/kwr017

Christiansen, P., Jennings, E., & Rose, A. K. (2016). Anticipated effects of alcohol stimulate craving and impair inhibitory control. *Psychol Addict Behav*, *30*(3), 383–388. doi:10.1037/adb0000148

Christiansen, P., Rose, A. K., Cole, J. C., & Field, M. (2013). A comparison of the anticipated and pharmacological effects of alcohol on cognitive bias, executive function, craving and ad-lib drinking. *Journal of Psychopharmacology*, *27*(1), 84–92.

Christiansen, P., Schoenmakers, T. M., & Field, M. (2015). Less than meets the eye: reappraising the clinical relevance of attentional bias in addiction. *Addictive Behaviors*, *44*, 43–50. doi:http://dx.doi.org/10.1016/j.addbeh.2014.10.005

Clark, L. (2014). Disordered gambling: the evolving concept of behavioral addiction. *Ann N Y Acad Sci*, *1327*, 46–61. doi:10.1111/nyas.12558

Clark, L., Studer, B., Bruss, J., Tranel, D., & Bechara, A. (2014). Damage to insula abolishes cognitive distortions during simulated gambling. *Proc Natl Acad Sci U S A*, *111*(16), 6098–6103. doi:10.1073/pnas.1322295111

Clark, W. H. (1968). Religious aspects of psychedelic drugs. *California Law Review*, *56*, 86–99.

Cloninger, C. R., Bohman, M., & Sigvardsson, S. (1981). Inheritance of alcohol abuse: cross-fostering analysis of adopted men. *Arch Gen Psychiatry*, *38*(8), 861–868.

Clotfelter, C. T., & Cook, P. J. (1993). Notes: The "gambler's fallacy" in lottery play. *Management Science*, *39*(12), 1521–1525.

Coe, J. W., Brooks, P. R., Vetelino, M. G., Wirtz, M. C., Arnold, E. P., Huang, J., ... O'Neill, B. T. (2005). Varenicline: an alpha4beta2 nicotinic receptor partial agonist for smoking cessation. *J Med Chem*, *48*(10), 3474–3477. doi:10.1021/jm050069n

Cohen, S. (2011). *Folk Devils and Moral Panics*. New York: Routledge.

Conklin, C. A., & Tiffany, S. T. (2002). Applying extinction research and theory to cue-exposure addiction treatments. *Addiction*, *97*(2), 155–167.

Corbett, D., & Wise, R. A. (1980). Intracranial self-stimulation in relation to the ascending dopaminergic systems of the midbrain: a moveable electrode mapping study. *Brain Res*, *185*(1), 1–15.

Costantino, C. M., Gupta, A., Yewdall, A. W., Dale, B. M., Devi, L. A., & Chen, B. K. (2012). Cannabinoid receptor 2-mediated attenuation of CXCR4-tropic HIV infection in primary CD4+ T cells. *PLoS ONE*, *7*(3), e33961. doi:10.1371/journal.pone.0033961

Cotton, N. S. (1979). The familial incidence of alcoholism: a review. *J Stud Alcohol*, *40*(1), 89–116.

Counotte, D. S., Smit, A. B., Pattij, T., & Spijker, S. (2011). Development of the motivational system during adolescence, and its sensitivity to disruption by nicotine. *Dev Cogn Neurosci*, *1*(4), 430–443. doi:10.1016/j.dcn.2011.05.010

Courtwright, D. (2015). 'The NIDA Brain Disease Paradigm: History, Resistance, and Spinoffs'. In R. Granfield & C. Reinarman (eds), *Expanding Addiction* (pp. 62–69). New York: Routledge.

Covault, J., Gelernter, J., Hesselbrock, V., Nellissery, M., & Kranzler, H. R. (2004). Allelic and haplotypic association of GABRA2 with alcohol dependence. *American Journal of Medical Genetics Part B-Neuropsychiatric Genetics*, *129B*(1), 104–109. doi:10.1002/ajmg.b.30091

Cox, W. M., Fadardi, J. S., Hosier, S. G., & Pothos, E. M. (2015). Differential effects and temporal course of attentional and motivational training on excessive drinking. *Experimental and Clinical Psychopharmacology*, *23*(6), 445.

# REFERENCES

Cox, W. M., Fadardi, J. S., Intriligator, J. M., & Klinger, E. (2014). Attentional bias modification for addictive behaviors: clinical implications. *CNS Spectrums*, *19*(03), 215–224.

Cox, W. M., Fadardi, J. S., & Pothos, E. M. (2006). The addiction-stroop test: theoretical considerations and procedural recommendations. *Psychological Bulletin*, *132*(3), 443.

Cox, W. M., Hogan, L. M., Kristian, M. R., & Race, J. H. (2002). Alcohol attentional bias as a predictor of alcohol abusers' treatment outcome. *Drug and Alcohol Dependence*, *68*(3), 237–243. doi:http://dx.doi.org/10.1016/S0376-8716(02)00219-3

Crabbe, J. C., Phillips, T. J., & Belknap, J. K. (2010). The complexity of alcohol drinking: studies in rodent genetic models. *Behav Genet*, *40*(6), 737–750. doi:10.1007/s10519-010-9371-z

Crabbe, J. C., Phillips, T. J., Harris, R. A., Arends, M. A., & Koob, G. F. (2006). Alcohol-related genes: contributions from studies with genetically engineered mice. *Addict Biol*, *11*(3–4), 195–269. doi:10.1111/j.1369-1600.2006.00038.x

Craig, A. D. (2009). How do you feel—now? The anterior insula and human awareness. *Nat Rev Neurosci*, *10*(1), 59–70. doi:10.1038/nrn2555

Crockford, D. N., & el-Guebaly, N. (1998). Psychiatric comorbidity in pathological gambling: a critical review. *Can J Psychiatry*, *43*(1), 43–50. doi:10.1177/070674379804300104

Croson, R., & Sundali, J. (2005). The gambler's fallacy and the hot hand: empirical data from casinos. *Journal of Risk and Uncertainty*, *30*(3), 195–209.

Crow, R., Gage, H., Hampson, S., Hart, J., Kimber, A., & Thomas, H. (1999). The role of expectancies in the placebo effect and their use in the delivery of health care: a systematic review. *Health Technol Assess*, *3*(3), 1–96.

Cumming, G. (2008). Replication and *p* intervals: *p* values predict the future only vaguely, but confidence intervals do much better. *Perspectives on Psychological Science*, *3*(4), 286–300.

Cummings, C., Gordon, J. R., & Marlatt, G. A. (1980). Relapse: prevention and prediction. *The Addictive Behaviors*, 291–321.

Curran, H. V., & Travill, R. A. (1997). Mood and cognitive effects of +/-3,4-methylenedioxymethamphetamine (MDMA, 'ecstasy'): week-end 'high' followed by mid-week low. *Addiction*, *92*(7), 821–831.

Curtin, J. J., McCarthy, D.E., Piper, M.E. and Baker, T.B. (2006). 'Implicit and Explicit Drug Motivational Processes: A Model of Boundary Conditions'. In R. W. Weirs and A. W. Stacy, (eds), *Handbook of Implicit Cognition and Addiction* (pp. 233–250). Thousand Oaks, CA: Sage.

Cuthbert, B. N. (2014). The RDoC framework: facilitating transition from ICD/DSM to dimensional approaches that integrate neuroscience and psychopathology. *World Psychiatry*, *13*(1), 28–35. doi:10.1002/wps.20087

Damsma, G., Pfaus, J. G., Wenkstern, D., Phillips, A. G., & Fibiger, H. C. (1992). Sexual behavior increases dopamine transmission in the nucleus accumbens and striatum of male rats: comparison with novelty and locomotion. *Behavioral Neuroscience*, *106*(1), 181.

Dansereau, D. F., & Simpson, D. D. (2009). A picture is worth a thousand words: the case for graphic representations. *Professional Psychology: Research and Practice*, *40*(1), 104–110. doi:10.1037/a0011827

Davies, J. (1997). *The Myth of Addiction* (2nd edn). Amsterdam: Harwood Academic.

Davis, D. R., Kurti, A. N., Skelly, J. M., Redner, R., White, T. J., & Higgins, S. T. (2016) A review of the literature on contingency management in the treatment of substance use disorders, 2009–2014. *Preventive Medicine*. doi:http://dx.doi.org/10.1016/j.ypmed.2016.08.008

Davis, L., Uezato, A., Newell, J. M., & Frazier, E. (2008). Major depression and comorbid substance use disorders. *Curr Opin Psychiatry, 21*(1), 14–18. doi:10.1097/YCO.0b013e3282f32408

Daw, N. D., & Doya, K. (2006). The computational neurobiology of learning and reward. *Curr Opin Neurobiol, 16*(2), 199–204. doi:10.1016/j.conb.2006.03.006

De Luca, M. A., Di Chiara, G., Cadoni, C., Lecca, D., Orsolini, L., Papanti, D., ... Schifano, F. (2017). Cannabis: epidemiological, neurobiological and psychopathological issues – an update. *CNS Neurol Disord Drug Targets, 16*(5), 598–609. doi:10.2174/1871527316666170413113246

Deng, X. D., Jiang, H., Ma, Y., Gao, Q., Zhang, B., Mu, B., ... Liu, Y. (2015). Association between DRD2/ANKK1 TaqIA polymorphism and common illicit drug dependence: evidence from a meta-analysis. *Hum Immunol, 76*(1), 42–51. doi:10.1016/j.humimm.2014.12.005

Di Chiara, G. (1999). Drug addiction as dopamine-dependent associative learning disorder. *European Journal of Pharmacology, 375*(1), 13–30.

Dick, D. M., & Agrawal, A. (2008). The genetics of alcohol and other drug dependence. *Alcohol Research & Health, 31*(2), 111–118.

Dick, D. M., Wang, J. C., Plunkett, J., Aliev, F., Hinrichs, A., Bertelsen, S., ... Goate, A. (2007). Family-based association analyses of alcohol dependence phenotypes across DRD2 and neighboring gene ANKK1. *Alcohol Clin Exp Res, 31*(10), 1645–1653. doi:10.1111/j.1530-0277.2007.00470.x

Dickinson, D., & Elvevag, B. (2009). Genes, cognition and brain through a COMT lens. *Neuroscience, 164*(1), 72–87. doi:10.1016/j.neuroscience.2009.05.014

Donoghue, K., Elzerbi, C., Saunders, R., Whittington, C., Pilling, S., & Drummond, C. (2015). The efficacy of acamprosate and naltrexone in the treatment of alcohol dependence, Europe versus the rest of the world – a meta-analysis. *Addiction, 110*(6), 920–930. doi:10.1111/add.12875

Dowling, N. A., Cowlishaw, S., Jackson, A. C., Merkouris, S. S., Francis, K. L., & Christensen, D. R. (2015). Prevalence of psychiatric co-morbidity in treatment-seeking problem gamblers: a systematic review and meta-analysis. *Aust N Z J Psychiatry, 49*(6), 519–539. doi:10.1177/0004867415575774

Drope, J., Cahn, Z., Kennedy, R., Liber, A. C., Stoklosa, M., Henson, R., ... Drope, J. (2017). Key issues surrounding the health impacts of electronic nicotine delivery systems (ENDS) and other sources of nicotine. *CA Cancer J Clin, 67*(6), 449–471. doi:10.3322/caac.21413

Ducci, F., & Goldman, D. (2012). The genetic basis of addictive disorders. *Psychiatric Clinics of North America, 35*(2), 495-+. doi:10.1016/j.psc.2012.03.010

Dunn, K., DeFulio, A., Everly, J. J., Donlin, W. D., Aklin, W. M., Nuzzo, P. A., ... Silverman, K. (2015). Employment-based reinforcement of adherence to oral naltrexone in unemployed injection drug users: 12-month outcomes. *Psychol Addict Behav, 29*(2), 270–276. doi:10.1037/adb0000010

Edenberg, H. J. (2007). The genetics of alcohol metabolism: role of alcohol dehydrogenase and aldehyde dehydrogenase variants. *Alcohol Research & Health, 30*(1), 5–13.

Edwards, A. C., Maes, H. H., Pedersen, N. L., & Kendler, K. S. (2011). A population-based twin study of the genetic and environmental relationship of major depression, regular tobacco use and nicotine dependence. *Psychological Medicine, 41*(2), 395–405. doi:10.1017/s0033291710000589

# REFERENCES

Edwards, G., & Gross, M. M. (1976). Alcohol dependence: provisional description of a clinical syndrome. *Br Med J, 1*(6017), 1058–1061.

Ehrman, R. N., Robbins, S. J., Bromwell, M. A., Lankford, M. E., Monterosso, J. R., & O'Brien, C. P. (2002). Comparing attentional bias to smoking cues in current smokers, former smokers, and non-smokers using a dot-probe task. *Drug and Alcohol Dependence, 67*(2), 185–191.

Ellis, A. (1962). *Reason and Emotion in Psychotherapy*. Oxford, England: Lyle Stuart.

Erickson, L. M., Tiffany, S. T., Martin, E. M., & Baker, T. B. (1983). Aversive smoking therapies: a conditioning analysis of therapeutic effectiveness. *Behaviour Research and Therapy, 21*(6), 595–611. doi:http://dx.doi.org/10.1016/0005-7967(83)90078-5

Ersche, K. D., Turton, A. J., Pradhan, S., Bullmore, E. T., & Robbins, T. W. (2010). Drug addiction endophenotypes: impulsive versus sensation-seeking personality traits. *Biol Psychiatry, 68*(8), 770–773. doi:10.1016/j.biopsych.2010.06.015

Everitt, B., & Wessley, S. (2004). *Clinical Trials in Psychiatry*. Oxford: Oxford University Press.

Everitt, B. J., Belin, D., Economidou, D., Pelloux, Y., Dalley, J. W., & Robbins, T. W. (2008). Review: neural mechanisms underlying the vulnerability to develop compulsive drug-seeking habits and addiction. *Philos Trans R Soc Lond B Biol Sci, 363*(1507), 3125–3135.

Fadardi, J. S., & Cox, W. M. (2009). Reversing the sequence: reducing alcohol consumption by overcoming alcohol attentional bias. *Drug and Alcohol Dependence, 101*(3), 137–145. doi:http://dx.doi.org/10.1016/j.drugalcdep.2008.11.015

Fantegrossi, W. E., Ullrich, T., Rice, K. C., Woods, J. H., & Winger, G. (2002). 3,4-Methylenedioxymethamphetamine (MDMA, 'ecstasy') and its stereoisomers as reinforcers in rhesus monkeys: serotonergic involvement. *Psychopharmacology (Berl), 161*(4), 356–364.

Fauth-Bühler, M., Mann, K., & Potenza, M. N. (2016). Pathological gambling: a review of the neurobiological evidence relevant for its classification as an addictive disorder. *Addiction Biology*, n/a-n/a. doi:10.1111/adb.12378

Fehr, C., Sander, T., Tadic, A., Lenzen, K. P., Anghelescu, I., Klawe, C., ... Szegedi, A. (2006). Confirmation of association of the GABRA2 gene with alcohol dependence by subtype-specific analysis. *Psychiatric Genetics, 16*(1), 9–17. doi:10.1097/01.ypg.0000185027.89816.d9

Fibiger, H. C., LePiane, F. G., Jakubovic, A., & Phillips, A. G. (1987). The role of dopamine in intracranial self-stimulation of the ventral tegmental area. *J Neurosci, 7*(12), 3888–3896.

Fiore, M. C., Jorenby, D. E., Baker, T. B., & Kenford, S. L. (1992). Tobacco dependence and the nicotine patch: clinical guidelines for effective use. *Jama, 268*(19), 2687–2694.

Fiorino, D. F., Coury, A., & Phillips, A. G. (1997). Dynamic changes in nucleus accumbens dopamine efflux during the Coolidge Effect in male rats. *Journal of Neuroscience, 17*(12), 4849–4855.

Fiorino, D. F., & Phillips, A. G. (1999). Facilitation of sexual behavior and enhanced dopamine efflux in the nucleus accumbens of male rats after D-amphetamine-induced behavioral sensitization. *Journal of Neuroscience, 19*(1), 456–463.

Fooks, G. J., & Gilmore, A. B. (2013). Corporate philanthropy, political influence, and health policy. *PLoS One, 8*(11), e80864.

Forbes, C. E., & Grafman, J. (2010). 'The Role of the Human Prefrontal Cortex in Social Cognition and Moral Judgment'. In S. E. Hyman (ed.), *Annual Review of Neuroscience, 33*, 299–324.

Foroud, T., Edenberg, H. J., & Crabbe, J. C. (2010). Genetic research: who is at risk for alcoholism? *Alcohol Res Health*, *33*(1–2), 64–75.

Foroud, T., Edenberg, H. J., Goate, A., Rice, J., Flury, L., Koller, D. L., ... Reich, T. (2000). Alcoholism susceptibility loci: confirmation studies in a replicate sample and further mapping. *Alcoholism: Clinical and Experimental Research*, *24*(7), 933–945. doi:10.1097/00000374-200007000-00001

Franken, I. H. (2003). Drug craving and addiction: integrating psychological and neuropsychopharmacological approaches. *Progress in Neuro-Psychopharmacology and Biological Psychiatry*, *27*(4), 563–579.

Franken, I. H., Hendriks, V. M., Stam, C. J., & Van den Brink, W. (2004). A role for dopamine in the processing of drug cues in heroin dependent patients. *European Neuropsychopharmacology*, *14*(6), 503–508.

Franken, I. H., Kroon, L. Y., & Hendriks, V. M. (2000). Influence of individual differences in craving and obsessive cocaine thoughts on attentional processes in cocaine abuse patients. *Addict Behav*, *25*(1), 99–102.

Frawley, P. J., & Smith, J. W. (1990). Chemical aversion therapy in the treatment of cocaine dependence as part of a multimodal treatment program: treatment outcome. *Journal of Substance Abuse Treatment*, *7*(1), 21–29. doi:http://dx.doi.org/10.1016/0740-5472(90)90033-M

Frazer, K. A., Murray, S. S., Schork, N. J., & Topol, E. J. (2009). Human genetic variation and its contribution to complex traits. *Nat Rev Genet*, *10*(4), 241–251. doi:10.1038/nrg2554

Freeman, C., & Tyrer, P. (2006). *Research Methods in Psychiatry* (3rd edn). London: RCPsych Publications.

Ganapathy, V. (2011). Drugs of abuse and human placenta. *Life Sciences*, *88*(0), 926–930. doi:10.1016/j.lfs.2010.09.015

Gates, P. J., Sabioni, P., Copeland, J., Le Foll, B., & Gowing, L. (2016). Psychosocial interventions for cannabis use disorder. *Cochrane Database of Systematic Reviews* (5). doi:10.1002/14651858.CD005336.pub4

Gaval-Cruz, M., & Weinshenker, D. (2009). Mechanisms of disulfiram-induced cocaine abstinence: antabuse and cocaine relapse. *Mol Interv*, *9*(4), 175–187. doi:10.1124/mi.9.4.6

Gelernter, J., Yu, Y., Weiss, R., Brady, K., Panhuysen, C., Yang, B. Z., ... Farrer, L. (2006). Haplotype spanning TTC12 and ANKK1, flanked by the DRD2 and NCAM1 loci, is strongly associated to nicotine dependence in two distinct American populations. *Hum Mol Genet*, *15*(24), 3498–3507. doi:10.1093/hmg/ddl426

Gelkopf, M., Levitt, S., & Bleich, A. (2002). An integration of three approaches to addiction and methadone maintenance treatment: the self-medication hypothesis, the disease model and social criticism. *Israel Journal of Psychiatry and Related Sciences*, *39*(2), 140.

Gigerenzer, G., Gaissmaier, W., Kurz-Milcke, E., Schwartz, L. M., & Woloshin, S. (2007). Helping doctors and patients make sense of health statistics. *Psychological Science in the Public Interest*, *8*(2), 53–96.

Gilovich, T., & Douglas, C. (1986). Biased evaluations of randomly determined gambling outcomes. *Journal of Experimental Social Psychology*, *22*(3), 228–241.

# REFERENCES

Glautier, S., & Spencer, K. (1999). Activation of alcohol-related associative networks by recent alcohol consumption and alcohol-related cues. *Addiction*, *94*(7), 1033–1041.

Glickman, S. E., & Schiff, B. B. (1967). A biological theory of reinforcement. *Psychol Rev*, *74*(2), 81–109.

Godfrey, C., Stewart, D., & Gossop, M. (2004). Economic analysis of costs and consequences of the treatment of drug misuse: 2-year outcome data from the National Treatment Outcome Research Study (NTORS). *Addiction*, *99*(6), 697–707. doi:10.1111/j.1360-0443.2004.00752.x

Goedde, H. W., Agarwal, D. P., & Harada, S. (1980). Genetic-studies on alcohol metabolizing enzymes: detection of isozymes in human-hair roots. *Enzyme*, *25*(4), 281–286.

Goh, E. T., & Morgan, M. Y. (2017). Review article: pharmacotherapy for alcohol dependence – the why, the what and the wherefore. *Aliment Pharmacol Ther*, *45*(7), 865–882. doi:10.1111/apt.13965

Goldman, D., & Ducci, F. (2007). Deconstruction of vulnerability to complex diseases: enhanced effect sizes and power of intermediate phenotypes. *ScientificWorld Journal*, *7*, 124–130. doi:10.1100/tsw.2007.210

Goldman, M., Brown, S. A., & Christiansen, B. (1987). 'Expectancy Theory: Thinking About Drinking'. In H. Blane & K. Leornard (eds), *Psychological Theories of Drinking and Alcoholism* (pp. 181–226). New York: Guilford Press.

Goldman, R. D. (2013). Caffeinated energy drinks in children. *Canadian Family Physician*, *59*(9), 947–948.

Goldstein, R. Z., Tomasi, D., Rajaram, S., Cottone, L. A., Zhang, L., Maloney, T., … Volkow, N. D. (2007). Role of the anterior cingulate and medial orbitofrontal cortex in processing drug cues in cocaine addiction. *Neuroscience*, *144*(4), 1153–1159.

Goldstein, R. Z., & Volkow, N. D. (2002). Drug addiction and its underlying neurobiological basis: neuroimaging evidence for the involvement of the frontal cortex. *American Journal of Psychiatry*, *159*(10), 1642–1652. doi:10.1176/appi.ajp.159.10.1642

Goodwin, D. W., Schulsin.F, Moller, N., Hermanse.L, Winokur, G., & Guze, S. B. (1974). Drinking problems in adopted and nonadopted sons of alcoholics. *Arch Gen Psychiatry*, *31*(2), 164–169.

Gossop, M. (2003). *Drug Addiction and its Treatment*. Oxford: Oxford University Press.

Gossop, M. (2015). The National Treatment Outcomes Research Study (NTORS) and its influence on addiction treatment policy in the United Kingdom. *Addiction*, *110*, Suppl 2, 50–53. doi:10.1111/add.12906

Gossop, M., Marsden, J., & Stewart, D. (2000). Treatment outcomes of stimulant misusers: one year follow-up results from the national treatment outcome research study (NTORS). *Addict Behav*, *25*(4), 509–522.

Gossop, M., Marsden, J., Stewart, D., & Kidd, T. (2002). Changes in use of crack cocaine after drug misuse treatment: 4–5 year follow-up results from the National Treatment Outcome Research Study (NTORS). *Drug Alcohol Depend*, *66*(1), 21–28.

Gossop, M., Marsden, J., Stewart, D., & Kidd, T. (2003). The National Treatment Outcome Research Study (NTORS): 4–5 year follow-up results. *Addiction*, *98*(3), 291–303.

Gottesman, II, & Gould, T. D. (2003). The endophenotype concept in psychiatry: etymology and strategic intentions. *Am J Psychiatry*, *160*(4), 636–645.

Gotti, C., & Clementi, F. (2004). Neuronal nicotinic receptors: from structure to pathology. *Prog Neurobiol*, *74*(6), 363–396. doi:10.1016/j.pneurobio.2004.09.006

Goudie, A. J. (1991). 'Animal Models of Drug Abuse and Dependence'. In P. Wilner (ed.), *Behavioural Models in Psychopharmacology: Theoretical, Industrial and Clinical Perspectives*. Cambridge: Cambridge University Press.

Grant, B., Hasin, D., Chou, S., Stinson, F., & Dawson, D. (2004). Nicotine dependence and psychiatric disorders in the United States: results from the national epidemiological survey on alcohol and related conditions. *Arch Gen Psychiatry, 61*, 1107–1115.

Grant, B., Stinson, F., Dawson, D., Chou, S., Durfour, M., Compton, W., … Kaplan, K. (2004). Prevalence and co-occurrence of substance use disorders and independent mood and anxiety disorders: results from the National Epidemiological Survey on Alcohol and related conditions. *Arch Gen Psychiatry, 61*, 807–816.

Grant, J. E., & Chamberlain, S. R. (2014). Impulsive action and impulsive choice across substance and behavioral addictions: cause or consequence? *Addict Behav, 39*(11), 1632–1639. doi:10.1016/j.addbeh.2014.04.022

Grant, J. E., Potenza, M. N., Weinstein, A., & Gorelick, D. A. (2010). Introduction to behavioral addictions. *Am J Drug Alcohol Abuse, 36*(5), 233–241. doi:10.3109/00952990.2010.491884

Gray, K. M., Carpenter, M. J., Baker, N. L., DeSantis, S. M., Kryway, E., Hartwell, K. J., … Brady, K. T. (2012). A double-blind randomized controlled trial of N-acetylcysteine in cannabis-dependent adolescents. *Am J Psychiatry, 169*(8), 805–812. doi:10.1176/appi.ajp.2012.12010055

Greenwald, G. (2009). *Drug Decriminalization in Portugal: Lessons for Creating Fair and Successful Drug Policies*. Washington, DC: Cato Institute.

Griffiths, M. D., Kuss, D. J., Billieux, J., & Pontes, H. M. (2016). The evolution of Internet addiction: a global perspective. *Addict Behav, 53*, 193–195. doi:10.1016/j.addbeh.2015.11.001

Grilo, C. M., & Shiffman, S. (1994). Longitudinal investigation of the abstinence violation effect in binge eaters. *Journal of Consulting and Clinical Psychology, 62*(3), 611.

Grinspoon, L., & Doblin, R. (2001). Psychedelics as catalysts of insight-oriented psychotherapy. *Social Research, 68*(3), 677–695.

Guo, S. W. (2001). Does higher concordance in monozygotic twins than in dizygotic twins suggest a genetic component? *Human Heredity, 51*(3), 121–132. doi:10.1159/000053333

Guze, S. B., Cloninger, C. R., Martin, R., & Clayton, P. J. (1986). Alcoholism as a medical disorder. *Compr Psychiatry, 27*(6), 501–510.

Haber, S. N., Fudge, J. L., & McFarland, N. R. (2000). Striatonigrostriatal pathways in primates form an ascending spiral from the shell to the dorsolateral striatum. *J Neurosci, 20*(6), 2369–2382.

Hadaway, P. F., Alexander, B. K., Coambs, R. B., & Beyerstein, B. (1979). Effect of housing and gender on preference for morphine-sucrose solutions in rats. *Psychopharmacology, 66*(1), 87–91. doi:10.1007/bf00431995

Haile, C. N., De La Garza, R., 2nd, Mahoney, J. J., 3rd, Nielsen, D. A., Kosten, T. R., & Newton, T. F. (2012). The impact of disulfiram treatment on the reinforcing effects of cocaine: a randomized clinical trial. *PLoS One, 7*(11), e47702. doi:10.1371/journal.pone.0047702

Hajek, P., & Stead, L. F. (2001). Aversive smoking for smoking cessation. *Cochrane Database of Systematic Reviews*, Issue 3. Art. No.: CD000546.

# REFERENCES

Hall, F. S., Drgonova, J., Jain, S., & Uhl, G. R. (2013). Implications of genome wide association studies for addiction: are our a priori assumptions all wrong? *Pharmacology & Therapeutics*, *140*(3), 267–279. doi:10.1016/j.pharmthera.2013.07.006

Hart, A. B., & Kranzler, H. R. (2015). Alcohol dependence genetics: lessons learned from genome-wide association studies (GWAS) and post-GWAS analyses. *Alcoholism: Clinical and Experimental Research*, *39*(8), 1312–1327. doi:10.1111/acer.12792

Hasin, D. S., O'Brien, C. P., Auriacombe, M., Borges, G., Bucholz, K., Budney, A., ... Grant, B. F. (2013). DSM-5 criteria for substance use disorders: recommendations and rationale. *Am J Psychiatry*, *170*(8), 834–851. doi:10.1176/appi.ajp.2013.12060782

Hayes, S., & Hirsch, C. R. (2007). Information processing biases in generalized anxiety disorder. *Psychiatry*, *6*(5), 176–182.

Heath, A. C., Bucholz, K. K., Madden, P. A. F., Dinwiddie, S. H., Slutske, W. S., Bierut, L. J., ... Martin, N. G. (1997). Genetic and environmental contributions to alcohol dependence risk in a national twin sample: consistency of findings in women and men. *Psychological Medicine*, *27*(6), 1381–1396. doi:10.1017/s0033291797005643

Heath, A. C., & Martin, N. G. (1994). 'Genetic Influences on Alcohol Consumption Patterns and Problem Drinking: Results from the Australian NH- and-MRC Twin Panel Follow-up Survey'. In T. F. Babor, V. Hesselbrock, R. E. Meyer, & W. Shoemaker (eds), *Types of Alcoholics: Evidence from Clinical, Experimental, and Genetic Research* (Vol. 708, pp. 72–85).

Heath, A. C., Whitfield, J. B., Madden, P. A. F., Bucholz, K. K., Dinwiddie, S. H., Slutske, W. S., ... Martin, N. G. (2001). Towards a molecular epidemiology of alcohol dependence: analysing the interplay of genetic and environmental risk factors. *British Journal of Psychiatry*, *178*, S33–S40. doi:10.1192/bjp.178.40.s33

Heather, N. (2013). A radical but flawed proposal: comments on Rehm et al. 'Defining Substance Use Disorders: Do We Really Need More than Heavy Use?'. *Alcohol and Alcoholism*, *48*(6), 646–647. doi:10.1093/alcalc/agt153

Heilig, M., Goldman, D., Berrettini, W., & O'Brien, C. P. (2011). Pharmacogenetic approaches to the treatment of alcohol addiction. *Nat Rev Neurosci*, *12*(11), 670–684. doi:10.1038/nrn3110

Heinz, A., Reimold, M., Wrase, J., Hermann, D., Croissant, B., Mundle, G., ... Mann, K. (2005). Correlation of stable elevations in striatal mu-opioid receptor availability in detoxified alcoholic patients with alcohol craving: a positron emission tomography study using carbon 11-labeled carfentanil. *Arch Gen Psychiatry*, *62*(1), 57–64. doi:10.1001/archpsyc.62.1.57

Herbert, B. M., & Pollatos, O. (2012). The body in the mind: on the relationship between interoception and embodiment. *Top Cogn Sci*, *4*(4), 692–704. doi:10.1111/j.1756-8765.2012.01189.x

Hermann, D., Hirth, N., Reimold, M., Batra, A., Smolka, M. N., Hoffmann, S., ... Hansson, A. C. (2017). Low mu-opioid receptor status in alcohol dependence identified by combined positron emission tomography and post-mortem brain analysis. *Neuropsychopharmacology*, *42*(3), 606–614. doi:10.1038/npp.2016.145

Hernstein, R. (1990). Rational choice theory: necessary but not sufficient. *Journal of the American Psychologist*, *45*, 356–367.

# REFERENCES

Hester, R. K., Lenberg, K. L., Campbell, W., & Delaney, H. D. (2013). Overcoming addictions, a web-based application, and SMART Recovery, an online and in-person mutual help group for problem drinkers, part 1: three-month outcomes of a randomized controlled trial. *J Med Internet Res, 15*(7), e134. doi:10.2196/jmir.2565

Heyman, G. M. (2009). *Addiction: A Disorder of Choice*. Cambridge, MA: Harvard University Press.

Heyman, G. M. (2013). Addiction and choice: theory and new data. *Front Psychiatry, 4*(31.10), 3389.

Higgins, S. T., Budney, A. J., Bickel, W. K., Hughes, J. R., Foerg, F., & Badger, G. (1993). Achieving cocaine abstinence with a behavioral approach. *Am J Psychiatry, 150*(5), 763–769. doi:10.1176/ajp.150.5.763

Higgins, S. T., Sigmon, S., & Heil, S. (2011). *Contingency Management in the Treatment of Substance Use Disorders: Trends in the Literature*. Philadelphia, PA: Lippincott Williams and Wilkins.

Higgins, S. T., & Solomon, L. J. (2016). Some recent developments on financial incentives for smoking cessation among pregnant and newly postpartum women. *Curr Addict Rep, 3*(1), 9–18. doi:10.1007/s40429-016-0092-0

Hill, A., & Paynter, S. (1992). Alcohol dependence and semantic priming of alcohol related words. *Personality and Individual Differences, 13*(6), 745–750.

Hoffmeister, F., & Wuttke, W. (1975). Psychotropic drugs as negative reinforcers. *Pharmacol Rev, 27*(3), 419–428.

Hogg, R. C., Raggenbass, M., & Bertrand, D. (2003). Nicotinic acetylcholine receptors: from structure to brain function. *Rev Physiol Biochem Pharmacol, 147*, 1–46. doi:10.1007/s10254-003-0005-1

Hollerman, J. R., & Schultz, W. (1998). Dopamine neurons report an error in the temporal prediction of reward during learning. *Nat Neurosci, 1*(4), 304–309.

Hong, L. E., Hodgkinson, C. A., Yang, Y., Sampath, H., Ross, T. J., Buchholz, B., ... Stein, E. A. (2010). A genetically modulated, intrinsic cingulate circuit supports human nicotine addiction. *Proc Natl Acad Sci U S A, 107*(30), 13509–13514. doi:10.1073/pnas.1004745107

Hrubec, Z., & Omenn, G. S. (1981). Evidence of genetic predisposition to alcoholic cirrhosis and psychosis: twin concordances for alcoholism and its biological end-points by zygosity among male veterans. *Alcoholism: Clinical and Experimental Research, 5*(2), 207–215. doi:10.1111/j.1530-0277.1981.tb04890.x

Hsu, L. G. (1990). Experiential aspects of bulimia nervosa implications for cognitive behavioral therapy. *Behavior Modification, 14*(1), 50–65.

Huang, W., Payne, T. J., Ma, J. Z., Beuten, J., Dupont, R. T., Inohara, N., & Li, M. D. (2009). Significant association of ANKK1 and detection of a functional polymorphism with nicotine dependence in an African-American sample. *Neuropsychopharmacology, 34*(2), 319–330. doi:10.1038/npp.2008.37

Hughes, J. R., Stead, L. F., Hartmann-Boyce, J., Cahill, K., & Lancaster, T. (2014). Antidepressants for smoking cessation. *Cochrane Database Syst Rev* (1), Cd000031. doi:10.1002/14651858.CD000031.pub4

Hukkanen, J., Jacob, P., 3rd, & Benowitz, N. L. (2005). Metabolism and disposition kinetics of nicotine. *Pharmacol Rev, 57*(1), 79–115. doi:10.1124/pr.57.1.3

# REFERENCES

Huxley, A. (1954). *The Doors of Perception*. New York: Harper & Brothers.

Hyman, S. E., Malenka, R. C., & Nestler, E. J. (2006). Neural mechanisms of addiction: the role of reward-related learning and memory. *Annual Review of Neuroscience, 29*, 565–598.

Imel, Z. E., Wampold, B. E., Miller, S. D., & Fleming, R. R. (2008). Distinctions without a difference: direct comparisons of psychotherapies for alcohol use disorders. *Psychology of Addictive Behaviors, 22*(4), 533–543. doi:10.1037/a0013171

Imperato, A., Mulas, A., & Di Chiara, G. (1986). Nicotine preferentially stimulates dopamine release in the limbic system of freely moving rats. *Eur J Pharmacol, 132*(2–3), 337–338.

Indave, B. I., Minozzi, S., Pani, P. P., & Amato, L. (2016). Antipsychotic medications for cocaine dependence. *Cochrane Database Syst Rev, 3*, Cd006306. doi:10.1002/14651858.CD006306.pub3

Insel, T. R. (2014). The NIMH Research Domain Criteria (RDoC) Project: precision medicine for psychiatry. *American Journal of Psychiatry, 171*(4), 395–397. doi:10.1176/appi.ajp.2014.14020138

Irvin, J. E., Bowers, C. A., Dunn, M. E., & Wang, M. C. (1999). Efficacy of relapse prevention: a meta-analytic review. *Journal of Consulting and Clinical Psychology, 67*(4), 563–570. doi:10.1037/0022-006X.67.4.563

Janis, I. L., & Mann, L. (1977). *Decision Making: A Psychological Analysis of Conflict, Choice, and Commitment*. New York: Free Press.

Jellinek, E. (1960). *The Disease Concept of Alcoholism*. Highland Park, NJ: Hillhouse Press.

Jentsch, J. D., & Pennington, Z. T. (2014). Reward, interrupted: inhibitory control and its relevance to addictions. *Neuropharmacology, 76 Pt B*, 479–486. doi:10.1016/j.neuropharm.2013.05.022

Jhanjee, S. (2014). Evidence based psychosocial interventions in substance use. *Indian Journal of Psychological Medicine, 36*(2), 112–118. doi:10.4103/0253-7176.130960

Job, V., Dweck, C. S., & Walton, G. M. (2010). Ego depletion – is it all in your head? Implicit theories about willpower affect self-regulation. *Psychol Sci, 21*(11).

Jordan, M. R., & Morrisonponce, D. (2017). Naloxone. In *StatPearls*. Treasure Island (FL): StatPearls Publishing. Available at www.ncbi.nlm.nih.gov/pubmed/2872293

Julien, R., Comaty, J., & Advokat, C. (2014). *Julien's Primer of Drug Action: A Comprehensive Guide to the Actions, Uses, and Side Effects of Psychoactive Drugs* (13th edn). New York: Worth.

Kalant, H. (2010). What neurobiology cannot tell us about addiction. *Addiction, 105*(5), 780–789. doi:10.1111/j.1360-0443.2009.02739.x

Kalivas, P. W., & Volkow, N. D. (2005). The neural basis of addiction: a pathology of motivation and choice. *American Journal of Psychiatry, 162*(8), 1403–1413. doi:10.1176/appi.ajp.162.8.1403

Kalivas, P. W., & Weber, B. (1988). Amphetamine injection into the ventral mesencephalon sensitizes rats to peripheral amphetamine and cocaine. *J Pharmacol Exp Ther, 245*(3), 1095–1102.

Karim, R., & Chaudhri, P. (2012). Behavioral addictions: an overview. *J Psychoactive Drugs, 44*(1), 5–17. doi:10.1080/02791072.2012.662859

Katz, J. L. (1989). 'Drugs as Reinforcers: Pharmacological and Behavioural Factors'. In J. M. Liebman & S. J. Cooper (eds), *The Neuropharmacological Basis of Reward*. Oxford: Oxford University Press.

Katzenschlager, R. (2011). Dopaminergic dysregulation syndrome in Parkinson's disease. *J Neurol Sci, 310*(1–2), 271–275. doi:10.1016/j.jns.2011.07.012

Kazdin, A. E., & Bootzin, R. R. (1972). The token economy: an evaluative review. *Journal of Applied Behavior Analysis*, *5*(3), 343–372.

Kelley, A. E., & Berridge, K. C. (2002). The neuroscience of natural rewards: relevance to addictive drugs. *Journal of Neuroscience*, *22*(9), 3306–3311.

Kelly, A. M. C., Scheres, A., Sonuga-Barke, E., & Castellanos, F. X. (2007). 'Functional Neuroimaging of Reward and Motivational Pathways in ADHD'. In M. Fitzgerald, M. Bellgrove, & M. Gill (eds), *Handbook of Attention Deficit Hyperactivity Disorder*. Chichester, UK: John Wiley & Sons Ltd.

Kelly, J. F., Stout, R., Zywiak, W., & Schneider, R. (2006). A 3-year study of addiction mutual-help group participation following intensive outpatient treatment. *Alcoholism: Clinical and Experimental Research*, *30*(8), 1381–1392. doi:10.1111/j.1530-0277.2006.00165.x

Kendler, K. S., Heath, A. C., Neale, M. C., Kessler, R. C., & Eaves, L. J. (1992). A population based twin study of alcoholism in women. *Jama-Journal of the American Medical Association*, *268*(14), 1877–1882. doi:10.1001/jama.268.14.1877

Kendler, K. S., Myers, J., & Prescott, C. A. (2007). Specificity of genetic and environmental risk factors for symptoms of cannabis, cocaine, alcohol, caffeine, and nicotine dependence. *Arch Gen Psychiatry*, *64*(11), 1313–1320. doi:10.1001/archpsyc.64.11.1313

Kendler, K. S., Neale, M. C., Sullivan, P., Corey, L. A., Gardner, C. O., & Prescott, C. A. (1999). A population-based twin study in women of smoking initiation and nicotine dependence. *Psychological Medicine*, *29*(2), 299–308. doi:10.1017/s0033291798008022

Kendler, K. S., Prescott, C. A., Neale, M. C., & Pedersen, N. L. (1997). Temperance board registration for alcohol abuse in a national sample of Swedish male twins, born 1902 to 1949. *Arch Gen Psychiatry*, *54*(2), 178–184.

Kenny, P. J. (2007). Brain reward systems and compulsive drug use. *Trends Pharmacol Sci*, *28*(3), 135–141.

Kessler, R. C., Hwang, I., LaBrie, R., Petukhova, M., Sampson, N. A., Winters, K. C., & Shaffer, H. J. (2008). The prevalence and correlates of DSM-IV Pathological Gambling in the National Comorbidity Survey Replication. *Psychological Medicine*, *38*(9), 1351–1360. doi:10.1017/S0033291708002900

Khan, A., Tansel, A., White, D. L., Kayani, W. T., Bano, S., Lindsay, J., ... Kanwal, F. (2016). Efficacy of psychosocial interventions in inducing and maintaining alcohol abstinence in patients with chronic liver disease: a systematic review. *Clinical Gastroenterology and Hepatology*, *14*(2), 191–202.e194. doi:http://dx.doi.org/10.1016/j.cgh.2015.07.047

Khantzian, E. J. (1985). The self-medication hypothesis of addictive disorders: focus on heroin and cocaine dependence. *American Journal of Psychiatry*, *142*(11), 1259–1264.

Khantzian, E. J., & Albanese, M. (2008). *Understanding Addiction as Self-Medication*. Maryland 20706, USA: Rowman and Littlefield.

Kim, S. H., Baik, S. H., Park, C. S., Kim, S. J., Choi, S. W., & Kim, S. E. (2011). Reduced striatal dopamine D2 receptors in people with Internet addiction. *Neuroreport*, *22*(8), 407–411. doi:10.1097/WNR.0b013e328346e16e

King, D. L., & Delfabbro, P. H. (2013). Issues for DSM-5: video-gaming disorder? *Australian and New Zealand Journal of Psychiatry*, *47*(1), 20–22.

# REFERENCES

Klosterhalfen, S., & Enck, P. (2006). Psychobiology of the placebo response. *Auton Neurosci, 125*(1–2), 94–99. doi:10.1016/j.autneu.2006.01.015

Ko, C., Yen, J., Chen, C., Yeh, Y., & Yen, C. (2009). Predictive values of psychiatric symptoms for internet addiction in adolescents: a 2-year prospective study. *Archives of Pediatrics & Adolescent Medicine, 163*(10), 937–943. doi:10.1001/archpediatrics.2009.159

Koepp, M. J., Gunn, R. N., Lawrence, A. D., Cunningham, V. J., Dagher, A., Jones, T., ... Grasby, P. M. (1998). Evidence for striatal dopamine release during a video game. *Nature, 393*(6682), 266–268.

Kolta, M. G., Shreve, P., & Uretsky, N. J. (1989). Effect of pretreatment with amphetamine on the interaction between amphetamine and dopamine neurons in the nucleus accumbens. *Neuropharmacology, 28*(1), 9–14.

Konkoly Thege, B., Colman, I., el-Guebaly, N., Hodgins, D. C., Patten, S. B., Schopflocher, D., ... Wild, T. C. (2015). Social judgments of behavioral versus substance-related addictions: a population-based study. *Addict Behav, 42*, 24–31. doi:10.1016/j.addbeh.2014.10.025

Konkoly Thege, B., Woodin, E. M., Hodgins, D. C., & Williams, R. J. (2015). Natural course of behavioral addictions: a 5-year longitudinal study. *BMC Psychiatry, 15*, 4. doi:10.1186/s12888-015-0383-3

Koob, G. F. (1987). 'Positive Reinforcement Properties of drugs: Search for Neural Substrates'. In J. Engel & L. Oreland (eds), *Brain Reward Systems and Abuse*. New York: Raven Press.

Koob, G. F. (2003). Neuroadaptive mechanisms of addiction: studies on the extended amygdala. *European Neuropsychopharmacology, 13*(6), 442–452.

Koob, G. F. (2010). The role of CRF and CRF-related peptides in the dark side of addiction. *Brain Research, 1314*, 3–14. doi:10.1016/j.brainres.2009.11.008

Koob, G. F., & Le Moal, M. (1997). Drug abuse: hedonic homeostatic dysregulation. *Science, 278*(5335), 52–58.

Koob, G. F., & Le Moal, M. (2001). Drug addiction, dysregulation of reward, and allostasis. *Neuropsychopharmacology, 24*(2), 97–129. doi:10.1016/S0893-133X(00)00195-0

Koob, G. F., & Le Moal, M. (2005). Plasticity of reward neurocircuitry and the 'dark side' of drug addiction. *Nat Neurosci, 8*(11), 1442–1444. doi:10.1038/nn1105-1442

Kosten, T. R., & George, T. P. (2002). The neurobiology of opioid dependence: implications for treatment. *Science & Practice Perspectives, 1*(1), 13–20.

Krebs, T. S., & Johansen, P. O. (2012). Lysergic acid diethylamide (LSD) for alcoholism: meta-analysis of randomized controlled trials. *J Psychopharmacol, 26*(7), 994–1002. doi:10.1177/0269881112439253

Kringelbach, M. L. (2005). The human orbitofrontal cortex: linking reward to hedonic experience. *Nature Reviews Neuroscience, 6*(9), 691–702.

Krupitsky, E. M., & Grinenko, A. Y. (1997). Ketamine psychedelic therapy (KPT): a review of the results of ten years of research. *J Psychoactive Drugs, 29*(2), 165–183. doi:10.1080/02791072.1997.10400185

Kuss, D. J., & Griffiths, M. D. (2011). Online social networking and addiction: a review of the psychological literature. *Int J Environ Res Public Health, 8*(9), 3528–3552. doi:10.3390/ijerph8093528

Kuss, D. J., Griffiths, M. D., Karila, L., & Billieux, J. (2014). Internet addiction: a systematic review of epidemiological research for the last decade. *Curr Pharm Des, 20*(25), 4026–4052.

Kuss, D. J., Griffiths, M. D., & Pontes, H. M. (2016). Chaos and confusion in DSM-5 diagnosis of Internet Gaming Disorder: issues, concerns, and recommendations for clarity in the field. *J Behav Addict*, 1–7. doi:10.1556/2006.5.2016.062

Lak, A., Stauffer, W. R., & Schultz, W. (2016). Dopamine neurons learn relative chosen value from probabilistic rewards. *Elife*, 5. doi:10.7554/eLife.18044

Lambert, N. M., McLeod, M., & Schenk, S. (2006). Subjective responses to initial experience with cocaine: an exploration of the incentive-sensitization theory of drug abuse. *Addiction*, *101*(5), 713–725.

Lawrence, A. J., Luty, J., Bogdan, N. A., Sahakian, B. J., & Clark, L. (2009). Problem gamblers share deficits in impulsive decision-making with alcohol-dependent individuals. *Addiction*, *104*(6), 1006–1015. doi:10.1111/j.1360-0443.2009.02533.x

Leeman, R. F., & Potenza, M. N. (2012). Similarities and differences between pathological gambling and substance use disorders: a focus on impulsivity and compulsivity. *Psychopharmacology*, *219*(2), 469–490. doi:10.1007/s00213-011-2550-7

Leith, N. J., & Barrett, R. J. (1981). Self-stimulation and amphetamine: tolerance to d and l isomers and cross tolerance to cocaine and methylphenidate. *Psychopharmacology (Berl)*, *74*(1), 23–28.

Lemere, F., & Voegtlin, W. L. (1940). Conditioned reflex therapy of alcoholic addiction: specificity of conditioning against chronic alcoholism. *Cal West Med*, *53*(6), 268–269.

Lessov, C. N., Martin, N. G., Statham, D. J., Todorov, A. A., Slutske, W. S., Bucholz, K. K., ... Madden, P. A. F. (2004). Defining nicotine dependence for genetic research: evidence from Australian twins. *Psychological Medicine*, *34*(5), 865–879. doi:10.1017/s0033291703001582

Leventhal, A. M., Strong, D. R., Kirkpatrick, M. G., Unger, J. B., Sussman, S., Riggs, N. R., ... Audrain-McGovern, J. (2015). Association of electronic cigarette use with initiation of combustible tobacco product smoking in early adolescence. *Jama*, *314*(7), 700–707. doi:10.1001/jama.2015.8950

Lieber, C. S. (1987). Microsomal ethanol-oxidizing system. *Enzyme*, *37*(1–2), 45–56.

Lilienfeld, S. O. (2014). The Research Domain Criteria (RDoC): an analysis of methodological and conceptual challenges. *Behav Res Ther*, *62*, 129–139. doi:10.1016/j.brat.2014.07.019

Lilienfeld, S. O., Smith, S., & Watts, A. (2013). 'Issues in Diagnosis: Conceptual Issues and Controversies'. In W. E. Craighead, D. J. Miklowitz, & L. W. Craighead (eds), *Psychopathology: History, Diagnosis, and Empirical Foundations*. Hoboken, New Jersey: John Wiley and Sons Inc.

Longman, H., O'Connor, E., & Obst, P. (2009). The effect of social support derived from World of Warcraft on negative psychological symptoms. *CyberPsychology & Behavior*, *12*(5), 563–566.

Lopez-Quintero, C., de los Cobos, J. P., Hasin, D. S., Okuda, M., Wang, S., Grant, B. F., & Blanco, C. (2011). Probability and predictors of transition from first use to dependence on nicotine, alcohol, cannabis, and cocaine: results of the National Epidemiologic Survey on Alcohol and Related Conditions (NESARC). *Drug and Alcohol Dependence*, *115*(1), 120–130.

Lorains, F. K., Cowlishaw, S., & Thomas, S. A. (2011). Prevalence of comorbid disorders in problem and pathological gambling: systematic review and meta-analysis of population surveys. *Addiction*, *106*(3), 490–498. doi:10.1111/j.1360-0443.2010.03300.x

# REFERENCES

Lovallo, W. R. (2006). Cortisol secretion patterns in addiction and addiction risk. *International Journal of Psychophysiology*, *59*(3), 195–202. doi:10.1016/j.ijpsycho.2005.10.007

Lubman, D., Peters, L., Mogg, K., Bradley, B., & Deakin, J. (2000). Attentional bias for drug cues in opiate dependence. *Psychological Medicine*, *30*(01), 169–175.

Luczak, S. E., Glatt, S. J., & Wall, T. L. (2006). Meta-analyses of ALDH2 and ADH1B with alcohol dependence in Asians. *Psychological Bulletin*, *132*(4), 607–621. doi:10.1037/0033-2909.132.4.607

Luijten, M., Schellekens, A. F., Kühn, S., Machielse, M. W., & Sescousse, G. (2017). Disruption of reward processing in addiction: an image-based meta-analysis of Functional Magnetic Resonance Imaging studies. *JAMA Psychiatry*, *74*(4), 387–398.

Lusher, J., Chandler, C., & Ball, D. (2004). Alcohol dependence and the alcohol Stroop paradigm: evidence and issues. *Drug and Alcohol Dependence*, *75*(3), 225–231.

Lussier, J. P., Heil, S. H., Mongeon, J. A., Badger, G. J., & Higgins, S. T. (2006). A meta–analysis of voucher–based reinforcement therapy for substance use disorders. *Addiction*, *101*(2), 192–203.

Lyons, M., Hitsman, B., Xian, H., Panizzon, M. S., Jerskey, B. A., Santangelo, S., ... Tsuang, M. T. (2008). A twin study of smoking, nicotine dependence, and major depression in men. *Nicotine & Tobacco Research*, *10*(1), 97–108. doi:10.1080/14622200701705332

MacKillop, J., & Munafo, M. (2013). *Genetic Influences on Addiction: An Intermediate Phenotype Approach*. Cambridge, MA: MIT Press.

Malhi, G. S., Byrow, Y., Cassidy, F., Cipriani, A., Demyttenaere, K., Frye, M. A., ... Tohen, M. (2016). Ketamine: stimulating antidepressant treatment? *BJPsych Open*, *2*(3), e5–e9. doi:10.1192/bjpo.bp.116.002923

Mann, K., Hoffmann, S., & Pawlak, C. R. (2016). Does acamprosate really produce its anti-relapse effects via calcium? No support from the PREDICT study in human alcoholics. *Neuropsychopharmacology*, *41*(3), 659–660. doi:10.1038/npp.2015.175

Manolio, T. A., Collins, F. S., Cox, N. J., Goldstein, D. B., Hindorff, L. A., Hunter, D. J., ... Visscher, P. M. (2009). Finding the missing heritability of complex diseases. *Nature*, *461*(7265), 747–753. doi:10.1038/nature08494

Marissen, M. A., Franken, I. H., Waters, A. J., Blanken, P., Van Den Brink, W., & Hendriks, V. M. (2006). Attentional bias predicts heroin relapse following treatment. *Addiction*, *101*(9), 1306–1312.

Markel, H. (2011). *An Anatomy of Addiction: Sigmund Freud, William Halsted, and the Miracle Drug Cocaine*. New York: Pantheon Books, Random House.

Marlatt, G. A. (1985). Cognitive factors in the relapse process. *Relapse Prevention*, 128–200.

Marlatt, G. A., & Gordon, J. (1985). *Relapse Prevention: A Self-control Strategy for the Maintenance of Behavior Change*. New York: Guilford. pp. 85–101.

Martinez, D., Orlowska, D., Narendran, R., Slifstein, M., Liu, F., Kumar, D., ... Kleber, H. D. (2010). Dopamine type 2/3 receptor availability in the striatum and social status in human volunteers. *Biol Psychiatry*, *67*(3), 275–278. doi:10.1016/j.biopsych.2009.07.037

Maté, G. (2008). *In the Realm of Hungry Ghosts: Close Encounters with Addiction*. Toronto, Ontario: Random House Canada.

Matsumoto, K., Suzuki, W., & Tanaka, K. (2003). Neuronal correlates of goal-based motor selection in the prefrontal cortex. *Science*, *301*(5630), 229–232.

Mattick, R. P., Breen, C., Kimber, J., & Davoli, M. (2009). Methadone maintenance therapy versus no opioid replacement therapy for opioid dependence. *Cochrane Database Syst Rev* (3), Cd002209. doi:10.1002/14651858.CD002209.pub2

Mattick, R. P., Breen, C., Kimber, J., & Davoli, M. (2014). Buprenorphine maintenance versus placebo or methadone maintenance for opioid dependence. *Cochrane Database Syst Rev* (2), Cd002207. doi:10.1002/14651858.CD002207.pub4

McClellan, J., & King, M. C. (2010). Genetic heterogeneity in human disease. *Cell*, *141*(2), 210–217. doi:10.1016/j.cell.2010.03.032

McCusker, C. G. (2001). Cognitive biases and addiction: an evolution in theory and method. *Addiction*, *96*(1), 47–56.

McCusker, C. G., & Gettings, B. (1997). Automaticity of cognitive biases in addictive behaviours: further evidence with gamblers. *British Journal of Clinical Psychology*, *36*(4), 543–554.

McHugh, R. K., Hearon, B. A., & Otto, M. W. (2010). Cognitive behavioral therapy for substance use disorders. *Psychiatric Clinics of North America*, *33*(3), 511–525. doi:http://dx.doi.org/10.1016/j.psc.2010.04.012

Meehan, S. M., & Schechter, M. D. (1998). LSD produces conditioned place preference in male but not female fawn hooded rats. *Pharmacol Biochem Behav*, *59*(1), 105–108.

Meerkerk, G. J., Van Den Eijnden, R. J., & Garretsen, H. F. (2006). Predicting compulsive Internet use: it's all about sex! *Cyberpsychol Behav*, *9*(1), 95–103. doi:10.1089/cpb.2006.9.95

Mellentin, A. I., Skøt, L., Nielsen, B., Schippers, G. M., Nielsen, A. S., Stenager, E., & Juhl, C. (2017). Cue exposure therapy for the treatment of alcohol use disorders: a meta-analytic review. *Clinical Psychology Review*, *57*, 195–207. doi:https://doi.org/10.1016/j.cpr.2017.07.006

Meng, Y., Deng, W., Wang, H., Guo, W., & Li, T. (2015). The prefrontal dysfunction in individuals with Internet gaming disorder: a meta-analysis of functional magnetic resonance imaging studies. *Addict Biol*, *20*(4), 799–808. doi:10.1111/adb.12154

Merikangas, K. R., Stolar, M., Stevens, D. E., Goulet, J., Preisig, M. A., Fenton, B., ... Rounsaville, B. J. (1998). Familial transmission of substance use disorders. *Arch Gen Psychiatry*, *55*(11), 973–979. doi:10.1001/archpsyc.55.11.973

Metcalfe, J., & Mischel, W. (1999). A hot/cool-system analysis of delay of gratification: dynamics of willpower. *Psychological Review*, *106*(1), 3.

Miedl, S. F., Wiswede, D., Marco-Pallares, J., Ye, Z., Fehr, T., Herrmann, M., & Munte, T. F. (2015). The neural basis of impulsive discounting in pathological gamblers. *Brain Imaging Behav*, *9*(4), 887–898. doi:10.1007/s11682-015-9352-1

Miller, E. M., Shankar, M. U., Knutson, B., & McClure, S. M. (2014). Dissociating motivation from reward in human striatal activity. *J Cogn Neurosci*, *26*(5), 1075–1084. doi:10.1162/jocn_a_00535

Miller, W. R. (1983). Motivational interviewing with problem drinkers. *Behavioural Psychotherapy*, *11*(02), 147–172.

Miller, W. R. (1998). Researching the spiritual dimensions of alcohol and other drug problems. *Addiction*, *93*(7), 979–990.

Miller, W. R. (2003). 'Comments on Ainslie and Monterosso'. In *Choice, Behavioural Economics and Addiction* (pp. 62–66). Oxford, UK: Elsevier.

# REFERENCES

Miller, W. R., & Baca, L. M. (1983). Two-year follow-up of bibliotherapy and therapist-directed controlled drinking training for problem drinkers. *Behavior Therapy*, *14*(3), 441–448.

Miller, W. R., & Rollnick, S. (2013). *Motivational Interviewing Helping People Change* (3rd edn). New York: Guilford Press.

Miller, W. R., Sovereign, R. G., & Krege, B. (1988). Motivational interviewing with problem drinkers: II. The Drinker's Check-up as a preventive intervention. *Behavioural Psychotherapy*, *16*(4), 251–268.

Miller, W. R., Taylor, C. A., & West, J. C. (1980). Focused versus broad-spectrum behavior therapy for problem drinkers. *Journal of consulting and clinical psychology*, *48*(5), 590.

Miller, W. R., & Wilbourne, P. L. (2002). Mesa Grande: a methodological analysis of clinical trials of treatments for alcohol use disorders. *Addiction*, *97*(3), 265–277. doi:10.1046/j.1360-0443.2002.00019.x

Miller, W. R., Zweben, A., DiClemente, C., & Rychtarik, R. (1992). *Motivational Enhancement Therapy Manual* (DHHS Publication No. ADM 92-1894). Washington, DC: US Government Printing Office.

Milton, A. L., & Everitt, B. J. (2012). The persistence of maladaptive memory: addiction, drug memories and anti-relapse treatments. *Neurosci Biobehav Rev*, *36*(4), 1119–1139. doi:10.1016/j.neubiorev.2012.01.002

Mineur, Y. S., & Picciotto, M. R. (2008). Genetics of nicotinic acetylcholine receptors: Relevance to nicotine addiction. *Biochem Pharmacol*, *75*(1), 323–333. doi:10.1016/j.bcp.2007.06.010

Minozzi, S., Amato, L., Vecchi, S., Davoli, M., Kirchmayer, U., & Verster, A. (2011). Oral naltrexone maintenance treatment for opioid dependence. *Cochrane Database Syst Rev* (4). Cd001333. doi:10.1002/14651858.CD001333.pub4

Mirza, N. R., Pei, Q., Stolerman, I. P., & Zetterstrom, T. S. (1996). The nicotinic receptor agonists (-)-nicotine and isoarecolone differ in their effects on dopamine release in the nucleus accumbens. *Eur J Pharmacol*, *295*(2–3), 207–210.

Monahan, J. (2007). Statistical literacy: a prerequisite for evidence-based medicine. *Psychological Science in the Public Interest*, *8*(2), i–ii.

Mora, F., Phillips, A. G., Koolhaas, J. M., & Rolls, E. T. (1976). Prefrontal cortex and neostriatum self-stimulation in the rat: differential effects produced by apomorphine. *Brain Res Bull*, *1*(5), 421–424.

Morgan, D., Grant, K. A., Gage, H. D., Mach, R. H., Kaplan, J. R., Prioleau, O., ... Nader, M. A. (2002). Social dominance in monkeys: dopamine D2 receptors and cocaine self-administration. *Nat Neurosci*, *5*(2), 169–174.

Naqvi, N. H., & Bechara, A. (2010). The insula and drug addiction: an interoceptive view of pleasure, urges, and decision-making. *Brain Struct Funct*, *214*(5–6), 435–450. doi:10.1007/s00429-010-0268-7

Naqvi, N. H., Gaznick, N., Tranel, D., & Bechara, A. (2014). The insula: a critical neural substrate for craving and drug seeking under conflict and risk. *Ann N Y Acad Sci*, *1316*, 53–70. doi:10.1111/nyas.12415

Naqvi, N. H., Rudrauf, D., Damasio, H., & Bechara, A. (2007). Damage to the insula disrupts addiction to cigarette smoking. *Science*, *315*(5811), 531–534. doi:10.1126/science.1135926

Nelson, A., & Killcross, S. (2006). Amphetamine exposure enhances habit formation. *J Neurosci*, *26*(14), 3805–3812. doi:10.1523/JNEUROSCI.4305-05.2006

Neville, M. J., Johnstone, E. C., & Walton, R. T. (2004). Identification and characterization of ANKK1: a novel kinase gene closely linked to DRD2 on chromosome band 11q23.1. *Hum Mutat*, *23*(6), 540–545. doi:10.1002/humu.20039

Newlin, D. B., & Strubler, K. A. (2007). The habitual brain: an "adapted habit" theory of substance use disorders. *Subst Use Misuse*, *42*(2–3), 503–526.

Nixon, R. (1971). Special message to the Congress on drug abuse prevention and control. *The American Presidency Project*.

Noble, E. P. (2003). D2 dopamine receptor gene in psychiatric and neurologic disorders and its phenotypes. *Am J Med Genet B Neuropsychiatr Genet*, *116B*(1), 103–125. doi:10.1002/ajmg.b.10005

Nocito Echevarria, M. A., Andrade Reis, T., Ruffo Capatti, G., Siciliano Soares, V., da Silveira, D. X., & Fidalgo, T. M. (2017). N-acetylcysteine for treating cocaine addiction: a systematic review. *Psychiatry Res*, *251*, 197–203. doi:10.1016/j.psychres.2017.02.024

Nutt, D. (2011). Perverse effects of the precautionary principle: how banning mephedrone has unexpected implications for pharmaceutical discovery. *Ther Adv Psychopharmacol*, *1*(2), 35–36. doi:10.1177/2045125311406958

Nutt, D., King, L. A., Saulsbury, W., & Blakemore, C. (2007). Development of a rational scale to assess the harm of drugs of potential misuse. *Lancet*, *369*(9566), 1047–1053. doi:10.1016/S0140-6736(07)60464-4

Nutt, D. J., King, L. A., & Nichols, D. E. (2013). Effects of Schedule I drug laws on neuroscience research and treatment innovation. *Nature Reviews Neuroscience*, *14*, 577. doi:10.1038/nrn3530

Nutt, D. J., King, L. A., Phillips, L. D., & Independent Scientific Committee on Drugs (2010). Drug harms in the UK: a multicriteria decision analysis. *Lancet*, *376*(9752), 1558–1565. doi:10.1016/S0140-6736(10)61462-6

O'Brien, C. (2011). Addiction and dependence in DSM-V. *Addiction*, *106*(5), 866–867. doi:10.1111/j.1360-0443.2010.03144.x

O'Connor, E. C., Chapman, K., Butler, P., & Mead, A. N. (2011). The predictive validity of the rat self-administration model for abuse liability. *Neurosci Biobehav Rev*, *35*(3), 912–938. doi:10.1016/j.neubiorev.2010.10.012

O'Dell, L. E. (2009). A psychobiological framework of the substrates that mediate nicotine use during adolescence. *Neuropharmacology*, *56*, 263–278. doi:10.1016/j.neuropharm.2008.07.039

O'Doherty, J., Dayan, P., Schultz, J., Deichmann, R., Friston, K., & Dolan, R. J. (2004). Dissociable roles of ventral and dorsal striatum in instrumental conditioning. *Science*, *304*(5669), 452–454. doi:10.1126/science.1094285

O'Doherty, J. P., Dayan, P., Friston, K., Critchley, H., & Dolan, R. J. (2003). Temporal difference models and reward-related learning in the human brain. *Neuron*, *38*(2), 329–337.

Olds, J., & Milner, P. (1954). Positive reinforcement produced by electrical stimulation of septal area and other regions of rat brain. *J Comp Physiol Psychol*, *47*(6), 419–427.

Oota, H., Pakstis, A. J., Bonne-Tamir, B., Goldman, D., Grigorenko, E., Kajuna, S. L. B., ... Kidd, K. K. (2004). The evolution and population genetics of the ALDH2 locus: random genetic drift, selection,

# REFERENCES

and low levels of recombination. *Annals of Human Genetics, 68*, 93–109. doi:10.1046/j.1529-8817.2003.00060.x

Orford, J. (2001). *Excessive Appetites: A Psychological View of Addictions*. Hoboken, NJ: John Wiley & Sons Ltd.

Orford, J. (2013). *Power, Powerlessness and Addiction*. Cambridge: Cambridge University Press.

Orford, J., Morison, V., & Somers, M. (1996). Drinking and gambling: a comparison with implications for theories of addiction. *Drug Alcohol Rev, 15*(1), 47–56.

Orgaz, C., Estevez, A., & Matute, H. (2013). Pathological gamblers are more vulnerable to the illusion of control in a standard associative learning task. *Front Psychol, 4*, 306. doi:10.3389/fpsyg.2013.00306

Oslin, D. W., Berrettini, W., Kranzler, H. R., Pettinati, H., Gelernter, J., Volpicelli, J. R., & O'Brien, C. P. (2003). A functional polymorphism of the mu-opioid receptor gene is associated with naltrexone response in alcohol-dependent patients. *Neuropsychopharmacology, 28*(8), 1546–1552. doi:10.1038/sj.npp.1300219

Page, P. B. (1997). EM Jellinek and the evolution of alcohol studies: a critical essay. *Addiction, 92*(12), 1619–1637.

Pahnke, W. N., Kurland, A. A., Unger, S., Savage, C., & Grof, S. (1970). The experimental use of psychedelic (LSD) psychotherapy. *Jama, 212*(11), 1856–1863. doi:10.1001/jama.1970.03170240060010

Palpacuer, C., Laviolle, B., Boussageon, R., Reymann, J. M., Bellissant, E., & Naudet, F. (2015). Risks and benefits of Nalmefene in the treatment of adult alcohol dependence: a systematic literature review and meta-analysis of published and unpublished double-blind randomized controlled trials. *PLoS Med, 12*(12), e1001924. doi:10.1371/journal.pmed.1001924

Pam, A., Kemker, S. S., Ross, C. A., & Golden, R. (1996). The 'equal environments assumption' in MZ-DZ twin comparisons: an untenable premise of psychiatric genetics? *Acta Geneticae Medicae et Gemellologiae, 45*(3), 349–360.

Pan, L., Yang, X., Li, S., & Jia, C. (2015). Association of CYP2A6 gene polymorphisms with cigarette consumption: a meta-analysis. *Drug Alcohol Depend, 149*, 268–271. doi:10.1016/j.drugalcdep.2015.01.032

Parhami, I., Mojtabai, R. M., Rosenthal, R. J., Afifi, T. O., & Fong, T. W. (2014). Gambling and the onset of co-morbid mental dosorders: a longitudinal study evaluating severity. *Journal of Psychiatric Practice, 20*, 207–219.

Park, C.-B., Park, S. M., Gwak, A. R., Sohn, B. K., Lee, J.-Y., Jung, H. Y., … Choi, J.-S. (2015). The effect of repeated exposure to virtual gambling cues on the urge to gamble. *Addictive Behaviors, 41*, 61–64. doi:http://dx.doi.org/10.1016/j.addbeh.2014.09.027

Parke, J., & Griffiths, M. (2006). The psychology of the fruit machine: the role of structural characteristics (revisited). *International Journal of Mental Health and Addiction, 4*(2), 151–179.

Parker, L. A. (1996). LSD produces place preference and flavor avoidance but does not produce flavor aversion in rats. *Behav Neurosci, 110*(3), 503–508.

Parrott, A. C. (2004). Is ecstasy MDMA? A review of the proportion of ecstasy tablets containing MDMA, their dosage levels, and the changing perceptions of purity. *Psychopharmacology (Berl), 173*(3–4), 234–241. doi:10.1007/s00213-003-1712-7

Parrott, A. C. (2013a). Human psychobiology of MDMA or 'Ecstasy': an overview of 25 years of empirical research. *Hum Psychopharmacol*, *28*(4), 289–307. doi:10.1002/hup.2318

Parrott, A. C. (2013b). MDMA, serotonergic neurotoxicity, and the diverse functional deficits of recreational 'Ecstasy' users. *Neurosci Biobehav Rev*, *37*(8), 1466–1484. doi:10.1016/j.neubiorev.2013.04.016

Parrott, A. C., Downey, L. A., Roberts, C. A., Montgomery, C., Bruno, R., & Fox, H. C. (2017). Recreational 3,4-methylenedioxymethamphetamine or 'ecstasy': current perspective and future research prospects. *J Psychopharmacol*, *31*(8), 959–966. doi:10.1177/0269881117711922

Pathan, H., & Williams, J. (2012). Basic opioid pharmacology: an update. *British Journal of Pain*, *6*(1), 11–16. doi:10.1177/2049463712438493

Pecina, S., Cagniard, B., Berridge, K. C., Aldridge, J. W., & Zhuang, X. (2003). Hyperdopaminergic mutant mice have higher 'wanting' but not 'liking' for sweet rewards. *J Neurosci*, *23*(28), 9395–9402.

Peele, S. (1985). *The Meaning of Addiction: An Unconventional View*. San Francisco, CA: Jossey-Bass.

Petry, N. M., Martin, B., Cooney, J. L., & Kranzler, H. R. (2000). Give them prizes and they will come: contingency management for treatment of alcohol dependence. *Journal of Consulting and Clinical Psychology*, *68*(2), 250.

Petry, N. M., Stinson, F. S., & Grant, B. F. (2005). Comorbidity of DSM-IV pathological gambling and other psychiatric disorders: results from the National Epidemiologic Survey on Alcohol and Related Conditions. *J Clin Psychiatry*, *66*(5), 564–574.

Pfaus, J., Damsma, G., Wenkstern, D., & Fibiger, H. (1995). Sexual activity increases dopamine transmission in the nucleus accumbens and striatum of female rats. *Brain Research*, *693*(1), 21–30.

Phillips, A. G., Brooke, S. M., & Fibiger, H. C. (1975). Effects of amphetamine isomers and neuroleptics on self-stimulation from the nucleus accumbens and dorsal noradrenergic bundle. *Brain Res*, *85*(1), 13–22.

Phillips, A. G., Carter, D. A., & Fibiger, H. C. (1976). Dopaminergic substrates of intracranial self-stimulation in the caudate-putamen. *Brain Res*, *104*(2), 221–232.

Phillips, A. G., & Fibiger, H. C. (1978). The role of dopamine in maintaining intracranial self-stimulation in the ventral tegmentum, nucleus accumbens, and medial prefrontal cortex. *Can J Psychol*, *32*(2), 58–66.

Phillips, H. (2003). The pleasure seekers. *New Scientist*, *180*, 36–40.

Picciotto, M. R., Caldarone, B. J., King, S. L., & Zachariou, V. (2000). Nicotinic receptors in the brain: links between molecular biology and behavior. *Neuropsychopharmacology*, *22*(5), 451–465. doi:10.1016/s0893-133x(99)00146-3

Pickard, H., Ahmed, S. H., & Foddy, B. (2015). Alternative models of addiction. *Front Psychiatry*, *6*, 20. doi:10.3389/fpsyt.2015.00020

Pickens, R. W., Svikis, D. S., McGue, M., Lykken, D. T., Heston, L. L., & Clayton, P. J. (1991). Heterogeneity in the inheritance of alcoholism: a study of male and female twins. *Arch Gen Psychiatry*, *48*(1), 19–28.

Planzer, S., Gray, H. M., & Shaffer, H. J. (2014). Associations between national gambling policies and disordered gambling prevalence rates within Europe. *International Journal of Law and Psychiatry*, *37*(2), 217–229. doi:http://dx.doi.org/10.1016/j.ijlp.2013.11.002

# REFERENCES

Pontieri, F. E., Tanda, G., Orzi, F., & Di Chiara, G. (1996). Effects of nicotine on the nucleus accumbens and similarity to those of addictive drugs. *Nature, 382*(6588), 255–257.

Popper, K. R. (2002). *The Logic of Scientific Discovery* (new edn). London: Routledge.

Posner, M. I., Snyder, C. R., & Davidson, B. J. (1980). Attention and the detection of signals. *Journal of Experimental Psychology: General, 109*(2), 160.

Premack, D. (1970). 'Mechanisms of Self-control'. In W. I. Hunt (ed.), *Learning Mechanisms in Smoking* (pp. 107–123).Chicago, IL: Aldine.

Prescott, C. A., & Kendler, K. S. (1995). Genetic and environmental influences on alcohol and tobacco dependence among women. *NIAAA Research Monographs, 30*, 59–87.

Price, D. D., Finniss, D. G., & Benedetti, F. (2008). A comprehensive review of the placebo effect: recent advances and current thought. *Annu Rev Psychol, 59*, 565–590. doi:10.1146/annurev.psych.59.113006.095941

Prochaska, J. O., & DiClemente, C. C. (1982). Transtheoretical therapy: toward a more integrative model of change. *Psychotherapy: Theory, Research & Practice, 19*(3), 276.

Prochaska, J. O., & DiClemente, C. C. (1992). Stages of change in the modification of problem behaviors. *Progress in Behavior Modification, 28*, 183.

Prochaska, J. O., DiClemente, C. C., & Norcross, J. C. (1992). In search of how people change: applications to addictive behaviors. *American Psychologist, 47*(9), 1102.

Prochaska, J. O., & Velicer, W. F. (1997). The transtheoretical model of health behavior change. *Am J Health Promot, 12*(1), 38–48.

Pryce, S. (2012). *Fixing Drugs: The Politics of Drug Prohibition*. Basingstoke, UK: Palgrave Macmillan.

Rash, C. J., Weinstock, J., & Van Patten, R. (2016). A review of gambling disorder and substance use disorders. *Substance Abuse and Rehabilitation, 7*, 3–13. doi:10.2147/SAR.S83460

Ray, L. A., & Hutchison, K. E. (2004). A polymorphism of the mu-opioid receptor gene (OPRM1) and sensitivity to the effects of alcohol in humans. *Alcohol Clin Exp Res, 28*(12), 1789–1795.

Ray, L. A., & Hutchison, K. E. (2007). Effects of naltrexone on alcohol sensitivity and genetic moderators of medication response: a double-blind placebo-controlled study. *Arch Gen Psychiatry, 64*(9), 1069–1077. doi:10.1001/archpsyc.64.9.1069

Raz, S., & Berger, B. D. (2010). Social isolation increases morphine intake: behavioral and psychopharmacological aspects. *Behavioural Pharmacology, 21*(1), 39–46. doi:10.1097/FBP.0b013e32833470bd

Redgrave, P., & Gurney, K. (2006). The short-latency dopamine signal: a role in discovering novel actions? *Nat Rev Neurosci, 7*(12), 967–975.

Redgrave, P., Gurney, K., & Reynolds, J. (2008). What is reinforced by phasic dopamine signals? *Brain Res Rev, 58*(2), 322–339.

Redish, A. D. (2004). Addiction as a computational process gone awry. *Science, 306*(5703), 1944–1947.

Redish, A. D., Jensen, S., & Johnson, A. (2008). A unified framework for addiction: vulnerabilities in the decision process. *Behavioral and Brain Sciences, 31*(04), 415–437.

Rehm, J. (2014). *Classification of addictions: a report examining the various classifications of addictions and extracting common elements of addiction classifications*. Retrieved from www.alicerap.eu/resources/.../297-ar-science-findings-41-heavy-use-over-time.html

Rehm, J., Marmet, S., Anderson, P., Gual, A., Kraus, L., Nutt, D. J., ... Gmel, G. (2013). Defining substance use disorders: do we really need more than heavy use? *Alcohol and Alcoholism, 48*(6), 633–640. doi:10.1093/alcalc/agt127

Reid, A., & Lingford-Hughes, A. (2006). Neuropharmacology of addiction. *Psychiatry, 5*(12), 449–454. doi:http://dx.doi.org/10.1053/j.mppsy.2006.09.006

Risch, N., & Merikangas, K. (1996). The future of genetic studies of complex human diseases. *Science, 273*(5281), 1516–1517. doi:10.1126/science.273.5281.1516

Risner, M. E., & Jones, B. E. (1975). Self-administration of CNS stimulants by dog. *Psychopharmacologia, 43*(3), 207–213.

Robbins, T. W., Cardinal, R., DiCiano, P., HAlligan, P., Hellemns, K., Lee, J., & Everitt, B. (2006). 'Neuroscience of Drugs and Addiction'. In D. J. Nutt, T. W. Robbins, G. V. Stimson, M. Ince, & A. Jackson (eds), *Drugs and the Future: Brain Science, Addiction and Society*. Burlington, MA: Academic Press.

Robbins, T. W., & Clark, L. (2015). Behavioral addictions. *Current Opinion in Neurobiology, 30*, 66–72. doi:http://dx.doi.org/10.1016/j.conb.2014.09.005

Robbins, T. W., & Everitt, B. J. (2007). A role for mesencephalic dopamine in activation: commentary on Berridge (2006). *Psychopharmacology, 191*(3), 433–437. doi:10.1007/s00213-006-0528-7

Roberts, D. C. S., & Ranaldi, R. (1995). Effect of dopaminergic drugs on cocaine reinforcement. *Clinical Neuropharmacology, 18* (suppl. 1), S84–S95.

Robins, L. N. (1993). Vietnam Veterans rapid recovery from heroin addiction: a fluke or normal expectation. *Addiction, 88*(8), 1041–1054. doi:10.1111/j.1360-0443.1993.tb02123.x

Robins, L. N., Helzer, J. E., & Davis, D. H. (1975). Narcotic use in Southeast-Asia and afterward: interview study of 898 Vietnam returnees. *Arch Gen Psychiatry, 32*(8), 955–961.

Robinson, T. E., & Berridge, K. C. (1993). The neural basis of drug craving – an incentive-sensitization theory of addiction. *Brain Research Reviews, 18*(3), 247–291. doi:10.1016/0165-0173(93)90013-p

Robinson, T. E., & Berridge, K. C. (2000). The psychology and neurobiology of addiction: an incentive-sensitization view. *Addiction, 95* Suppl 2, S91–117.

Rogers, C. (1959). A theory of therapy, personality and interpersonal relationships, as developed in the client-centered framework. In S. Koch (ed.), *Psychology: A Study of a Science*, Vol. 3. New York: McGraw-Hill.

Rogers, C. (1980). *A Way of Being: The Latest Thinking on a Person-centered Approach to Life*. Boston, MA: Houghton Mifflin.

Rolles, S., & McClure, C. (2009). *After the War on Drugs: Blueprint for Regulation*. Bristol: Transform Drug Policy Foundation.

Room, R., Turner, N. E., & Ialomiteanu, A. (1999). Community effects of the opening of the Niagara casino. *Addiction, 94*(10), 1449–1466.

Rosner, S., Hackl-Herrwerth, A., Leucht, S., Lehert, P., Vecchi, S., & Soyka, M. (2010). Acamprosate for alcohol dependence. *Cochrane Database Syst Rev*(9), CD004332. doi:10.1002/14651858. CD004332.pub2

# REFERENCES

Rosner, S., Hackl-Herrwerth, A., Leucht, S., Vecchi, S., Srisurapanont, M., & Soyka, M. (2010). Opioid antagonists for alcohol dependence. *Cochrane Database Syst Rev*(12), Cd001867. doi:10.1002/14651858.CD001867.pub2

Rothkirch, M., Schmack, K., Schlagenhauf, F., & Sterzer, P. (2012). Implicit motivational value and salience are processed in distinct areas of orbitofrontal cortex. *Neuroimage*, *62*(3), 1717–1725.

Rovaris, D. L., Mota, N. R., Bertuzzi, G. P., Aroche, A. P., Callegari-Jacques, S. M., Guimarães, L. S. P., ... Grassi-Oliveira, R. (2015). Corticosteroid receptor genes and childhood neglect influence susceptibility to crack/cocaine addiction and response to detoxification treatment. *Journal of Psychiatric Research*, *68*, 83–90. doi:http://dx.doi.org/10.1016/j.jpsychires.2015.06.008

Rubens, M., Ramamoorthy, V., Attonito, J., Saxena, A., Appunni, S., Shehadeh, N., & Devieux, J. G. (2015). A review of 5-HT transporter linked promoter region (5-HTTLPR) polymorphism and associations with alcohol use problems and sexual risk behaviors. *J Community Genet*. doi:10.1007/s12687-015-0253-1

Saccone, N. L., Culverhouse, R. C., Schwantes-An, T. H., Cannon, D. S., Chen, X., Cichon, S., ... Bierut, L. J. (2010). Multiple independent loci at chromosome 15q25.1 affect smoking quantity: a meta-analysis and comparison with lung cancer and COPD. *PLoS Genet*, *6*(8). doi:10.1371/journal.pgen.1001053

Saccone, S. F., Hinrichs, A. L., Saccone, N. L., Chase, G. A., Konvicka, K., Madden, P. A., ... Bierut, L. J. (2007). Cholinergic nicotinic receptor genes implicated in a nicotine dependence association study targeting 348 candidate genes with 3713 SNPs. *Hum Mol Genet*, *16*(1), 36–49. doi:10.1093/hmg/ddl438

Samson, C. (2004). 'The Disease over Native North American Drinking: Experiences of the Innu of Northern Labrador'. In R. Coomber & N. South (eds), *Drug Use and Cultural Contexts Beyond the WEST* (pp. 137–157). London, UK: Free Association Books.

Sanchis-Segura, C., & Spanagel, R. (2006). Behavioural assessment of drug reinforcement and addictive features in rodents: an overview. *Addict Biol*, *11*(1), 2–38.

Sarbin, T. R., & Nucci, L. P. (1973). Self-reconstitution processes: a proposal for reorganizing the conduct of confirmed smokers. *Journal of Abnormal Psychology*, *81*(2), 182.

Satel, S., & Lilienfeld, S. O. (2013). Addiction and the brain-disease fallacy. *Front Psychiatry*, *4*, 141. doi:10.3389/fpsyt.2013.00141

Saunders, J. B. (2013). The concept of substance use disorders: a commentary on 'Defining substance use disorders: Do we really need more than heavy use' by Rehm et al. *Alcohol and Alcoholism*, *48*(6), 644–645. doi:10.1093/alcalc/agt146

Schenk, S., Gittings, D., Johnstone, M., & Daniela, E. (2003). Development, maintenance and temporal pattern of self-administration maintained by ecstasy (MDMA) in rats. *Psychopharmacology (Berl)*, *169*(1), 21–27.

Schoenbaum, G., Chiba, A. A., & Gallagher, M. (1998). Orbitofrontal cortex and basolateral amygdala encode expected outcomes during learning. *Nat Neurosci*, *1*(2), 155–159.

Schubiner, H., Tzelepis, A., Milberger, S., Lockhart, N., Kruger, M., Kelley, B. J., & Schoener, E. P. (2000). Prevalence of attention-deficit/hyperactivity disorder and conduct disorder among substance abusers. *J Clin Psychiatry*, *61*(4), 244–251.

Schultz, W. (1998). Predictive reward signal of dopamine neurons. *J Neurophysiol, 80*(1), 1–27.

Schultz, W. (2001). Reward signaling by dopamine neurons. *Neuroscientist, 7*(4), 293–302.

Schultz, W. (2006). Behavioral theories and the neurophysiology of reward. *Annu Rev Psychol, 57*, 87–115.

Schultz, W. (2007). Behavioral dopamine signals. *Trends Neurosci, 30*(5), 203–210.

Schultz, W. (2013). Updating dopamine reward signals. *Current Opinion in Neurobiology, 23*(2), 229–238.

Schultz, W., Dayan, P., & Montague, P. R. (1997). A neural substrate of prediction and reward. *Science, 275*(5306), 1593–1599.

Schultz, W., Tremblay, L., & Hollerman, J. R. (1998). Reward prediction in primate basal ganglia and frontal cortex. *Neuropharmacology, 37*(4–5), 421–429.

Schwarz, N. (2000). Emotion, cognition, and decision making. *Cognition & Emotion, 14*(4), 433–440.

Sescousse, G., Barbalat, G., Domenech, P., & Dreher, J. C. (2013). Imbalance in the sensitivity to different types of rewards in pathological gambling. *Brain, 136*(Pt 8), 2527–2538. doi:10.1093/brain/awt126

Sessa, B. (2007). Is there a case for MDMA-assisted psychotherapy in the UK? *Journal of Psychopharmacology, 21*(2), 220–224. doi:10.1177/0269881107069029

Sessa, B. (2017a). Why MDMA therapy for alcohol use disorder? And why now? *Neuropharmacology*. doi:10.1016/j.neuropharm.2017.11.004

Sessa, B. (2017b). Why psychiatry needs 3,4-Methylenedioxymethamphetamine: a child psychiatrist's perspective. *Neurotherapeutics, 14*(3), 741–749. doi:10.1007/s13311-017-0531-1

Shaw, S. G., & Rolls, E. T. (1976). Is the release of noradrenaline necessary for self-stimulation of the brain? *Pharmacol Biochem Behav, 4*(4), 375–379.

Siegel, S., Baptista, M. A., Kim, J. A., McDonald, R. V., & Weise-Kelly, L. (2000). Pavlovian psychopharmacology: the associative basis of tolerance. *Exp Clin Psychopharmacol, 8*(3), 276–293.

Siegel, S., Hinson, R. E., Krank, M. D., & McCully, J. (1982). Heroin 'overdose' death: contribution of drug-associated environmental cues. *Science, 216*(4544), 436–437.

Sigmon, S. C., & Higgins, S. T. (2006). Voucher-based contingent reinforcement of marijuana abstinence among individuals with serious mental illness. *Journal of Substance Abuse Treatment, 30*(4), 291–295. doi:http://dx.doi.org/10.1016/j.jsat.2006.02.001

Sigvardsson, S., Bohman, M., & Cloninger, C. R. (1996). Replication of the Stockholm Adoption Study of alcoholism: confirmatory cross-fostering analysis. *Arch Gen Psychiatry, 53*(8), 681–687.

Singh, I., Morgan, C., Curran, V., Nutt, D., Schlag, A., & McShane, R. (2017). Ketamine treatment for depression: opportunities for clinical innovation and ethical foresight. *The Lancet Psychiatry, 4*(5), 419–426. doi:https://doi.org/10.1016/S2215-0366(17)30102-5

Skinner, B. F. (1953). *Science and Human Behavior*. New York: Simon and Schuster.

Skinner, M. D., Lahmek, P., Pham, H., & Aubin, H. J. (2014). Disulfiram efficacy in the treatment of alcohol dependence: a meta-analysis. *PLoS One, 9*(2), e87366. doi:10.1371/journal.pone.0087366

Slutske, W. S. (2006). Natural recovery and treatment-seeking in pathological gambling: results of two U.S. national surveys. *Am J Psychiatry, 163*(2), 297–302. doi:10.1176/appi.ajp.163.2.297

# REFERENCES

Slutske, W. S., Caspi, A., Moffitt, T. E., & Poulton, R. (2005). Personality and problem gambling: a prospective study of a birth cohort of young adults. *Arch Gen Psychiatry*, *62*(7), 769–775. doi:10.1001/archpsyc.62.7.769

Slutske, W. S., Moffitt, T. E., Poulton, R., & Caspi, A. (2012). Undercontrolled temperament at age 3 predicts disordered gambling at age 32: a longitudinal study of a complete birth cohort. *Psychol Sci*, *23*(5), 510–516. doi:10.1177/0956797611429708

Smith, J. L., Mattick, R. P., Jamadar, S. D., & Iredale, J. M. (2014). Deficits in behavioural inhibition in substance abuse and addiction: a meta-analysis. *Drug and Alcohol Dependence*, *145*, 1–33. doi:http://dx.doi.org/10.1016/j.drugalcdep.2014.08.009

Smith, J. W. (1982). Treatment of alcoholism in aversion conditioning hospitals. In E. M. Pattison & E. Kaufman (eds), *Encyclopedic Handbook of Alcoholism*. New York: Gardner Press.

Soyka, M. (2016). Nalmefene for the treatment of alcohol use disorders: recent data and clinical potential. *Expert Opin Pharmacother*, *17*(4), 619–626. doi:10.1517/14656566.2016.1146689

Soyka, M., & Muller, C. A. (2017). Pharmacotherapy of alcoholism – an update on approved and off-label medications. *Expert Opin Pharmacother*, *18*(12), 1187–1199. doi:10.1080/14656566.2017.1349098

Soyka, M., Preuss, U. W., Hesselbrock, V., Zill, P., Koller, G., & Bondy, B. (2008). GABA-A2 receptor subunit gene (GABRA2) polymorphisms and risk for alcohol dependence. *Journal of Psychiatric Research*, *42*(3), 184–191. doi:10.1016/j.jpsychires.2006.11.006

Spanagel, R., Vengeliene, V., Jandeleit, B., Fischer, W. N., Grindstaff, K., Zhang, X., ... Kiefer, F. (2014). Acamprosate produces its anti-relapse effects via calcium. *Neuropsychopharmacology*, *39*(4), 783–791. doi:10.1038/npp.2013.264

Spanagel, R., Vengeliene, V., & Kiefer, F. (2016). Reply to: Does acamprosate really produce its anti-relapse effects via calcium? No support from the PREDICT study in human alcoholics. *Neuropsychopharmacology*, *41*(3), 661–662. doi:10.1038/npp.2015.263

Spear, L. P. (2000). Neurobehavioral changes in adolescence. *Current Directions in Psychological Science*, *9*(4), 111–114. doi:10.1111/1467-8721.00072

Spencer, T. J., Biederman, J., Ciccone, P. E., Madras, B. K., Dougherty, D. D., Bonab, A. A., ... Fischman, A. J. (2006). PET study examining pharmacokinetics, detection and likeability, and dopamine transporter receptor occupancy of short- and long-acting oral methylphenidate. *Am J Psychiatry*, *163*(3), 387–395.

Spyraki, C., Fibiger, H. C., & Phillips, A. G. (1982). Dopaminergic substrates of amphetamine-induced place preference conditioning. *Brain Res*, *253*(1–2), 185–193.

Squeglia, L. M., Jacobus, J., Nguyen-Louie, T. T., & Tapert, S. F. (2014). Inhibition during early adolescence predicts alcohol and marijuana use by late adolescence. *Neuropsychology*, *28*(5), 782–790. doi:10.1037/neu0000083

Squeglia, L. M., Pulido, C., Wetherill, R. R., Jacobus, J., Brown, G. G., & Tapert, S. F. (2012). Brain response to working memory over three years of adolescence: influence of initiating heavy drinking. *Journal of Studies on Alcohol and Drugs*, *73*(5), 749–760.

Squeglia, L. M., Rinker, D. A., Bartsch, H., Castro, N., Chung, Y., Dale, A. M., ... Tapert, S. F. (2014). Brain volume reductions in adolescent heavy drinkers. *Developmental Cognitive Neuroscience*, *9*, 117–125. doi:10.1016/j.dcn.2014.02.005

Stacy, A. W., Leigh, B. C., & Weingardt, K. (1997). An individual-difference perspective applied to word association. *Personality and Social Psychology Bulletin, 23*(3), 229–237.

Stahl, S. M., Pradko, J. F., Haight, B. R., Modell, J. G., Rockett, C. B., & Learned-Coughlin, S. (2004). A review of the neuropharmacology of Bupropion, a dual norepinephrine and dopamine reuptake inhibitor. *Primary Care Companion to The Journal of Clinical Psychiatry, 6*(4), 159–166.

Starcevic, V., & Aboujaoude, E. (2017). Internet addiction: reappraisal of an increasingly inadequate concept. *CNS Spectr, 22*(1), 7–13. doi:10.1017/s1092852915000863

Stead, L. F., Perera, R., Bullen, C., Mant, D., Hartmann-Boyce, J., Cahill, K., & Lancaster, T. (2012). Nicotine replacement therapy for smoking cessation. *Cochrane Database Syst Rev, 11*, Cd000146. doi:10.1002/14651858.CD000146.pub4

Stephens, M. A., & Wand, G. (2012). Stress and the HPA axis: role of glucocorticoids in alcohol dependence. *Alcohol Res, 34*(4), 468–483.

Sterling, P., & Eyer, J. (1988). Allostasis: A new paradigm to explain arousal pathology. In S. Fisher & J. Reason (eds), *Handbook of Life Stress, Cognition and Health* (pp. 629–647). New York: John Wiley.

Stewart, D., Gossop, M., & Marsden, J. (2002). Reductions in non-fatal overdose after drug misuse treatment: results from the National Treatment Outcome Research Study (NTORS). *J Subst Abuse Treat, 22*(1), 1–9.

Stewart, D., Gossop, M., Marsden, J., Kidd, T., & Treacy, S. (2003). Similarities in outcomes for men and women after drug misuse treatment: results from the National Treatment Outcome Research Study (NTORS). *Drug Alcohol Rev, 22*(1), 35–41. doi:10.1080/0959523021000059811

Stitzer, M. L., Bickel, W. K., Bigelow, G. E., & Liebson, I. A. (1986). Effect of methadone dose contingencies on urinalysis test results of polydrug-abusing methadone-maintenance patients. *Drug and Alcohol Dependence, 18*(4), 341–348. doi:http://dx.doi.org/10.1016/0376-8716(86)90097-9

Stitzer, M. L., & Higgins, S. (1995). Behavioral treatment of drug and alcohol abuse. *Psychopharmacology: The Fourth Generation of Progress, 1807–1819*.

Stitzer, M. L., Iguchi, M. Y., & Felch, L. J. (1992). Contingent take-home incentive: Effects on drug use of methadone maintenance patients. *Journal of Consulting and Clinical Psychology, 60*(6), 927–934. doi:10.1037/0022-006X.60.6.927

Stolerman, I. (1992). Drugs of abuse: behavioural principles, methods and terms. *Trends Pharmacol Sci, 13*(5), 170–176.

Strang, J., Groshkova, T., Uchtenhagen, A., van den Brink, W., Haasen, C., Schechter, M. T., ... Metrebian, N. (2015). Heroin on trial: systematic review and meta-analysis of randomised trials of diamorphine-prescribing as treatment for refractory heroin addiction†. *Br J Psychiatry, 207*(1), 5–14. doi:10.1192/bjp.bp.114.149195

Stroop, J. R. (1935). Studies of interference in serial verbal reactions. *Journal of Experimental Psychology, 18*(6), 643.

Styles, E. (1998). *The Psychology of Attention*. Hove, Sussex, UK: Psychology Press Limited.

Subramaniam, M., Chua, B. Y., Abdin, E., Pang, S., Satghare, P., Vaingankar, J. A., ... Chong, S. A. (2016). Prevalence and correlates of Internet gaming problem among Internet users: results from an Internet survey. *Ann Acad Med Singapore, 45*(5), 174–183.

# REFERENCES

Swanson, J. M., & Volkow, N. D. (2003). Serum and brain concentrations of methylphenidate: implications for use and abuse. *Neurosci Biobehav Rev*, *27*(7), 615–621.

Sylva, D., Safron, A., Rosenthal, A. M., Reber, P. J., Parrish, T. B., & Bailey, J. M. (2013). Neural correlates of sexual arousal in heterosexual and homosexual women and men. *Horm Behav*, *64*(4), 673–684. doi:10.1016/j.yhbeh.2013.08.003

Taurah, L., & Chandler, C. (2003). Elevated depression scores following abstinence from MDMA. *Addiction Biology*, *8*, 244–245.

Taurah, L., Chandler, C., & Sanders, G. (2014). Depression, impulsiveness, sleep, and memory in past and present polydrug users of 3,4-methylenedioxymethamphetamine (MDMA, ecstasy). *Psychopharmacology (Berl)*, *231*(4), 737–751. doi:10.1007/s00213-013-3288-1

Thoma, N., Pilecki, B., & McKay, D. (2015). Contemporary cognitive behavior therapy: a review of theory, history, and evidence. *Psychodynamic Psychiatry*, *43*(3), 423–461. doi:10.1521/pdps.2015.43.3.423

Thomasson, H. R., Edenberg, H. J., Crabb, D. W., Mai, X. L., Jerome, R. E., Li, T. K., ... Yin, S. J. (1991). Alcohol and aldehyde dehydrogenase genotypes and alcoholism in Chinese men. *American Journal of Human Genetics*, *48*(4), 677–681.

Thorgeirsson, T. E., Gudbjartsson, D. F., Surakka, I., Vink, J. M., Amin, N., Geller, F., ... Stefansson, K. (2010). Sequence variants at CHRNB3-CHRNA6 and CYP2A6 affect smoking behavior. *Nat Genet*, *42*(5), 448–453. doi:10.1038/ng.573

Tiffany, S. T. (1990). A cognitive model of drug urges and drug-use behaviour: role of automatic and nonautomatic processes. *Psychological Review*, *97*(2), 147–168. doi:10.1037/0033-295x.97.2.147

Tobler, P. N., Dickinson, A., & Schultz, W. (2003). Coding of predicted reward omission by dopamine neurons in a conditioned inhibition paradigm. *J Neurosci*, *23*(32), 10402–10410.

Tobler, P. N., Fiorillo, C. D., & Schultz, W. (2005). Adaptive coding of reward value by dopamine neurons. *Science*, *307*(5715), 1642–1645.

Townshend, J., & Duka, T. (2001). Attentional bias associated with alcohol cues: differences between heavy and occasional social drinkers. *Psychopharmacology*, *157*(1), 67–74.

Turner, N. E., Zangeneh, M., & Littman-Sharp, N. (2006). The experience of gambling and its role in problem gambling. *International Gambling Studies*, *6*(2), 237–266. doi:10.1080/14459790600928793

Tusa, A. L., & Burgholzer, J. A. (2013). Came to believe: spirituality as a mechanism of change in alcoholics anonymous: a review of the literature from 1992 to 2012. *J Addict Nurs*, *24*(4), 237–246. doi:10.1097/jan.0000000000000003

Tversky, A., & Kahneman, D. (1974). Judgment under uncertainty: heuristics and biases. *Science*, *185*(4157), 1124–1131. doi:10.1126/science.185.4157.1124

Tyce, F. A. (1968). Influence of methylphenidate hydrochloride on self-stimulation of the brain by rats. *Psychol Rep*, *23*(2), 379–385.

Tyler, M. W., Yourish, H. B., Ionescu, D. F., & Haggarty, S. J. (2017). Classics in chemical neuroscience: ketamine. *ACS Chem Neurosci*, *8*(6), 1122–1134. doi:10.1021/acschemneuro.7b00074

Tyrer, P. (2014). A comparison of DSM and ICD classifications of mental disorder. *Advances in Psychiatric Treatment*, *20*(4), 280–285.

Uhl, G. R., Drgon, T., Johnson, C., Li, C. Y., Contoreggi, C., Hess, J., ... Liu, Q. R. (2008). Molecular genetics of addiction and related heritable phenotypes: genome-wide association approaches identify 'connectivity constellation' and drug target genes with pleiotropic effects. *Ann N Y Acad Sci, 1141*, 318–381. doi:10.1196/annals.1441.018

Uhl, G. R., Liu, Q. R., & Naiman, D. (2002). Substance abuse vulnerability loci: converging genome scanning data. *Trends Genet, 18*(8), 420–425.

Urbanoski, K. A., & Kelly, J. F. (2012). Understanding genetic risk for substance use and addiction: a guide for non-geneticists. *Clinical Psychology Review, 32*(1), 60–70. doi:10.1016/j.cpr.2011.11.002

Vaillant, G. E. (2003). A 60-year follow-up of alcoholic men. *Addiction, 98*(8), 1043–1051. doi:10.1046/j.1360-0443.2003.00422.x

Valle, S. K. (1981). Interpersonal functioning of alcoholism counselors and treatment outcome. *Journal of Studies on Alcohol, 42*(9), 783–790.

Valleur, M., Codina, I., Venisse, J. L., Romo, L., Magalon, D., Fatseas, M., ... Challet-Bouju, G. (2016). Towards a validation of the Three Pathways Model of pathological gambling. *J Gambl Stud, 32*(2), 757–771. doi:10.1007/s10899-015-9545-y

van Holst, R. J., Lemmens, J. S., Valkenburg, P. M., Peter, J., Veltman, D. J., & Goudriaan, A. E. (2012). Attentional bias and disinhibition toward gaming cues are related to problem gaming in male adolescents. *J Adolesc Health, 50*(6), 541–546. doi:10.1016/j.jadohealth.2011.07.006

Vanyukov, M. M., Tarter, R. E., Kirillova, G. P., Kirisci, L., Reynolds, M. D., Kreek, M. J., ... Ridenour, T. A. (2012). Common liability to addiction and 'gateway hypothesis': theoretical, empirical and evolutionary perspective. *Drug and Alcohol Dependence, 123*, S3–S17. doi:10.1016/j.drugalcdep.2011.12.018

Verhulst, B., Neale, M., & Kendler, K. (2015). The heritability of alcohol use disorders: a meta-analysis of twin and adoption studies. *Psychological Medicine, 45*(05), 1061–1072.

Vitaro, F., Arseneault, L., & Tremblay, R. E. (1999). Impulsivity predicts problem gambling in low SES adolescent males. *Addiction, 94*(4), 565–575.

Volkow, N. D., Baler, R. D., Compton, W. M., & Weiss, S. R. B. (2014). Adverse health effects of marijuana use. *New England Journal of Medicine, 370*(23), 2219–2227. doi:10.1056/NEJMra1402309

Volkow, N. D., Baler, R. D., & Goldstein, R. Z. (2011). Addiction: pulling at the neural threads of social behaviors. *Neuron, 69*(4), 599–602. doi:10.1016/j.neuron.2011.01.027

Volkow, N. D., Ding, Y. S., Fowler, J. S., Wang, G. J., Logan, J., Gatley, J. S., ... et al. (1995). Is methylphenidate like cocaine? Studies on their pharmacokinetics and distribution in the human brain. *Arch Gen Psychiatry, 52*(6), 456–463.

Volkow, N. D., Fowler, J. S., & Wang, G. J. (2003). The addicted human brain: insights from imaging studies. *Journal of Clinical Investigation, 111*(10), 1444–1451. doi:10.1172/jci200318533

Volkow, N. D., Fowler, J. S., & Wang, G. J. (2004). The addicted human brain viewed in the light of imaging studies: brain circuits and treatment strategies. *Neuropharmacology, 47* Suppl 1, 3–13.

Volkow, N. D., Fowler, J. S., Wang, G. J., Ding, Y. S., & Gatley, S. J. (2002). Role of dopamine in the therapeutic and reinforcing effects of methylphenidate in humans: results from imaging studies. *Eur Neuropsychopharmacol, 12*(6), 557–566.

Volkow, N. D., Fowler, J. S., Wang, G. J., Hitzemann, R., Logan, J., Schlyer, D. J., ... Wolf, A. P. (1993). Decreased dopamine D2 receptor availability is associated with reduced frontal metabolism in cocaine abusers. *Synapse, 14*(2), 169–177.

# REFERENCES

Volkow, N. D., & Swanson, J. M. (2003). Variables that affect the clinical use and abuse of methylphenidate in the treatment of ADHD. *Am J Psychiatry, 160*(11), 1909–1918.

Volkow, N. D., Wang, G. J., Fischman, M. W., Foltin, R., Fowler, J. S., Franceschi, D., ... Pappas, N. (2000). Effects of route of administration on cocaine induced dopamine transporter blockade in the human brain. *Life Sciences, 67*(12), PL1507–PL1515.

Volkow, N. D., Wang, G. J., Fowler, J. S., Logan, J., Gatley, S. J., Gifford, A., ... Pappas, N. (1999). Prediction of reinforcing responses to psychostimulants in humans by brain dopamine D2 receptor levels. *Am J Psychiatry, 156*(9), 1440–1443.

Volkow, N. D., Wang, G. J., Fowler, J. S., Logan, J., Gatley, S. J., Hitzemann, R., ... Pappas, N. (1997). Decreased striatal dopaminergic responsiveness in detoxified cocaine-dependent subjects. *Nature, 386*(6627), 830–833.

Volkow, N. D., Wang, G. J., Fowler, J. S., Logan, J., Hitzemann, R., Ding, Y. S., ... Piscani, K. (1996). Decreases in dopamine receptors but not in dopamine transporters in alcoholics. *Alcohol Clin Exp Res, 20*(9), 1594–1598.

Volkow, N. D., Wang, G. J., Ma, Y., Fowler, J. S., Wong, C., Ding, Y. S., ... Kalivas, P. (2005). Activation of orbital and medial prefrontal cortex by methylphenidate in cocaine-addicted subjects but not in controls: relevance to addiction. *J Neurosci, 25*(15), 3932–3939.

Volkow, N. D., Wang, G. J., Telang, F., Fowler, J. S., Logan, J., Childress, A. R., ... Wong, C. (2006). Cocaine cues and dopamine in dorsal striatum: mechanism of craving in cocaine addiction. *J Neurosci, 26*(24), 6583–6588.

Volkow, N. D., Wang, G. J., Telang, F., Fowler, J. S., Logan, J., Childress, A. R., ... Wong, C. (2008). Dopamine increases in striatum do not elicit craving in cocaine abusers unless they are coupled with cocaine cues. *Neuroimage, 39*(3), 1266–1273.

Waddington, G. (1977). Stabilisation in systems: chreods and epigenetic landscapes. *Futures, 9*(2), 139–146.

Wall, M. M., Poh, E., Cerdá, M., Keyes, K. M., Galea, S., & Hasin, D. S. (2011). Adolescent marijuana use from 2002 to 2008: higher in states with medical marijuana laws, cause still unclear. *Ann Epidemiol, 21*(9), 714–716.

Walsh, J., & Ramsey, G. (2016). *Improving Global Drug Policy: Comparative Perspectives and UNGASS. Brookings Institution, 2016.* Uruguay's Drug Policy: Major Innovations, Major Challenges.

Wang, S., Yang, Z., Ma, J. Z., Payne, T. J., & Li, M. D. (2014). Introduction to deep sequencing and its application to drug addiction research with a focus on rare variants. *Mol Neurobiol, 49*(1), 601–614. doi:10.1007/s12035-013-8541-4

Warner, C., & Shoaib, M. (2005). How does bupropion work as a smoking cessation aid? *Addict Biol, 10*(3), 219–231. doi:10.1080/13556210500222670

Warner, L. A., Kessler, R. C., Hughes, M., Anthony, J. C., & Nelson, C. B. (1995). Prevalence and correlates of drug use and dependence in the United States: results from the National Comorbidity Survey. *Arch Gen Psychiatry, 52*(3), 219–229.

Wassenaar, C. A., Dong, Q., Wei, Q., Amos, C. I., Spitz, M. R., & Tyndale, R. F. (2011). Relationship between CYP2A6 and CHRNA5-CHRNA3-CHRNB4 variation and smoking behaviors and lung cancer risk. *J Natl Cancer Inst, 103*(17), 1342–1346. doi:10.1093/jnci/djr237

Waters, A. J., Shiffman, S., Sayette, M. A., Paty, J. A., Gwaltney, C. J., & Balabanis, M. H. (2003). Attentional bias predicts outcome in smoking cessation. *Health Psychology, 22*(4), 378.

Weinstein, A., & Cox, W. M. (2006). Cognitive processing of drug-related stimuli: the role of memory and attention. *Journal of Psychopharmacology, 20*(6), 850–859.

Welte, J. W., Tidwell, M. C., Barnes, G. M., Hoffman, J. H., & Wieczorek, W. F. (2016). The relationship between the number of types of legal gambling and the rates of gambling behaviors and problems across U.S. states. *J Gambl Stud, 32*(2), 379–390. doi:10.1007/s10899-015-9551-0

West, R., & Brown, J. (2013). *Theory of Addiction*. New York: Wiley.

West, R., & European Monitoring Centre for Drugs and Drug Addiction (2013). *Models of Addiction*. EMCDDA Insights, Series No. 14. Luxembourg: Publications Office of the European Union.

Westermeyer, J. (2005). 'Historical and Social Context of Psychoactive Substance Use Disorders'. In R. J. Frances, S. I. Miller, & A. H. Mack (eds), *Clinical Textbook of Addictive Disorders* (3rd edn, pp. 16–34). New York: Guilford Press.

Wetherill, R. R., Squeglia, L. M., Yang, T. T., & Tapert, S. F. (2013). A longitudinal examination of adolescent response inhibition: neural differences before and after the initiation of heavy drinking. *Psychopharmacology, 230*(4), 663–671. doi:10.1007/s00213-013-3198-2

Wetter, D. W., Smith, S. S., Kenford, S. L., Jorenby, D. E., Fiore, M. C., Hurt, R. D., ... Baker, T. B. (1994). Smoking outcome expectancies: factor structure, predictive validity, and discriminant validity. *Journal of Abnormal Psychology, 103*(4), 801.

Wiers, R. W., Bartholow, B. D., van den Wildenberg, E., Thush, C., Engels, R. C., Sher, K. J., ... Stacy, A. W. (2007). Automatic and controlled processes and the development of addictive behaviors in adolescents: a review and a model. *Pharmacol Biochem Behav, 86*(2), 263–283.

Wiers, R. W., Cox, W. M., Field, M., Fadardi, J. S., Palfai, T. P., Schoenmakers, T., & Stacy, A. W. (2006). The search for new ways to change implicit alcohol-related cognitions in heavy drinkers. *Alcoholism: Clinical and Experimental Research, 30*(2), 320–331.

Wiers, R. W., & Stacy, A. W. (eds) (2005). *Handbook of Implicit Cognition and Addiction* London: Sage.

Williams, J. M. G., Mathews, A., & MacLeod, C. (1996). The emotional Stroop task and psychopathology. *Psychological Bulletin, 120*(1), 3.

Willner, P. (1991). 'Behavioural Models in Psychopharmacology'. In P. Willner (ed.), *Behavioural Models in Psychopharmacology: Theoretical, Industrial and Clinical Perspectives*. Cambridge: Cambridge University Press.

Willner, P., James, D., & Morgan, M. (2005). Excessive alcohol consumption and dependence on amphetamine are associated with parallel increases in subjective ratings of both 'wanting' and 'liking'. *Addiction, 100*(10), 1487–1495. doi:10.1111/j.1360-0443.2005.01222.x

Winstock, A., Mitcheson, L., Ramsey, J., Davies, S., Puchnarewicz, M., & Marsden, J. (2011). Mephedrone: use, subjective effects and health risks. *Addiction, 106*(11), 1991–1996. doi:10.1111/j.1360-0443.2011.03502.x

Wise, R. A. (1996). Addictive drugs and brain stimulation reward. *Annu Rev Neurosci, 19*, 319–340.

Wise, R. A. (2005). Forebrain substrates of reward and motivation. *J Comp Neurol, 493*(1), 115–121.

# REFERENCES

Wise, R. A., & Bozarth, M. A. (1987). A psychomotor stimulant theory of addiction. *Psychol Rev, 94*(4), 469–492.

Wolff, P. H. (1972). Ethnic differences in alcohol sensitivity. *Science, 175*(4020). doi:10.1126/science.175.4020.449

Wong, D. F., Kuwabara, H., Schretlen, D. J., Bonson, K. R., Zhou, Y., Nandi, A., … London, E. D. (2006). Increased occupancy of dopamine receptors in human striatum during cue-elicited cocaine craving. *Neuropsychopharmacology, 31*(12), 2716–2727.

Wonnacott, S., Kaiser, S., Mogg, A., Soliakov, L., & Jones, I. W. (2000). Presynaptic nicotinic receptors modulating dopamine release in the rat striatum. *Eur J Pharmacol, 393*(1–3), 51–58.

Yalachkov, Y., Kaiser, J., & Naumer, M. J. (2012). Functional neuroimaging studies in addiction: multisensory drug stimuli and neural cue reactivity. *Neurosci Biobehav Rev, 36*(2), 825–835. doi:10.1016/j.neubiorev.2011.12.004

Yang, B. Z., Kranzler, H. R., Zhao, H., Gruen, J. R., Luo, X., & Gelernter, J. (2007). Association of haplotypic variants in DRD2, ANKK1, TTC12 and NCAM1 to alcohol dependence in independent case control and family samples. *Hum Mol Genet, 16*(23), 2844–2853. doi:10.1093/hmg/ddm240

Yang, B. Z., Kranzler, H. R., Zhao, H., Gruen, J. R., Luo, X., & Gelernter, J. (2008). Haplotypic variants in DRD2, ANKK1, TTC12, and NCAM1 are associated with comorbid alcohol and drug dependence. *Alcohol Clin Exp Res, 32*(12), 2117–2127. doi:10.1111/j.1530-0277.2008.00800.x

Yang, J., Manolio, T. A., Pasquale, L. R., Boerwinkle, E., Caporaso, N., Cunningham, J. M., … Visscher, P. M. (2011). Genome partitioning of genetic variation for complex traits using common SNPs. *Nat Genet, 43*(6), 519–525. doi:10.1038/ng.823

Yen, C. F., Yen, J. Y., & Ko, C. H. (2010). Internet addiction: ongoing research in Asia. *World Psychiatry, 9*(2), 97.

Young, K. S. (1998). Internet addiction: the emergence of a new clinical disorder. *CyberPsychology & Behavior, 1*(3), 237–244.

Zhang, J., Berridge, K., & Aldridge, J. W. (2012). Computational models of incentive-sensitization in addiction: Dynamic limbic transformation of learning into motivation. In B. Gutkin & S. H. Ahmed (eds), *Computational Neuroscience of Drug Addiction* (Vol. *10*, pp. 189–203): Springer New York.

Zhang, L., Amos, C., & McDowell, W. C. (2008). A comparative study of Internet addiction between the United States and China. *Cyberpsychol Behav, 11*(6), 727–729. doi:10.1089/cpb.2008.0026

Zimmermann, P., Wittchen, H. U., Hofler, M., Pfister, H., Kessler, R. C., & Lieb, R. (2003). Primary anxiety disorders and the development of subsequent alcohol use disorders: a 4-year community study of adolescents and young adults. *Psychological Medicine, 33*(7), 1211–1222. doi:10.1017/s0033291703008158

Zinberg, N. (1986). *Drug Set and Setting: The Basis for Controlled Intoxicant Use*. Yale University, USA: Yale University Press.

# INDEX

α4β2 nAChR, 149
μ-opioid receptor (MOR), 141-2
AA (Alcoholics Anonymous), 106, 136, 171–3, 216
ABC form, 169
abstinence, 135–6, 141, 142
abstinence violation effect, 120
Acamprosate, 139, 141
acetaldehyde, 93, 140
acetaldehyde dehydrogenase (ALDH), 31, 93, 99–100, 140
acetylcholine receptors, 34, 61, 63, 94
acquired emotional regulation cycles, 122
addiction
   addictive cycle, 6
   case studies, 2–4
   components, 6–8
   definitions, 4–6, 7
   role of cognition in, 8–9
   vulnerability factors, 10–13
addiction-Stroop test, 116
adenosine receptors, 34
ADHD (Attention Deficit Hyperactivity Disorder), 26, 37, 85
adjuvant therapy, 138
adolescents, 10–11, 181, 182–3, 186, 195
adoption studies, 87–9
Advisory Council on Misuse of Drugs, 205
affective processing model, 114
affinity, 30, 70
agonists, 27–8, 34, 38, 39, 40, 143–4
alcohol
   adolescents *see* adolescents
   adoption studies, 87–9
   alcohol metabolising enzymes, 93–4
   alcohol use disorders (AUDs), 17–18, 89, 93, 106, 139, 142, 152, 165
   alcoholism, 31, 87–9, 91, 92, 93, 95, 100, 106, 139, 142, 163, 173
   ANKK1 (repeat and kinase domain containing 1) gene, 95–6
   case studies, 2–4
   chemical aversion therapy, 164
   cognitive behavioural therapy, 170–1
   cue exposure therapy (CET), 165
   disease model, 106
   dopamine, 32
   DRD2 gene, 95–6
   family studies, 87
   GABA, 32, 92, 140
   genes for alcohol metabolising enzymes, 93–4
   genetic predisposition, 10, 31
   harm caused by, 30, 205, 207fig, 208
   impulsitivity, 187, 188
   industry, 216–17
   MDMA, 139
   metabolism, 31
   motivational interviewing (MI), 162
   pharmacodynamics, 31–2, 61
   pharmacokinetics, 31
   pharmacotherapy, 138–2
   research, 7
   withdrawal symptoms, 42, 139–1
Alcohol Attention Control Training Program (AACTP), 165–6
alcohol dehydrogenase (ADH) enzyme, 31, 93, 99–100
Alcoholics Anonymous (AA), 106, 136, 171–3, 216
Alexander, B.K., 12, 202
alleles, 82, 91
allostasis, 70–1, 108
alpha-2 adrenergic drugs, 143
alprazolam (Xanax), 42
American Society of Addiction Medicine, 5
amphetamines
   Class B, 204
   dopamine, 29fig, 38
   harm, 209
   intracranial self-stimulation (ICSS), 60, 61
   mechanism of action, 38
   medical usage, 37
   pharmacokinetics, 37–8

# INDEX

pharmacological effects, 38
pharmacological treatments, 150, 151
psychological addiction, 7
self-administration, 63
vulnerability to addiction, 9
amygdala, 32, 43, 62fig, 70, 74, 77, 115, 193
anabolic steriods, 204
analgesia, 39–40, 44, 45, 56, 145
animal models, 52–8, 89–90
ANNKK1 (repeat and kinase domain containing 1) gene, 95–6
antagonists, 27–8, 34, 39, 145–7
anterior cingulate gyrus, 77, 115
antidepressants, 148–9, 218
antipsychotics, 151
antisocial impulsivist gamblers, 185, 186, 187
antisocial personalities, 88
anxiety disorders, 11, 13, 42, 43, 46–7, 85, 97, 184
Argentina, 203
aryl cyclohexylamines, 17
*Asp398ASn*, 94
association studies, 89, 98
associative learning, 8, 64, 67, 72, 74–5, 183
Ativan (lorazepam), 42, 139
Attention Deficit Hyperactivity Disorder (ADHD), 26, 37, 85
attentional bias hypothesis, 115, 120–1, 165, 166, 195
attribution theory, 110
autoreceptors, 29fig
aversion therapy, 165

Baclofen, 139
Bandura, Albert, 164
barbiturates, 42
Beck, Aaron, 168
Becker, Howard, 211
behaviour therapy, 163–7, 168
behavioural addictions, 17, 178–1, 195
    *see also* Gambling Disorder
behavioural genetics, 86–9
behavioural inhibition, 73fig, 74, 75
behavioural skills training, 164
behaviourally conditioned gamblers, 185
behaviourism, 57
benzodiazapines
    anxiety disorders, 42, 43
    Class C, 204
    overview, 41–2
    pharmacokinetics, 42

pharmacological effects and mechanism of action, 42–3
for treating addiction, 139–40
benzoylecgonine (BE), 36
Berridge, K.C., 66–7, 115
biological theories
    *see also* conditioned place preference (CPP); intracranial self-stimulation (ICSS); self-administration
biomarkers, 19
Black Mamba, 210
Blood Alcohol Concentration (BAC), 30, 31
blood brain barrier (BBB), 26, 27, 30, 41
*Blueprint for Regulation*, 210
Booth Davies, John, 109
Bozarth, M.A., 64–5, 66
Bradley, K.A., 21
brain
    adolescent, 10–11
    blood brain barrier (BBB), 26, 27, 30, 41
    brain disease model, 6
    circuitry, 5, 6, 9, 20, 105
    dopamine, 61
    reward, 9, 11, 34, 70
Brazil, 203
buprenorphine, 41, 107, 144–7
bupropion (Zyban), 148–50, 150, 152
butyrylcholinesterase, 36

caffeine
    Caffeine Dependence Syndrome, 35
    Caffeine Use Disorder, 17, 35
    physiological effects, 34–5
    withdrawal symptoms, 17, 35
Cambridge Gambling Task, 187, 188
Canadian Indians, 12
cancers, 30, 33, 45, 94, 105, 147, 218
candidate genes, 91, 92–3, 97
cannabinoids
    receptors, 32, 43–5
    synthetic, 210
cannabis
    cannabis use disorder, 168
    Class B, 202
    mechanism of action, 43–4
    medical uses, 45, 218–9
    overview, 43
    pharmacokinetics, 44
    pharmacological effects, 44–5

260

# INDEX

receptor sites, 61
recreational use, 43
smoking, 44, 45
THC (delta-9-tetrahydrocannabinol), 44
Uruguay, 210, 215
withdrawal symptoms, 17, 45
capillaries, 26, 27
capitalism, 12
cardiovascular disease, 33, 140, 144, 147
case studies, 2–4
catechoaminergic neurotransmitters, 38
CB1 and CB2 cannabinoid receptors, 43–4, 45
cell membranes, 26–7
chemical aversion therapy, 164
chlordiazepoxide (Librium), 42, 140
choice impulsivity, 187, 198
choice models, 105, 109–12
CHRNA5-CHRNA3-CHRNB4 gene, 94, 95
chromosomes, 80, 81fig, 82–4
cigarettes, 33, 34
Class A drugs, 203
Class B drugs, 204
Class C drugs, 204
classical conditioning, 8, 55–6, 163, 185
classification systems, 18–19
clinical trials, 131–5, 150
clonazepam (Klonopin), 42
cocaethylene, 36
cocaine
    Class A, 203
    dopamine, 26, 29fig, 36, 71–2, 151
    family studies, 87
    GABA, 36
    harm, 207fig, 208, 209
    historical usage, 35
    impulsivity, 187, 189
    intracranial self-stimulation (ICSS), 60, 61
    mechanism of action, 36–7
    methamphetamine, 152
    pharmacodynamics, 26, 61
    pharmacokinetics, 26, 35–6
    pharmacotherapy, 140, 150–2
    psychological addiction, 7
    self-administration, 63
    withdrawal symptoms, 42
codeine, 41, 204
cognition, 8–9
cognitive behavioural therapy, 69, 163, 168–1, 174
cognitive bias modification (CBM), 165–6

cognitive bias theories, 111–19
cognitive dissonance, 120
cognitive distortions, 191–3
cognitive impairment, 16, 42, 44, 45, 179
cognitive model, drug urges and
    drug-use behaviour, 113–14
cognitive restructuring, 170
Cohen, Stanley, 212
Collaborative Study on the
    Genetics of Alcoholism (COGA), 91
coma, 36
common disease/common variant hypothesis, 98
common liability to addiction (CLA), 85
co-morbidity, 13, 17, 69, 85, 99, 181, 184, 188, 190
compulsive eating, 5
COMT gene, 97
concordance, 88, 89
conditioned place preference (CPP), 59–60, 63
conditioned response (CR), 55, 56, 59
conditioned stimulus (CS), 55, 56, 59, 163, 165
conduct disorder, 85
confidence intervals, 129–1
construct validity, 54
consumption level, 21
contingency management (CM), 166–7
continuous reinforcement (CRF) schedule, 57, 58
control mechanisms, 72–4
control theory, 201
controlled drugs, 203–4
coping skills training, 170
cortisol, 13, 88
crack, 35, 207fig, 208
craving, 6, 7, 8, 17, 20, 32, 38, 66–7, 76, 114, 115, 141, 143, 145, 148, 149, 181, 193
crime, 200, 201, 203, 206
cue exposure therapy (CET), 165, 166
cue reactivity, 8, 113, 165
cues, 118
Cultural and Economic Capital argument, 216–17
culture, 12
cynomolgus macaques, 71–2
CYP-2A6 enzyme, 34, 95
CYP-2D6 enzyme, 41, 46
cytisine (Tabex), 149

decisional balance, 157, 159–160, 161
decriminalisation, 202, 203, 205, 212, 213–14
delay discounting task, 74, 189
*delta* (DOP) receptors, 39, 142, 146

# INDEX

delta-9-tetrahydrocannabinol (THC), 44 reverse
dependence, 14, 15–16, 21, 40, 206
depression, 16, 36, 38, 46–7, 48, 85, 97, 148, 149, 184, 220
development factors, 10–11
deviance, 211–12
dexamphetamine, 152
diagnosis
   current classification systems, 18–19
   DSM, 13–14, 16–19, 20, 53–4, 178–9, 181, 193, 194
   Gambling Disorder, 181–2
   heavy use over time, 20–1
   ICD-10, 13, 14–16, 17, 18, 19, 20
   overview, 13–14
   research domain criteria (RDoC), 19–20
Diagnostic and Statistical Manual of Mental Disorders (DSM) *see* diagnosis, DSM
diazepam (Valium), 42, 61, 69, 140
disease model, 105–9, 135
dislocation theory, 12
Disruptive, Impulse-Control and Conduct Disorders (DSM-5), 179
dissociative anaesthetics, 48
disulfiram, 93, 139, 140–1, 152
DMT (dimethytryptamine), 47
DNA, 80–2, 90–1
dominant, 82
dopamine
   alcohol, 32
   allostasis, 71fig
   amphetamines, 29fig, 38
   brain regions, 61
   bupropion (Zyban), 149
   cocaine, 26, 29fig, 36, 71–2, 151
   drug cues, 116
   Gambling Disorder, 191
   Internet Gaming Disorder (IGD), 195
   MDMA, 47
   mesotelencephalic dopamine system, 9
   methylphenidate, 26
   nicotine, 34, 63, 94
   opioids, 39–40
   phasic dopamine response, 75–6
   receptors, 9, 10, 70–2, 95, 195
   *see also* mesolimbic dopamine system; mesolimbic pathway
dose response curves, 29–30
dot-probe task, 115, 117–18
DRD2 gene, 95–6

drink-driving, 31
Drinker's Checkup, 162
drugs
   administration, 24–5
   crime, 200, 201, 203, 206
   cues, 116
   elimination, 27
   harm caused by, 201, 205–8
   historical usage, 200
   industry, 221
   laws, 107, 202–5, 208–09, 210, 211–12, 213
   prohibition, 106, 200, 202, 213
   self-administration *see* self-administration
   tolerance *see* tolerance
DSM, 13–14, 16–19, 20, 53–4, 178–9, 181, 193, 194

e-cigarettes, 148
ecstasy *see* MDMA
Edwards, Griffith, 106
electronic gaming machines, 192–3
electronic smoking, 33
Ellis, Albert, 168
Emotional Stroop Test, 115, 116–7, 117, 118, 120
emotionally vulnerable gamblers, 185, 186
empathic engagement, 161–2, 219
encephalin, 40
endocannabinoids, 44, 61, 139
endogenous opioids, 141, 142
endophenotypes, 99–100
entactogens, 46
environmental stress, 12
epigenetics, 86, 88, 123
ethnic minorities, 182, 183
Ethylphenidate, 210
euphoria, 7, 30, 35, 36, 38, 40, 41, 45, 56, 69, 145
   *see also* highs
excessive appetite model, 119–2, 179
extinction, 55, 72
Eyer, J., 70

face validity, 53–4
familial vulnerability, 9
family studies, 87
fentanyl, 41, 143, 146
foetal alcohol spectrum disorders (FASD), 30
formication, 36
Franken, I.H., 115
free market legalisation, 215–16
Freedom to Choose argument, 217

# INDEX

frontal lobes, 11, 72, 74
full agonists, 27–8
functional magnetic resonance imaging (fMRI), 19, 189–190, 195

GABA (gamma-aminobutyric acid)
  alcohol, 32, 92, 140
  cocaine, 36
  mesolimbic DA system, 77fig
  mood, 70, 71fig
  nicotine, 34
  receptors, 32, 42–3, 61, 92, 141
GAM-Anon, 171
gambler's fallacy, 191, 192
gambling
  cue reactivity, 165
  GAM-Anon, 172
  Gambling Disorder *see* Gambling Disorder
  industry, 216–17
  neurotransmitters, 5
  social deprivation, 121
Gambling Commission, 183
Gambling Disorder
  antisocial impulsivist gamblers, 185, 186, 187
  behaviourally conditioned gamblers, 185
  cognitive distortions in, 191–3
  comorbidity, 184
  diagnostic criteria, 181–2
  dopamine, 191
  DSM, 17, 178
  emotionally vulnerable gamblers, 185, 186
  neurobiology of, 187–91
  nicotine, 184
  prevalence and socio-demographic variables, 182–4
  Three Pathways Model of Pathological Gambling, 185–6
  vulnerability factors, 185, 187, 188
genes
  alcohol metabolising enzymes, 93–4
  ANNKK1 (repeat and kinase domain containing 1) gene, 95–6
  candidate genes, 91, 92–3, 97
  CHRNA5-CHRNA3-CHRNB4 gene, 94, 95
  COMT gene, 97
  DRD2 gene, 95–6
  gene expression, 83, 85
  gene variants, 96–7
  genetic association studies, 89, 98
  genetic predisposition, 10, 19, 31, 64

HTR2B gene, 98
  methods for identifying, 89–92
  research challenges, 97–9
  SLC6A4 gene, 97
  smoking behaviour, 94–5
  structure, 80–1, 82
genome-wide association studies (GWAS), 92, 94, 97, 98
genotype, 82, 91
GHB, 204
glass, 37
glutamate, 9, 32, 34, 36, 40, 48, 140, 141
Goldstein, R.Z., 77
Go/No-go Task, 73fig, 74, 187, 188
Gossop, Prof. Mike, 69–70
Gramsci, A., 216
Gross, Milton, 106

half-life, 27, 36, 37–8, 41
hallucinogens, 17, 46, 47–8, 63, 139, 220
HapMap project, 89
harm
  alcohol, 30, 205, 207fig, 208
  amphetamines, 209
  cocaine, 207fig, 208, 209
  drugs, 201, 205–8
  heroin, 207fig, 208
  MDMA, 205, 207fig, 208
  methamphetamine, 207fig, 208
  nicotine, 206
  reduction, 110, 136, 138, 142, 210, 213, 214, 217
  smoking, 33, 207fig, 208
harmful use (ICD-10), 14
Harmless Entertainment discourse, 216
head shops, 210
heart attacks, 36, 45
Heather, N., 21
heavy use over time, 20–1
hepatitis, 14, 143
heritability, 86–7, 88–9
heroin
  Class A, 203
  harm, 207fig, 208
  historical usage, 39, 105
  intravenous (IV) use, 25
  methadone maintenance therapy (MMT), 145–4
  pharmacokinetics, 41
  processing of drug cues, 116
  receptor sites, 61
  research, 7

# INDEX

use as deviance, 211–12
Vietnam War, 12
withdrawal symptoms, 7
heteroreceptors, 29fig
heterozygous, 82
Heyman, Gene, 109, 110–12
highs, 25–6, 35, 41, 181
*see also* euphoria
hindsight bias, 191
hippocampus, 32, 44, 77
*His48Arg*, 93
HIV, 143, 214, 218
homeostasis, 7, 56, 70, 71fig, 152
homozygous, 82
hot information processing, 114
HTR2B gene, 98
HTTLPR region, 97
Human Genome Project, 89
Huxley, Aldous, 200
hydrocodone, 40, 41, 146
hyperbolic discounting, 111
hypo-thalamic-pituitary adrenal (HPA) axis, 13, 139

ICD (International Classification of Diseases), 13, 14–16, 17, 18, 19, 20, 182
ice, 37
illusion of control, 191–2
impaired response inhibition and salience attribution (I-RISA) syndrome, 108
Impulse Control Disorders, 182
impulsivity, 7, 11, 53, 62fig, 74, 97, 100, 180, 184, 187–91
impulsive aggression, 98
incentive salience, 66–9, 76, 188
incentive-sensitisation theory, 8, 65–9, 76, 108
Information Sampling Test, 188
inhalation, 25, 35, 44
inhibitory functioning, 11
Institute of Public Policy Research (IPPR), 183
instrumental conditioning, 8, 57, 163, 166–7, 185
*see also* operant conditioning
insula, 193
intermediate phenotypes, 99–100
International Classification of Diseases (ICD) *see* ICD (International Classfication of Diseases)
International Conference on Harmonisation of Technical Requirements for Registration of Pharmaceuticals for Human Use (ICH), 132
International Statistical Classification of Diseases and Related Health Problems (ICD) *see* ICD (International Classification of Diseases)
Internet
gambling, 182–3
Internet Addiction, 194
Internet Gaming Disorder (IGD), 17, 178, 193–6
use, 5
intracranial self-stimulation (ICSS), 59, 60, 61, 62fig
intranasal administration (snorting), 35
intravenous (IV) drug use, 25, 26, 35, 36, 37, 143
inverse agonists, 27–8
ι-opioid receptor (MOR),
CHECK page 141 – four lines from bottom
Iowa Gambling Task (IGT), 187, 188–89

Jellinek, E.M., 106
Jones, Afron, 210

K2, 45
*kappa* (KOP) receptors, 39, 142, 145, 146
ketamine, 48, 139, 204, 218, 220
Klonopin (clonazepam), 42
Koob, G.F., 69–70, 71fig, 76
Kuhn, Thomas, 137

laws, 107, 202–5, 208–09, 210, 211–12, 213
learning, 66, 74–6, 77, 170, 185, 187, 191
learning deficit theories, 189
learning theories, 54–8
legal highs, 37, 202, 209–10
legalisation, 212, 214–17, 221
legislation *see* laws
levo-alpha acetylmethadol (LAAM), 41, 144
Librium (chlordiazepoxide), 42, 140
liking, of drugs, 66–9
linkage studies, 89, 90–1, 92
liver damage, 16, 20–1, 30
Logan, Frank, 72
lorazepam (Ativan), 42, 140
losses disguised as wins (LDWs), 192–3
low mood, 8, 9, 40
*see also* depression
LSD (lysergic acid diethylamide), 47, 63, 139, 203, 205, 206, 208, 218, 220
lung disease, 33, 152

malignant hyperthermia, 46–7
MAOA enzyme, 97, 98

# INDEX

marijuana
  adolescents, 10–11
  contingency management (CM), 167
  family studies, 87
  psychological addiction, 7
Massively Multiplayer Online Role
    Player Games (MMORPGs), 195
matching law, 111
Maté, G., 202, 211, 214
Matthew, Father, 216
MDMA
  anxiety disorders, 46–7
  Class A, 203
  depression, 46–7
  dopamine, 47
  harm, 205, 207fig, 208
  impulsivity, 187
  mechanism of action, 47
  medical uses, 219–220
  overview, 46
  pharmacokinetics, 46
  pharmacological effects, 46–7
  Post-Traumatic Stress Disorder, 218
  purity, 209
  self-administration, 63
  therapy in AUD, 139
medical uses
  cannabis, 45, 218–19
  hallucinogens, 220
  ketamine, 220
  MDMA, 219–220
medicalisation, 221
Medicines Act (1968), 203
Medicines and Healthcare Products
    Regulatory Agency (MHRA), 132
meiosis, 83–4
melioration, 111
membranes, 26–7
memory, 32, 45, 96, 118, 188, 189, 219
Mendel, Gregor, 82
mental health problems, 11, 85, 99, 140, 150, 167, 181,
    184, 218, 219
mephedrone, 211–12
mescaline, 46, 47
mesolimbic dopamine system, 40, 45,
    63–4, 65, 66, 74–6, 77–8, 120, 149
mesolimbic pathway, 61, 62fig, 63
mesotelencephalic dopamine system, 9
meta-analyses, 137

methadone maintenance
    therapy (MMT), 41, 107, 143–4, 167
methamphetamine
  Class A, 203
  cocaine addiction treatment, 152
  global use, 37
  harm, 207fig, 208
  impulsivity, 187
  withdrawal symptoms, 42
Methiopropamine (MPA), 210
methylphenidate (Ritalin), 26, 76, 152
mice, 68, 90–1
microarray technology, 92
microsomal ethanol-oxidising system, 31
Miller, W.R., 72, 161
Milner, P., 59
mindfulness, 168
Mindfulness-Based Relapse Prevention, 170
Misuse of Drugs Act (1971), 203–4
mitosis, 82
MMORPGs (Massively Multiplayer Online Role Player
    Games), 195
MMR vaccine, 130
Moderation Management, 173–4
monoamine neurotransmitters, 96–7
monoamine oxidase, 38
mood
  mood disorders, 13, 184, 185
  mood states, 70, 71fig, 185, 186
MOR (opioid receptor), 141–2
moral panics, 209, 212, 219
morality, 211
morphine, 39, 41, 107
morphine-6-glucoronide, 41
mortality, drug-related, 206
motivation, 54, 59, 63, 66, 67, 70, 76, 77,
    118, 122–4, 161
Motivational Enhancement Therapy (MET), 162–3,
    170, 174
motivational interviewing (MI), 161–3
*mu* (MOP) receptors, 39, 40, 41, 77fig, 96, 107, 142,
    143, 144, 145, 146
mutations, 83, 90
*The Myth of Addiction*, 109–10

N-acetylcysteine (NAC), 152
nalmefene, 41, 139, 142, 145, 146
naloxone (Narcan), 40, 145, 146
naltrexone, 40, 96, 107, 139, 141–2, 145–6

INDEX

narcolepsy, 26
National Institute of Alcohol Abuse and Alcoholism (NIAAA), 163
National Institute of Mental Health (NIMH), 19
National Treatment Outcome Research Study (NTORS), 136, 136fig
near misses, 192, 193
negative reinforcement, 8–9, 57, 69–72, 180
neoliberalism, 215
neural plasticity, 122, 123
neuroimaging, 9, 19, 20
neurotransmitters, 5, 9, 10, 27, 28–9, 32, 34, 36, 37, 38, 181
New Psychoactive Substances (NPS), 202, 203, 208–09
nicotinamide adenine dinucleotide (NAD), 31
nicotine
   adolescents, 11
   aversion therapy, 164
   dopamine, 34, 63, 94
   GABA, 34
   Gambling Disorder, 184
   harm, 206
   mechanism of action, 34
   metabolism, 34
   pharmacokinetics, 33–4
   receptors, 29fig, 61, 149, 151fig
   smoking, 34
   susceptibility genes, 10, 94–5
   tobacco use, 33
   withdrawal symptoms, 33–4, 148, 149
   see also smoking
nicotine replacement therapy (NRT), 147–48, 149, 150
nicotinic acetyl choline receptors (nAChR), 34, 94
nigrostriatal system, 62fig, 65
NMDA (N-methyl-D-aspartate) receptors, 32, 48
Node-Link Mapping, 169
noiceptin (NOP) receptors, 39
non-substance addictions, 178–96
noradrenaline, 36, 38, 40, 47, 140, 149
nucleotides, 80–2, 84, 90
nucleus accumbens (NAcc), 32, 43, 61, 62fig, 63–4, 65, 68, 70, 74, 77fig, 115, 141
Nutt, David, 202, 205–8, 29

Obsessive-Compulsive and Related Disorders (DSM-5), 179
OCD, 70
Olds, J., 59

operant conditioning, 57–8, 61, 166–7
   see also instrumental conditioning
opioids
   allostasis, 70, 71fig
   contingency management (CM), 167
   dependence, 40
   disease model, 106–7
   dopamine, 39–40
   endogenous, 141, 142
   historical usage, 38–9
   metabolism, 40
   opioid sparing action, 45
   opioid use disorder (OUD), 143
   painkillers, 41
   peptides, 71fig
   pharmacotherapy, 143–6
   prescription drug abuse, 39
   psychomotor stimulant theory, 65
   receptors, 29fig, 39–40, 61, 77fig
   transmitters, 32, 36
   withdrawal symptoms, 40, 42, 145
   see also heroin; morphine
opium, 106–7
OPRM1-G polymorphism, 96
oral administration, 25, 35, 37
orbitofrontex cortex, 74, 75, 76–7
Ordinary Business discourse, 216
Orford, J., 119–2, 200, 202, 215, 216–17
outcome measures, 135–6
*Outsiders: Studies on the Sociology of Deviance*, 211
overdose, 39, 40, 41, 56, 132, 143, 144, 146, 152, 214
oxycodone, 40, 41, 146

P value, 129, 130
pain, 39, 40, 41, 45
parenteral administration, 25
Parkinsons disease, 191
Parrott, Andy, 209, 219
partial agonists, 27–8, 39, 144-5
Pathological Gambling, 182
Pavlov, Ivan, 55, 59, 64
PCP (phencyclidine), 48
peptides, 71fig
personal responsibiity, 6
Personal Responsibility discourse, 217
personality disorders, 13
PET (positron emission topography), 19, 141–2, 191
pharmaceutical companies, 221
pharmacodynamics, 26, 27–30, 31–2, 61

pharmacokinetics
  alcohol, 31
  amphetamines, 37–8
  benzodiazapines, 42
  cannabis, 44
  cocaine, 26, 35–6
  heroin, 41
  MDMA, 46
  nature of, 24–7
  nicotine, 33–4
pharmacy model, 212, 221
phasic dopamine response, 75–6
phenotype, 82, 91
  *see also* intermediate phenotypes
physical dependence theories, 69–72
placebos, 131
placental barrier, 26, 30, 36, 38, 40, 42, 45
Plato, 200, 217
PMA, 209
polymorphisms, 90, 92, 93
Popper, Karl, 137
Portugal, 203, 212, 213, 214
positive reinforcement, 57, 59, 64–5, 69–70, 72, 18-
Positive Valence Systems, 20
positron emission topography (PET), 19, 141–2, 191
postsynaptic receptors, 28–9
Post-Traumatic Stress Disorder (PTSD), 46, 218, 219
power, 121, 138, 216
predictive validity, 53
prefrontal cortex, 48, 61, 62fig, 75, 77, 188, 193, 195
pregnancy, 30, 42
prescription drugs, 39
presynaptic terminals, 28–9, 34, 40
primary processes, 119–120
PRIME theory, 119, 122–4
prisons, 201, 210, 214
prohibition, 106, 200, 202, 213
Project Match, 163
proof, 128
protein synthesis, 83
psilocybin, 47, 141, 203, 207fig, 208, 218, 220
psychedelics, 139
Psychoactive Substance Bill, 208, 210
psychological addiction, 7
psychomotor stimulant theory, 64–5, 66
psychopharmacology, 23, 53
psychosis, 36, 38, 45, 48
psychosocial integration, 12
psychostimulants, 33–7, 64–5, 150–2

PTSD (Post-Traumatic Stress Disorder), 46, 218, 219
publication bias, 136–7

quantification, 21

randomised controlled trials (RCTs), 133, 134
rare variants common disease model, 98
Rational Emotive Therapy, 168, 174
rats, 52, 54, 57–8, 59, 62fig, 63
raves, 46–7
receptors
  cannabis, 61
  dopamine, 10, 70–1
  GABA, 32, 42–3, 61, 92, 141
  heroin, 61
  nicotine, 29fig, 61, 149, 151fig
  opioids, 29fig, 39–40, 61, 77fig
  receptor affinity, 30
  receptor binding sites, 27
recessive, 82
recombination, 83, 90, 91
recovery, 136, 157
rectal administration, 25
reflection impulsivity, 188
reinforcement, 8–9, 57–8, 64–5
relapse, 5, 69, 96, 166
Relapse Prevention (RP) model, 169–1, 174
relatives, 10
religion, 211
remission, 5
repeat and kinase domain containing 1 (ANKK1) gene, 95–6
research domain criteria (RDoC), 19–20
research methodology, 130
respiratory depression, 42, 145, 146
response impulsivity, 187
reward
  adolescent brains, 11
  brain systems, 9, 34, 70
  intracranial self-stimulation (ICSS), 61
  pathways, 71
  reward deficiency theories, 62fig, 189
  reward prediction errors, 75–6, 190, 191
  reward processing, 20, 32
  role in addiction, 5, 7
  *see also* mesolimbic dopamine system; mesolimbic pathway
risk factors, 10–13
Ritalin (methylphenidate), 26, 76, 152

# INDEX

Robbins, T.W., 74, 115
Robinson, T.E., 66–7
Rubinsky, A.D., 21

Safrole, 209
Saunders, J.B., 21
SBM-NTX, 146
schizophrenia, 45, 97, 219
science, 128, 130–1, 132, 134–5, 136–7
secondary processes, 119–120
seizures, 32, 35, 36, 38, 42, 149
self-administration, 54, 61, 63–4, 71–2
self-efficacy, 112, 157, 160, 161, 170
self-empowerment strategies, 122
self-help groups, 121–2
   *see also* twelve-step approaches
self-medication, 13, 69
self-report research methods, 115
sensation seeking, 100
sensitisation, 8, 65–9
sentencing guidelines, 204–5
serotonin, 9, 32, 34, 36, 38, 40, 47, 94
Sessa, B., 219–220
shaping, 58
shopping, 5
signal transduction, 95
single nucleotide polymorphism (SNP), 90, 91, 92, 95–6
Skinner, B.F., 57, 59, 64
SLC6A4 gene, 97
slot machines, 182, 183, 186, 192, 193
Slutske, W.S., 187
SMART Recovery, 174
Smith, Bob, 171
smoking
   cannabis, 44, 45
   contingency management (CM), 167
   delivery of nicotine, 34
   family studies, 87
   genes linked to smoking behaviour, 94–5
   harm caused by, 33, 207fig, 208
   impulsivity, 187
   insula, 193
   pharmacotherapy for cessation, 147–50
   transtheoretical model of behaviour change (TTM), 160
   *see also* nicotine; tobacco
social context, 11–12
social deprivation, 121, 183
social dislocation, 12

social networking, 194
social status, 72
social stress, 12
socio-demographics, 182–4
speed of entry, to brain, 26
Spice, 45, 210
spontaneous recovery, 55–6, 58, 109
stages of change model, 156–61
state monopoly legalisation, 215
statistical significance, 128–130
Sterling, P., 70
stigma, 109, 213
Stop Signal Reaction Time Task, 73fig, 187, 188
stress, 12–13, 36, 70, 71fig, 76, 144
striatum, 26, 32, 61, 62fig, 72, 75, 76–7, 141, 189–190, 191, 195
stroke, 36, 38, 45
Stroop tasks *see* Emotional Stroop Test
Suboxone, 145
Substance-Related and Addictive Disorders (DSM-5), 16, 178, 181, 182
Subutex, 145
susceptibility genes, 10, 94–5
synapses, 28–9, 38
synthetic cannabinoids, 210
synthetic drugs, 37, 208–10

Tabex (cytisine), 148
Taiwan, 15
teenagers *see* adolescents
temporal difference
   reinforcement learning theories, 190, 191
THC (delta-9-tetrahydrocannabinol), 44
third wave CBT, 168
Three Pathways Model of Pathological Gambling, 185–6
Tiffany, S.T., 113–14
tobacco
   industry, 217
   nicotine, 33
   tobacco use disorder, 17
   *see also* smoking
token economies, 166
tolerance, 7, 15–16, 18, 20, 32, 34, 36, 38, 45, 56, 66fig, 67fig
Transform, 210
transmucosal administration, 25
transporters, 29fig, 38
transtheoretical model of behaviour change (TTM), 156–61, 173

twelve-step approaches, 163, 171–4
twin studies, 87, 88–9

unconditioned response (UCR), 55, 56, 59
unconditioned stimulus (UCS), 55, 56, 59, 163
unstable mind, 122, 123–4
Uruguay, 203, 210, 214, 215, 221
USA, 215, 218, 219, 221

validity, 53–4
Valium (diazepam), 42, 61, 69, 140
varenicline (Chantix), 139, 147, 149–150, 151fig, 153
variability, 86, 90, 92, 98
variable number tandem repeats (VNTRs), 97
ventral tegmental area (VTA), 32, 61, 62fig, 63–4, 65, 77fig, 151fig
video gaming, 193–6, 195
Vietnam War, 12

virtual reality, 60, 165
Volkow, Nora, 70–1, 77
vulnerability, 9, 10–13, 185, 17, 188

wanting, of drugs, 66–9
West, Robert, 122–4
Willner, P., 53, 54, 68–9
Wilson, Bill, 171
Wise, R.A., 64–5, 66
withdrawal symptoms, 7, 15, 17, 20, 32, 33–4, 35, 40, 42, 45, 69, 139–140, 143, 145, 148, 149
women, 31

Xanax (alprazolam), 42
XR-NTX, 146

Yellow Card system, 132

Zyban (bupropion), 148–9, 150, 152